PIMLICO

785

WILLIAM KENT

Timothy Mowl is Reader in Architectural and Garden History at the University of Bristol. His recent publications include biographies of two eighteenth-century aesthetes, *Horace Walpole* (1996) and *William Beckford* (1998), and a polemical study, *Stylistic Cold Wars*, of John Betjeman and Nikolaus Pevsner (2000). He is currently writing an historic gardens series of the English counties.

'[Mowl's] accounts of actual buildings and gardens are full of subjective intensity as well as subtle observations... Engrossing.' Alan Hollinghurst, *Guardian*

'Provocative... We tend to admire what received opinion admires, whereas Mowl's book reverses the process, and healthily advises us to "draw back from praising past culture simply because it happened." ' John Carey, *Sunday Times*

'Engaging... I was reminded, above all, of Sacheverell Sitwell's evocations of the Baroque. *Kent* is as much a work of stylistic art.' Christopher Woodward, *Literary Review*

'Although Kent is an influential figure, he left little in writing but Mowl does a fine job of recreating his life, and personality... An honest account of Kent's genius and failings.' *BBC History Magazine*

'Gloriously opinionated Tim Mowl blasts our pre-conceptions flat revealing his hero to be a joker-genius whose work changed the direction of English architecture, interior decoration and garden design, sometimes, he admits, for the worse, but often for the better.' Sir Roy Strong

WILLIAM KENT

Architect, Designer, Opportunist

TIMOTHY MOWL

Timothy Mowl

PIMLICO

Published by Pimlico 2007

2 4 6 8 10 9 7 5 3 1

First published in Great Britain in 2006 by
Jonathan Cape

Pimlico edition 2007

Pimlico
Random House, 20 Vauxhall Bridge Road,
London SW1V 2SA

www.randomhouse.co.uk

Addresses for companies within The Random House Group Limited can be found at:
www.randomhouse.co.uk

The Random House Group Limited Reg. No. 954009

A CIP catalogue record for this book
is available from the British Library

ISBN 9781844135394

The Random House Group Limited makes every effort to ensure that the papers used in its books are made from trees that have been legally sourced from well-managed and credibly certified forests. Our paper procurement policy can be found at:
www.randomhouse.co.uk/paper.htm

Printed and bound in Great Britain by
William Clowes Ltd, Beccles, Suffolk

For John Harris
In record of a generous, sometimes embattled, friendship

Contents

List of Illustrations

Black & White Sections

Colour Section

Acknowledgements

My first thanks go to John Harris, to whom this book is dedicated, for a long and often combative intellectual friendship. His research and writings on Kent and Burlington have been my benchmark for a revision of Kent's influence and importance as a multi-disciplinary designer. Then, of course, I owe a debt of gratitude to Michael I. Wilson, whom I have not met, but whose 1984 book on Kent was a constant source of information, and to John Dixon Hunt, whose insights into Kent as a garden designer were so valuable. David and Susan Neave were very helpful on Kent's origins in Bridlington, Fr Hugo Vanermen was a most courteous and enthusiastic guide to Kent's fresco at San Giuliano dei Fiamminghi in Rome, Michael Symes shared with me his extensive and detailed research on Esher Place and Oatlands Park, and Susan Gordon, a former Ph.D. student of mine at Bristol, was illuminating about the underlying sexual iconography of Kent's most poetic garden layout at Rousham.

I have been indebted to many scholars over the years for their insights into Kent in particular and the early eighteenth-century period in general, so I would like to thank the following for their advice and encouragement: Sir Howard Colvin, Eileen Harris, John Wilton-Ely, Geoffrey Beard, Andor Gomme, Steven Parissien, Bruce Bailey, Malcolm Airs, Roger White, Edward Impey, Tom Williamson, David Lambert, Stewart Harding, Mavis Batey, Giles Worsley, Richard Hewlings and Richard Wheeler. Other scholars and friends to whom I owe a debt of gratitude are: Pete Smith, Richard Morrice, Hal Moggridge, Philip White, Jeremy Musson,

Helen Langley, Carole Fry, Kate Felus, Julia Ionides, Andrew Eburne, Neil Porteous, John Borron, Fiona Cowell, Tim Richardson, Paul Bancroft and Verity Smith.

Administrators, curators and archivists who have helped with Kent-related sources include Christopher Lloyd, Jo Brooks, Annabet Roellig, Joanna Parker, Katy Myers, Jane Cunningham, Susan Palmer, Diane Naylor, Paula Minchin, Christine Hiskey, Helen Trompeteler, Laura Turner, Mike Daley and Laura Valentine.

All the owners or custodians of Kent buildings I have met have been more than willing to share with me their personal view of the man and his work and I would like to make a special mention of Mrs Cottrell-Dormer at Rousham, the late Duchess of Beaufort at Badminton, the late Earl of Shaftesbury at St Giles House, Wimborne St Giles, Lady Nutting at Chicheley, Chris Galloway at Ditchley Park, Lee Prosser at Kensington Palace, Philip and Tibouche Gunn at the Euston Temple and Mrs J. H. Richmond-Watson at Wakefield Lodge.

I have had generous support from academic colleagues at Bristol University, particularly from Michael Liversidge, Stephen Bann, Mike and Claire O'Mahony, Mark Horton and Kate Robson Brown. Michael Richards of the University Library Special Collections has been as helpful as ever in finding for me published sources for Kent material and Ann Pethers has produced many photographs of the archival images for the book.

At Jonathan Cape I have been fortunate to have a commissioning editor in Will Sulkin whose idea it was that I tackled Kent and who, together with Rosalind Porter and Neil Bradford, has handled the book with professionalism and imagination. My agent, Sara Menguc, has been as encouraging as ever about the project, Douglas Matthews has provided an exhaustive index, my good friend and academic colleague Brian Earnshaw has carried out some of the more pleasurable aspects of the research and, together with Clare Hickman, has edited the draft manuscript with care and precision.

Finally, my wife Sarah, my son, Adam, and my daughter, Olivia, have been a tremendous support and have weathered cheerfully all my tempestuous storms over footnotes and computer glitches.

Bristol, Summer 2005

Preface

William Kent was the greatest designer of the eighteenth century. This book is a record of his life and activities, and an assessment of their significance and consequential impact. It does not attempt a definitive account of all his works: that would be twice the length and a tedious repetition of writings already published. There are earnest discussions of the influence of Domenico Parodi, Giovanni Foggini and Giovanni Giardini on Kent's designs, with little regard to whether that influence was good, bad or remotely significant. For most scholars it is enough that Kent simply existed; what he created seems to justify laboured analysis even though, as so often in his early years, it was third rate or disastrous.

As a result of his Italian experience, Kent himself had a shrewd critical awareness of the insular provincialism of English eighteenth-century artistic standards. He was deeply involved in them and, together with Lord Burlington, he must share much of the blame for the confusion and the often poor quality of design. In a letter he wrote to Burlington on 16 November 1732 he commented on a conversation he had just had in London with a French bookseller who 'sayes he wonders whats the matter with the English, but his observation has been whe are a hundred yeer behind them always (I think for a Frenchman hes in the right) as for what you and I do, it may be esteem'd a hundred yeer hence, but at present does not look like it'.[1] If he had said two hundred years, bringing it to 1932, he would have been nearer the mark. By that time a sugary reverence for all things 'Georgian' had settled upon the critical establishment, and his century had managed to pass itself off, retrospectively, as the 'Age of Reason', despite its gentry wearing powdered white wigs, enjoying heroic couplets and hailing mediocre portrait painters as great artists.

Kent was right. There *was* something the matter with the English. He knew that he and his forceful, not very intelligent, partner, Burlington, were part of the problem. It is time to accept that and to draw back from praising past culture simply because it happened. By his detachment and his improvisatory brilliance, Kent did much to ease his country out of complacency and to compensate for his early malign compromises. His true inspiration came, not from obscure Italians, but from Queen Caroline, a German intellectual with a flair for public image, and from a randy old general, James Dormer, with a talent for ruthless self-analysis. We are far enough away from the early eighteenth century to be as honest about it as Kent was himself. That is the aim of this book.

Introduction
Yet another royal wedding

When a few minor misadventures, a papal funeral, civil licences and the moral reservations of the Head of the Church of England disturbed the programme for the wedding of Prince Charles and Mrs Camilla Parker Bowles for a day or two in April 2005, there was much wringing of hands and talk of unkind Fate, jinxes and adverse omens. Surprisingly no one mentioned the infinitely more traumatic royal wedding of 14 March 1734 when Anne, the Princess Royal and favourite daughter of King George II and Queen Caroline, married the Dutch Stadtholder, Wilhelm Karl Heinrich, Prince of Orange. That was a ceremony and an official bedding that reads like something from the Hammer House of Horror, and the decorations for the wedding were supplied by William Kent.[1] He had arrived, but what a destination!

A royal wedding is usually unnatural and interesting because it is likely to be a compromise between the desires of the flesh and the requirements of the state. That wedding of 1734 was not so much a compromise as a head-on collision. Princess Anne was reasonably attractive. She had a lively, clean look and a very fine complexion, although she was marked a good deal by smallpox. Though she was running to fat like her mother, she was not crippled in any way. This meant that in the royal marriage market she was a relatively hot property. The problem was that there were very few princes in Europe at the time who were of her age, twenty-five, unmarried and Protestant, a Catholic spouse being out of the question. In fact, there was just one, the Prince of Orange, who was not only Protestant but the ideal age, twenty-three. Where the British public was concerned, this would be a popular match because the last Dutchman of the House of Orange on the English scene had been William III. Ruling with his wife, Mary, they had been the most popular monarchs since Queen Elizabeth I: the couple who had saved their nation from Catholic plots and put the Irish in their place at the Battle of the Boyne (1690).

There were other problems: the Prince was a hunchbacked dwarf. Royalty tried to keep well informed on physical matters because there was always the question of an heir, and informed reporters, who had met the young Dutch Prince, claimed that, while his face was not bad, and his countenance was sensible, his breath was more offensive than it was possible for those who had not been offended by it to imagine. Poor Princess Anne was in a quandary. As her mother's bisexual male companion, Lord Hervey, put it, she could go to bed with this piece of deformity in Holland, or die an ancient maid in her royal convent of St James's Palace. The balancing factor was Anne's pride. She was the proudest of all her family and her family the proudest of all the proud, status-hunting German aristocracy. Germany was not like England. The English aristocracy married for money and then invested that money in trade, which was how it had contrived to colonise a quarter of the globe's surface, and the most profitable quarter at that. But if you were an aristocrat in the Holy Roman Empire of the German people then birth and status were everything, and Princess Anne was German through and through.

She argued it out at length with her father the King. Hervey, who spent his court life listening at keyholes and spying though windows, still had a sympathetic awareness of human predicaments; and one afternoon he just happened, as usual, to be snooping around Richmond Lodge, Queen Caroline's house by the Thames, when he looked out and saw the Princess walking with her father in the garden, her hand constantly in his, King George speaking with great earnestness and seeming affection, and she listening with great emotion and attention, the tears falling so fast all the while that her other hand went every moment to her cheek to wipe them away. At the end of their conversation he embraced her, and she kissed his hand with great fondness and respect. That, Hervey concluded, must have been when the decision was made to marry a prince who, unfortunately, was an oddly shaped dwarf. Anne would at least be the wife of the hereditary Stadtholder of a rich and reasonably powerful country. Her husband might have halitosis, but he would also have a controlling interest in the spice islands of Indonesia; lose one, gain some others.

The House of Orange being a good deal more popular in England than the House of Hanover, Parliament gave its blessing. Anne's elder brother, Frederick, Prince of Wales, was put out because his sister was marrying before him, but his parents detested him so much that the snub made the situation all the more satisfying for them. Negotiations dragged out with the indifference of the English ministers and the tardy phlegm of the Dutch, but eventually terms were agreed and a royal yacht was sent over to Helvoetsluys to collect the bridegroom. On 7 November 1733 the Prince of Orange arrived and was lodged in Somerset House, which was where the problems began.

King George II was a confidently unintelligent, though physically courageous man; and, being as status conscious as his beloved daughter, he considered a Prince of Orange to be a nothing until the pair were married. So no salutes were fired from the Tower, and no guard of honour was turned out in welcome. To bring the Prince to St James's Palace the next day for inspection, only one miserable leading coach with two horses and two footmen was sent. It was, therefore, mortifying for the Hanoverians to observe that the Prince's coach passed through streets crowded with cheering Londoners, while the Palace was so crammed with courtiers that the Prince and his retinue had difficulty making their way to the Throne Room. It was observed that, though the Prince's body was as bad as possible, his face was far from disagreeable and his actual address was engaging, even noble. He had that trick of being so personally confident and indifferent to his physical limitations that people talking with him soon forgot about them. Queen Caroline insisted, in private conversation, that neither she nor the King had pressed the Princess Royal into accepting the match, and that the Princess was so committed to it that she had declared that if he was a monkey she would marry him. Certainly she appeared completely at ease when the couple first met the following day.

The next Monday was fixed for the marriage ceremony, in the French Chapel which Inigo Jones had built in Charles I's reign for his Queen, Henrietta Maria, to celebrate her Catholic faith. The usually parsimonious King George was resolved to do his best for a favourite child, even if she was only marrying a Dutchman, and no expense was to be spared for the decorations of the Chapel.[2] Hervey, as Vice Chamberlain, a highly appropriate double entendre, was in charge of the arrangements, but he had developed a jealous dislike of William Kent, London's leading interior decorator, who by his position as Master Carpenter to the Board of Works, was the obvious man for the job. Anyone who got on well with Queen Caroline was a threat to Hervey's position as her personal confidant, the son she wished she had had instead of the frenetic Prince Frederick. Hervey dismissed Kent as: 'A man much in fashion as a gardener, an architect, a painter and about fifty other things, with a very bad taste and little understanding, but had the good luck to make several people who had no taste or understanding of their own believe that they could borrow both of him';[3] also as someone who ruined his patrons' fortunes building houses that nobody could live in and everybody made fun of. It was an unkind appraisal that had, nevertheless, certain elements of truth in it. Kent was a very complex influence on English art and design, a positive and negative force whose worth will always be contentious. He was given the prestigious commission to decorate the wedding chapel in the teeth of Hervey's disapproval. Queen Caroline and Kent had recently caught the imagination of the entire country with a weird new garden building at Richmond and the Queen did not forget her friends.

Throughout the week running up to the ceremony the workmen and upholsterers hammered and sewed to make Inigo Jones's handsome single-cell chapel into a theatre as faery-like as the church in Parma where Kent had, back in 1714, witnessed the betrothal of the Duke of Parma's daughter, by proxy, to the King of Spain.[4] The huge sum of £15,000 was spent on the hangings and everything was complete by the Sunday. But on the day of the wedding the Prince fell very ill, possibly as a result of English cooking. For several days his life was despaired of and Hervey recorded that not a single member of the royal family visited him in his lodgings at Somerset House or even enquired about his health, while his prospective bride showed not the least concern or interest. On an accidental encounter the Prince met Princess Anne and her younger sisters, had dinner with them and also a game of backgammon with the King. But the girls were forbidden to see him again and he was packed off first to Kensington Palace for the fresh air there, then to Bath, where he slowly tottered back to health, taking the waters. Meanwhile the marvellous drapes and screens of Kent's decorations hung unused in the St James's Chapel. When in decorative doubt Kent usually fell back on white and gold, and with £15,000 in hand any amount of cloth of gold and silver tissue could be hung about in long drapes and swags with rosettes of brocade and silken tassels. Green velvet was another of his favourite materials.

This scene was a temptation to William Hogarth, England's greatest living artist. Always short of money, Hogarth was a man of wicked wit. He had shamelessly chauvinistic views on an artist like Kent, who had trained abroad in Italy and painted the ceiling of a Catholic church in Rome for the Catholic Cardinal Ottoboni. Indifferent to Kent's authorship of the Chapel decorations, he determined to make a quick killing on souvenir prints of the happy couple taking their vows at the altar before the event actually took place.[5] Living a life of cheerfully indiscriminate mockery it would not have worried him that he had already ridiculed Kent's schemes and artistic achievements three times and with malicious accuracy. In February 1724, following a foolishly sycophantic poem by John Gay describing Kent, a dreadful painter incapable even of catching a likeness, as England's 'Raphael', Hogarth published an engraving, *Masquerades and Operas*, commonly known as *The Taste of the Town*.[6] This showed Kent as a statue standing on the gateway of Burlington House with Michelangelo and Raphael kneeling adoringly at his feet. To push the attack beyond the bounds of decency he inscribed the Kent statue with 'KNT', an accepted standard abbreviation for a woman's genitalia.

That really hurt Kent. Because his baptismal surname had been Cant, he had changed it, deliberately, to avoid mockery, to Kent, with its respectable county implications. Another print, *Taste, or Burlington Gate*, probably from Hogarth's ready pen, illustrates the same scene, with Kent directing and Pope sloshing whitewash wildly about on the rival Baroque architectural patron, the Duke of Chandos and Buckingham.[7] But the deadliest cartoon of all was Hogarth's parody of the altarpiece that Kent had painted for St Clement Danes.[8] The original was a sickly representation of The Celestial Choir. Hovering above with a scatter of cherubs was the Holy Spirit; down below, two large winged angels were playing an organ and a harp while another sang. This unfortunate object had been taken down to preserve peace and unity among the parishioners after an *agent provocateur* had claimed that the face of one of the angels, the harpist, was a disloyal portrait of Princess Sobieski, the wife of Prince Charles, the Young Pretender.[9] The Bishop of London had intervened in person, such was the political sensitivity of the accusation and the times.[10]

Hogarth's engraving reminded viewers of that possibly treasonous representation and added insult to injury by lettering bits of the angels' anatomies with an explanatory key underneath, as:

> F the inside of his Leg but whether right or Left is yet undiscover'd
> H the other leg judiciously omitted to make room for the harp.

The attack had been telling, and now this mocking enemy was intending to make money by copying Kent's decorations just as Kent was considering producing the same scene as a print with the same mercenary end in view. The Lord Chamberlain, the Duke of Grafton, Kent's patron, found Hogarth drawing in the Chapel and asked him to stop. When the outraged Hogarth claimed that he had Queen Caroline's permission to sketch the scene, ruthlessly, but justifiably, the Lord Chamberlain had him thrown out. Caroline was brought in and, embarrassed by it all, backed Kent, not Hogarth. Kent seems to have had a way with the ladies.

By this time the unhappy Prince of Orange had been given a hero's welcome on his arrival in Bath, spent several weeks taking the waters and had a public square dedicated to his name. Now he returned to London to find that his wedding would be celebrated on 14 March 1734, but that a terrible row had broken out with the Irish peers. They were protesting against Hervey's decision that for the ceremony they should file into the Chapel in procession after all the English and Scottish peers, regardless of their rank. Irish peers were, with the honourable exception of a few Celtic–Norman titles, a disgraceful group of placemen who had been recently ennobled in order to pack the Irish House of Lords and give Catholic Irishmen a bad time. Hervey claimed at first that they should all be away in Dublin carrying out Irish business. When that failed, because there was very little Irish business to carry out, he offered them a chance to process by themselves the day after the wedding was over and no one else was in the Chapel. Under the early Hanoverians, England often lapsed into such comic opera absurdities. All that was missing was Gilbert and Sullivan to capture its buffooneries, though John Gay managed that quite well with his *Beggar's Opera*, where the leader of the thieves is clearly meant to portray the Prime Minister, Sir Robert Walpole. It was a world in which William Kent, a clown of lively genius, was perfectly at home. The Irish peers capitulated, agreed to bring up the rear and, at long last, the royal wedding was on.

Led by a band comprising one fife, sixteen trumpets and a kettle drum, the multiple processions made their several ways into a chapel which, even Hervey had to admit, Kent had fitted up with extreme good taste: as much finery as velvets, gold and silver tissue, fringes, tassels, gilt lustres and candle sconces could give it. Kent's taste in decoration ran to theatrical excess and he revelled in upholstery.

What had happened, once the native Stuart line of monarchs had either been drummed out of the country, like James II, or died without heirs, like Queen Anne, was that royal court taste and direction in style had virtually collapsed and cheerful opportunists like Kent had taken over. The new German kings and queens were as opportunistic as Kent, which might explain his success with them. They had no great stylistic commitment to offer the prosperous island nation that had surprisingly adopted them but never really respected them; and the aristocrats, who really ruled the country, were perfectly willing to take their culture from someone who could claim not only to have trained in Italy, but to have practised there. It was not, as this wedding ceremony indicates, a very serious country but, almost accidentally, it worked efficiently. It was rich and powerful, though a blank canvas in terms of style. Kent is the key to England's subsequent hit-or-miss, experimental stylistic history for the rest of the eighteenth century. England was a wildly amateur, provincial island, moored out in the North Sea with men like Kent at the helm.

As the wedding service proceeded, with only one anthem – 'This is the Day' – music by Handel, words chosen by the Princess Royal herself, the King behaved well as he loved a show; but his wife and daughters were on the edge of tears. Their entry into the Chapel had put observers in mind of Iphigenia being led to the sacrifice with mournful pomp rather than a royal celebration. The bridegroom, supported by the Dukes of Richmond and Rutland, had not cut too grotesque a figure. He had worn his hair long, like a wig, flowing down his back and largely concealing the hump; so since his face was quite agreeable there was nothing visibly odd about him except his stature. After the service the processions repeated themselves, this time with the married women leading and the unmarried ones walking behind. The King and Queen gave the couple their blessing at a private ceremony in the lesser Drawing Room and supper was taken in public in the great State Ballroom, with the Countess of Hertford carving the meat. If that had been the end of it no one would have been upset, but the happy pair then had to be ceremonially and publicly put to bed in rich undress.

The Prince of Orange entered the bedroom in nightgown and nightcap, this time with no music and no Kentian decorations to distract the witnesses. The appearance he made was as indescribable as the astonished faces of the courtiers. In his brocaded gown he looked from behind as if he had no head, and from the front as if he had no neck and no legs. The curtains of the bed were drawn over what happened next, but the following morning Queen Caroline was still traumatised by the fate of her favourite child. 'Oh my God', she exclaimed to Lord Hervey, 'when I saw that monster come in, to lie with my child, I thought I was going to faint; I was staggered before, but this blow was the limit. Tell me, Lord Hervey, didn't you notice the monster and think about him at that point? Weren't you sorry for my poor Anne. Dear God! I know it's stupid but I am going to cry again!'[11] Hervey assured her, from his own experience, that after six months one gets used to anything in bed, but the Queen was still shattered at the thought of those first six months and what the Princess Royal would have to suffer. Princess Emily insisted that she would never have gone through with it, but Princess Caroline, another sister, said she could probably have weathered the experience. Princess Anne herself took the only possible course and behaved adoringly to her new husband, praised everything he said and acted as if she had married an Adonis.

Once the pair had been shipped back to Holland the royal family settled down to squabbling about music and their favourite composers. Did one back Handel or the Italian opera? King George, who was a natural philistine, declared that setting oneself at the head of a faction of fiddlers was not an honourable preoccupation for persons of quality. Life was back to normal. This was William Kent's England, in the Age of Reason, elegance and taste

1
Gothic Bridlington – the birthplace

There has to be a suspicion that not many who have written on William Kent have ever bothered to visit Bridlington where he was born, late in 1685. If they had they would surely have commented on the strong aesthetic conditioning that the place must have exerted on him. It looks, on a map, like a small seaport, halfway between much larger Hull and more historic Scarborough, just south of the chalk cliffs of Flamborough Head on the East Riding coast of Yorkshire. But it has to be experienced to appreciate its binary oddity. Even today, when straggling late Victorian and Edwardian suburbs link them, it is two entirely different communities of sharp social and architectural contrasts. In Kent's day almost a mile of fields separated The Quay from the Old Town where he was born and brought up. The Quay clusters on low cliffs around a sizeable commercial harbour, workaday and scruffily undistinguished, but with a violent history of storms, shipwrecks and heroic rescues. On either side of it the terraces of an Edwardian seaside resort spread out, now searching for a more convincing identity in an age of package holidays.

There is not a breath of salty air in the Old Town. With its handsome High Street curving up east to a widening green and the astonishing wreck of an apparent cathedral, it is at least as Barchester and godly in ambience as Tewkesbury or Sherborne, but with little of neighbouring Beverley's bustle and consequence, more a place of tea shops, parked cars and the prestige Georgian premises of doctors, lawyers and architects. On that High Street are the offices of the thirteen Lords Feoffees, an arcane, enjoyable body which, in default until quite recently of the normal mayor and council, has manipulated Bridlington's fortunes since the Dissolution of the Monasteries.[1] The Feoffees are a self-perpetuating oligarchy like the Merchant Venturers of Bristol, but more inland-looking in their character and generally benign. They have considerable land holdings, including the house on the High Street, Number 45, in which William Kent was brought up: a cosy, modestly elegant bourgeois nest. The Secretary of the Feoffees was most helpful in researching this book and it would be satisfying to link the Lords Feoffees with William Kent's projection into fame. They have their fingers in so many Bridlington pies, but the connecting evidence has not been found. 45 High Street and Bridlington Old Town seem exactly the comfortable surroundings where the only son of a prosperous joiner might have settled down for married life. The interesting fact is that William Cant, as he was born, bred, and on the first day of 1686, christened, never made a career in the town and never married. Bridlington's Gothic architecture imprinted itself on his visual imagination, but its social life seems to have bored him to tears. Some reservation has, however, to be made for the impact of Bridlington's characteristic tone of voice and accent.

It is accepted, though not often evident in dramatic and film presentations, that eighteenth-century England was a Babel of regional accents with no standard English pronunciation. Both Houses of Parliament reflected this rich oral soup and it took the broad Jamaican English of Alderman William Beckford, the equivalent of today's Brixtonese, to arouse laughter and amused comment. William Kent, so dull in his letters, appears to have been the life and soul of witty company, the 'Signior', a boisterous jester in the flow of his speech. While anxious not to offend present-day Bridlingtonians, from whom I have received nothing but help, interest and kindness, they do still retain (the older townspeople more than the younger) a distinctive, almost aggressive joshing pitch of voice, wary yet warm, that probably still preserves, not just William Kent's register, but also that of his patron-friend, Lord Burlington. He, for all his aristocratic assurance and stylistic sophistication, was brought up by his mother and her servants at Londesborough, the family seat of the Boyles, less than twenty miles south-west from Bridlington.

In that sharp, ejaculatory accent, Bridlington, Brillington and Burlington were accepted variants, so Lord Burlington was really Lord

Bridlington, the title his grandfather, Richard Boyle, had selected in 1665 to honour Charles I's widowed Queen Henrietta Maria.[2] She had chosen the town as a safe port of loyal subjects where she could land arms and reinforcements from Holland during the civil wars of the 1640s. Shared accents would have been at least one factor in the later bonding between Kent and Burlington.

One afternoon in a café at The Quay I sat listening to two old working-class men arguing at the next table. Their conversational pitch was perfect for the quick, slightly camp, delivery of two comedians, mocking yet amused and cordial. But I realised that it was still so regional that I could hardly follow it. What, for instance, did 'oo ee don't know now, the woman a says' precisely mean? The old Danelaw connection had not quite melted away. In his *Blood of the Vikings*, a local history book, Bryan Waite quotes two parallel passages, one actually modern Danish, the other modern East Riding. The latter is: 'Fost efther Ah was wed, we lived I Olbro me an mi weyf. We lived in a raw of houses, an Ah was sadly plagued wi owd gossapin wimmen', while the Dane said: 'Fost etter A wer gift, boed we i Aalborre, moe o mi huen. We boed i en rai hicks. A wer tit slest plawed aw gammel sladderkwind'.[3]

The idea that Kent and Burlington would have almost been able to make themselves understood in Jutland is of little stylistic importance, but it does set something of the tone of lost voices, a roughness to the speech of men whose voice patterns might otherwise be recreated as polished and effete. Let us try to imagine, for a moment, the two men talking together and Burlington beginning: 'Oo ee, that Alexander Pope a says to aye', and Kent responding sharply: 'Never i this world tha don't say'. It is an effort, but one worth making. We shape the past in accents of the polite present to our loss.

Kent's visual education, as well as his voice patterns, was moulded at Bridlington. By both nature and nurture he was an East Riding boy. If the architectural residue of the Industrial Revolution is ignored, any alert southerner going up to Yorkshire today will be struck by the subtle differences in building design, variations at least as strong as those between southern England and Scotland, and indeed much richer than those of Scotland, which destroyed so much more in its turbulent Reformation and later relative poverty. Yorkshire's Gothic is far more linear, defined and fresh, its domestic buildings pantiled and faintly picture-book in their cottage classicism.

Kent's father, William senior, who never changed his surname from Cant to Kent, unlike his more sensitive son, was a prosperous local joiner who rebuilt 45 High Street in 1693 and filled it with sound but undistinguished woodwork at a time when his only son and first-born was an impressionable eight years old. Esther, William's mother, born Esther Shimmings and married in 1684, died in 1697 leaving young William and his sister, another Esther, six years his junior, to be brought up by their father, who would live to a ripe old age, dying in 1739, only nine years before his son.[4]

As he would have lacked a mother's influence from the age of eleven onwards, that half-orphaned state makes the strikingly Gothic environment of William's schooling doubly important. It is here that Bridlington's rich Gothic visuals are likely to have made their impact. The High Street is a shallow curve of good building, with some late seventeenth- and early eighteenth-century brick houses with classical pilaster strips. In its western extension, Westgate, The Avenue is a more commanding classical house built in 1714 for a wealthy lawyer. Most of the original houses must have been characterfully vernacular, like the original surviving rear gable to the Cant house,[5] before they were refronted with symmetrical façades and multi-paned sash windows. A dual carriageway now severs the eastern flow of the street, but in Kent's schooldays it broadened out gracefully into Priory Green with The Bale, the Priory's massive 1388 gatehouse, in the foreground and then, unexpectedly vast, the cathedral-sized wreck of the Priory itself. It was built over the fourteenth and fifteenth centuries in a warm brown stone with a tremendous pattern-book range of clerestory windows, five in the easily copied, compass-drawn geometric tracery of Decorated Gothic and another three at its west end in fussy angular Perpendicular. Huge as the church still is, it is disturbingly obvious that this is only part of what was once raised. The great central tower, transepts, choir and saint's shrine in the east-work have all gone without leaving a trace; even the two west towers are Victorian of 1876, though by Sir Gilbert Scott at his thoughtful best and daringly contrasted.

The west front, the great battery of ornate porches from which Scott's towers now rise, was, however, there in Kent's time to make a lasting impression upon the schoolboy. Not only does it unroll from left to right like some ideal child's guide to the sequence of medieval styles in their correct chronological order – Norman, Early English, Decorated and

Perpendicular – its dominant motif, the curvaceous ogee arch, usually quite rare in English Gothic, is here profusely displayed in uninhibited ornate virtuosity of carving. Ogees shape two of the three cavernous porches, perfect shelters for schoolboys in wet or cold weather, and they are overcarved with niches and leafy crocketed forms.

These are the seductive flourishes of the Decorated Gothic style which peaked in the disorderly reign of King Edward II. While monarch and barons brawled over the King's generosity to his successive male lovers, the bishops and abbots built the Gothic into its flowering time: the nodding ogees of Ely's Lady Chapel, the matchless leaves of the Southwell Chapter House, Exeter Cathedral's lush symmetries, the experimental hall vaults of St Augustine's at Bristol. What this Decorated work was to the Gothic era, the Rococo would be, centuries later, to the classical: a self-indulgence of curving detail, crammed with lively copies of natural forms, leaves and flowers, a time for the sensuous after the purity and restraint of Early English lancet forms. And it would be this west front of ogee porches that William Kent would have faced every day of his school life, for Bridlington's Free or Grammar School was sited in the long room over the two gate arches of The Bale; and The Bale looks, not squarely, but at a dramatic angle focused down a grove of trees, to the west front of the Priory.

As a natural result of this visual indoctrination, when Kent came later to design a historicist Gothic or to draw Gothic illustrations for Edmund Spenser's *The Faerie Queene* he drew, not normal pointed-arched Gothic, but his own Bridlington ogee Gothick. That exquisitely inauthentic, playful style created Shobdon Church in Herefordshire, the screen for Gloucester Cathedral, a pulpit for York Minster and the castle where, in Book 5 of Michael Drayton's *Poly-Olbion*, Artegal fights the Saracen Pollente. For most of the remaining eighteenth century medieval revival work would be Kent's Gothick, not the real Gothic of the past; simple pointed arches were out, ogee arches were in. Horace Walpole, for all his superficial scholarship, saw the Middle Ages through Kentian spectacles. His Strawberry Hill Gothick is essentially ogee Gothic. Where Kent had shown the way, building ogee-arched Esher Place as the country house of Henry Pelham, later to become a successful prime minister, England would follow until an accurate, but less rewarding, truly scholarly, medievalism was imposed in the next century.

In his notes on Kent, George Vertue, the malicious gossip and chronicler of the arts and artists of the early eighteenth century, describes sketching and drawing as 'the root & foundation of fruitfull Genius'.[6] There is little to suggest in Kent's writing – the hit-or-miss spelling, the dyslexic syntax, the ugly, though legible, handwriting – that he was a responsive delight to his schoolmasters in The Bale. 'The truth is', he wrote in an apologetic letter of 3 June 1713 to his financial sponsor, Burrell Massingberd of Ormsby Park, Lincolnshire, 'I had as leave make a drawing as write a letter.'[7] So how many sketches of ogee arches and crocketed details did he sketch on Priory Green to fix those sinuous curves into his visual vocabulary? The same young man, whose written response to Paris on his first visit in 1719 was a listless sentence devoid of effective nouns – 'I think to stay here a fortnight, to see the things'[8] – could never have been a prize pupil of Usher John Topham, the Cambridge-educated head teacher at The Bale in Kent's time. But then, in strict accuracy, there is no concrete proof that Kent ever attended Bridlington's Free School: no class lists of its seventeenth-century pupils have survived. But Kent's father was a townsman of some substance. He was a constable of the manor in 1691 and served on the manorial court jury in 1688, 1697, 1698 and 1701.[9] He and his wife Esther both signed their names clearly on a deed of 1693,[10] so it is unthinkable that they would not have ensured that their only son should be equally literate, and there was only the one school in Bridlington, just up the road, which he could have attended.

There is, however, one oddity in William Kent's religious direction in his twenties that needs to be explained. His Bridlington was a hotbed of nonconformity, with Quakers, Baptists and Independents all drawing their congregations and setting up their little tabernacles, indications that the Church of England clergy officiating in the great Priory Church were an ineffectual team. Yet Kent, once he had tired of his father's joinery business and taken a coasting ship, a mere twenty-four-hour journey with favourable winds, to London, became closely involved with an ardent Roman Catholic convert and spent the next ten years very contentedly in Catholic Italy, an eager spectator at canonisation ceremonies in St Peter's.

There are several possible explanations for this devotional flexibility. It could have been a case of Catholicism by visual osmosis. In its prime Bridlington Priory had produced its very own saint, in competition, possibly, with St John of neighbouring Beverley. John of Thwing was born in about 1320, studied at Oxford, 'shrank from all vainglory as from deadly poison',[11] became Prior of Bridlington in 1362, died in 1379 and was the last Englishman before the Reformation to be canonised, in 1401. St John of Bridlington was a favourite saint of Henry V, who attributed his victory at Agincourt (1415) to the intercession of the two East Riding St Johns and paid a second pilgrimage of gratitude to the two great churches in April 1421. Yorkist kings were equally devoted. Renewing a grant, Edward IV wrote of 'the special respect which we have & bear towards the glorious confessor, the holy John, formerly prior of the aforesaid place',[12] while in 1499 Bridlington's Prior was mitred by the Pope. In Kent's day nothing would have remained of the saint's medieval shrine, but only a few miles down the road in Beverley Minster, the Percy Tomb, which Nikolaus Pevsner salutes as 'the most splendid of all British Dec funerary monuments',[13] was and remains gloriously intact, an explosion of nodding ogees, angels, hazel and vine leaves, musical instruments and fighting beasts. Again there is this parallelism of the figurative detail in ornate forms of the early fourteenth century with that mid-eighteenth-century Rococo-Gothick, to which Kent would be drawn as a counter to the austere disciplines of Burlington's ill-conceived Palladian.

Only a visit to this East Riding area of Humberside can convey the curious dominance of Gothic forms in that entirely unremarkable, level countryside. Not just Bridlington Priory and Beverley's two great churches, but St Patrick, Patrington, Holy Trinity, Hull, St Augustine, Hedon, and St Peter, Howden, are all Gothic giants towering up out of the dull fields and muddy rivers, memorable in contrast to an uninventive Nature, and every one of them splendid enough to have served as a cathedral. An almost medieval religiosity of visual outlook would have come readily to the Bridlington boy.

There is, in addition, the strong possibility that, in that vacant period between ending school and leaving for London, Kent could have fallen under the influence of Richard Fiddes, author, priest, dipsomaniac, Tory and High Churchman, teacher for a time at Bridlington Free School, though probably not while Kent was a boy there. The evidence is only circumstantial, but it does offer an explanation for Kent's refusal to do the obvious thing: to follow in his father's well-established joinery business, marry and settle down to raise a family in that almost empty house on the High Street. When Kent reached London he was introduced to a leading member of the Whig government, the 3rd Earl of Sunderland, by an MP, Sir William Hustler. That would be in 1709. Back in May 1704 the same William Hustler,

> Patron of the School att Bridlington in this County. Do hereby Nominate constitute and appoint Mr Richard Fiddes Master of the Sd Schoull. In Witness thereof I hereunto put my hand and Seal.[14]

This is not proof of a Fiddes–Kent connection. Fiddes was no Catholic, but the married and impecunious vicar of Halsham down in Holderness; nevertheless he brought to quiet and provincial Bridlington a strong gust of the larger world of politics and influence. He was the faithful chaplain to Robert Harley, 1st Earl of Oxford, and would later visit the fatally indecisive Earl when the triumphant Whigs had imprisoned him in the Tower after the Hanoverian accession of 1714. Fiddes was to lose his own chaplaincy to the Garrison at Hull in the same political reversal. He was eccentric, loyal and scholarly enough to be a friend of Jonathan Swift, Dean of St Patrick's, Dublin, and there is something about Fiddes, a humorous absurdity of nature, that suggests he and William Kent would have been attracted to each other in the tedious reaches of Bridlington society. Who else could have recommended the twenty-four-year-old Kent to a London MP with access to the inner circles of government? We should at least consider Fiddes's credentials for Kent's company.

Fiddes was born at Hunmanby a few miles south of Scarborough, the home of a possible later patron of Kent, Sir Richard Osbaldeston, who was Hustler's brother-in-law.[15] In 1687 he entered Corpus Christi College, Oxford, but, for unexplained reasons, transferred to University College. Absent-mindedness led him one evening, when studying for his BA in the Bodleian Library, to forget the way out and he was locked in all night. But he was alert enough to marry the reasonably affluent Mrs Jane Anderson in 1693. In 1694 he took Holy Orders and was given the living, at £66 a year, of Halsham, but was soon complaining of poverty. His voice was weak and it seems that he could only articulate distinctly when he had been drinking wine in convivial company. This casts doubts upon his performance in either pulpit or schoolroom.

As a writer he was much more impressive. Nineteen books are credited to him in the British Library catalogue, all written after 1708. Some, like his *Life of Cardinal Wolseley* (1724) and his *Practical Discoveries on*

Several Subjects (1720), went through many editions. His *Sermon on Proverbs XVIII, v. 16, preach'd to the criminals in York Castle, July 4, 1708, principally on occasion of the murder of Major T. Foulkes*, went through only one. His *Wolseley*, written at a time of strong anti-Catholic prejudice, is not only scholarly, with a full appendix of sources, but also impressively broad-minded about a Catholic prelate of uncertain moral background. Fiddes died in Putney in 1725, leaving his wife and six children ill provided for. This was not a good time for High Church Tories, even those without a drink problem. But Richard Fiddes does come across as a whimsical oddity, one who, in quite a small town, could well have been a congenial companion for the much younger and perhaps easily influenced Kent and, therefore, the source of the Hustler introduction.

All we have to rely on for Kent's early years is Vertue's often spiteful account:

> when young unexpectedly he demonstrated his youthful inclinations to drawing. (being apprentice. of a coach painter. & house painter. – from him he came to London without leave. or finishing his apprenticeship) His parents or Friends circumstances being not in a Condition to forward his practice & the expence of a profession . . .[16]

However, no record has been found in the apprenticeship lists of Hull or York of Cant or Kent's name. His father was not poor and could have employed his son in his own business. The coach or house painter story sounds like a malicious jibe from a hostile narrator, and Vertue was hostile. From the few hard facts emerging from this ill-chronicled area of Kent's life it seems likely that he was much more in command of his own direction than Vertue chose to imply.

2

Politics and a pick-up in London

The long years of unrecorded life, which only reasonable speculation can cover, came to an end in February 1709 when 'William Cant of the City of London Limner' witnessed three deeds conveying land in Bridlington from the recently widowed Susanna Prudom, and her eldest son, Robert, a London mercer, to another son, David Prudom, a Bridlington resident.[1] Three months later there would be a second and far more interesting written record of Kent's activities, but at least this first signature proves a move to the capital and a profession of sorts. Kent's fellow witnesses to the deeds were John Grimston, the local attorney who would eventually draw up Kent's father's will, and a clerk, Robert Popplewell, the son of a clergyman and a graduate of St John's College, Cambridge, whom Kent would remember respectfully in a letter from Italy three years later.[2] So the range of his social acquaintances was widening, though the implication of Bridlington-born Robert, the London mercer, is that Kent was still keeping within an East Riding circle, even in a London of enchantingly various Wren steeples and bland, repetitive brick façades that had risen since the Great Fire of 1666.

In view of Kent's later friendship with John Talman, an ardent convert to Catholicism, his closeness to the Prudoms is surprising, as they were a vigorously nonconformist family; the Prudom father, who had died in 1709, having been a founder, after many years as a Quaker, of Bridlington's first Baptist congregation. It has been suggested that Kent may have lodged in London with the younger Robert Prudom, but this is mere speculation.[3] Exhaustive research has not even revealed the Prudoms' London address though it did reveal the fact that Kent, with what would become his characteristic self-confidence, never bothered to become apprenticed to the Painter Stainers' guild.

This profession of 'Limner' is tantalisingly vague, particularly so as in the next written reference Kent has changed his name from the unfortunate associations of 'Cant', which was always used deprecatingly at the time,[4] to the more feudal sounding 'Kent' and is now listed as a 'Painter'.[5] The term 'limner' often described someone working in watercolours, as in Thomas Robins, the 'Limner of Bath', who painted delicate garden views in the 1740s.[6] There was also some implication of portraiture as in Samuel Foote's satirical comedy *Taste* of 1752: 'how do you limners contrive to overlook the Ugliness, and yet preserve the Likeness?' So Kent could have been making a modest reputation and living for himself in London by ink and wash portraiture of citizens and their wives. He could, however, just as easily have become a commercial artist decorating legal documents with delicate watercolour heraldry and scroll work, which would have been less romantic, but is more probable.

What is far more revealing is the next written reference. It is found in a fat, leather-bound letter book in the Bodleian Library in Oxford.[7] This had been kept by John Talman to create a lively journal, apparently for posterity, by selecting copies of the many letters which he wrote on his Italian expedition between 1709 and 1711. Talman's complex character and confused aims will emerge over the course of the next chapter; for now it suffices to say that he was the son of William Talman, who was the Comptroller of Works, and a favoured court architect in the reign of William III. Talman had been dismissed as soon as the Tories came to power in 1702 under Queen Anne, and his son John, a draughtsman of some ability, trained as an architect; but with no buildings to his credit, he seems to have been planning his second Italian trip (the first had been in 1699–1702) in order to revive his father's career by a spectacular injection of Italian designs into the world of English architecture.

He had made his first well-informed, beautifully drawn and coloured demonstration of continental forms, half of them Italian classical, but the more imaginative ones Italian Gothick, a year earlier. All Souls College, Oxford, had been planning extensions to its medieval quadrangle since 1703. Six schemes had been proposed and John Talman's was arguably more impressive even than Nicholas Hawksmoor's designs, which were eventually adopted. It is easy to see why Talman's scheme must have frightened the dons. As a convert to Roman Catholicism, burning with zeal, Talman could not control his delight in the vestments of the Roman Church nor his exuberant Baroque imagination. Recently returned from Italy, his mind was still full of the tremendous frescoes, like Pietro da Cortona's *Triumph of Divine Providence* in the Barberini Palace or Annibale Carracci's *Triumph of Bacchus and Ariadne* in the Farnese.

For the new 'Refectory' at All Souls, Talman described and roughly sketched out a wall.

> painted from end to end, w: ye Muses Surrounding Apollo, who sits in a round temple, from whence he orders divers Praemium's to be distributed to multitudes of Students in yir prop. habits (whose faces are to be drawn from ye life) in ye air are to be Cupids flying about, holding tablets w: motets &c. ye Country very fertil w: fruits, flowers, grove of mirtle.[8]

There would have been nothing else like it in Oxford: cupids flying over groves of myrtle and students drawn from the life, all the joyful animation of the Italian Baroque, but what English painter could have projected such a composition? Inevitably it was passed aside, but it is quite probable that one of John Talman's aims in taking the young William Kent off to Italy was to ensure that at some future date there would be at least one English fresco painter capable of realising that scene of groves around a classical temple. While Kent never painted it he did, with the help of Capability Brown, who was gardening at Stowe in his first promotion, plant and build such a scene in the Elysian Fields.

Even more stimulating and revolutionary were the exteriors which Talman had drawn for All Souls: six great bays for the Refectory; the windows pointed to the outside, round-headed to the interior. Each buttress was to have its statue, and Talman's obsession with ecclesiastical gear was to be given full expression: the Founder 'in his pontifical mantle', 'Romish Bishops' in chasubles and mitres, other statues in gilt brass and 'foliage alla Romana'.[9] In an Oxford so recently saved from the Romish intentions of King James II it would have been enough to give nervous Protestant clerics heart failure. But Talman, young, brash and optimistic, was preparing for a return of the Old Pretender to the throne as James

III. His was an artistic gamble which would fail, yet this was the man who now took Kent, young and impressionable, under his wing, to sweep him off on a splendid hare-brained project to Rome itself, the very citadel of hostile art forms.

Kent would have ten years of indoctrination, before he met Lord Burlington, not only in the Italian Baroque as it edged over into the Rococo, but in John Talman's highly sophisticated eclecticism. Coming from the ogee curves of the Gothic west front of Bridlington Priory, Kent fell straight into the cheerfully eccentric clutches of a man who had already projected an impressive major scheme in a weird compromise: 'Italian Gothick' with 'Tuscan' tracery for an Oxford college. Kent's was no ordinary artistic apprenticeship. Talman was his first master; Burlington was merely the second.

How the two men came together in London is not known. Kent is most unlikely to have shared Talman's Jacobite sympathies, but they are likely to have recognised each other as kindred spirits: ebullient, unmarried, adventurous, dextrous with paint or pencil; and Kent was to prove himself consistently as a charmer, not of women, but of men, witty, pliable and good company. There is no doubt from some of his letters that Talman grew very fond of him and exerted much influence to advance his Italian career. Kent, for his part, used Talman and moved on, but not without the imprint of that Gothick eclecticism which would continue to modify and enliven his later Palladian phase.

Writing from London on 12 May 1709 to his notoriously quarrelsome and frustrated father at the family home in Ranworth, Norfolk, Talman mentioned, airily and without significant comment (he could, after all, hardly tell his father that he had picked up a new boyfriend from Yorkshire, who might just possibly turn out to be a genius):

> Y other day Mr Kent y Painter who goes w: me, was carried by Sr. Wm Usher member of Parliament to my Lord Sunderland, who enquired of him how he went to Rome & whom, & making answer w: me, what? (says my Ld) Talman is going to Rome again to bring home a Design for Whitehall.[10]

So in three months' space, between February and May, Cant, the onetime Bridlington boy, now aged twenty-four, had moved from the company of Bridlington lawyers, clerks and mercers to that of Sir William

Hustler,[11] an MP, albeit a local one, of Acklam in the North Riding, and Charles Spencer, 3rd Earl of Sunderland and Secretary of State for the South, a post that usually implied a governmental control of foreign affairs. The Earl was a leading member of the Whig junta that governed the country from 1706 to 1710. To grace the occasion William Cant had become William Kent and the 'Limner' had become a painter.

Hustler's patronage of Kent can be explained. His grandfather was a wealthy Bridlington draper who had endowed the town's grammar school in 1636, and Sir William was now a patron of the school and a substantial property owner in the town.[12] He could, therefore, have been recommending a promising old boy of the school to the Foreign Secretary immediately before Kent set off abroad. What is more probable is that Richard Fiddes, whom Hustler had nominated as a master at Bridlington Free School, had noticed Kent's talents in the 1704–9 period and personally recommended him to Sir William. How Kent had managed to impress John Talman so much that Talman recruited him for his second Italian visit is harder to explain. But it is possible that Fiddes was again responsible. While in no way a Catholic, Fiddes was a Tory and High Churchman, likely, therefore, to have been as hesitant over the question as to who would succeed Queen Anne as was his friend and patron, Edward Harley, 2nd Earl of Oxford. If, as seems likely, he was a Jacobite sympathiser, he could have recommended Kent to Talman, a fellow Jacobite.

What is interesting about the meeting and Lord Sunderland's comments are the politics and nuances behind them. Queen Anne's short but triumphalist reign covered twelve years of the most intense and febrile political manoeuvring in English history. In May 1989, the art historian Jane Clark published an article in *Apollo*, 'The Mysterious Mr Buck'. This argued, with a wealth of convincing scholarly evidence, that Lord Burlington, Kent's future patron, was not, as had always been assumed, a pillar of the Whig party, but a closet Jacobite who had paid a generous annual subsidy to the exiled court of the Old Pretender in France through all the years when Burlington was dancing attendance at the Court of St James's. The shock and alarm that ran through the world of architectural history on the publication of the article was some indication of how shallow and unsound was most people's historical understanding of the period. There can, in fact, have been very few prominent aristocratic politicians who were not hedging their bets on Stuarts and Hanoverians at this time. Any notion of two solid political blocks in the Lords from 1700 to 1730, or even into the second Jacobite Rebellion of 1745, is an error. William Kent was caught up in the guessing game and, as events turned out, made a bad move from a political point of view in 1709, but a profitable one from an artistic angle.

In that year England was, as a result of its experiences over the previous sixty years, an unusually sophisticated country in its political responses. It had suffered the trauma, acute in a conservative, insular society, of the public execution of a king, God's Annointed, after an open judicial process. There had followed eleven years of a republic when the House of Lords had been juggled at the whim of a gentleman farmer turned soldier, Oliver Cromwell. The Restoration of 1660 had left the monarchy dependent upon the fluctuating will of a Parliament with a strong republican minority of the Whigs descended from the Cromwellian elite. One foolish move from James II, appointing a Catholic to be head of Magdalen College, Oxford, thus threatening a Catholic takeover, had resulted in an extraordinarily perverse decision. Rather than continue with the rightful, but Catholic, King, the country accepted, grimly but firmly, the Stadtholder of Holland as its new monarch and saviour, even though Britain had just fought three savage little wars with Holland in the previous forty years. It was basically a Whig party decision, but taken with reluctant Tory backing, because the Tory party supported the Church of England and that Magdalen College appointment had undercut the whole Church of England establishment.

The experiment, unexpectedly, had been a resounding success. Bringing in a foreign king had resulted in military triumphs abroad, Ireland subjugated and the House of Lords ruling the country under a president-king. But then, thanks to William III's sexual reluctance to sire an heir, and his sister-in-law, Queen Anne's, failure to rear a child to adulthood even after seventeen pregnancies, the political game was wide open again. Should Queen Anne be succeeded by a very old German woman, the Electress Sophia of Hanover, merely because she was a Protestant and, via Elizabeth, the Winter Queen, of Bohemia, the grandchild of King James I? That was the Whig party's preferred option. Or should, now the exiled James II had died in France in 1701, his son, James the Old Pretender, be brought back, under strong anti-Catholic safeguards, to rule as James III, Parliament's obedient puppet? That was what the Tory party would, ideally, have liked to do.

An octogenarian German woman on the throne of the United Kingdom was a dispiriting prospect, but the Old Pretender had refused, when tested by secret Tory embassies, to give up his Catholic faith. London was apparently not worth an Anglican Communion Service. Queen Anne was another part of the problem. Her habit of referring to her half-brother, the Old Pretender, as 'the Prince of Wales', hinted at a disturbing inclination towards a Stuart rather than a Hanoverian successor. She hated the two-party system that had emerged since 1660, and attempted with some success to balance Tories and Whigs in the ministers she entrusted with power. Tories tended to dominate except for the years between 1706 and 1710, when the 1710 general election, which had at this time by the Triennial Act to be held every three years, had put the Whigs back in power, with Lord Sunderland as a Secretary of State. But the extreme uncertainty of political allegiances at this time is best demonstrated by the position of the Duke of Marlborough, the hero of Blenheim and scourge of Louis XIV. He was by instinct a Tory, yet he relied upon his wife to control the whims and prejudices of the Queen, and his Duchess was a Whig. In Parliament there were both outright Jacobite Tories and Hanoverian Tories. Indecision was in the air. Even leading and ostensibly Tory politicians like Lord Godolphin and the Earl of Oxford hesitated in their loyalties and their decision making. Though Queen Anne was only in her mid-forties, her health was poor and the prospect of a very old German grandmother succeeding her as Queen Sophia did not offer much promise of stability.

In all this uncertainty and equivocation the two men with whom William Kent was associating in May 1709 were striking exceptions. Lord Sunderland was a determined and entirely committed pro-Hanoverian Whig. He had, as early as 1706, bypassed the Electress Sophia and made a personal promise of loyalty to her son, the Elector Georg, thereby setting his republican principles aside in the pursuit of power. John Talman was equally committed to the opposite side. As a devout Catholic, with all the enthusiasm of a convert, he was for a return of the Stuarts' true male line. His Catholic faith and the reason for his forthcoming visit to Italy were clearly well known to Sunderland and would have provoked his instant hostility and suspicion. That comment about Talman going to Rome again 'to bring home a Design for Whitehall' would have been delivered either with an angry snarl or with sarcastic contempt. Sunderland would have realised that the Catholic and Jacobite Talman was going to pick up an Italian Baroque palace design, ostensibly to flatter Queen Anne, but really to prepare for the Old Pretender's return and so curry future royal favour for his unemployed architect father.

Sir William Hustler, if he was not politically astute, may have thought he was doing his Bridlington protégé a favour by securing the audience with Lord Sunderland. In reality it was like introducing a mouse to a cat. Sunderland, thirty-five years old, of fair complexion and middle height, inclined to corpulency and with a fixed and settled sourness to his face, was the most dangerous and thrusting member of the Whig junta which was enjoying a precarious five-year interlude of government. An instinctive republican, he despised the monarchy, dictated to the Queen and looked forward to a time when titles would be abolished and he would become plain Charles Spencer.[13] He may have had his statue carved in Roman senatorial costume but, having earlier pledged support for the Elector Georg, he would in 1714 organise Georg's smooth succession to the throne and be rewarded in 1718 by being appointed First Lord of the Treasury, or Prime Minister.

Sunderland would immediately have marked Kent down as a dangerous Jacobite. John Talman was surely alert enough to realise what had been the tone of the interview and had passed the remark on to his father without glossing it. William Talman had, under William III, been a natural Whig; but after quarrelling with virtually every Whig lord he had worked for in the 1680s and 1690s – the Duke of Devonshire and Lords Carlisle, Normanby, Coningsby, Portmore and Kingston – he was now financing his son's second visit to Italy as part of his plan to be restored by the Tories to his old post of Comptroller of Works. The proof of this would come in 1713 when he appealed for reinstatement to Lord Oxford, the hesitant Tory leader who had been returned to power in 1710. To back his claim Talman urged that he had made, and was 'still collecting by his son abroad, the most valuable Collection of Books, Prints, Drawings & etc, as is in any one person's hands in Europe, as all the artists in Towne well know'.[14]

The petition failed – Sir John Vanbrugh was reinstated in 1715 – but the elder Talman's words are very revealing about the mission for which Kent had been enlisted. It implies that stylistic taste was generally considered to be in the air. Instead of drawing Lord Oxford's attention to the superbly assured palace façade in modified French Baroque that he had designed for the south front of Chatsworth in his glory days, William Talman was now suggesting that the extensive collection of Italian designs that his son was making, with some assistance from Kent, would be relevant to England's stylistic advance in the eighteenth century. The Talman collection would contain some drawings by Palladio and some by Inigo Jones, but these were not explicitly mentioned. There is no stress on pure classical antiquity, but rather on a general free-for-all of continental enrichments. In their eagerness to follow continental fashions the Talmans, father and son, were missing out on the future Palladian and neo-classical stylistic direction of their own insular society.

It is only possible to speculate on whether Kent had been sufficiently alert to tone and nuance to see that the introduction to Lord Sunderland had not been a success. But the two written records do throw further doubt on George Vertue's later account of Kent's early years. According to Vertue, Kent's parents

> had the Good fortune to find some Gentlemen of that Country. [Yorkshire] to promote his studyes, raisd a contribution and recommended him to propper persons at London, to direct him to Italy, where he went with Mr J. Talman & Mr W. Locke aged about 20 (certainly 1710 by sea).[15]

As a limner working in the City with respectable friends in the legal profession, he was obviously making his own career. Sir William Hustler is the only local Yorkshire gentleman who could be said to be promoting his studies, and that indirectly and extremely tactlessly. What may have confused Vertue is the fact that Kent would owe his profitable later connection with Sir William Wentworth in Italy to the Hustler connection.[16] Sir William Hustler was Wentworth's uncle, which would have been enough to bring the two young men, Kent and Wentworth, together when Wentworth's Grand Tour brought him to Rome in 1710. Wentworth's subsequent promise of £40 a year to support Kent in his studies, in exchange for certain services, would enable Kent to escape his ties with John Talman.

It is obvious, however, that in 1709 those ties were strong. Kent was about to venture off to Italy in the employment and close company of an impulsive Catholic Jacobite. There was no Yorkshire connection; such a connection would not develop until Kent was settled in Italy and looking around for other means of support and further sponsorship. What it does prove is a remarkable self-confidence, a spirit of cheerful adventure and only secondarily a quest to obtain professional, artistic training. Talman had chosen his team: there was Kent whose talents for drawing could be put to copying Italian stylistic models, helping to create the collection, which the elder Talman would boast about in 1713; and there was Daniel Locke, an architect, though with no recorded buildings to his credit and of roughly the same age as Kent. Locke would presumably advise John Talman on appropriate Italian palace models. Talman himself was fluent in Italian, had studied law at Leiden, travelled in Holland, Germany and Italy between 1698 and 1702 and was himself an able enough draughtsman in a heavy-handed style of thick black lines.

There is a distinct sense of eccentric improvisation about the expedition. Three bachelors: Talman aged thirty-two and reasonably affluent through subsidies from his father; Locke, twenty-seven and paying his own way on a first visit to Italy; and Kent, twenty-four and financed, according to a later Talman letter,[17] by John Talman himself. John Talman's character will appear from his personal revelations, but if there is any clue as to how he came to employ an unknown limner on an ambitious, ill-organised project, it may lie in his tendency to sudden eccentric impulses. For instance, shortly after the curious threesome had set sail from Deal their boat was held up for several weeks off Portsmouth. As if the prospect of a long voyage in the company only of Locke and Kent had suddenly overwhelmed him, Talman wrote an urgent letter to a Mr Oddy imploring him 'to join the party'.[18] It would cost him eighteen shillings to come down on the coach from London, and then £10 to the captain would cover the cost of the voyage to Leghorn; 'bring in specie [gold] w, you', Talman added.[19] Mr Oddy never turned up. Three years later he was still being anticipated in Rome.

It seems likely that Kent was taken on after a similar impulsive offer which, unlike Oddy, he eagerly accepted, being a young man ready to take chances, to risk a perilous sea voyage during a war with France, with a persuasive talker who had taken a fancy to either his person or his quick sketches, or to both. Whether there was, as Vertue claims, any intent 'to promote his studyes',[20] thereby improving those quick sketches into great art, is doubtful. That ambition seems to have developed later as the personable and friendly Kent picked up Yorkshire and Lincolnshire gentlemen sponsors in Rome by the same arts that he had picked up Talman in London. Vertue was under no illusions about Kent who, he claimed, had 'engrossd' Lord Burlington's 'favours – by merrit or cunning'.[21] What has to be admired is Kent's mixture of confidence and vulnerability. He may have freed himself from Talman's monetary patronage, but in a stylistic sense he would never escape, nor wish to escape, from the influence of those early years abroad. Talman's enthusiasm for Italian decorative excess, for a proto-Rococo that would prove refreshingly at odds with the austerity of Palladianism, would have a lasting impact on the design career of William Kent.

3
A foolish voyage

To claim that the threesome – Talman, Locke and Kent – actually set sail for Italy on 22 July 1709 would be optimistic, for the voyage would be one of many delays; but at least by that day they were on board the merchantman *Swallow* in hopes of a departure from Deal. 'We are now in y. Downs', Talman wrote dutifully to his paymaster father, 'waiting for a wind & some moor of Man of War going w. stores to Lisbon; if they come within 2 or 3 days we shall stay for ym otherwise we go without . . . our boat just going now a shoar.'[1]

The war with France, which had been fought successfully on land by the great Duke of Marlborough, had not proved one of the brightest chapters in the annals of the Royal Navy. No Blake, Rodney or Nelson had emerged to sweep the French off the seas and the English Channel was perilous. Back in April, John Talman had been anxious. 'I labour hard to find out a ship', he had written to Dr Hudson at University College, Oxford, 'now ye year is so far advanced, ye more inconvenient will it be to travel in yt hot country to Florence, where I shall make some stop before I reach Rome.'[2]

He need not have worried. It would be mid-October before the party landed at Leghorn, after almost three months at sea. They were going the cheap way, £10 for the passage, but crammed together on hard bunks in a tiny cabin with no enlightening visits to the great cities of the Low Countries, Germany or France, no exciting foreign foods and wines. It must have been a formidable test of personal relationships, and once they were in Italy the two younger men, Kent and Locke, tended to travel together on their own timetable, apart from Talman, the two sharing lodgings in Rome.

Talman believed he was in love with a married woman and was very wrapped up in the affair, squeezing every last drop of emotion out of it. Before they sailed he had written a terrible poem to 'My Dearest Dear', and been pleased enough with the composition to include it in his letter book:

> Do not torment this heart of mine
> Don't cause me still to sigh & pine
> O how happy might we always be,
> To live in Rome in sure sincerity!
> Hearken to my prayers and let love
> The same desires in yr Passion move:
> Let us on y subject talk together,
> Don't be cruel, Dearest tell me whether
> We shall meet, & when, pray tell me soon
> Let me know without delay my Doom;
> Let me Dearest soul, in't silence of ye night
> Hear yr mind & melt me wt delight;
> Don't deny me, hear me, don't abuse me
> Hasten y happy minuit, don't refuse me.
> Yr Dearest Charmer
> Tuesday 12 o'clock at night. Jn. Talman[3]

When that boat was going ashore to Deal with the letter to his father, it also carried a letter to Mrs Gardner, 'Ma Cara Bella',

> To let you know by letter how much you reign in my heart, and how often I kiss your Dear pretty lip. I have only time to wish you all happiness; and to send you ten thousand kisses.
> I am, dear wife in life
> Yr real lover Jn. Talman

Eventually the *Swallow* did set off, only to drop anchor again in Spithead, off Portsmouth, where it remained, confined by weather and the French, for the greater part of August. This gave Talman time to write four more letters to Mrs Gardner. An emotional crisis, never exactly defined, had arisen and he was concerned about her mental condition. 'Poor dear love', he wrote,

> Methinks I embrace thee in my arms & kiss thee a thousand times while yu are telling me w. tears yu'l retire into y country to yr father, pretty innocent fool! methinks I see yr tears trickle down yr dear cheeks! but don't suffer passion to overcome reason, but the strongest argument of all to persuade yu to be easy, is yr own innocence; wch makes me love thee as much as thy dear pretty eyes charm me.[4]

There is much more in this vein, so apparently the affair had been platonic. It could be that Talman's letter-appeal, mentioned earlier, to Mr Oddy, pleading with him to load his pockets with gold and join the party, had been written in the hope that Oddy would lend Talman sympathy and moral support in his lovelorn condition. Kent and Locke seem to have lured him into laddish behaviour. Something shameful had taken place when Talman next wrote on 7 August, still from Portsmouth: 'This world', he complained to his father, 'is full of turns & changes; ye vicissitudibility of sublumary affairs causes much trouble & anxiety: nothing is certain, nothing is to be depended on. On fryday last ah! fatal day, our long boat carryd us three passengers to Portsmouth.'[5]

But there, frustratingly, the confession ends, or at least that part which Talman thought safe to copy into the letter book. If *Tristram Shandy* had been published in 1709 rather than 1759, Talman could be accused of mimicking its style. Did they meet Mrs Gardner, or her angry husband, visit a brothel or merely get drunk in a Portsmouth ale house? Whatever the answer the three men appear to have been the only passengers on the brig and to have achieved sufficient male bonding to carry them over two more months of close confinement. From later comments the voyage, though prolonged, was blessed with good weather and no one was seasick. The delays were due to a mixture of unfavourable winds and threats from French privateers.

The *Swallow* reached Gibraltar on 22 September and finally made Leghorn, as the English insisted on calling Livorno, the port for Pisa, on 15 October. 'I shall bring yu something from every town I go to', Talman promised his father;[6] and immediately became industrious for a whole month in Pisa with a side trip to Lucca. Apparently Kent helped him in his recording of details of high altars, choir stalls, pulpits and organs, though a Signor Santucci of Pisa was also similarly employed. It is hard to see how such details would be impressive or useful back in England. Perhaps Talman was anticipating, in his habitual Toad-like enthusiasm, a mass national reconversion to the Roman Church; but a certain type of recent convert does tend to a trainspotting delight in the minutiae and accessories of any correct Catholic observance.

It would be the same in Florence. In a letter to his father of 21 November he wrote rapturously:

> In y Chapel of St Laurence are urns of most valuable stones on which are crowns and cussions set all over with precious stones, y altar & tabernacle are so rich yt I can't describe it in words, but I hope in God you will see it in draught w. many other curiosities.[7]

There can be no question about Talman's sincerity, only his judgement. Writing to Signor Magnolfi in Rome on 31 May 1710 he expressed his sorrow because 'I shall see on the feast of Corpus Dei an immense treasure & ye most glorious ornament of ye Christian Church without being so happy as to have a representation of it to preserve a lively veneration of ye Majesty of ye Catholick Ch. when I am returned to my own country.'[8]

The intriguing question is where, in all this blaze of rapturous piety, did William Kent stand? One of his later Yorkshire patrons, Burrell Massingberd, quizzed him on the issue and received the smooth reply:

> I have been with the cardinal [Ottoboni] since I came. I imagine by a word in your letter you are afraide I should change my religion but there's no fear of that though I am just now a going to do a little ceiling of a church, my countrymen wonder at it but you may imagine my one reason I do it for a small matter both to force my invention & to have practice, to paint in fresco.[9]

That sounds plausible; but he did also win a prize in a papal competition for young artists,[10] though it was only a second award in the second class, and Talman had secured the patronage of Cardinal Ottoboni for him. Kent was adept at being all things to all men, and it seems most likely that in his nine Roman years he was a practising Catholic to his Italian 'master' and patrons, while remaining blandly Protestant to his

English friends. He would have seen to it that the question of spiritual allegiance never came up; fish-like he could swim in all waters and eventually return to England apparently still a conventional, and convenient, Protestant.

What would have attracted Kent to John Talman's service and friendship would have been Talman's Baroque mind, his enthusiasm for pomps, ceremonies, local decorative detail, all that mind-set which would make Talman's enormous collection of drawings a mere show of rarities back in England, a one-day wonder, in a land now dedicated to a revived Palladian austerity. Something of Talman's blundering organisation appears from a letter he wrote from Pisa asking Lords Somers and Halifax: 'yt I may be further instructed concerning yr Lordships commands & in a more determined manner yt I may give all satisfaction I am capable of; I have hinted likewise concerning y method of payment, & to whom I must apply'.[11] Surely these were matters which he should have clarified when he was in London, not in Pisa. Apparently he was referring to the project for a bronze statue of Queen Anne, to be set up on a column in London, and to that scheme for the grand new Italian Baroque palace for Whitehall at which Lord Sunderland had sneered.

On arrival in Florence on 18 November, Talman was writing again to Mr Topham about other projects, some extremely wild, that he should have sewn up before he left England. He urged Topham to patronise, that is, finance, a project to draw and engrave 'a compleat corpus of y antick statues gems & etc', which would be 'an honour to our Kingdom'; and continued:

> I do not mention what fine marbles, shafts of pillars & statues yt might from time to time be brought for Blenheim . . . & more especially for y adorning a noble Palace suitable if such a one can be built, to ye greatness of a Qn. who has a soul to do as glorious things in Arts at home as she has done in arms abroad.[12]

Scholarly studies of a serious subject can easily miss the truth just by being too serious. It would be inaccurate to project John Talman, who was obviously Kent's mentor at a most impressionable period in his life, as anything but a comic figure. Kent would have liked and appreciated him precisely because Talman was often ridiculous and wildly camp, quite over the top in his art appreciation and his excesses of interior decoration. Kent had a common, lavatorial sense of humour. He thought that pissing up walls was comic and that dogs pissing on their masters' legs were hilarious, and in one sense he was right.[13] John Talman, who slavered over ornate chasubles and overwrought reliquaries, yet walked from Florence to Rome to save money, was an eccentric in a grand tradition. For Kent to meet Italy in Talman's company, rather than in that of some nervously reserved young milord, was a great stroke of luck, an education in itself. The greatness of Kent – and sometimes he was going to be truly great as well as truly inferior – lay in his sponge-like ability to play Protestant and Catholic, to accord closely with a would-be Palladian, Lord Burlington, so soon after learning from a would-be Baroque, Talman. He would humour whoever paid him. As for carting off antique columns to improve Blenheim Palace, that was more or less what Robert Adam did with verd-antique columns salvaged from the Tiber to enrich the Anteroom at Syon House. The notion was excellent; it was just fifty years premature. Decorative excess is not a sin; pure simplicity is only a passing fashion. Great designers can ride both the sin and the fashion, but they need a sense of humour, as do their critics.

Settled comfortably in Florence, at the Casa di Signor Mingardi al insegna di S. Filippo Nere near San Firenze, with five men, Kent apparently included, all working for him on his expanding programme of Baroque record, John Talman had time to pass sexual advice on to his Cousin Betty, who had just got married back in England:

> Each minuit of y tedious hour a Passionate wife has to wait for her husband, in ye most secret recess of yr shady grove. let them dare a Bower fit only for love & blushes wch are only seen wn ye eyes rould w. quickest motion. at each palpitation of y heart strike fire, & set at once in a flame wch terminates in convulsive milky joys and Swimming extasy. Not to trespass too much on yr patience I hope Y are marryd well & wt is still better yt yu are w. child.[14]

In an earlier letter, to his Uncle ap Price, Talman had included an aphrodisiac present of a rhinoceros horn, intended presumably for the cousin, not the uncle, with a rhetorical warning, worthy of Robert Burton's *Anatomy of Melancholy*, against bad-tempered women who 'thrust fingers in butter, slap hoods against walls, cast fur caps in ye fire, split tables, jumble stools together & clinck fingers together & roll eyes round as if y were fire balls'.[15] This was nothing; in another letter, to his cousin Benjamin Talman at Lisbon, he had ordered Benjamin 'never go into a woman's company if possible; for it is very dangerous & yr Portuguese are all eyes & ears'.[16] Remembering that Poor Kent had been cooped up for three months on a small brig with this neurotic bachelor, it is small wonder that Kent's only recorded venture into sexual relations in later life was to imply in his will his paternity of two children born to the actress Elizabeth Butler.[17] A safe and respectable bachelor's life, living in the household of the happily married Lord Burlington, would have preserved him from the possibility of fingers thrust into butter dishes, caps hurled into fireplaces, tables split in half and eyes rolling like fire balls!

While drawing and recording in Florence, absorbing Italian decorative detail in the most direct possible way, Kent found time to cultivate and impress the English envoy to Tuscany, Dr Henry Newton (1651–1715), a scholarly and important diplomat who gave Kent his first commission to paint a picture in Italy and later corresponded with his young protégé.[18] Kent owed that introduction to John Talman, the first of several such influential contacts; but it was also a clear proof of Kent's personable charm.

Talman's party remained in Florence from November 1709 to April 1710. Whether Locke and Kent followed their leader's example and, to save money, walked from Florence to Rome via Siena, is not recorded, though it seems likely. They settled in Rome in separate lodgings, Locke and Kent in the house of an old English painter, Thomas Edwards, in the Strada Paolina, round the corner from Santa Maria Maggiore. Talman, however, claimed 'we agree very well and every Thursday we spend in seeing fine palaces as last Thursday we saw Borghese Palace'.[19] Kent may still have been working for Talman and there was still a good relationship between the three men, but a social gap was widening now and it was in these months between April and August of 1710 that Kent demonstrated how easily he could make his own way among English visitors to Rome when a Yorkshire or Lincolnshire connection could be claimed. Talman, while still keeping an eye on developments, noted nervously in a letter of 5 July to Henry Newton: 'For the keeping of poor Mr Kent abroad at study for some years our English gentlemen have been so publick spirited (which humour I pray God encrease for the honour of England) as to give him generous assistance. his bashful temper and inexperience in writing has been the cause of his not troubling you with a letter of thanks for your favours.'[20]

John Talman's anxiety to make excuses for Kent's churlishness, in not writing to thank Dr Newton for his patronage, indicates how fond he had become of the younger man. A series of letters written later in the same year of 1710 hints that Talman felt Kent slipping away from him and was trying hard to revive their emotional closeness. What is significant about the letters is, not that they were written, but that Talman chose to preserve copies in his letter book. They have none of the absurd, dramatic gush of those letters to his Mrs Gardner; instead they betray real concern. 'Dear Billy', the first began. It was written from Naples on 8 November and would be the only time when anyone addressing Kent would ever reduce his Christian name down to its intimate form:

> I hope you don't take it ill I have not writt, wch hasn't proceeded from forgetfulness of my Friend, but from ye abundance of curiositys I note down every night. I hope you study hard; by Xmas I hope to be in Rome, y situation of ye city is not to be imagined; I find ye Churches rich to excess.[21]

Neapolitan church interiors had, understandably, quenched even Talman's thirst for Catholic sumptuosities. He ended with an appeal for a reply. Kent being Kent, no reply was written; so on 6 December, still in Naples, Talman wrote again, this time to plain 'Mr Kent':

> I wrote yu nov 8 but have had no answer, I am sorry you forget yr friend, if yu had so much to write at nights as I have yu & Mr Lock might be excused. I hope yu Study very hard.
> immediately after Xmas yu'll see yr huble Ser:
> & true friend J. Talm Service to all friends.[22]

Even more revealing was the next letter from Naples on 20 December, this time to Locke, who had had the courtesy to write back to Talman on the twelfth of the month. But its theme was still 'Billy'. Talman would not be back in Rome until 31 December,

for wch reason if it would not be a violent trouble I would ask yu to assist Mr Kent w. me for a week by wch I will pay interest if required. My return will be very soon to see an opera in Capronica. tho Naples is more a siren y can yu imgin. Keep my Bill safe & fra tanta lei Sta Felice godendo
Ca Bella gioia! Roma!
Saluta Theophilus & Boanerges Servo vostra Sempre fidele Gio: Talman
w: a holy kiss.[23]

The flippant humour of the conclusion cannot hide the concern, even the panic, that motivated its writing. The implication is that if Talman does not continue to pay Kent, someone else will; those weekly subs have ended and 'my Bill' may be looking elsewhere for support. Talman was even prepared to pay interest if Daniel Locke would keep Kent in pocket money for the three weeks before Christmas.

These letters suggest, but in no way prove, a close intimacy between Talman and Kent, one that could well explain Kent's presence on the team. They suggest also that Kent could be bought. Benedetto Luti's portrait of Kent aged thirty-three invites speculative attention: the plump, self-satisfied face, those huge, knowing eyes and those trim, pouting lips.[24] If one were obliged to make a guess as to Kent's sexual identity, as in a biography an author is, a tentative judgement would be that he was a cheerful rogue, confidently manipulative, ready to adapt to whichever role might serve the occasion, but with no strong drive in any direction. The signs were, in the winter of 1710, that John Talman was beginning to outwear his usefulness.

Kent was beginning a course of studies under an impressive master, Giuseppe Chiari. Did Kent take his artistic talents as seriously as did his sponsors? Whatever the degree of self-deception, Chiari would allow him to enjoy Rome for five years, independent of John Talman.

4

Silk stockings from the Philosopher Earl

The mystery man among Kent's associates, patrons and friends in Italy is Sir William Wentworth of Bretton in the West Riding.[1] Wentworth was almost Kent's contemporary. He arrived in Rome in April 1710, the same month as Kent, but only stayed in the city until August. Yet in those five months he became sufficiently impressed by Kent's artistic potential to promise to fund him with £40 a year for the next seven years, with the apparent understanding that Kent would study under Giuseppe Chiari. The oddity of the relationship is that Wentworth, who had been in Italy some years earlier,[2] had been directed by his kinsman, the British ambassador to Prussia, Lord Raby, to make contact with and rely upon, not Kent, but an Irish artist, Henry Trench, who had been studying in Rome under Chiari ever since 1704. Wentworth did, in fact, contact Trench as soon as he reached Rome and went along with the Irishman to check that the paintings of Roman scenes that Raby had ordered were being executed. He assessed Trench as 'a pretty good judge of painting', expert enough to have advised the Italian artist 'to make him now and then some little alterations & put in some figures where he thought their [*sic*] wanted'.[3] A year earlier Trench had been almost destitute, writing to his patron, Sir John Perceval, that he was 'in so great Want that I cannot do anything except I am helped Speedily'.[4] But it was not Trench whom Wentworth helped out with £40 a year, but William Kent, newly arrived in Rome and apparently entirely unrecommended, unless Wentworth's uncle, Sir William Hustler, had put in a word.

That has to be a possibility. Wentworth was from the West Riding, Kent from the East Riding and Hustler from the North Riding, so all three were Yorkshiremen, united by much the same accent, while Henry Trench was Irish and a Catholic. Virtually every writer who mentions him misspells his name, suggesting that he spoke with his lips half-closed, changing any initial 't' to a 'th' in a fast, soft Dublinese. Voice and religion could explain Kent's rise to favour with Wentworth.

The known facts about Wentworth do not add up to an entirely plausible character. Why should he have been eager to sponsor Kent's artistic education, ensuring a steady flow of antique fragments and copies of celebrated paintings for Bretton Hall, when his response, on 20 March 1710, to Raby's advice on paintings was a sturdy philistinism? He had, he claimed, no money for art:

> I shall be well content with the walls of Bretton just as they are, so that I have but a good glass of Ale and Bear [*sic*] to make my friends welcome with, when they honour me with his company, which is all I desire.[5]

Lord Raby's doting raptures over his kinsman, fourteen years his junior, ring curiously in contrast with such stolid squirearchical poses of homely simplicity: 'I look upon you as a brother', Raby wrote from Berlin on 17 December 1709,

> to whom it is more natural to be free than to be complaysant; & I believe I really love & esteem you so much that instead of being weary, I really wish'd you could have staid much longer, for as your company was easy & agreeable, I shou'd desire the perpetual continuation of it.[6]

On 12 April 1710 he was still writing in this intimate vein: 'I really don't love you alone as a relation but as my own brother.'[7]

Raby would be created Earl Strafford in 1711, Duke of Strafford in 1722 (a Jacobite title) and he was anxious to collect paintings for the palatial Franco-Prussian entrance range that General Jean de Bodt had designed for him at Wentworth Castle. For his part Sir William was dutiful in carrying out the various errands in the Roman art world that Raby had asked him to perform, but he deliberately ignored his would-be brother's general old-maidish tourist advice, which explains how he fell in with Kent, the eager networker. His kinsman had urged him to stay in Rome with 'one Charles Brown a Scotchman who has the best lodgings' and warned him against 'one Edwards an English painter who is very officious to his countrymen but wonderfully Sharp and loves to get as much from them as he can'.[8] Making the excuse that Brown's was full, Wentworth stayed at Edwards's lodgings where Kent was a fellow boarder.

Thomas Edwards lived in the Strada Paolina from 1705 to his death in 1720. A Catholic and himself a painter, he was one of those English guides to Rome who kept a stable of young artists at hand whose works he would tout, for a commission, to his clients. Two of Kent's future patrons, Burrell Massingberd in 1713 and Thomas Coke in 1717, bought from Edwards, so he and Kent probably came to an arrangement. It is even possible that Edwards had talked up Kent's potential as a future genius to Wentworth, resulting in the £40 sponsorship.

While Kent would treat his next two sponsor-patrons – Massingberd and Sir John Chester – with a mixture of sycophantic gratitude and irritated impatience, he seems to have held Sir William Wentworth in nervous respect. Kent's very first letter surviving from his Roman period was to his London antiquary friend, James Gale, begging him to send on 'this picture & drawings for Sir William Wentworth not knowing where to find him'. 'Sir Wm', he urged, 'is my very good patron.'[9] He had, nevertheless, forgotten his address. Poor Massingberd, a natural victim of life and of people like Kent, complained several times in plaintive letters that 'Sir Wm' was getting preferential treatment with prompt acknowledgement of money received and 'you have very much neglected me though Sir William Wentworth sais you are long enough to him, his pictures came all safe but mine was very much damaged'.[10]

So Kent's patrons back in England did exchange information on their prodigy. This raises a puzzling question of judgement. How could a whole sequence of reasonably cultivated gentlemen have become persuaded that William Kent had latent genius? Talman could have been emotionally motivated and Giuseppe Chiari will have taken Kent on simply for the money; but Sir William Hustler, Henry Newton, Wentworth, Massingberd and Sir John Chester are an impressive muster, with Thomas Coke, Earl of Leicester, and Lord Burlington even more prestigious. Granted that Kent had usually to supply them in addition with Neapolitan soap and Italian treacle, but there was always the hope that they were sponsoring an English Raphael. What could he have shown them to raise their expectations so absurdly high?

His drawings have an undeniable saucy charm; he could have illustrated the *Adventures of Tintin* admirably. In a few lines he could convey the rigid walk of a Negro gardener or the reflection in a canal of a naked man towelling himself dry; but he could not even draw trees sensitively. As for figurative fresco painting, that group on the ceiling above the King's Staircase at Kensington Palace has three men and one woman looking down from a balcony. It should be a composition in the classic *de sotto in su* perspective, as seen in foreshortening from below. Kent does foreshorten the balustrading, but not the figures above it. All three men look like fat, sly versions of Kent himself as Luti painted him, and even the lady has the same unattractive leer. It is both charmless and incompetent, and by the time he came to paint it Kent had had nine years of study and practice under Chiari.

The explanation for this almost national mood of credulous sponsorship that would, by 1713, leave Kent comfortable on £70 or £80 a year, could only be the impact upon the English ruling classes of the one book of philosophy which, in three centuries, they have ever taken to their hearts. *Characteristicks of Men, Manners, Opinions, Times* was published in parts between 1708 and 1712 by Anthony Ashley Cooper, 3rd Earl of Shaftesbury. He was the grandson and spiritual heir of the 1st Earl, a Cromwellian soldier and Dorset country gentleman who had been the founder of the Whig party, the 'false Achitophel' of Dryden's satirical poem 'Absalom and Achitophel', and a pillar of the republican left in British politics under Charles II.

It is impossible to overestimate the influence of this persuasively optimistic book upon English eighteenth-century attitudes. Addressed in the form of a letter to his friend, John Lord Somers, the recently retired Lord Chancellor, it took the sting out of Christian doctrines, virtually banished the idea of original sin, valued cheerful moderation and established an educated elite of virtuosi gentlemen as the natural rulers and pilots of the United Kingdom. Putting aside for a moment its irresistible appeal to a landed aristocracy, Shaftesbury's second volume with its paean of praise for wild, natural gardens was instrumental in raising Kent to the level of genius when, in the later 1720s, he would have an opportunity to design gardens himself. So far its influence was positive. But the 3rd Earl's *Letter concerning Design*, written and widely circulated in 1709, though not published until 1732, indirectly crippled Kent's career as an architect by its malign influence on his patron Lord Burlington.

If the earlier books of the *Characteristicks* had not been so intoxicatingly acceptable, so much the world view that the English aristocracy and gentry wanted to believe in, then the prejudiced nonsense which Shaftesbury poured out in his last *Letter concerning Design* would not have been so disastrously influential. But it contained an entirely unsupported attack on the architecture of Sir Christopher Wren and Sir John Vanbrugh. As a Whig arbiter of virtuosi taste Shaftesbury despised automatically any buildings produced in what he called 'The long Reign of Luxury and Pleasure under King Charles the Second', when the Tory party had ruled.[11] His foolish prejudice blinded him to the reality that the period had been, with Wren and Vanbrugh, one of the great ages of English architecture. While he was entitled to sneer at Carolean painting and at most Carolean music,[12] his book was responsible for the eighteenth century's general failure to rate the poetic invention of Wren's London church steeples or the achievement of St Paul's Cathedral, which had been raised after two centuries during which no great church had been attempted anywhere in England. In addition, because of Shaftesbury's facile and spiteful attack, England failed to take the escape route that Vanbrugh's Baroque spatial handling of houses as well as palaces had opened up.[13] Instead, the platitudinous, two-dimensional simplicities of a second-hand Palladianism prevailed, stripped of most of the inventive qualities that Palladio had deployed. Shaftesbury dismissed, without quite naming it, Blenheim Palace, scorned Wren's additions to Hampton Court and asserted that 'the many Spires arising in our great City with such hasty and sudden growth . . . shall be hereafter censur'd as retaining much of what Artists call the *Gothick* Kind'.[14]

Colen Campbell, who featured St Paul's and Vanbrugh's buildings generously in the volumes of his *Vitruvius Britannicus* (1715), was never so dismissively crass; but because of Shaftesbury's prestige and his vague earlier appeal of 1709 for a return to the neo-classical forms of the Roman republic, the tame Palladian designs in the same volumes were what prevailed. To Shaftesbury, 'enthusiasm' in design, as in all aspects of human behaviour, was ungentlemanly. Reserved, and, therefore, usually boring, architectural simplicity was the goal. In many respects the English aesthetic outlook has never recovered from this snobbery, which equated good design with economic cost-cutting: an irresistible combination.

Equally irresistible was the philosophy which had preceded the *Letter concerning Design*. In the unfortunate past of seventeenth-century religious conflicts, Christian divines had tended to denigrate human nature: 'we are afraid of bringing good Humour into Religion'.[15] Shaftesbury believed that morality should not be based upon rewards in the hereafter, but on all those virtues of kindness, friendship, sociableness, love of company, conversation and natural affection, that Thomas Hobbes had left out of his gloomy *Leviathan* of 1651. We should be honest without thought of heaven or hell. Atheists and believers alike united to condemn human nature when it was, the Earl proposed, in reality generous and good.

So much for the Fall of Man: Shaftesbury virtually dismissed Christianity; we should concentrate upon Nature, where the goodness and beauty of the Divine creation is evident. Addison seized upon this notion and popularised it in May 1712 in *The Spectator* in his essay on 'Cheerfulness':

> Such an habitual Disposition of Mind consecrates every Field and Wood, turns an ordinary walk into a morning or evening Sacrifice, and will improve those transient Gleams of Joy, which naturally brighten up and refresh the Soul on such Occasions, into an inviolable and perpetual State of Bliss and Happiness.[16]

So at the beginning of the century the poetry of Wordsworth at its ending was exactly foreshadowed, as were, more immediately, the semi-natural gardens that Kent would have the genius to improvise at Stowe, at Richmond, Esher, Holkham, Claremont and Rousham and, though against the grain of Burlington's previous blinkered formalism, at Chiswick. All that would come in response to Shaftesbury's journalism.

This last skill should never be underestimated. The old Earl had a magical power over words. In his evocation of the beauty of deep woodland glades in the second section of volume two of *The Moralists* he anticipated Edmund Burke's *A Philosophical Treatise into the Origin of our Ideas of the Sublime and the Beautiful*, published forty years later, in 1757:

> And here a different Horror seizes our shelter'd Travellers, when they see the Day diminish'd by the deep Shapes of the vast Wood; which closing thick above, spreads Darkness and eternal Night below. The faint and gloomy Light looks horrid as the Shade it-self: and the profound Stillness of these Places imposes Silence upon Men, struck with the hoarse Echoings of every Sound within the spacious Caverns of the Wood. Here *Space* astonishes. *Silence* it-self seems pregnant; whilst

an unknown Force works on the Mind, and dubious Objects move the wakeful Sense.[17]

Shaftesbury was consciously reviving the old gods, creating a desire for 'sacred sylvan scenes, such as of old gave rise to temples, and favoured the religion of the ancient world'.[18] Kent would be the man to satisfy such a desire. That was not the only mood of Shaftesbury's journalism. He could anticipate Winston Churchill in his appeals for national effort, not to repel the enemy (Marlborough had just done that) but to make Britain as great in the arts as on the battlefield:

> I can, with some assurance, say to your Lordship [Lord Somers] in a kind of spirit of Prophecy, from what I have observ'd of the rising Genius of our Nation, That if we live to see a Peace in any way answerable to that generous Spirit with which this War was begun, and carry'd on, for our *own* Liberty and that of Europe; the Figure we are like to make abroad, and the Increase of Knowledg, Industry and Sense at home, will render *united* BRITAIN the principal Seat of Arts; and by her Politeness and Advantages in this kind, will shew evidently, how much she owes to those Counsels, which taught her to exert herself so resolutely on behalf of the *common Cause*, and that of her own *Liberty* and happy *Constitution*, necessarily included.[19]

That is why Kent's sponsors were so ready to be generous. Art was patriotic; Kent was to be a creator of 'her Politeness and Advantages'.

As a journalist, Shaftesbury was a glorious hypocrite. In one section of his book he could damn enthusiasm as ungentlemanly; but when Theocles, one of his neo-Platonic moralists, apostrophises '*Nature*! supremely Fair, and sovereignly Good! All-loving and All-lovely, All-divine!',[20] he shamelessly piles on the rhetorical enthusiasm and indeed admits as much when Theocles is pressed in argument: enthusiasm is fine when applied to the right objects. The passage in which Shaftesbury advocates a new style of garden design is well known, but it deserves repetition. It comes, like so much of his best writing, in *The Moralists* when Theocles has anticipated Wordsworth and aimed a deadly blow at formalism:

> The Wilderness pleases. We seem to live alone with Nature. We view her in her inmost Recesses, and contemplate her with more Delight

> in these original Wilds, than in the artificial Labyrinths and feign'd Wildernesses of the Palace.[21]

It is then that he comes to the details of an ideal garden

> of a *natural* kind; where neither *Art*, nor the *Conceit* or *Caprice* of Man has spoil'd their *genuine Order*, by breaking in upon that *primitive State*. Even the rude *Rocks*, the mossy *Caverns*, the irregular unwrought *Grotto's*, and broken *Falls* of Waters, with all the horrid Graces of the *Wilderness* it-self, as representing NATURE more, will be the more engaging, and appear with a Magnificence beyond the formal Mockery of princely Gardens.[22]

In his last writings on the Beautiful of 1712, from Naples, it is apparent that, for all his handling of 'Caves, Grottos, Rocks, Urns & Obelisks in retir'd places',[23] Shaftesbury had not entirely thrown off seventeeth-century formal planting. He wants them 'disposed at proper distances and points of Sight, with all those Symmetrys which silently express a reigning order, Peace, Harmony and Beauty'. Symmetry still lurks at the back of his vision of an ideal garden. But what he was offering, to opportunists as free-spirited and confident as Kent to reorder, were the adjuncts, the parapher-nalia of classicism to be disposed romantically. Shaftesbury himself was very nearly a Romantic, perhaps because he had abandoned his ancestral acres and settled in Naples. But then he died, leaving the actual decorative forms of Romanticism for men like Kent to evolve out of Robert Castell's semi-formal gardens as mapped out in the plans of his *Villas of the Ancients* (1728). These would become the English 'Arcadian' gardens that first swept this country and then enchanted Western Europe. Romanticism always had its roots in the picturesque appeal of classicism in decay.

What has to be remembered is that when Shaftesbury's moralists, Philocles and Theocles, go out for their evening walk, it was in fields 'from whence the laborious Hinds were now retiring'.[24] His was no demo-cratic ideal. The free play of mind to which his virtuosi should aspire was aristocratic and elitist, a moral and aesthetic freedom to be shared only among gentlemen who know one another well: 'the mere Vulgar of Mankind often stand in need of such a rectifying Object as the *Gallows* before their eyes'.[25] This was from his *Essay on the Freedom of Wit*, and the appeal of such 'Wit' to country gentlemen vexed with 'Hinds', who were poaching their deer and their pheasants, hardly needs to be stressed. Rousseau and the long slide towards the French Revolution were still a comfortable fifty years distant. Kent was born at the right time.

What is so dramatically satisfying in this Italian summer and autumn of 1712 is that Kent and the great 3rd Earl, whose garden aspirations Kent would realise, actually came, if not precisely face to face, at least into a very close personal contact; so close that the Earl gave Kent a pair of silk stockings. The man who brought this about was Henry Trench, or, as Shaftesbury called him, misled by Dublin aspirates, 'Mr Thrence'.

Shaftesbury was dying, but gracefully and in no hurry. Plagued by an asthmatic condition, he had decided to leave England for ever and seek health in the mild climate and grotto-rich gardens of Naples. He had made a late marriage and fathered a boy, the future 4th Earl, now two years old. But with true philosophic detachment, he took his wife with him to nurse his asthmatic bouts, leaving his son at Wimborne St Giles, the Ashley Coopers' family seat in Dorset. Such was his prestige that two hostile armies parted on the Franco-Prussian border to allow his party to pass.

On his way down through Italy he called at Florence to consult with the British envoy to the Grand Duke of Tuscany, the Hon. John Molesworth, who was not only the son of an old friend but, incidentally, an admirer of Kent's budding artistic talents. Lord Shaftesbury corresponded with Molesworth from Naples until his death two years later. It was no coincidence that when Molesworth gave up his diplomatic post he returned to England with the Florentine architect Alessandro Galilei in tow and set up the New Junta for Architecture with himself, Galilei, Sir Thomas Hewett and Sir George Markham as its members.

The New Junta would be dedicated to realising Lord Shaftesbury's ill-thought-out ideas for a revived noble simplicity of correct classical architecture. By themselves they might have had little influence, but there can be no doubt that they had the open backing of the King, George I, who was eager to make some kind of cultural impression on a country more inclined to regard him as a German joke figure with unusually ugly mistresses and a shady record of wife abuse. The King would make Molesworth a Viscount in 1725 and knight Hewett in 1719 to celebrate his appointment to the influential position of Surveyor General of the King's Works in the same year. In 1717 Hewett would join the growing band of Kent's admirers, brought into contact by his friendship with

Massingberd who was a landowner in the next county to Hewett's Nottinghamshire.

Yet again, often by quite obscure contacts, Lord Shaftesbury directed Kent's career. On 6 November 1711, he was briefly in Rome, sharing the Eternal City with Kent for only one day, though unaware of the proximity. He reached Naples with his party of eleven on 15 November, settled in the Palazzo Mirelli, and there, under the attentions of the Spanish Viceroy's own doctor,[26] his health improved so much that he was able to prepare a second edition of the *Characteristicks*, illustrated this time with elaborately symbolic headpieces and a frontispiece of Shaftesbury himself, posing as a senator of republican Rome in a voluminous toga like an extra large nightgown.[27] This antique fashion had been current in England since at least 1660 among Whigs and Tories alike, though normally only for statuary and funeral monuments.

The Italian artist Magliar, who began work on the headpieces, fell ill and, after careful enquiries, Shaftesbury employed Henry Trench to realise his allegorical schemes. A Catholic Irish priest, Dr Fagan, had recommended Trench and the Earl made his neo-classical leanings very clear, commanding Trench to study 'the antient Originals . . . & drawing after the noble models of Statuary and Painting here in Italy to copy ancient Basso Relievi both for the sake of the Figures as well as the Draperys, Dresses, Arms, Instruments and Ornaments civil, military and religious, which accompany the antient historical Pieces'.[28]

Henry Trench, informed upon all these scholarly details, took up residence in Shaftesbury's palazzo from 6 April to 16 September 1712. There he drew the headpieces to the Earl's detailed specifications. Their engraver's name, Simon Gribelin, appears in the second edition, but not Trench's; the vain old Earl had claimed that they were drawings 'Which I in a manner designed and drew', merely because he had stipulated their details.[29] One headpiece in particular, portraying the various ages of the Arts, does seem to anticipate the eclectic garden buildings – pyramid, obelisk, domed temple and even a Gothic cathedral – that eventually graced the grounds of Stowe where Kent and Capability Brown would design together on the Elysian Fields.

Trench's influence is implied in the purchase of paintings which the Earl made while Trench was in residence: two wild landscapes by Salvator Rosa, a landscape in oils and another in black chalk by Gaspar Dughet, an Annibale Carracci of the Holy Family in a landscape and the Claude landscape that Shaftesbury prized above the others, describing it at length in a letter of 8 November 1712 to Sir John Cropley:

> A Campanian or Bayan sea shore; forming a Bay: a Promontory with a beautiful Castle or Villa and Architecture: Nothing Gothick or ruinous. Everything smiling: sea calm: a Brease only playing on it: the Trees and Shrubs of a Wood making Shade at hand: and the Sun's heat abated by being near set and half in cloud. The Nymphs are already come out of their Grots to joyne in Dance, with the Fauns and Satyrs: an old one of this kind with his young Stripling sitting by and performing as Musicians to their Country-Dance . . . If this be not found a *Pleasant Piece*, I can have no idea what is pleasant in painting.[30]

This was Shaftsbury's ideal model for the new gardens. With his seductive landscapes of great trees and smiling waters set with classical temples and medieval castles, Claude was their inspiration, so it is accurate to describe the gardens which evolved from his writing as 'Arcadian'.

As he was leaving in September, Trench was given a memorandum by the Earl requiring him to find out in Rome 'What Painters, Sculptors or Engravers of any note or young men who promising arrive at Rome from other Places or are sent for to England, France, Germany, or taken into Princes or great Peoples Service? In particular concerning Ioseppe Cari [Chiari]. What single Piece of his (being one of his best sort) may be had at an easy Price?'[31] This sounds as if Trench had put in a good word for his master, Chiari, and also, by subsequent events, for William Kent, a word to which, however, Kent seems to have responded ill advisedly. The Earl's accounts read:

> Paid Mr Trench by Order (just at his going away) for a pair of silk Stockings presented to Mr Kent at Rome for a Draught of King Attila 2 ducats 2 carlins 0 grains. Paid Mr Trench as a Present from my Ld five Pistoles at 45 carlins each.[32]

To send, as a specimen of his work, the scowling Hunnish head of Attila to an old gentleman who delighted in classical bas-reliefs would not have been a tactful gesture, though it does sound very Kentian: grotesque and even mischievous. He had taken Attila from Alessandro

Algardi's celebrated history painting of Pope Leo I persuading the Huns to give up their siege of Rome simply by the holy awe of his presence. A pair of silk stockings was Shaftesbury's courteous put-down to a young man who had not hugely impressed him. Another memorandum of accounts, dated 5 September, had noted that 'in Mr Brown's last Accot. (folded up in Mr Moreau's Bills) he has charged 7 Crowns in one article and 7 Crowns and 6 Julios in another for Prints bought by Mr Kent'.[33] So Kent had been busy. However, the 'Accot.' continues: 'The whole sum according to ye Note hereunto annexed ought to be 16 Crowns & 4 Julios . . . overcharged 6 Julios'.[34] Brown was a Roman art dealer and Kent had been less than careful with the money, daring to short-change the Philosopher Earl himself.

Whether Kent ever met the Earl face to face is not made clear, but, at a guess, and judging from the implication of those effete silk stockings, it seems very likely that the philosopher and the gardener, who would eventually realise the philosopher's aims, did actually get together. Kent was not a man to let opportunities, social or commercial, slip past him. He must have realised that he owed it to Shaftesbury's urgent appeal for painting, architecture and music to flourish in England alongside its military triumphs, that so many young gentlemen in Rome were prepared to put money into his training in the art of painting. Shaftesbury had made such sponsorship seem a patriotic duty. Another comment in the *Letter concerning Design*, that 'the Publick has of late begun to express a Relish for Ingravings, Drawings, Copyings, and for the original Paintings of the chief Italian Schools (so contrary to the French)',[35] hints that on his Naples trip John Talman could have hidden his Tory loyalties long enough to have asked Shaftesbury to support his projects. Kent would have been wide open to second-hand information on Shaftesbury's views on architecture and garden design from Henry Trench, who had been an intimate of the dying Earl for almost six months. This meant that, to the eccentric, Gothick-Baroque influence of John Talman were now added the grand, neo-classical public projects of Shaftesbury, who maintained that: 'Tis the good Fate of our Nation in this particular, that there remain yet two of the noblest Subjects for Architecture; our Prince's *Palace* and our *House of Parliament*.'[36] All these possibilities Kent was storing away for future reference and for wider networking.

5
Playing the patrons

Kent enjoyed Rome; it was his kind of city, not necessarily in its architecture, where the scale of its palaces was too grand and its streets were too narrow to serve as useful models, but in its gardens, those of the Villa Borghese, with their scatter of classical temples over lawns and short avenues of trees, being very close to the formula Kent would work out eventually in England. He would also have relished the city's lively social buzz. In June 1711 John Talman staged a lavish and exquisitely precious 'Symposium', which resulted in a papal audience for him, with access to 'y Popes Secret Sacristy in y Vatican'.[1] As a personal favour for Talman's engaging young artist friend, it also gained Kent the patronage of Cardinal Ottoboni, with modestly prestigious commissions for paintings and even for a fresco in a church. Talman wrote excitedly to his father on 6 June:

> I had an entertainment wch is the talk of the whole town, in a scene in one of y rooms was a compliment to y Pope & Cardinal Ottoboni who already knew of it & ye latter sent ye next morning one of his Chamberlains to thank me. I had ye best musick in Rome composed on purpose & a poem of about 400 verses composed on ye occasion in praise of arts & commending several persons yre present who were all top virtuosi.[2]

There had been forty-three guests in rooms 'illuminated & hung w. festoons of myrtle flowers, round y room were 12 heads painted representing

Vitruvius, Fabius y Painter, Glycon y Sculptor; on ye opp. side were Palladio, Rafael & Bonarotta, on an other side, Inigo Jones, Fuller & Pierce'.[3]

This ranking of three Englishmen with the three great Italians – Palladio, Raphael and Michelangelo – was revealing. Isaac Fuller and Edward Pierce were a Baroque artist and a Baroque sculptor-architect respectively. Talman's father William had been Pierce's 'very good friend', mentioned in Pierce's will as having 'the choise and picking of what therein shall seeme to make up the worthy collection he intends'.[4] But Inigo Jones could hardly be described as a Baroque architect. John Talman, who would later sell a number of Palladio's drawings to Lord Burlington, must, therefore, have been broader in his stylistic tastes than at first appears because he included Palladio's more correct and neo-classical designs in the vast and generally Baroque, or 'incorrect', Talman collection. It is not precisely stated in Talman's letter, but it seems likely that Kent painted these '12 heads' for the entertainment, and would, therefore, have become familiar with Inigo Jones's fame and his idealised representation of features.

The company seated beneath this display was served with 'hot meats all round' at two tables; the Prince of the Academy or Symposium was Lord Cornbury whose health was drunk 'in richly perfumed Rosoli during wch a trumpet sounded a martial air'. Fifty double flasks, including eight sorts of rare wines, were drunk at a cost to Talman of £15. 'I do not ask', he wrote to his father, 'to be paid for it extraordinary, but if yu please to send me £20 free of exchange to make another' it would help.[5]

On 15 August he wrote again in triumph to his apparently indulgent father: 'I beg leave to inform yu yt next Wednesday I shall have audience with y Pope. Leave will be asked to see his Highnesses fine collection of drawings from y Anticks.'[6] It was a formidable achievement in ecclesiastical trainspotting, but soon Talman was back to his old form: the lecherous, boastful Mr Toad. In a 13 June letter to his friend Conrad Fleetwood, a son of the British Consul in Naples, he reminisced gleefully over past conquests: 'I hope to enjoy a little more of Mrs Betty's flesh managed just as it was at Resina, y savory relish makes me still licking lips, tho' I ly most nights alone. O sweet Mrs Betty w: pepper and salt.'[7] This heterosexual rapture makes it unlikely that, unless Talman was bisexual, his relationship with Kent was anything more than that of a friend and patron.

Interwoven with this culinary bawdy talk were Talman's sincere eclectic interests, which later events prove he was passing on to the impressionable

Kent. His letter of 1 August in the same year quizzed a Mr Della Motray, again of Naples, for

> Your views of ye Greek & Turkish temples very large, yt all ye parts as also ye figures may be easily distinguished . . . I thank yu also for yor care concerning ye Moskees. I should be glad to have ym large & w: all exactness possible on paper in y. colours w. y. fine marbles, y foldages & y Ceremonies performed in ym . . . ye Priests habits both of y Turks & y Greeks; w particular views of y parts of ym temples, viz y altars, belles, y Crosses, mitres, chalices or any other religious furniture.[8]

John Talman's fevered activities in Italy go some way to explain the awareness of eclectic cultural influences which mark out the world of early eighteenth-century garden designers, Kent of course included, with their Turkish tents, mosques and classical temples.[9] Time and again one is reminded in Kent's design career of Talmanesque exuberance, striving for release from the Burlingtonian disciplines of an austere neo-classicism.

Kent was even a little influenced by Talman's leering and laddish attitudes to women. Now that he was collecting patrons and had to squeeze out the occasional letter, brief rays of light begin to fall on the social life of a Roman lodging house for young English gentlemen, and Kent himself becomes less of a two-dimensional figure reacting passively to others' manipulations. His next catch as a sponsor, after Sir William Wentworth, was the Lincolnshire gentleman, Burrell Massingberd of Ormsby. In early spring 1712, Massingberd was travelling in the prim, conventional company of Charles Baldwyn of Stokesay Castle, Shropshire. Both were part of an informal group of young Englishmen, travelling sometimes together, sometimes apart. It included Henry Lord Herbert, the future 'Architect' 9th Earl of Pembroke, co-designer with Roger Morris of the Palladian Bridge in the garden of Wilton House, near Salisbury. The group appears to have come together in Thomas Edwards's lodging house on the Strada Paolina, where Kent was living; so it was probably Kent who persuaded Lord Herbert to buy a Chiari painting.

In his first letter to Massingberd, Kent refers knowingly, in an uneasily assumed manly style, to a young woman, probably a laundry maid, living in 'the family above', who seems to have had hopes of a match with one of the English group: 'Mr Harvey's french man gave her a serinade & M'Ld Herbert's Gent. which makes much of her'.[10] The laundry maid seems to have become something of an obsession with Kent, being mentioned in the Massingberd letters many times over a period of several years. Revelations on Kent's sexual identity are so rare that it is worth following the affair through to its end for hints on his moral responses. By his next letter the situation has deteriorated: 'as for the family above no body goes to them but my Ld Caminen who my hope is will make her his wife, but I believe he will go into her body first'.[11] While Kent's 'hope' is anything but bawdy, more in fact naively moral, the phrase 'will go into her body', exudes a certain nervous distaste, as if he wanted to sound worldly-wise but had not mastered the correct spit-and-sawdust terminology, even though he was twenty-seven years old. Was he trying to humour Massingberd who had expressed an interest in the laundry maid upstairs? By the time of the letter of 5 November, posted to Massingberd at Searle's coffee house in Lincoln's Inn, the affair has taken its predictable course: 'I had almost forgot to tell you of misses being in love with m'Lord Camiere & likewise he very much with her, who parted last with much sorrow, but in hopes of returning ye next carnavale as he told her.'[12]

When he was writing three years later, Kent, now fluent in Italian, would sound a little more at ease on sexual matters. The 'Sigra Lavandera', he informed Massingberd knowingly, was still a virgin, 'but not much frequented by ye English, there is too many Italians about her though now & then si poul bacciare la mana' – he got to kiss her hand.[13] This was hardly the mark of an avid lecher. The girl's eventual marriage to a violinist seems to have pleased the moral Kent thoroughly. So he was being naive rather than ironic in his conclusion to the earlier letter that Lord Camiere would be back for the next carnival.

His letter of 5 November 1712 had ended: 'if I can serve you in anything here please to command me, I have drawn you some statues wh. I shall send by my Ld Herbert for I am to send him some things'.[14] Obviously Kent had begun to refine that process of making himself useful to the most promising young aristocrats which would first net him Thomas Coke, the future Earl of Leicester, and finally Lord Burlington himself. Massingberd was too minor a gentleman to warrant serious pursuit, but the relationship was warm. He signed off to Kent as 'Your Loving friend & humble servant'. Like Kent he was, it appears, more by nature a man's man than a woman's. In a letter to his fellow antiquary and collector William Stukeley, who was considering marriage, Massingberd struck a smug, self-congratulatory note:

> I freely own I am not fond of matrimony, but whosoever advances I am none of Love's votarists, does me an injury of such magnitude yt no charity can forgive it. 'To have and to hold' are words I like well, for they always suggest land, but 'for better or worse' & 'till death doth part' are such killing sort of phrases yt I wonder ye pronouncers of ym fall not lifeless at yr Parson's feet.[15]

It would not, however, be long before he would be asking Kent to purchase three Roman fans, confessing bashfully that they were for a lady with whom he was going to 'commit matrimony'.[16]

Some of Massingberd's phrases, such as 'when an impertinent correspondent breaks in upon your lucubrations', suggest an orotund pomposity.[17] Though only Kent's senior by a year, he sometimes adopted a very paternal tone in his writing: 'Good Dear Kent, study hard if you may answer ye character I have given you' and 'I beg you to study & not think of coming over donec Raphael secundus eris [until you have become a second Raphael], don't stint yourself in study or ambition and another 7 years may produce wonders & yr advancement shall always be ye desire & endeavour of Burrell Massingberd and Sir John Chester'.[18]

Kent had met Sir John Chester in Rome in May 1712, but it was Massingberd who had recruited him as another £40 sponsor on their return to England. For the next seven years the two men would badger Kent by the slow post, grumbling about marbles that failed to arrive, paintings that came in bad condition and 'thank-you' letters that were never sent. But, quite apart from what Massingberd received, Sir John was sent copies of Correggio's *Leda*, Domenichino's *Diana and her Nymphs*, a Poussin, Maratta's *Daphnis and Apollo* and his *Madonna*, together with a ceiling centrepiece by Kent on canvas of *Herse and her Sisters a sacrificing to Flora & Mercury a flying when he fell in love with her.*[19] So the protégé had not been completely idle. Kent would pay them out for their sniping comments when he eventually returned to England. After many assurances of a visit loaded with copies, and what Massingberd called 'knick knacks' from Italy, once he was back on English soil Kent ignored his two benefactors completely in a show of cool ingratitude.

When Massingberd suggested that Kent might paint an altarpiece for Ormsby church he was told: 'the very lowest I can possibly do it for will be £250 for the picture'.[20]

The altarpiece was never painted. Yet between them Massingberd and Chester must have paid out at least £560 to Kent over his Roman years and, as Kent assured Samuel Gale, each year 'you may live for fifty pounds & buy books and prints as our friend Mr Lock does'.[21] So they had kept him in comfort for nine years. Kent arrived in Rome as a rather gauche young Yorkshireman, marvelling at the pavements of St Peter's and sending unsuitable drawings of a ferocious Hun to the Philosopher Earl dying in Naples. But by the time he left the city he had developed a shrewd eye for the main chances in life and was stalking great lords of the correct Whig political persuasion, not lesser gentry who pestered him for soap, treacle and copies of Guido Reni's sugary nudes to gloat over in country house galleries.

Reading between the lines of exchanged letters and the accounts of Thomas Coke's party on their prolonged Grand Tour, it is clear that Kent had found an Italian friend and co-conspirator in this game of 'fleece the patron'. This was another very minor artist, a Signor Giacomo Mariari, not otherwise known to art history. Kent had introduced him to Massingberd and in May 1713 persuaded his patron to make a gift to Mariari of artist's materials, a box of mezzo tints, black and red chalks and black lead pencils, not readily available in Italy. Then, when Coke first descended on Rome and found in Kent an obliging art dealer, he also hired Mariari as an architecture master for a month, paid him for drawing the high altar in the Gesù and, on a return visit in 1717, paid him for making a plan of the Palazzo Farnese. Henry Trench was another friend of Kent who did some work for Coke, though he would have been the most retiring member of the predatory artistic threesome sharing possible patrons and introductions.

In his letters from Rome Kent often comes across as a simple Yorkshire lad, a little out of his social depth, desperate to better himself and full of doubts about his artistic range and ability. But when he eventually got back to London his Italian pursuit of seriously rich aristocrats would be revealed as extraordinarily prescient. In Florence and in Rome he was making good impressions on just those men who would be abreast of the current fashions in art of George I's London, and in the position to give Kent his first, second and third steps up the ladder of fame and success. He had been a shrewd operator in his Italian years; contacts rather than skills were what counted: his easy deferential ways and homely, unthreatening Yorkshire charm made English gentlemen abroad feel safe with him, even paternalistic. He required encouragement and invited care, but behind that façade he was a calculating opportunist.

Parallel with this hunting down of seriously rich aristocrats was Kent's much more testing campaign to win acceptance as a painter in Rome's virtuosi circles. It is unlikely that, with his limited talents, he would have got very far among sophisticated Italians without John Talman's influence on Cardinal Ottoboni following the great Symposium of June 1711. Talman and Locke had both left Rome in 1712, but Talman did not quit Italy until 1717 and, from Kent's letters, it appears that he often made brief visits to his protégé offering wise advice, such as that, for the Sir John Chester ceiling, it might be better to rely on 'grottesque' work rather than any more demanding figurative compositions.[22] He must have come to recognise Kent's limitations as a painter some years before anyone except perhaps Chiari and Kent himself. Kent was never brimming with self-confidence about his artistic talents. Indeed throughout his career he would always be happier with the moral support and encouragement of another man. In an early letter to Massingberd he had written: 'I will endeavour within a little time to send you some of my work; though my best may not be extraordinary',[23] and Talman, who was, 'continually apreaching to me yt I may be a great painter,[24] must have felt that gross flattery was the only way to bolster up 'dear Billy's' hesitant drive for fame. The mystery is why quite so many men over the years felt that they should do this. At first it must have been a vulnerable charm that won him supporters; later perhaps that same charm was carried by the witty self-projection of an apparently confident, amusing 'Signior', peppering his English with Italian phrases and Italian anecdotes. Not until he was back in England and on the edge of middle age, when he was confident enough to follow his own instincts, unmoved by the whims and pressures of patrons, would true flashes of real genius reveal themselves.

In June 1713, quite early in his Roman years, Kent had won a prize at the Accademia di S. Luca for a drawing of the 'Miracle of S. Andrea Avellino', and had 'the honour of a Cardinal telling ye Pope a Protestant had drawn a miracle better than a Roman Cattish'.[25] The prize was a silver medal with a bust of the Albani Pope, Clement XI, on one side and St Luke on the other. But it was only a second prize in the second class, while his rival Henry Trench had won a first prize in the third class in 1795, a first prize in the second class in 1706 and second prize in the first class in 1711. Trench was living just up the Corso from Kent who was conscious of competition from the erratic Irishman. It will have come as some satisfaction for him to note that in 1718 Trench only achieved a second prize in the third class. George Vertue, who rarely missed an opportunity to denigrate Kent, noted that it was 'generally allowed that Trench was the better designer'.[26] Trench was, however, far less skilled at handling patrons.

On 16 May 1714 Kent mentioned casually in a letter to Massingberd, 'Here is one Mr Coke a bying a Collection and has bespoke six of the best painters and pictures & one I am to do as big as y life – please my obedient respects to Sir John and wherein I can be serviceable to him or you shall always be ready to observe with care.'[27] There followed a long, seven-month, gap before Massingberd heard anything more from Rome. Kent had his second important aristocrat in his sights after losing Lord Herbert. He had been touring northern Italy in the lavish entourage of Coke, the future Earl of Leiçester and the builder, partly to Kent's design, of Holkham Hall, Norfolk, one of the largest and, in its exterior elevations, one of the least attractive Palladian houses in England. A long and complex relationship had begun between the two men, one which would prove very profitable financially to Kent. It would also be the beginning of his slide away from the Baroque and proto-Rococo enthusiasms of John Talman and Kent's Italian patrons. In their place he would be drawn towards the amateurish neo-classicism that gripped the English upper classes after the Hanoverian succession. The English aristocracy's obsessive identification of themselves with the senators of republican Rome was occasioned in part by the Earl of Shaftesbury's basically republican writings, but largely by a half-concealed guilt complex. Whereas the original Roman senators had got rid of their kings completely and ruled without a royal figurehead, Whigs and Tories alike had colluded to jettison the direct royal line of the Stuarts, but then replaced them with faintly ridiculous Germans, more interested in Hanover than in the United Kingdom. Kent's own career as a designer would depend in future upon the extent to which he could handle political pressures, and it would not be easy.

Thomas Coke should logically have become Kent's major patron and a controlling influence on his artistic development. He was very rich, a dedicated collector of paintings, sculpture, books and medals, and ambitious to build a great country house at his family seat, at Holkham. In addition he was unusually young for the Grand Tour, aged only fifteen when he set off from London in August 1712 on an expedition that would last until May 1718 and include two separate Italian tours as well as visits to Switzerland, Germany and France. Unfortunately for Kent, Coke's mind was already shaped by his formidable tutor, Dr Thomas Hobart. Coke's guardian had written in 1711: 'His passions are strong and violent and should be early regulated, civilised and softened.'[28] Dr Hobart was that regulator, directing his driven and wilful charge into scholarly collecting. Thomas Coke was the perfect virtuoso that Shaftesbury had idealised, except that he lacked the sense of humour which Shaftesbury considered an essential leaven to intelligence. Coke's collections were prodigious. Whether he was ever a man of judicious taste, able to distinguish beauty from mere rarity, is most doubtful.

Before the Coke caravan reached Rome on 7 February 1714 it had made an initial pass through Italy – Turin, Genoa, Pisa, Florence and Venice. Announcing himself 'a perfect virtuoso and a great lover of pictures'[29] Coke proved himself in Rome by spending 4500 pauls on paintings. (For an indication of the value of a paul, William Patoun's advice, in the first half of the eighteenth century, was 'look upon a Sequin as half a Guinea and Pauls as Sixpenses . . . pay no more than Eight Pauls a head for your Dinners in Common at Rome'.) This must have been the time when Kent was introduced and began to share in the loot. After two weeks in Naples, Coke was back in Rome, leaving for northern Italy on 6 June with Kent in his train in an unstated advisory role. Kent was sufficiently impressed by the adventure to keep a diary of its progress.[30] This can be compared usefully with the very detailed accounts kept by Coke's valet and treasurer, Edward Jarret; though to be strictly honest Jarret's accounts are both more revealing and humanly interesting than Kent's desperately dull list of places visited and paintings seen.[31] What does make his dreary diary well worth appraisal, however, is its revelation of his interest in architecture: not in classical or Baroque buildings, but Byzantine, Romanesque and Gothic work. Here is the proof of John Talman's influence. Those requests for notes on mosques, Greek Orthodox ceremonial and holy slippers will have given Talman an unusual depth of knowledge about eclectic styles, and his interest has clearly brushed off on Kent.

In Siena he admired the cathedral, 'a Gothic pile', finding the sgrafitti work of its pavement 'most wonderful'.[32] He ignored Michelangelo's set pieces in Florence in favour of 'two boys a singing' by Raphael and demonstrated his early delight in gardens, noting 'a villa Call'd Prattolini a very fine situation and very fine Grotos adorn'd with Shells & petrified stone work with pretty water works a Galatea coming out of her grotto drawn by Delfini'.[33] Curiously he fails to mention Pratolino's outstanding feature. Was the great stone Apennine giant a little too sixteenth century and excessive for his taste?

After making long dutiful lists of painters whose works he had observed without comment in Bologna, he was taken by Coke's republican leanings to the comic opera republic of San Marino, a strange detour. There Kent's attention was caught, as it would be throughout his journey, by picturesque human activity: 'We returned from ye Bright republick with ye sounding of Trumpets & came to our Callash & set out for Ravenna.'[34] The party was travelling in style in double-seated, four-wheeled carriages, open but with folding hoods. Edward Jarret's accounts of money spent on 'Cloaks, Necessaries, Extraordinarys, Travelling expenses and other payments' record endless consumption of drinking chocolate, coffee, biscuits and sugared almonds, as well as the fortune that Coke lavished, first on paintings, then on sculptures and books. Entrance fees to the various palaces and gardens varied wildly, Cardinal Ottoboni's palace was 4 pauls, the Pitti Palace was 9 pauls, but 'paid for seeing the Great Duke's gallery at Florence' was a remarkable 99 pauls.[35] In between endless accounts of sugar for making cooling lemon drinks, Jarret drops mysteriously large sums, no doubt to pay for prostitutes, 'to my master for his pocket'.[36]

After San Marino, Byzantium seized Kent's imagination with the atmospheric melancholy of Ravenna: 'ye famous church of St Vitale ye plan being an octagonal & they say ye form of St Sabbea at Constantinople, in one chapel there is 3 fine pictures one of Guido, Barrocci, Cingiani – in ye garden is ye sepolera Galla placida & Theodosio Cesare Imperatori'.[37] Enraptured with the Dark Ages he wrote on in far more detail than he had done in any previous visit:

> a little way out of the town is y famous stone thicknesse 4 foot, cerconference CXIV, diametro XXXI & tow inches – Amalasanta only daughter of Teodorico King of y Gote she built it y year DXXXVI for a sepulcre of her father, upon which was an urne of porferi – in

ye Dome are several Greek bishops as these yt they tell you were inspired by y St Spirito.[38]

After discoursing more in the mood of a Victorian than an early eighteenth-century traveller he seems to have collected himself and made a rare contemporary comparison:

with a Dove upon ye chappell all apinted by Guido Rine y Alter repr Mosses stricking y rock – in ye Couploi our Saviour in y middle of yt maddonna with saints – St Michael looks as if Cigniani had taken his thought from Guido for his at Forli.[39]

This little interlude of Kent at Ravenna is most revealing. Because he had come up the hard way with no university education, no Latin probably and no Greek, he was wide open to influences off the beaten tourist track, a most improbable candidate, therefore, for training in pure neo-classicism. He was far more a genuine original mind nurtured by Talman.

St Mark's in Venice puzzled him: 'very much Gotic but ye great arches are round & all mossake upon the frount, without are four noble horses of a Green Gusto'.[40] John Ruskin might have found him a kindred spirit. Sansovino's Library he thought was built by Scamozzi, Palladio's pupil, and 'very fine'. He valued paintings by their size rather than any other quality, so Tintoretto's *Paradiso* in the Doge's Palace and his *Raising of the Cross* in the School of St Rocque were both mentioned approvingly, along with human spectacle again: 'ye Doge in prosession in cloth of gold'.[41]

At Padua Kent parted company with Coke and his entourage. In Jarret's notes on expenditure there are hints of a certain reserve felt towards Mr Kent. Thomas Coke had paid him 750 livres for pictures he had bought, and it may have been that he was regarded as a commercial outsider in a tight group of loyal servants. Henry Trench, Kent's private Nemesis, was also occasionally with the company and receiving payments. What is so satisfying about the episode, for all the strange spelling and the failures to communicate, is the sense that an odd and independent personality is emerging here in the Italian years, before the Burlington connection brought Kent back to heel and to conventional stylistic responses. But he would never quite lose that creative apartness, which was to make him a shaper of styles rather than a follower.

As he journeyed back to Rome alone, supported by Coke's generous allowance, it was Palladio's Teatro Olimpico at Vicenza that caught his interest. He merely noted without admiration 'several other pallaces'.[42] This meant that he would be in no position, once back in England, to moderate Lord Burlington's equal ignorance of Palladio's practical work on modest town houses and villas. It would be a disastrous weakness for the development of the Palladian revival. Kent, who could and should have positively influenced his patron Burlington, was largely ignorant as to how creative, lively and human in scale Palladio's invention had been. He could hardly have missed the rich elevations of the Palazzo Chiericati, yet he made no mention of that or of the Villa Capra a mile outside the town.

At Mantua he was impressed by the paintings, 'David cutting Golia's head' and 'Samson with ye Lion' in the Palazzo del Tè, two curious choices;[43] but again it was the garden that he really fancied: 'In grotta at ye end of ye garden are very fine grottesquees.' But writing them up 'at y peacock in Parma upon my bed not having more room' he was still so angry at the grotto's decay that he burst into dyslexic Italian: 'ma per disgratia eper la vertu va tutte in ruina – sopra vey onzi cosa are mai ha fata Julio':[44] it was unfortunate that such fine work should be ruined with fragments falling off.

Kent's strangest obsession on this tour, one that would haunt him for several years, was with the Correggio frescoes in the Renaissance dome of Parma's, otherwise Romanesque, cathedral. They would bring him back to the city for a two-week sketching visit, during which he caught his only bout of Italian fever. On this 1714 visit his fondness for fabrics and the pomps of a court were to the fore. It was the human theatre of 'ye Duke of Parma's daughter being sposata to ye King of Spain' that delighted him.[45] The young queen, wearing flowered cloth of gold, was led by her mother, wearing cloth of silver lined with red velvet to a throne of silver tissue. This was Kent the dressmaker in his Versace mood, but even during the ceremonial he had time to make a mental note for future reference of Correggio's early (1534) *Assumption of the Blessed Virgin*, spiralling up into the cupola in a terrible tangle of bare flesh and soft porn. The Virgin Mary is viewed up her bare legs and her skirt. It is a disaster of a composition, with soft, billowing clouds used to stuff up any awkward gaps.

That Kent must have considered it high art says little for his judgement. He could, even this early in 1714, have been plotting to use Cardinal

Ottoboni's influence to let him paint his own cupola fresco in a Roman church, as he would do in 1717. That would be the perfect badge of professionalism when reported in London. Kent's impudent ambition explains why he would succeed in life and why Henry Trench would die disappointed in 1726, without even decorating, as he had hoped, the staircase in Mavisbank House, Midlothian. The encouraging element to Kent's career in design is that he rose beyond his ability and then justified that unjustifiable rise.

That night of 16 September 1714 the great Farnese Theatre, grander even than the Teatro Olimpico in Vicenza, 'was illuminated & ye Actors sung upon ye stage as rivers – intermedia dancing & finest ye Ladys & Gents danced'.[46] For all his interests in the Gothic and the Byzantine, Kent was no social rebel, but entirely and uncritically happy with the artistocratic pomps of his times. Only the neglect of a good grotto could enrage him.

Once he was back in Rome, Kent was obliged to soothe his neglected patron Massingberd by claiming that his master Chiari had advised the excursion with Coke and by assuring him that he was still very poor and grateful: 'after by travelling I had ruind all my clothes & had nothing to by more, which money you sent me has set me up again'.[47] No mention was made of the commissions from selling all those paintings to Coke. By way of encouragement for his sponsors he reported that 'my master will have me do things of my invention',[48] which would not have been unreasonable after four years' training. But he had begun a historical painting, one stage up in prestige from portrait painting, a phase he chose to skip. The subject was from Homer, 'when Agamemnon sent to Achilles for Briseises a subject never has been done & I hope will do very well'.[49] Later there would be another easel painting with a Homeric theme – 'Venus a-conducting Helena to Paris' – and a conventional Holy Family.

It was in this autumn of 1714 that Lord Burlington, twenty years old and on his first, quite brief, tour of Italy, had arrived in Rome via Turin, Genoa, Pisa and Siena, only to fall seriously ill there and be confined to bed for three months. Presciently, Massingberd had suspected that when Lord Burlington arrived in Italy 'full of money . . . you will I hope have his encouragement because he loves pictures mightily'.[50] Whether or not Kent did have this 'encouragement' is a real mystery, a frustrating void in the Kent–Burlington relationship. The Pope's own doctor was attending Burlington and Kent reported that 'my Ld Burlington is here but none has seen him yet but a Prussian & they say he has been sicke ever since he came'.[51] But Kent tended to keep his best contacts, men like Coke, close to his chest. Vertue claims that they did meet.[52] The young Burlington lying sick in a foreign country would have been vulnerable to Kent's charm and eager for an informed account of the Roman art scene delivered in the familiar Bridlington accent.

James Lees-Milne has suggested that Kent must have been the agent responsible for Lord Burlington's purchase of two paintings, an Annibale Carracci and a Viveano, because they were both bought when Burlington was still lying in bed, sick of the fever and, therefore, unable to act for himself. Lees-Milne makes a plausible case for Kent having used his friendship with Coke as a means of securing a first meeting with Burlington.[53] Nothing, however, can be absolutely certain. It is hard to believe that, when Burlington made his next Italian visit in 1719 and opened it with an interview with Kent in Genoa, where he proposed an apparently pre-arranged contract, he was not dealing with someone he already liked and trusted. In the autumn of 1714, however, Kent would only have sold himself as a painter and art dealer, nothing more, and Burlington had yet to become fixated upon Palladio as the best route to the neo-classical for a pseudo-republican England.

In 1715 Talman was back in Rome and Kent was complaining that gentlemen were getting his sketches 'and then leave me so I get nothing for my loss of time or for my drawings'.[54] He had been caught up again in Talman's frenetic activity and 'forced to draw one drawing from Rafael for him'.[55] But he still needed Talman, who could be a potent influence on Cardinal Ottoboni, for the fresco project. Coke had, for the time being, retired to an academy in Turin, so it was time to mend bridges in Rome. Kent told Massingberd in his 20 July 1715 letter that he hoped to spend another four years in Rome 'so am resolved to study very hard'.[56] He had a fine collection of prints and drawings and 'if I live to come home', he declared plaintively, 'they will be a pleasure to you to see & what you like shall be at your service'.[57] Needless to say neither Massingberd nor Chester ever set eyes on them. Kent offered to design a summerhouse for Ormsby Hall and he had copied 'with great difficulty' a seductive *Leda* by Correggio for Sir John Chester.[58] But Sir William Wentworth, his most formidable sponsor, was getting restless and wanted his Yorkshire genius back in England: 'I shall be ye more oblig'd', Kent pleaded to Massingberd, 'if you & Sir John will pleas to continue a year or tow longer.'[59] Cardinal Ottoboni had at last commissioned a painting from him. It was to be Cyrus ordering the Jews to rebuild the Temple in Jerusalem: 'if I succeed the honour may be something but ye profit no great matter', he claimed with a noble air of being above such low concerns as money.[60]

In October 1716 the action had begun to speed up. Cyrus and the Jews had gone on show anonymously at the feast of St Roche and been much praised. The Cardinal had made Kent a handsome present and hung the painting in his own palace. What Kent did not report to his sponsors was that he had been working very profitably for Thomas Coke again, first in Naples in May, where Coke had paid for his lodgings, and then in Rome where Coke had been spending money like water on paintings and, for the first time, on sculpture: an ominous sign of his growing interest in neo-classicism. Kent must have been closely involved in all this. His friend Signor Mariari took Coke to Frascati and Caprarola; Kent could have been with them as he sent sketches of the belvederes at both palaces, the Aldobrandini at Frascati and the Farnese at Caprarola, to Massingberd. Coke's purchases were so ambitious that when he attempted to export a headless statue of Diana from the Casa Consiglieri to England, both he and Kent were threatened with imprisonment and Kent with expulsion from the Papal States. Money soon eased the problem and Coke went on buying, with Kent helping him.

Commissions from all these transactions left Kent so rich that he set off on another tour of north Italy with Cardinal Ottoboni's approval. He visited Florence, Bologna, Modena, Reggio and Parma, sketching, or so he claimed. But in Parma again, for a prolonged copying session of Correggio's show of bare legs, his luck ran out. 'In ye Coupolo', he told Massingberd in a letter of 15 February 1717, 'I got such a cold & an ague which put me out of all patience was resolved to come back to Rome & by moving & by Jesuits powder I thank God have got out of the distemper.'[61] So at last he could attend to 'ceiling pieces'[62] for both his long-suffering, and by this time probably quite unnecessary, sponsors. He must already have been very well provided for through his dealership transactions. It is unlikely that Kent would ever again be short of money from 1716 to the end of his life in 1748. He would never be less than moderately prosperous, saving and investing.

The reward for all those hours sketching Correggio in the cathedral of Parma came in the summer of 1717. Devious as ever, on 15 June

Kent had written to Massingberd that he was 'quite wery with liveing this power melancholy life, but I hope to be revived when I see all my friends in England. Your humble servant Wills Kent.'[63] In reality he was on the crest of success. His Cardinal, who was a patron of the church of the Flemish community in Rome, San Giuliano dei Fiamminghi, must have put in a word for him. In a semi-legal document, drawn up by the Flemish community and signed on 12 July, Kent offered to paint the centrepiece ceiling of the church. It had been newly built in 1681 by Antonio Maria Borioni, an assistant of Bernini who had worked on and learnt from Bernini's small 1658 masterpiece, San Andrea al Quirinale.[64] Kent would work 'per mia devotione' – for no fee – but the church's officials would pay for the necessary scaffolding. On 16 July the scaffolding tower was being erected and on 4 September the plasterer, Maestro Domenico, began to prepare the vault for the Englishman's fresco.[65]

To give Kent his due, it was quite an achievement for a Protestant, if that was really what he was still claiming to be, to paint the centrepiece of even a quite small church in the heart of Catholic Rome. Seven years of preparation, of currying favour and of concealing a general lack of talent had ended in *The Apotheosis of St Julian*. On 9 December the work was completed and on 13 March 1718 the congregation awarded Kent an honorarium of 15 golden scudi. Untrustingly they emphasised that the painter would have no further right to remuneration or gifts in kind. Kent had taken it all most seriously and two pages survive, dated 17 September 1717, written at the back of his diary for the Coke expedition, recording how he made and used the various colours, all in his usual mangled English:

> After well dry'd which require time as ye place is damp – retuch with temper an Egg broke into a cup of well beat, with a quantity of tow eggs of water put in after beat & then cut ye stalk of fig leaves, or if not ye peel of lemon.[66]

San Giuliano, the official church in Rome of the Kingdom of the Belgians, is nowadays only open on a Thursday evening and for Mass at 10.30 a.m. on a Sunday. Its exterior to the Via del Sudario, a dark, narrow street, is unpromising, just a doorway with a bronze of St Julian above it, inset within the apartment block, originally built to house and care for Flemish pilgrims. But once inside, and with the lights on, the aesthetic shock is one of the most unexpected in Rome. Borioni was a genius of the Baroque. An oval is enclosed within an octagon, a miniature of San Andrea, but even more impressive because the spatial movement is so intimate in scale. Bernini used red and cream Sienese marble for the columns, Borioni made do with scagliola, but the effect is just as rich. San Giuliano is a jewel and in the centre of its oval ceiling is Kent's fresco, another oval with a richly gilded surround, broken twice to allow Kent's clouds to escape and give an illusion of activity, which does not succeed.

It is an adequate centrepiece, but no more than that. Examined in detail the brushwork is rough, but the composition – a female figure representing Flanders, not St Julian – is supported by a quintet of five angels playing musical instruments, as in the Parma *Assumption*. A number of cherubs, one of them playing a horn, romp on the clouds that fill any awkward spaces. It does not look from their features as if Kent was very charmed by small children; but there it is, warm, rosy and golden with a cloudy sunrise. What other English Protestant painter can claim to have done as much in Rome? This is where students of Kent must come to appreciate that a designer, who would soon be constrained to work in neo-classical dimensions and with neo-classical decorative motifs, once painted for three months in a wonderfully subtle and successful space of the Baroque. Such a visit is likely to create a feeling of regret that he was given so little opportunity in England to convey the spatial sophistication that he had learnt here in San Giuliano.

6

The wilful impatience of a would-be Palladian lord

Once he had painted in 1717 his apotheosis of a female Flanders rising to the sound of an angel orchestra, William Kent had peaked in Rome. It had been a modest triumph: 'my Ld Burford did me ye honour with other Gentlemen to come upon y scaffold to see me paint', he wrote to Massingberd.[1] On paper his curriculum vitae was already most impressive: prizes from the Pope, presents from a cardinal, paintings exhibited anonymously and admired, and then a young Protestant artist frescoes the ceiling of a Roman church. There was no way now but downwards, yet still he hesitated. 'I long to see you', he wrote insincerely to his loyal patron in June 1718, '& if please God next summer at farthest to leave Rome, my invention makes me improve dayly.'[2] But he still looked around for excuses to delay:

> Am resolved to do something here & not to do as others of our country, stay here a great many years without doing one picture. I am resolved to have a tryal here of ye difficult & different parts of painting & not run ye hazard to begin when I come home. I long to see England but ye desire I have to do something makes me delay y more.[3]

Then he came to what was really disturbing him: 'Signor Giacomo & I desire one favour if you could procure us a design of ye church made in y Strand & to hear how Mr Trench succeeds in his painting, for he has not done one picture here.'[4] If Trench was in London and if James

Gibbs's new church, St Mary-le-Strand, required an altarpiece then Kent was idling his time away in the wrong city. Two months later he had begun to clear his backlog. Sir John Chester's 'ceiling piece upon two large cloths' was under way and Kent was 'still longing to see you which I hope to keep my resolution for next spring without fail & then if please God to see my most oblig'd friends, & shall accept of yr kind offer to come to you before I go to make myself known in London'.[5] That was written on 16 August, so Lord Burlington had apparently not yet made Kent the offer he could not refuse. But his attention was, nevertheless, turning away from painting towards architecture. He was collecting ornaments in stucco 'after an Italian gusto . . . & continually a drawing ornaments & Architecture & getting things I think will be necessary for me in England'.[6]

This suggests that Kent was already preparing to fall back on interior decoration and architecture if painting failed. It was hardly a self-confident gesture, but surely, after nine years' familiarity in Rome with the breathtaking competence of even second-ranking Italian painters, Kent must have been experiencing doubts about his own abilities with a paintbrush. He had no doubts, however, about the power of impudence to undo purse strings. After all the money he had been coining in Rome he was still shameless enough on 18 December 1718 to write to Massingberd hoping 'you'll be so kind to send me some assistance to come home, which I am resolved makes me still more desire to see my friends, & will content myself to see france alone, & not go into Flanders'.[7] It would be eleven months later before Massingberd would receive his next letter, dated 15 November 1719, and by that time Kent was in Paris, firmly in the grip of Lord Burlington and stylistically brainwashed, fuming vaguely against 'that Dam'd Gusto that's been for this sixty years past now'.[8] If we count back sixty years from 1719 we get the date 1660, the restoration of Charles II, when it was architecture, not painting, that fell into a new 'Gusto': the timid but civilised second-hand French Baroque of Hugh May and Christopher Wren. Kent's little rant implied that he was definitely thinking of an about-turn in architecture rather than in painting. Pressure may have been put upon him; so it becomes important to trace exactly what had been going on since a message from Sir William Wentworth had prised Kent away from Rome to a rendezvous with Lord Burlington at Genoa.

In that letter from Paris, presumably the first Massingberd had received since the previous December, Kent had the grace to sound mildly apologetic: 'Hond Sir', he began,

> I beg your excuse for not writing sooner being continually in coming towards England and waiting longer for Sir William Wentworth at Florence than I expected. I came with him as far as genoa & since have been about twenty days on my journey here, & being alone & not speaking the language has disterbd me very much, but I hope in a little time to see my good friends in England that will be a great satisfaction to me for all my troubles'.[9]

After the appeal for sympathy – poor William alone in a strange land – came the truth, or at least some of it: 'I think to stay here a fortnight to see the things, if my Lord Burlington does not hinder me. I met him at Genoea & he would make me promise to stay for him here.'[10] Then comes the most illogical detail of the entire plot: 'he was a going towards Vicenza & Venice to get Architects to draw all the fine buildings of Palladio, & return back here which I expect every day, his lordship likd my designs so well both painting and architecture that he would make me promis at least to begin to paint for him the first when I came over, which if he comes soon may be'.[11] At that point Kent's always tortured syntax breaks up completely: 'with his good Lordship since I have left Rome & Florence cannot beare to see anything except tow fine Pallaces of Vitruvius a Genova that my Ld caryd me to see which he has ordered to be drawn'.[12]

Whether these palaces were drawn by Kent or by some other is not clear, and Kent writes as if Vitruvius were a contemporary Italian architect rather than an ancient Roman authority on the subject. Burlington's explanation of the Vitruvian correctness behind the palace design by Galeazzo Alessi must have confused him. But what does emerge from the letter is a sense of passive excitement. An irresistible personal force has swept up an irresolute object. Burlington had given orders and, no doubt, funds to carry out those orders. There was no need now to wait around Lincolnshire or Yorkshire hoping for employment from minor country gentlemen. A rich and confident aristocrat had taken Kent over and Kent was obviously eager to be converted to a dynamic new crusade in the arts. For the last nine years he had been enjoying Italy, preparing courageously for a career in painting to which he was thoroughly unsuited, putting off the evil day when the patience of sponsors would be exhausted and his bluff would be called back in England. But here was a wealthy patron, nine years his junior, an impulsive and not always very intelligent young man who could be humoured, amused, instructed, and perhaps directed, by a tactful fellow Yorkshireman.

Kent, desperate to please now that he had let Lord Herbert and Mr Coke slip away from him, made his first bad mistake in the Kent–Burlington partnership. He let Burlington ride off at a furious pace without him to Venice and Vicenza to research Palladio's buildings, writings and drawings, while Kent, destined in Burlington's ambitious scheme for the resurgence of the arts of Great Britain, as a painter not an architect and certainly not as a garden designer, travelled alone to Paris. As a direct result of that characteristically thoughtless decision, neither Burlington nor Kent ever had time to absorb in the Veneto the essence of Palladio's genius. The Palladian revival which would grip Britain for at least the next forty years, and often longer, as revival followed revival, would be based on a disastrous misapprehension by an amateur in a hurry.

Richard Boyle, 4th Earl of Cork and 3rd Earl of Burlington, never revealed himself freely and openly in writing. He has become a legendary figure in architectural history: impulsive, manipulative, hugely influential, imposing almost single-handed on his country the version of Palladianism, a revival of a revival of a revival, that could, such was early eighteenth-century scholarship, pass as an authentic neo-classicism. But no convincing and satisfying biography is ever likely to be written of him.[13] He lived his middle years in a whirl of activity, but never left a key to his own assessments of personal failures and successes. In the end he died one of the most mysterious figures in eighteenth-century cultural history, and some of that mystery attaches to his relationship with Kent, whom he both projected and deflected from his true career.

In October 1718, if it was in October that they met in Genoa, no one is quite sure, Kent caught Burlington in a hurry that has never been convincingly explained. At certain periods of his life Burlington seems to have had much to hide and 1718 was one of those periods. His father, the 2nd Earl, had died when his only son was not quite ten years old; consequently, instead of being reared by a father to the political ambitions natural to someone with wide estates in Ireland and Yorkshire, and very valuable property in west London, it was always assumed that Burlington had little interest in politics. Instead he was supposed to have been directed to music, painting and architecture, in that order of priority, by his mother, the Countess Juliana. But then in that sensational piece of detective scholarship came Jane Clark's *Apollo* article, already mentioned, which proposed that, far from being a relatively inactive Whig supporter of the Hanoverian succession, the young Burlington was a secret but highly active Jacobite, working for a return of the exiled Stuarts to the throne.[14] His code name in Jacobite records was 'Mr Buck'. He contributed generously to the support of the Old Pretender's court in France and used his 1714–15 Grand Tour as a cover for frequent contacts with Jacobite agents in the Low Countries and with various friars when in Rome. According to Clark, the abject failure of the 1715 Jacobite Rebellion had barely quenched his enthusiasm for the Stuarts and his brief, two-month, trip to Italy in the autumn of 1719 was a second round of plotting, concealed behind its overt purpose of researching Palladio's buildings, writings and origins.

What was so revolutionary and disturbing about this new theory was that it had become accepted in architectural history circles that the Palladian revival had been staged by Lord Burlington expressly to create a house style and badge of party allegiance to the Whigs and the House of Hanover. Now the alternative proposal was that Palladian building had been a gesture of loyalty to the Stuarts who had projected the first revival of the style under Inigo Jones in Charles I's reign. To complicate the debate there was an alternative argument that King George also naturally favoured the revived Venetian style because his family name, 'Welf', was derived from the Italian 'Guelph' and originated in the Veneto. He had followed some at least of its principles in his palace at Herrenhausen, and appointed William Benson to succeed Sir Christopher Wren as Surveyor to the King's Works in 1718 because Benson claimed, on very little evidence, to be able to design in the style of Palladio and Inigo Jones.

The only reservation to be made against Burlington as an ardent Jacobite is that in the years before and after the accession to the throne of a faintly comical German princeling, who could speak little English, at least half the aristocracy, and probably more, must have been hedging their bets on a return of the rightful Stuart line. We tend now to look upon the Hanoverian succession as a natural event, but in 1715 it must have seemed a most improbable stop-gap solution. Only the dull public image of James, the Old Pretender, and the folly of launching the first Jacobite Rebellion among the Scots, whom the English generally disliked and mistrusted, kept King George on his uncertain throne. A landing with a small force at Preston in Catholic Lancashire would probably have succeeded with little bloodshed.

Assuming that there is some truth in Clark's theory, where would that have left William Kent? He must, in his time with John Talman, have become familiar with Jacobite arguments and loyalties. Yet he expressed unreserved delight at hearing of the collapse of the 1715 Rebellion:

> Ye Scotch yt were so bright at our Café House are never seen now & when they appear seem to have fasted ever since there pretender left Scotland – I have such an aversion against ym yt ever since I came from Mont Vesuvio I fancy they all stanch of Brimstone.[15]

Did he hold his nose to avoid the smell of Jacobite brimstone whenever he came near Lord Burlington, or does his easy relationship with the young rich lord prove that the 'Mr Buck' theory is all wrong, and that Burlington's Palladian quest was exactly what it claimed to be: a search for a Whig house style in building appropriate to the senators of a modified Roman republic with a hereditary German president?

Examined closely the Burlington itinerary that wet autumn is suspect in the extreme and, as so often in these years, the 3rd Earl of Shaftesbury, though six years in his tomb, was the presiding influence. He had foolishly dismissed the organic growth of a native English classicism through Wren's inspired, if eccentric, Franco-Dutch neo-classicism to Vanbrugh's exuberant castellar Baroque. Instead Shaftesbury had called for something noble, Roman and antique, though with only a hazy amateur's notion of what he was envisaging. But at the same time he had not asked for a new domestic neo-classicism. He had particularised Britain's architectural need: a new royal palace to replace battered, fire-blown Whitehall and a new home for Lords and Commons to replace their converted premises in the so-called 'palace' of Westminster. In emphasising these two prime requirements Shaftesbury had merely been echoing the national consciousness, but his was an unusually potent voice.

It was ostensibly to find a Palladian-inspired solution for these two architectural projects, not to reshape the homes of the English aristocracy, that Burlington was touring northern Italy in general and the Veneto in particular. He may well have had other treasonable objects in mind, conferences with exiled Jacobites, soundings, even of papal sympathies, but as far as Palladio went, his aim was to find suitable Palladian models for grand public buildings. There was just one problem: Palladio had never built any. He had designed a grand 'Egyptian' hall interior and he had wrapped a magnificent Serlian-style double arcading around the existing medieval fifteenth-century civic Basilica at Vicenza. But while he had designed and built superb churches, he left no complete public buildings on a scale senatorial enough to satisfy London's needs, though there was his rejected design for the Doge's Palace in Venice. John Webb had plundered that to draw designs for Whitehall that would have made the Escorial look modest.[16] Webb's drawings had been under Lord Burlington's nose back in England in William Talman's collection. They would have suited him admirably and, guided probably by Kent, he did later hunt them down and buy them. But in 1719 Burlington was young, impetuous and questing politically as much as artistically.

That explains most convincingly why he did not take Kent, who was fluent in Italian, and already eagerly researching architectural possibilities, to the Veneto with him. He did not yet trust him and he had too much to hide. It remains one of the great lost opportunities in English architectural history. Palladio's existing villas had so much to offer if the two men could have toured them together, discussing and analysing Palladio's infinitely flexible and humane deployment of original Roman motifs. They could have absorbed the way in which his villas used artists to fresco walls with relaxed compositions working around door frames and windows, not to paint remote triumphs on canvas that were then slung up on ceilings. Burlington had that rare and valuable quality: he made things happen, his influence was hard to resist. He was an ardent idealist; but he had bad judgement and he imposed that bad judgement on his country. To appreciate the disastrous effect that the Burlingtonian fake-Palladian solution had on English domestic architecture it is only necessary to visit Chatsworth and then to go quickly, while the impressions of the serene richness of William Talman's 1687 Baroque south front are still fresh in the mind, to Wentworth Woodhouse in the next county to take in the straggle of unabsorbed and barely related details of its supposedly 'Palladian' east font of 1734.[17] Between these two dates lies Burlington's second Italian visit. England already had an integrated Baroque classicism which could range easily between the modest and the magnificent. Burlington persuaded the country to throw all that away for a staccato arrangement of 'correct' detail which was supposed, by its aggressive awkwardness, to assert an antique authenticity. A country gets the art and the architecture that its education and sophistication deserve. It is hard not to draw a parallel between what Burlington did in the 1720s with what another skilled and confident manipulator of the public taste, Charles Saatchi, did in the 1990s. The price of public taste, like that of democracy, is constant vigilance.

Scholarly authorities like Rudolf Wittkower and John Wilton-Ely have assumed – and their error was completely natural – that on his second journey Burlington must have had, to use Wilton-Ely's phrase, 'six months of intense collecting and formal analysis [in Italy] behind him'.[18] That was before the implications of a letter from Burlington in Turin to Sir Andrew Fountaine in London, discovered and quoted by Clark, had penetrated the architectural establishment. It proved that Burlington had, at the most, spent two days in Vicenza, the city of Palladio, and those in very bad weather, and that he had despised the local nobility and missed out on the great arc of villas in the hill country.

That letter to Sir Andrew has to be quoted in full, but equally interesting was the discovery that Sir Andrew Fountaine was involved with both Burlington and Kent. There has always been some uncertainty about that meeting between a fever-wracked Burlington and a picture-touting Kent in the Roman autumn of 1714. If it ever actually took place, how did Kent contrive to impress Burlington so deeply with his artistic talents that five years later Burlington would take the trouble to use Sir William Wentworth to escort Kent to a meeting in Genoa and a spoken contract? The link with Sir Andrew makes it much easier to understand.

Fountaine had been, back in 1716, one of Kent's more unusual social conquests in Rome. With a letter to Massingberd of 14 January of that year Kent had enclosed a print,

> I have grav'd in Aqua Fortis myself & without vanity to you since I have not come nigh any of our English, they begin to think I am

> worth something, & desir'd immediately if I hade printed my plate to give yn one, Sir Andey Fountain was so pleas with yt he has done me ye honour to send on to my Ld Pembroke.[19]

This was a genuine accolade. Fountaine was no brash young Grand Tourist but a mature and seasoned diplomat and Italophile. With Lord Macclesfield he had delivered a copy of the Act of Succession to the Court of Hanover in 1701. He was the friend of men of such diverse distinction as the philosopher Leibniz, the numismatist Cardinal Enrico Noris, the archaeologist Monsignor Bianchini, and the Grand Duke Cosimo III of Tuscany. Fountaine had persuaded Giuseppe Chiari to donate his self-portrait to the Grand Duke's gallery and, as a frequent patron of Kent's master-tutor, Fountaine's approval of a print would have been significant. Once again Kent had exercised that charm which appears so rarely in his letters. 'Sir Andrew Fountain', he reported proudly to Massingberd, 'is making a Collection of Drawings we are very good friends because he brings his drawings to shew me not being willing to trust to ye Italians.'[20] That was on 20 March; and Massingberd must have been impressed and written back quickly to apprise Kent of Fountaine's reputation in England, because on 9 June Kent was writing: 'Sir Andrey answers ye character you give him he seems to be mightily pleas'd that I begin to get credit amongst ye Italians.'[21] This was at the time of the Cyrus painting for Cardinal Ottoboni when John Talman was predicting that Kent 'may be a great painter'. 'This head [with which] I seal my letter', Kent boasted, 'is a gift of Sir Andrey as a ring set in gold.'[22] If it was the seal Kent used to emboss his letters to Lady Burlington in the 1730s it was engraved with an oddly nineteenth-century seeming face of a severe man with a drooping moustache, possibly Fountaine himself.[23]

Sir Andrew had returned to England and his seat, Narford in Norfolk, in 1716. There, or in London, Burlington had apparently met him to benefit from his judgement. Fountaine must have confirmed whatever first impressions Burlington had gained, deciding him to entrust Kent with the Shaftesbury-imposed task of raising England's profile in the art of painting. Because he had left Rome in April 1716, Fountaine would have missed Kent's performance on the ceiling of San Giuliano in 1717 and his Cyrus painting for Ottoboni.

Lord Burlington's letter to Fountaine from Turin reveals that the two men had become very close in England, with Sir Andrew approving and fostering Burlington's project to use Palladio as the model for a pure and reformed British neo-classicism. But the visit had not gone as Sir Andrew had hoped. The letter makes it unlikely that Burlington had spent more than a day in Vicenza while travelling from Genoa to Venice in October.[24] He had passed the last twelve days of the month in Venice, observed by the British Consul and left on 1 November, arriving in Turin, at the very latest, on 6 November, the date of his letter to Fountaine. He must have been in Vicenza on 3 November as that is the date inscribed on the copy of the *I Quattro Libri dell'Architettura* that he bought there and which he annotated with notes on the Villa Capra.[25] So there are only five days to account for, including travelling time, between leaving Venice and reaching Turin. Burlington had a reputation, which he prized, as a hard rider, but, even so, one day must be allowed from Venice to Vicenza and then another two between Vicenza and Turin. The letter explains why Burlington is most unlikely to have spent more than one night in a Vicenza which could not even offer him a bed:

> Dear Knight
>
> I ought to ask ten thousand pardons for not having thanked you sooner for the favour of your letter, which I received the day before I left Paris, but I am sure, if you knew the constant hurry that I have been in, you would be so good to forgive me, I was forced to make my stay in Vicenza much shorter than I intended for the waters were so out that there was no possibility of seeing any of the villas at any distance from the town besides that I was forced to sleep in a chair, there being but one bed in the house and that so bad that no creature but a frenchman would have gone into it so that you will easily imagine to whose share it fell, the town is so poor that I question whether your letter could have procured me one, you must pardon me for bringing of it back again, for I own I took such an impression of the Nobili from the few with whom I was acquainted that I did not deliver it, here has been such violent rains that the road from Venice to this place looks like a sea, I left a great many passengers upon the road and I was the only one that ventured to come on, *Cosucci* [curios] are so scarce since you drained Italy that I could find nothing but some tables at Genova and some drawings of Palladio at Venice.[26]

By the notes on three city palazzi that Burlington inscribed carefully into his *Quattro Libri* it is evident that he had studied the Palazzo Thiene, whose heavy, blockish simplicities he admired enormously, and the Palazzo Chiericati where he was told a cock-and-bull story by a local bricklayer who claimed 'that he built this house from the ground after Palladio's design, about thirty years ago'. The truth is that the place was largely standing and inhabitable by 1570, when Valerio Chiericati moved in, but that some work did go on after Valerio's death in 1609. The palace is so beautiful and complex in its columned galleries that it would not have fitted comfortably into Lord Burlington's preconceived notions of the simple, noble antique. This he had acquired from an opinionated Scot, Colen Campbell, who had never set foot in Italy nor seen a Roman antique structure more sophisticated than Hadrian's Wall.

Bad weather did not prevent a visit to the Villa Capra, or Rotunda, as that masterpiece stands less than a mile outside the town, high and dry above any floodwaters. It impressed Burlington 'by the ornaments and exquisite taste that is in the most minute part of it', but its Mannerist interior decorations upset him. 'The present owner of it has done it a great injury by inlarging the chamber doors, and dressing them in a most extravagant manner.'[27] This finicky, critical concern with 'correct' proportions and exact details was to become the bane of English neo-Palladianism, not just in the eighteenth century, but again in the twentieth century when a foolish reverence for correct use of classical orders was often a substitute for a true appreciation of an elevation's aesthetic impact. What is sometimes described as a 'Germanic' critical pedantry is, in fact, very English, a product of one-upmanship acquired in bad schools, a nervous reliance upon an authority figure.

What is evident from the tone of the letter to Fountaine is that Palladio's style of building, where classical motifs are treated as a starting point for inspired improvisations of round arches, oculi, Michelangelesque reclining figures and wild rustication, was not what Burlington was expecting after his memories of Roman remains. Nor would it be what he intended to introduce to the English aristocracy. He had acquired, possibly in his weeks in Venice, possibly from the Barbaro's town palazzo in Vicenza, some personal papers of the architect who had been a friend of the brothers Marcantonio and Daniele Barbaro. There is, sadly, no indication that, in a wet November, he had braved the floods and got out to the brothers' beautiful Villa Maser near Treviso.[28] If he had he would have begun to appreciate what Palladio was all about: a relaxed classical humanism for confident, aristocratic farmers, where fat-bellied giants and gently straining naiads support an exquisitely poetic nymphaeum, and a largely single-storey house extends its golden stuccoed, barely classical arms out to windowless, curvaceous pavilions.

Unaware of or indifferent to villas he had missed up on the hills – Godi, Piovene and Forni-Cerato – or the perversely inventive villas on the plains – Poiana and Caraceno – that defiantly enliven a drab, horizontal landscape, Lord Burlington had what he wanted. This was Palladio's very own reconstruction of a whole series of grand imperial Roman baths. These would be the blueprints for the palace and the parliament house that Lord Shaftesbury had required. Any further domestic developments on 'Palladian' lines could be extensions of those 'authentic' Roman buildings. In the meantime there were, no doubt, pressing appointments to be kept with Jacobite malcontents. For the moment Lord Burlington had done his duty by the arts and his duty to the dead Earl of Shaftesbury. From various details on the plans of the baths – Diocletian windows, Serlian tripartite features and shallow domes – smaller structures could be improvised in a true antique gusto. Bad weather and a day and a half of intensive tourist activity had, however, left him with the entirely false impression that Palladian buildings were usually urban structures lining narrow streets and built on confined sites with relatively formal classical details. With his disdain for the Vicenzan 'Nobili' and his terror of their bug-ridden beds he is unlikely to have gained any lasting impression of the playful beauty of their well-proportioned rooms, enlivened with frescoes of landscape and the loves of the Gods that sprawl artfully around door frames or create, in clever perspective, doors, windows, children at play, servants at work, that do not really exist. Burlington had come to Palladio with misconceptions and did not stay long enough in Vicenza or the Terrafirma to correct them. If Kent had been with him to laugh, to mock and to appreciate, it could all have been so different.

7
In Paris 'to see the things'

While Lord Burlington was missing his opportunities in the Veneto, William Kent was in Paris with a chance to catch up on the realities of Western European design. So much of Kent's life and his responses are unwritten, and then, when he does write, his words are anticlimactic. The man who was soon to leap the fence and find all Nature to be a garden crossed the Alps in late October 1719, but left not a word of response to the scenery of the Mont Cenis pass, if that was the way he had been directed to go, on the twenty-day journey from Genoa to Paris which, 'being alone and not speaking the language well, has disturbed me very much'.[1]

It would be too much to expect any anticipations of Edmund Burke's *Sublime* from the man whose eventual strength would be the deft dramatisation of pastoral landscapes. But then to arrive in Paris, fortunate to spend at least a fortnight in the most glittering capital in Europe, and to record nothing more than a glum resolution 'to see the things'[2] is a disappointment indeed. Under the Régence, Paris was in a mood of high-spirited rejuvenescence, which should have fired Kent's imagination and sent him on to an England of solemn senescence in a spirit of lively rebellion. The boy King, Louis XV, reigned but did not yet rule. Philippe, Duke of Orleans, was at the helm as Regent, an appallingly mistreated epidemic of measles having carried off two whole generations of Louis XIV's heirs apparent. Self-indulgent, uncombative and fashion-conscious, the Regent had ushered in a rare twenty-year interlude of Anglo-French co-existence, when the French chief Minister,

Cardinal Fleury, could hunt and dine at Richmond as the guest of the English Prime Minister, Sir Robert Walpole.

If ever there was a time for England to be impressed by the inventive genius of France this was it. While the English, led by a Scot, Colen Campbell, and a German monarch, George I, were hesitating on the edge of an unenterprising return to Palladian neo-classicism, which was no more than an eighteenth-century revival of a sixteenth-century attempt at true Roman manners, France was beginning to reshape classical style in a modern idiom, giving it contemporary reference and figurative vigour.[3] The nineteenth century would christen the style mockingly, 'Rococo', from its fondness for *rocaille* (rock work) and *coquille* (shell work). In its time it was known, rightly, as 'le Style Moderne', innovative, curvaceous and vibrant with living forms. Even though he was dead, Louis XIV was still in command. In 1698 he had had the insight, rare in someone of his age, to see that the predictable half-Baroque neo-classicism which had been adequate to express the mood of 'la Grande Nation' for the first fifty-five years of his long reign (1643–1715) was played out and needed to be revitalised. He had told Jules Hardouin-Mansart, his Premier Architecte: 'Il faut qu'il y ait de la jeunesse mêlée dans ce que l'on fera' (There has got to be a youthful element worked into what is going on). It was an unexpected but entirely admirable moment, like that incident in General Charles de Gaulle's last election campaign when *Le Canard Enchaîné* featured the aged general beaming under a Beatle-style haircut over the slogan 'Votez de Gaulle! Votez Jeune!'

It had its effect, not with an instant, airily elegant, full-blown Rococo, but with two decorative devices: a revived Raphaelesque Grotesque work and a surge in those auricular forms that suggest the whorls of the ear. These would lead, by the end of the Régence in 1723, to a true Rococo. The Grotesque had been fashionable in the sixteenth century. Now, inspired by the frescoes discovered in the ruins of the Emperor Nero's Domus Aurea on the Esquiline Hill in Rome, the Grotesque was a style made for William Kent.[4] It ignored perspectives, its pavilions tilted but never fell, gravity made ninety-degree bends at an artist's whim; men, monkeys, parrots and squirrels all appeared in roughly equal stature, womens' necks tended to be as long as the rest of their bodies. Irreverence brims over from its figurative juxtapositioning. In Claude III Audran's 1704 ceiling at Anet, male fairies perch on symmetrically sited squirrels' backs, monkeys with guns shoot at flying birds, rats brandish C-scrolls among slender armatures, and everywhere interlaced scroll work prevails.[5] On Jean-Baptiste Monnoyer and Guy-Louis Vernansul's tapestries of 1700 parrots perch on these scrolls, other birds offer branches to a sphinx and acrobats walk tightropes at impossible angles.[6] As interpreted in France, the world of the Grotesque was one of clowns where Don Quixote finds his natural place hunting honour in vain among the maze of the arabesque.[7]

Two years before Kent reached Paris he had been urged, by the vastly more sophisticated John Talman, to deploy the Grotesque for that much delayed ceiling which he was supposed to be designing for Sir John Chester at Chicheley in Buckinghamshire. On that occasion, unaware perhaps of the style's potential for caricature and eclectic charm, Kent had written grudgingly to Massingberd: 'Mr Talman was here this morning & would have me done this ceiling after ye Grotesk manner, but I think it will not be well.'[8] Instead he produced the impressive brooding composition, one of his best historical paintings, *Mercury watching Herse and her Sisters before the Temple of Minerva*, which now hangs in the Entrance Hall at Chicheley. Kent could usually handle composition, whether in these paintings or, later, in landscapes. His weaknesses were crude brushwork and an inability to capture convincing likenesses of attractive models. Back in Italy he had nursed a Colonel Blimpish anti-Gallicanism that automatically prejudiced him against any artistic movement originating in France. He had written to Massingberd on 28 January in a drearily English spirit of negative patriotism:

> I am informed yt in England we are inclined a little to ye French gusto in painting but can assure you I never designe to follow it – for if they understood painting as well as they do Musick If consider ye difference between French musick & ye Italiane I can assure y there is just ye same in painting as yn French Musick is most ungrateful to ye Eare, so is there painting to ye Eiyy.[9]

This is a passage that deserves to be savoured for the stumbling syntax of Bridlington Grammar School and for its confident, hobbledehoy ignorance. Even the distribution of its capital letters betrays prejudice, yet Kent was a mature thirty-year-old when he penned these lines. Nine years in Rome had done little to broaden his mind or open him up to influences, and now he was dependent on the favour of a younger man,

Burlington, who was himself in the stylistic grip of Colen Campbell, a half-trained Scots lawyer turned architect. John Talman had been a safer patron and Kent was heading towards a crisis in an already uncertain career.[10]

It is not possible to say exactly how open to Parisian influences the sullen, isolated, tongue-tied William Kent would have been in the fortnight he spent there. He would have had no one to offer him entry to the great town houses of the nobility until Lord Burlington caught up with him; and then Burlington, obsessed with the noble, the austere and the antique, is unlikely to have been an enthusiast for male fairies or academic apes. Yet it does seem that this was when Kent was converted to the Grotesque and, therefore, had his mind opened to the Rococo which would follow on from it. After rejecting the Grotesque in Rome in 1717 he would splash it out confidently over a principal ceiling at Kensington Palace in 1722, and win royal approval for it from King George I.

By 1719 the style was well established in Paris. Jean Bérain had been painting lively Grotesque work in the 1680s before Louis XIV's call for 'la jeunesse'; and Claude Audran had picked up the style eagerly. Gilles Marie Oppenord had redecorated the notorious Appartement des Roués at the Palais Royal for the pleasure-loving Regent Orleans in 1714.[11] But would anyone in Parisian upper circles have invited Bridlington Kent to join the Roués? It is hardly likely, unless he had an entrée to the sexual underworld of the city. Though that was always a possibility for a man who had been nine years in Rome practising his talents for striking up useful relationships with young unmarried gentlemen.

It was well known in Paris that the Regent Orleans had climbed a scaffolding in the Appartement and amateurishly daubed away at a ceiling. One of the great attractions of the Grotesque was its eclectic iconography, which allowed personal choice; patrons would become flatteringly involved in the subject matter. There were no confining rules of classical precedent; anything could be included among those spiralling garlands. Just as England was preparing to trap its decorated interiors in the trite motifs of an outworn revival, France was moving in an exactly opposite direction, towards wit, invention and charm. Neo-classicism confines, but satisfies the conservative and the unsure. Grotesque work, and the Rococo which developed from it, leaves the artist and the designer free to invent or borrow every theme from Olympus to the circus. It was

Giuseppe Grisoni's predictably Baroque and pietistic representation of John Talman (centre), with his father, William, Frances Cockayne and Hannah Talman, painted in 1719, ten years after his meeting with William Kent.

(*Below left*) *The Story of Latona* by Giuseppe Chiari, who was Kent's master and teacher for five years in Rome.

(*Below right*) Anthony Ashley Cooper, 3rd Earl of Shaftesbury, poses as a Roman senator for the frontispiece of his *Characteristicks of Men, Manners, Opinions, Times.*

This headpiece from Shaftesbury's *Characteristicks* (1732 edition) features most of the eclectic garden buildings in a park like Stowe. It illustrates the Ages of the Arts.

FACING PAGE

(*Above*) The true flamboyant 'gusto' of Italian Baroque painting – Sebastiano Ricci's *The Triumph of Galatea* (1713-15), on the staircase of Burlington House.

(*Below*) Kent's *Assembly of the Gods* (1719-20), oil on plaster, Burlington House.

Bartholomew Dandridge's portrait of Kent in relaxed and confident mood.

The entrance front of Chiswick House drawn by Kent with a statue of Palladio. Kent, walking stick in hand, expounds as a dog pisses on Burlington's ankle.

The Obelisk at Chiswick with Kent and his dog relieving themselves against the west entrance archway.

A Kent drawing of an idealised Plunge Pool and Temple with nude bathers.

England's Rococo moment – John Rocque transposes the cast from Watteau's *Embarkation for the Island of Cythera* to the banks of the Thames opposite Queen Caroline's Richmond Gardens.

Richard Boyle, 3rd Earl of Burlington, with the Bagnio at Chiswick in the background, which he designed in 1719.

The interior of the Ante-Room at Chiswick Villa (1726-29) illustrates the febrile intensity which Kent was able to infuse into normally calm Palladian decorative details.

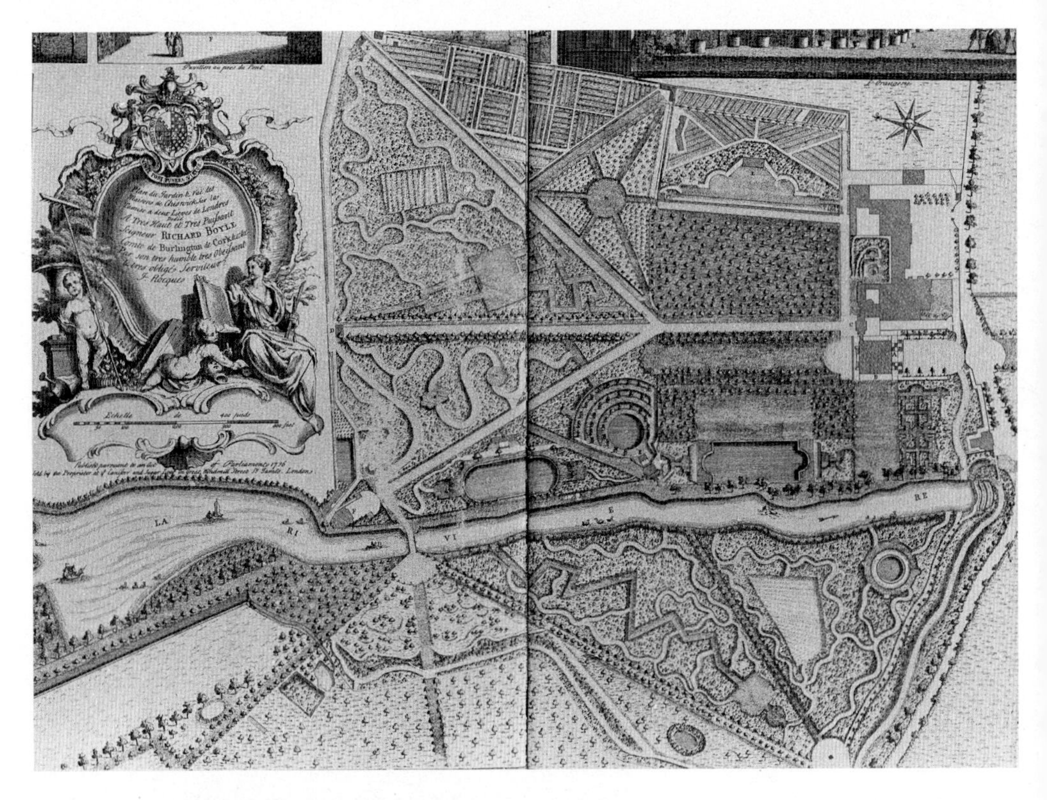

In Rocque's 1736 Plan of Chiswick the winding woodland paths and natural seeming course of the Bollo Brook lie in complete contrast with Charles Bridgeman's geometry of the principal avenues.

Little dogs scamper, a negro servant brings wine and a lady curtseys in Kent's sketch for the Exedra and Ionic Temple at Chiswick.

for the rebels, the innovators and the bored. Here, quite early in the new century, European art was exploring the preliminary tensions between classical control and Romantic freedom. Kent's design career would be alive with these tensions, at no time more than in London over the next two years.

The auricular – *rocaille* forms favoured by the new style – twisting, perverse asymmetries – would have been commonplace to Kent after his Italian years. Stefan della Bella had been experimenting with the auricular for some years before his death in 1664, and his followers in Italy only lacked the airy grace of the ultimate French Rococo. Kent would simply need to recall the gilded auricular riot of late seventeenth-century Italian tables and chairs that he had seen in Roman palaces and he would have the designs for what the English think of as 'Kentian' furnishings.[12]

Only the calibre of French artists in overdoors, ceiling paintings and framed work might have given Kent a pause by its sheer professionalism. Painters who would have become renowned and wealthy in England were, if not quite two-a-penny, readily accessible in France as a result of generous royal patronage. Hyacinthe Rigaud, François Le Moyne, Jean Restout, Guillaume Martin, Charles de la Fosse, Antoine Coypel[13] and Nicolas Lancret were all active, turning out, in sumptuous colour, effortless erotic elegances in the shape of nymphs, shepherd swain and Olympian goddesses. Breasts rose from tumbling folds of silk and shepherds flaunted their sleekly muscled nudity with just a saving drape over the thigh. This was when France really asserted its sexual ascendancy in Europe.

It was all a far cry from that fully clothed *Spirit of Flanders* on the ceiling of San Giuliano dei Fiamminghi. Kent, who was personally plump, never really let himself go on a female, or for that matter a male, nude. If he noticed that French nudity had a domestic immediacy, which was absent from Italian set piece nudes like Correggio's *Danaë* in the Galleria Borghese, he would opt, when he came to his own *Danaë* at Kensington Palace, for the more heightened Italian model, as being less disturbing. Nine years of Roman training would easily outweigh a Parisian fortnight of artistic tourism.

What would be most satisfying would be if there were evidence that Kent came, in that fortnight, into contact with the second element in France's new painting, the Romantic. He is likely to have seen at least a print of Jean Antoine Watteau's *Embarkation for Cythera*. It was painted in 1717, two years before Kent arrived. More than any other single painting it established the idea of the *fête galante*, where exquisitely informal ladies and gentlemen pose in woodland glades and by shallow waters for elegantly al fresco meals. With that one captivating scene Watteau realised Sir Philip Sidney's *Arcadia* and seduced the aristocracy away from pompous formalism to an idealised real life. Now the true '*douceur de la vie*' could, and indeed should, be casually framed within apparently natural woodland settings with hints of classical reference: the statue of a faun or a garlanded urn among the trees. The French were the first to achieve in paint this ideal setting for a *fête galante*; but it would be the English who, despite the handicap of their climate, first realised those Arcadias in their parks. No one would design them more convincingly than Kent, though Henry Hoare would exceed him in eclectic range at Stourhead in the 1740s and Alderman Beckford would create in the 1750s a practical voyage to Cythera on his new lake at Fonthill.

While edging perilously into counter-factual history it is impossible not to feel some frustration that neither Kent nor Burlington appears to have experienced, and absorbed, the interior decoration of Palladio's own villas. On his travels with Coke's party Kent seems to have observed only the exteriors of the villas, while the perpetually impatient Burlington allowed flood waters to cut him off from their inspiration on his hasty second tour. No artistic advance in the culturally interlocked states of Europe is ever completely isolated or without ancestry. Watteau perfected the setting for the *fête galante*, but such refined and artfully incident-strewn landscapes had been frescoed on the walls of many, even most, of Palladio's villas: Forni Cerato, Emo, Barbaro, Pisani. These landscapes are not trapped, however, on canvas in frames or suspended away from natural visual sight-lines up on a ceiling. They are splashed out on the plaster of the walls of dining rooms and entrance halls like vibrant wallpaper, casually and playfully. They are often illusionistic. Landscapes with classical ruins are viewed as over a painted balcony balustrade; in Paolo Veronese's frescoes for the Villa Barbaro a little painted girl stands in a half-open painted door, but under a real projecting pediment. Art was part of real life in Italy because frescoes came easily to artists. England was more grudging in talent and so kept art on a pedestal or, more literally, in a carved frame.

Lord Burlington was not aiming so much at the revival of Palladio's domestic architecture of the sixteenth century as at the supposed architecture of senatorial Rome, sixteen hundred years earlier. He assumed, in his ignorance, that Palladio's Orders in his *First Book*, together with his semi-scholarly reconstructions of Roman public bath houses, would provide an easy route to an authentic neo-classical revival. The fact that, when he came to devise his own 'Roman' villa at Chiswick, he used some of Vincenzo Scamozzi's villas as a model and not one by Scamozzi's master, Palladio, indicates how far Burlington was from reverential copying. Very little in the British love affair with Palladio and Palladianism is what it seems.

For the rest of his life Kent would be caught up in this half-scholarly quest, reacting to and modifying Burlington's initiatives, prejudices and misconceptions. Because his new patron-friend had drawn him into the very heart of the English establishment he was prepared to go along for the ride. Without Burlington's wealth, contacts and drive, he would have had no influence, but together the two men were, artistically, 'an item'. Burlington was positive, Kent was passive, but he relished being taken on, hurried away and made a part of the stylistic movement which, however retrograde and ill-thought out, was at least dynamic.

After those few Paris weeks, unrecorded though not without influence, Burlington, the Earl with a mission, hard riding and weather-beaten, came galloping up from Turin. Now he was armed with his own copy of the *Quattro Libri* and with Palladio's version of what the great Roman municipal baths might have looked like. It did not occur to him that a bath house for an idle, lecherous citizenry might not be the happiest possible model for a new royal palace or new Houses of Parliament.

Lord Burlington's mode of travel on this, his second and shorter Italian tour, has no architectural relevance, but it does indicate how the aristocrat, nine years Kent's junior, must have impacted upon plump, nervous William, lost in a strange city. On his first, true Grand Tour, Burlington had journeyed with a mini-orchestra in tow and a whole convoy of carriages. But now, as Dr James Hay reported after observing Burlington's departure from Venice, the Earl was 'in a constant hurry. I wish', Hay added, 'we could afford to travel after his manner but without his train',[14] referring apparently to speed rather than to pomp. So when Burlington swept down on Paris to hurry Kent along to London he was probably not in a carriage but riding on horseback, mud-bespattered, with a group of mounted attendants carrying his *cosucci* and precious papers. The party had left Turin on 6 November and by 24 November they would be in

London: a mere eighteen days to cover some six hundred miles at roughly thirty-three miles a day, in winter and including a sea crossing. Those figures give some idea of what life with the young Burlington must have been like. They explain Kent's reference, in his letter of 10 December to Massingberd from London, to 'a dismal journey from Paris'. It will have brought him breathless and critically bemused to lodge in an architectural paradox and to face a stylistic confrontation.

8

What good thing ever came from a Campbell?

When, at the end of their long, fast journey, the group of horsemen finally clattered into the forecourt of Burlington House,[1] William Kent could have been excused for finding the architectural contradictions of the great courtyard disturbing. Unless, that is, Lord Burlington had found time to explain his problems with the Dowager Countess Juliana, his mother.

Ever since 1704, when his father, the 2nd Earl, had died, leaving his only son not quite ten years old, Burlington had been under his mother's firm direction. It is always accepted that she was responsible for her son's enthusiasm for music and opera; what has not been emphasised so much is the way she had pitched him headlong into an architectural confusion over the exterior of his London town house. At the same time she had trapped him into rigid and not entirely fortunate assumptions about how paintings should function in an interior. Both her architecture and her art patronage would present Kent with problems.

The Burlington House which the Countess's husband had inherited had been large, unassuming and Carolean, eleven bays long and brick-built. It had been designed by Sir John Denham and Hugh May after 1644, out on the edge of west London, with long gardens that would soon become a gold mine for developments. In 1715, while her son was still under-aged, she had commissioned from James Gibbs, a Catholic architect of wide Italian experience, this *cour d'honneur* so monumental in its Baroque grandeur that she must have been intending eventually to give the dull house a makeover in something of the same style. Before that, in 1714, she had called in Sebastiano Ricci and Giovanni Pellegrini to paint Baroque canvases to enrich the sober interior. Neither artist was, by Italian standards, of the very first rank, but both were good and, by William Kent's standards, shatteringly competent. Even today, re-sited and badly lit, Ricci's *Triumph of Galatea* and *Diana and her Nymphs* raise, by their sheer Baroque exuberance and overt eroticism, a sense of cheerful anticipation on the climb up to the Fine Rooms on the first floor.

By May 1717, when Burlington got back from his sickness-plagued Grand Tour, the artwork was in place and Gibbs's grand colonnade had been built. It was immediately recognised as one of the sights of the capital. Horace Walpole attended a reception there one night and 'At day-break, looking out of the window to see the sun rise, I was surprised by the vision of the colonnade that fronted me. It seemed one of those edifices in fairy tales that are raised by genii in a night's time.'[2] But Burlington, characteristically, took against it. To him it was an example of 'that damn'd gusto', the Baroque apparently, against which he was fighting in his quest for a republican simplicity of classicism which would symbolise the aristocratic order that the Whigs were about to construct under the docile figurehead of their German King-President. Burlington was now twenty-one, so he was able to disengage himself from his mother's Catholic architect, bringing in a plausible Scot, Colen Campbell, to design a new entrance front for the house which would outface, by the cool reserve of its chaste, staccato classicism, the splendid half-circle of Gibbs's Doric colonnade.

Campbell was laird of the unhappily named Boghole, a small estate in Nairnshire.[3] Little is known about his early architectural training, probably because he kept discreetly quiet about its limitations. He had studied law at Edinburgh University and actually practised as a lawyer. His tenuous connection with Palladianism seems to have been through a Scottish architect, James Smith, who fathered, by two wives, thirty-one children and built around Glasgow a few dull, regular classical houses that could charitably be described as Palladian in character.[4]

Smith's style and his influence, via Campbell, on England's revived Palladianism needs to be emphasised as it was from Smith that a plain, correct regularity, so remote from Palladio's lively invention, settled like a stylistic blight upon many eighteenth-century English houses, which claim to be Palladian but are in reality mere classical boxes, built on the cheap and devoid of imagination. Through his dire influence upon the impressionable young Burlington, Colen Campbell would prove to be the bane of William Kent's career. From Campbell's time onwards, and even today, many Georgian enthusiasts appraise a classical building as 'correct' or 'incorrect' rather than as alive, inventive, dull or predictable.

In its time Campbell's Burlington House façade[5] was so admired that a carefully accurate 1746 painting of it in a sylvan setting by Zuccarelli and Visentini became a valued item in the Royal Collection, and it remains today in Buckingham Palace.[6] This innovatory new façade had just come out of its scaffolding when a saddle-sore Kent rode into that court of stylistic confrontations. Confusing the complex even further was Campbell's gatehouse in the middle of Gibbs's colonnade. Anxious to assert his links with Inigo Jones, Campbell had modelled this on the Water Gate of York House, supposing that its rusticated columns and grotesque heads were authentic works of the great master. In fact it was a Jacobean conceit by either Nicholas Stone or Sir Balthasar Gerbier;[7] so that added a third stylistic element to the courtyard which could hardly, therefore, be considered a clear stylistic manifesto.

Kent had been hurried up to London, not just to continue the sequence of Cupid and Psyche paintings that Ricci had begun with his *Cupid before Jove on Olympus*.[8] His second and more pressing task was to design interiors for the house in a style that would reflect Campbell's supposedly 'Palladian' entrance front. As that elevation was meant to act as a striking demonstration of the Whigs' new order in a fashionable quarter of the capital, Kent was expected to pick up the essentials of Campbell's style and create equally distinctive interiors that would be copied across the country. From being a moderately successful Roman guide, art dealer and painter he was now in a position of artistic influence in a very rich, stylistically disorientated country, required to devise coordinates with Campbell's staccato exterior.

That Kent was able to come up with exactly what Burlington was looking for in the Fine Rooms on the first floor – a pure, distinctive style of interior decoration that could be easily copied without requiring much craftsmanship or experience – explains his sudden remarkable impact upon the limited world of English design. Kent was adaptable and perfectly ready to cut aesthetic corners if that meant pleasing a not very sensitive patron. The parallel between Kent's work for Burlington and Albert Speer's work on the Reich Chancellery for Adolf Hitler comes readily to mind. One version of neo-classicism or another will always suggest a reassuring reminder of past imperial order, together with a stripped-down cleanliness of line and a wholesome simplicity. The subsequent tedium will take a while to settle.

It is arguable that, coming after Sir Christopher Wren and Sir John Vanbrugh, both giants of creativity, Colen Campbell was one of the most malign influences ever to work in English architecture. But his façade for Burlington House achieved exactly that iconic influence that his patron had intended; and because Kent caught up its staccato styling to devise matching architectural interiors it requires some analysis. No one knows how much actual experience of Roman architecture Campbell had acquired or even if he had travelled in Italy at all. The 'Palladianism' he introduced to England was not truly Palladian. Far from being light-hearted and humane, it depended upon setting correct copies of original Roman details in staccato isolation on plain wall surfaces. It was, in fact, architecture for nervous pedants, often resulting, as on that Burlington House entrance front, in a chilling institutionalised air, a textbook of detail rather than a connected composition conceived in a generally classical spirit. The features – windows, pediments, columns, doorways – of a Baroque front connect with each other to produce movement; the features of Campbell's pseudo-Palladianism demand to be appraised in isolation. It says very little for the visual sophistication of eighteenth-century aristocrats that they took so readily to a scholarly rather than a living, evolving classicism; but Kent knew what was required and he delivered it with confidence.

It is irresistible to speculate on his first reactions as he went through that absurdly understate Campbellian central doorway and moved sideways into the Countess Juliana's overwhelming stair hall.[9] Was there a 'Lucky Jim' moment of despair as he sized up the competition and considered a speedy retreat back to Rome? Above him on the ceiling was Sebastiano Ricci's *Cupid on Olympus*, on three walls were the same artist's *Triumph of Bacchus*, *Triumph of Galatea* and *Diana and her Nymphs*. Even the overdoors were brilliantly erotic. As the Countess Juliana welcomed him, did she gesture to the master works which he was now required to follow and equal?

Fortunately we have some record of Kent's state of mind, as he continued to write letters to Massingberd until he felt confident that Burlington was not going to cast him adrift in a hostile London. On 10

December 1719 he broke the news that Massingberd must have been expecting for some time:

> Got safe here with my Ld. Burlington & am Lodg'd in his house, & he will have me begin to paint for him the furst thing I do is the fine room in his new building. I have already made the designs wch he seems to be much pleasd with.[10]

This was a hopeful rather than a confident note, and he was still keeping an escape route open to Massingberd in Lincolnshire: 'I hope it will not be long before I have the happiness to see you though the season is a little troublesome & the change of aire from that of Italy yt since I came I have had a great cold but hope it will be nothing.'[11] The London fogs were obviously taking their toll on his sinuses. A month later, writing on 19 January 1720, he was still tentatively scrounging on his old paymaster and beginning to realise the hostile opposition gathering around him: 'I hope I shall not have too much to pay at the custom house for I may take the liberty to tell you am forc'd to make y best show I can & not to seem to these great people as if I wanted money.'[12] This was as fair an indication as any that he was not Burlington's paid companion, but a vulnerable, independent artist putting on a brave show in pinched financial circumstances, though surely someone with his eager interest in money would have come to some kind of agreement over a salary by this time. He continued, appealing for sympathy,

> How I come of I can't tell you may imagine I am not a little disturbed at the hurry of this countery, for being quite a stranger to the extravagant tast of ye English vertuosi in Painting Sculpt Arch that I don't now were I am when I am once out of the gates of Ld Burlington's hous were I think you may see a true Palladian front.[13]

This was evidence as to how little attention Kent had paid to Palladian houses when he was in Italy. Far from being, as some authors claim, a version of Palladio's town palace in Vicenza for Iseppo da Porta, which Campbell is unlikely ever to have seen,[14] the Scot had put together an original composition with Venetian windows at each end bay, something Palladio never did. Burlington House was, in effect, a sandwich of English slices. Its rustic, or ground, floor, was copied from that of the Queen's

House, Greenwich; its principal storey from the first floor of the Whitehall Banqueting House minus its rustication; and its window surrounds were modelled on those of the Grand Gallery at Somerset House.[15] All its emphasis was horizontal, not vertical, and its lack of a bedroom or attic floor gave it the institutional air of a town hall.

In his letter Kent gave a clear indication that he was being employed, not simply as an artist, but as a designer: 'I have made a sketch in Coloers for the great room in the front [the Saloon] & all the rest of the ornaments are to be al Italiano I waite only to get my things & then hope shall get to work.'[16] Eleven days later he was beginning to find his feet, still in a 'continual hurry', but 'twice a week yt I go to ye Opera where I am highly entertained & yn think myself out of this Gothick country'.[17] There was no opera on in London at that date and Kent must have been referring to a popular concert-vaudeville performance, which suggests that he rarely attended the opera in Italy. His disparaging use of the term 'Gothick' is intriguing as he would soon make it, by his own ingenious designs, a term of quaint praise for an exotic historicist style of ogee arches and quatrefoils. The commissions which Burlington was giving him 'makes all these power spirited English Daubers raile & make partys against me, but I hope to overcome them all'.[18] The letter ended with a note which again appears to contradict those who consider his relationship with his patron to have been sexually suspect: 'Lord Burlington is going to be marry'd to Lady Dorothy Saville so I hope ye vertue will grow stronger in our house & architecture will flourish more.'[19] Interestingly, it is not painting that will flourish, but architecture; his interests were already beginning to shift, even before he was launched on his dreadfully third rate *Cupid and Psyche* cycle.

Burlington's mother had fixed upon the sugary sentiment of the Cupid legend when Ricci was working for her five years earlier.[20] If it was chosen in an attempt to persuade her son to marry and fill the house with children, rather than with foreign artists, then her campaign had succeeded: Kent appears to have been delighted by the engagement. He remained, however, challenged by the visual presentation of young love. His paintings at Burlington House are of infinitely less influence and importance than the decorative architectural scheme which he evolved around them for the Fine Rooms, but they have to be noticed. It was Kent's bad luck, then as now, that visitors come to his ceilings after a passage between the rosy vitality of Ricci's seductive *Nymphs* and the billowing, airy lines of his *Galatea*. Kent's figures for Cupid and Psyche seem, in contrast, reluctant to touch each other or even to make effective eye contact.

His oil upon plaster on the ceiling of the present 'Lee and James C. Slaughter Room' represents Jove giving consent to the marriage of Cupid and Psyche. It is a revealing piece of work. The human figures are weak, the artist seeming to lack that lustful relish in human flesh that brings nude and semi-nude studies to life. A certain sexless quality runs through Kent's life and work so that it comes as a surprise to read in his will that he had a mistress all the time, by whom he fathered a son, George, and a daughter, Elizabeth.[21] His Psyche in this painting is limp and listless; Mercury is only half-realised, he floats when he should be flying. Jove has a good bearded head on a weak body, but Kent never mastered human eyes: all his eyes are slits. The horses, in contrast, are excellent, great muscular beasts with kindly eyes and faces, cheerfully dappled. Is it possible that Kent liked horses more than humans? The answer leaps out from Ricci's *Triumph of Galatea. His* horses are great muscular beasts with kindly eyes and faces. Kent must have copied them in almost every detail; if only he had copied Ricci's nymphs as faithfully. For some reason now lost to us Kent did not relate well to human models. His eyes and his paintbrush did not connect any more than his subjects' hands and bodies connect; his compositions are static; Baroque Rome had influenced him remarkably little.

That static, un-Baroque quality became an asset when Kent had to devise an 'antique gusto' to accord with Campbell's pseudo-Palladian, neo-classical exterior. The Fine Rooms at Burlington House have recently been restored to their pristine Kentian condition.[22] On pure, creamy white walls the plaster frames, the pier glasses under their pediments and the pedimented doorcases are all lavishly gilded and stand out as strictly isolated incidents of classical purity with no connecting lines. It is the 'gusto Italiano' that Kent had been brought over to create. The upholstery is crimson silk damask, otherwise all the relieving colour is up on the ceiling; there were decorative lunettes in the coving of the central Saloon, but these are being restored. Over the pedimented doorways stand oddly gesticulating cherubs, sculpted by one of Burlington's tame artist imports, Giovanni Guelfi.

The effect is cold, expensive, tasteful and unmoving, like Campbell's architecture, but the strangest features are the empty frames. They cry out for paintings, lively and readily accessible, but Kent left them empty.[23] There is nothing to record whether the vacancy was his choice or Burlington's rueful decision, but they do seem to make a negative point about Kent's art. He had, nevertheless, come up with what his patron was looking for. The Fine Rooms have a grudging elegance, but they could pass as a notional ancient Roman simplicity and they could be easily copied: white, gold and crimson. Soon any number of white and gold interiors with crimson touches would be created in English houses, parodies of the true frescoed Palladian interiors. Kent had complemented Campbell's exterior forms perfectly. Whether that was a positive design step depends upon assessments of Campbell's style, which must be personal.

Kent had returned to England at a most unusual point in the nation's history: the very middle of the reign of one of the least noticed yet most influential kings – George I – ever to occupy the throne. It was a time when good precedents were broken, bad precedents were set, great architects and good artists were snubbed, but knaves with an eye to the main chance flourished. Both Burlington and Kent came perilously close to belonging to the knaves' party and that reality has to be faced. Because Lord Shaftesbury had effectively assassinated him in print,[24] Wren was retired from his key position as Surveyor of the King's Works in 1718, and Vanbrugh was sidetracked by being denied promotion in 1719; Hawksmoor suffered a similar fate. As Sir Howard Colvin makes clear in his authoritative *History of the King's Works*, the accession of a foreigner to the English throne marked a time when merit no longer had any place in the appointment to the great artistic offices of state. From 1714 onwards cronies and political placemen took most of the high offices. Colen Campbell and his devious, half-German friend, William Benson, were prime examples of this tendency, yet they were men with whom Kent had to work closely in these early years of his return to England. Campbell, and quite probably King George himself, had as much influence on Kent at this time as had his protector, Lord Burlington.

Campbell had become, in 1715, the fashionable architect of the new reign thanks more to his publishing activities than to the large, ugly house that he began building in 1714 at Wanstead in Essex, for Sir Richard Child, later created Earl Tylney. It was in 1714 that Campbell's luck had really turned. Not only was work begun on Wanstead, whose dreary horizontal façade could be seen as a simplistic counterblast to Vanbrugh's towered Blenheim, but that was the year when he hijacked the *Vitruvius Britannicus* project. This was a commercial scheme to publish, in several magnificently produced and illustrated volumes, a record of English architectural achievement in recent years. George I had come to the throne in 1714 and, because he was known to favour Palladio from his own ancestral origins in the Veneto, it was considered expedient to inject a strong Palladian element into the first volume of *Vitruvius Britannicus*.[25] That would require some ingenuity as there had been virtually no Palladian revival building in England for the last fifty years, but much in the Baroque style. Campbell was called in on the strength of his unfinished Wanstead and he proceeded to introduce Palladianism of a peculiarly limited vintage by a publishing confidence trick. It was one, however, that completely took in the impulsive Lord Burlington and that consequently dragged William Kent, for all his background of the Roman Baroque, into the forefront of a Palladian revival.

With an impudence that may explain how he had obtained the Wanstead commission, Campbell opened the first volume of his *Vitruvius* with distorted perspectives of St Paul's Cathedral and St Peter's in Rome, followed immediately by a correctly perspectived engraving of a church, domed to link it with the first two, that he claimed he was going to build in Lincoln's Inn Fields, though there was not the slightest chance of one stone of it ever being laid upon another. Among the impressive illustrations that followed he slyly inserted three more palatial and memorably vulgar designs of his own, one for the Duke of Argyll, a fellow Campbell, one for the Earl of Islay, Argyll's brother, and one for the Earl of Halifax. None of the three was likely to be commissioned, but they flattered their dedicatees and were themselves flattered by being ranked alongside Greenwich Palace, Blenheim, Castle Howard, Chatsworth and several more of the greatest houses in the country. Not just his Wanstead design as built, but a second, expensively domed, alternative design also had pride of place.

The architectural historian Carole Fry's analysis of the subscribers to that first, 1715, volume of Campbell's *Vitruvius Britannicus* reveals a wave of national interest in the book among the country's ruling classes.[26] What is puzzling is that the contents of the volume, the splendidly illustrated plates, give few clues as to why the style Campbell was advocating, a Jonesian–Palladian composite, actually caught the aristocracy's imagination. Of the subscribers, 60 per cent were Whig, 40 per cent were Tory.

Most of the peerage subscribed, exiled Jacobites like the Earl of Mar proving as ardent for a revival of Palladianism as they understood the term, as were Whig lords in office. Almost as many Tory MPs as Whig subscribed. Intellectuals and high army officers were well represented, as were German statesmen and even King George's loyal Turkish secretary-bodyguards, Mustapha and Mehemet von Königstren. Only Cambridge University was a little withdrawn: Oxford supplied fifty-seven subscribers to Cambridge's nineteen. Twenty-five of the Oxford contingent were from Christ Church, which was where, from 1706 to 1714, Dean Aldrich had pioneered the country's first major Palladian building, his Peckwater Quad. Aldrich was a Tory, which suggests that there was a general national impatience with the stylistic indecisiveness of the post-1660 years together with some revulsion against any classicism that smacked of French influence, as Wren's St Paul's undoubtedly did.

Everything that Inigo Jones was supposed to have designed was included by Campbell in order to make Palladian forms seem patriotic and native to England. In a particularly clever device Campbell included among all these grand and historic buildings a view of Burlington House as built in 1664 and looking very plain and dowdy by contrast. Lord Burlington took the point and, moving at his usual brisk, social pace, took Campbell under his wing. Quite how he was able to reconcile these ornate and vulgar 'Inventions' that Campbell was proposing for the Argylls and Halifax with Lord Shaftesbury's quest for a new architecture of noble simplicity is hard to explain. Campbell's preface to the first volume, with its patriotic appeal, its scorn for 'the affected and licentious' forms of the Baroque and its praise for the 'Antique Simplicity' of 'the renowned Palladio' and the 'famous Inigo Jones', must have won his trust. One underlying implication of the Kent–Burlington interaction is that, while Burlington was a man of great influence, dynamic, determined and a hero to any twentieth-century scholars with a taste for authoritarian solutions, he had little analytical intelligence and narrow aesthetic judgement. Then there was his vanity.

Kent eventually became the dominant partner in the relationship by his charm and by his ability to provide solutions, but initially Kent's problem was that Burlington had been flattered by the wily Campbell into thinking himself a Palladian architect. The confidence trick had been carried out in 1717, long before Burlington's second Italian visit. Campbell had coaxed Burlington into producing a pretty little design for a garden bagnio, or bath house, at Chiswick – a domed turret over a room with a Venetian window – the whole perched elegantly over an arch.[27] It was actually built and Burlington had himself painted by Jonathan Richardson leaning on a stone pedestal with the Bagnio in the background and a self-satisfied look on his long aristocratic face.[28] The incident explains why, in 1720, Burlington and Campbell were still close and why Kent would have had to tread warily in questioning Campbell's designs.

By 1719, however, both Campbell and William Benson had been exposed as the rogues and charlatans they really were. It is a most satisfying story. Sir Christopher Wren had been sacked as Surveyor General of the King's Works in 1718 and the prestigious office was given to Benson with Campbell as his Deputy. Benson's only claim to the office was that, being half-Prussian, he could speak German with the King. He had also been quick witted enough to pick the brains of a Dorset curate, the Revd Thomas Holland, an amateur in hydraulics, and then to direct a skilled mechanic to create a fountain with a supposed 100-foot jet in the garden of George's Herrenhausen Palace in Hanover.[29] His house at Wilbury in Dorset may have given him some faint claim to Palladian credentials as it had been built on the sandwich slice principle. It was a single-storey box, a virtual replica of the attic storey of Amesbury Abbey which Benson mistakenly thought had been designed by Inigo Jones, rather than by his protégé, John Webb.

Once ensconced in the Surveyor's office, this precious pair claimed that the building, a converted chapel, housing the Lords in the Palace of Westminster, was in imminent danger of collapsing on the heads of the assembled peers. They had probably some ambitious plan ready for rebuilding the Houses of Parliament to a Palladian design at great expense and much profit to themselves. Their dishonest plot was exposed by alarmed Treasury officials and in July 1719 both men were obliged to retire in some disgrace, having held office for only fifteen months.

A sub-plot to this scandal deserves to be mentioned. Who had been working closely with Campbell on a Palladian-style bagnio in 1717? Who was dedicated to carrying out the 3rd Earl of Shaftesbury's injunction to rebuild the Houses of Parliament in a style of simple classical dignity, and who left England abruptly in the summer of 1719 to seek out a new architect–painter–designer in Italy? The answer, of course, is Lord Burlington, and it is most likely that he was as involved in Benson and Campbell's plot as they were themselves, and that he left England to avoid awkward questions, while at the same time searching out some useful designs by Palladio so that he could launch the next rebuilding of Parliament scheme in person.

This episode needs to be digested in preparation for Kent's royal commission in the following chapter, where King George, Lord Burlington, Campbell and Benson were all involved in a Kentian projection that managed to combine the noble, the ridiculous and the dishonest in roughly equal measure. Kent rose to fame and success in some dubious company and in 1720 his glory days were still some way ahead. It is broadly safe to say that in the reign of King George I only the unscrupulous rose to the top – William Kent included.

9
Kensington – Kent's innovative but unfortunate palace

It would be sensible to count Kent's work on the new rooms at Kensington Palace as a learning experience as there is very little else favourable that can be said about it. The rooms are important, despite their indeterminate and often clumsy styling because they were royal and, therefore, influential. They are markers to an actual turning point in national fashions of design, so Kensington needs to be separated from its romantic associations with the young Queen Victoria and Princess Diana and considered as an experimental building of largely botched neo-classical intentions. A new wave of less than competent architects and designers were struggling there to satisfy an old German Elector-King who had had some personal experience of classical re-visionism himself back in Hanover. But the truth is that neither King George, nor Benson and Campbell his architects, nor Kent his painter-designer, nor the manipulator Burlington, nor the New Junta for Architecture knew exactly what kind of design and architectural break-through they were aiming at. The dead puppet master, Lord Shaftesbury, had never been very clear either; all he had wanted was a symbolic change of style. And that, at Kensington, was what they were groping towards.

It would be fascinating to know more about the apparently cordial relationship which Kent established with King George once Burlington had effected an introduction and a contract. Unfortunately little is recorded, apart from royal approval, as Kent went from 1722 to 1727 designing one interior after another at the Palace.[1] He would be paid a small fortune, £3250, for this work, so he would never again be poor, but become instead an investor in property. The Kensington commissions made Kent permanently fashionable, a figure in the English artistic establishment with a licence to take risks, to experiment and to surprise. Subsequent critical interest has, therefore, tended to concentrate on Kent rather than on the King, whose experience in his previous fifty-four German and Italian years could well have enabled him to impose a direction on his artistically uncertain and even demoralised realm. We know what Kent had to offer from his experiences in Baroque Italy; we know how absurdly Burlington overrated his collection of Palladio's drawings of Roman baths; what is less known is what the Electoral Prince Georg Ludwig Guelph brought from his considerable experience of the Veneto, the Palladian heartland and original homeland of the Guelph or Welf family.[2]

Georg Ludwig's years before his accession in 1714 to the English throne, which he inherited as one of James I's great-grandsons, had been marked by a mixture of luck and solid determination.[3] That luck has not extended to his posthumous reputation in Britain. He is widely believed to have inaugurated the cabinet system of government because of his inability to speak English or preside, as a consequence, at the principal councils of his ministers. In addition, he is supposed to have murdered Count Philipp Christoph von Königsmark, the lover of his wife, Sophia Dorothea, and concealed the body. More seriously, from the point of ridicule, he is supposed to have favoured two ugly mistresses, one very thin, one very fat. Even worse, one of them, the fat one, Sophia Charlotte was his half-sister. Following Stuart precedent he advanced both of them in the peerage – the thin one, Melusine, to be a duchess; the supposedly incestuous Sophia, to a countess. He is very rarely given much credit for advancing the Palladian revival; Lord Burlington is usually accorded that distinction.

The truth is quite different. King George I was an accomplished linguist speaking fluent German, French, Latin and Dutch, with some Italian and some English. He held cabinet councils throughout his reign,[4] wrote English notes on English memoranda,[5] attended performances of English plays, including some by Shakespeare at Hampton Court, but, like his mother, the Electress Sophia, preferred to write in French, the polite language of Europe. It was in the reign of his son, George II, that Sir Robert Walpole refined the powers of a prime minister and the cabinet system. Sophia Charlotte, Countess of Darlington and George

I's half-sister, was never his mistress and Melusine von der Schulenburg, Duchess of Munster and Kendal, nicknamed 'the Maypole' in England, was his morganatic wife, as Madame de Maintenon was of Louis XIV. She was a kindly, sophisticated woman, the mother of George's two daughters, and she made him very happy. Count Königsmark was murdered on the orders of Ernst August, George's father, because he was carrying on an open sexual affair with George's wife Sophia Dorothea. At the time of the murder George was away in Berlin visiting his sister, though that was convenient and probably arranged.

Most relevant to this study is the Italian, Venetian and Palladian connection. From 1679 onwards Georg and his father Ernst August had been conducting a determined diplomatic campaign to raise Hanover to become the 9th Electoral state in the German Empire with the right to join the other eight Electoral Princes and Bishops in deciding the next Emperor of the Holy Roman Empire of the German People. Their Italian links were already strong; they took holidays regularly in Italy and emphasised their historic Guelph origins in the Veneto. Georg's mother, the Electress Sophia, spent the whole of 1684 in Italy. In the same year Georg, who had fought the Turks in the siege of Vienna the previous year, led an army of Hanoverian troops again to fight the Turks, this time for the relief of the Venetian Republic, his ancestral homeland. The reward for all this military support for the Empire was the ceremonial presentation of the Electoral Cap, ermine-lined and crowned with an arch, in 1693. Ernst August died in 1698, whereupon Georg became the second Electoral Prince. He was received into the Electoral College in 1708. That was three years after the death of his uncle, Georg Wilhelm, had allowed him to unite at last the separate duchies of Celle and Hanover into the new Hanoverian principality.

Architectural prestige had been a third element in the three-pronged campaign for electoral dignity. A two-thousand-seat opera house, the largest in northern Europe, was opened in Hanover in 1689. Between 1694 and 1698 the Galerie, twenty-five bays long and with many Palladian details, almost a palace in itself, was raised next to the main building at Herrenhausen to a design by Johann Peter Wachter. Its 200-foot-long hall was frescoed by the Venetian artist Tommaso Giusti with the history of Aeneas, and, though this is wildly Rococo, each side elevation is austerely centred on a simple Palladian-style doorcase with strictly correct classical enrichments.[6] The main entrance has an ornate Corinthian portico, again correctly enriched, and is topped by a simplified Venetian window. Georg's favourite hunting palace at Göhrde has Palladian stables for three hundred horses. These were built to another simple porticoed design, entirely un-Baroque, by the French Huguenot architect Rémy de la Fosse, working from 1705 to 1710; they still survive in the present seminar centre at Göhrde.[7] Another structure, the Garden Theatre in the grounds of Herrenhausen with its glittering array of gilded nude statues, is worth recalling when the decorative details of Kensington Palace are considered.[8]

King George I was a north German, little influenced by the brilliant Baroque excesses of south Germany and his Italian links again were not Baroque, but Palladian Venetian. When he was settled in England and Kent was working inside Kensington, the architect 9th Earl of Pembroke, Lord of the Bedchamber to George's son, George Augustus, the Prince of Wales, built, in conjunction with Roger Morris, two Palladian villas of jewel-like perfection. One was for the Prince of Wales's mistress, Lady Suffolk, at Marble Hill, Twickenham, in 1724, and the other was for King George himself, the White Lodge in Richmond Park,[9] begun in 1727 and completed in the next reign for George II. The two buildings, of the classic 1/3/1 villa bay design, were more influential and far more copied than Burlington's Palladian designs of the same period: Burlington House (1719), Tottenham Park, Wiltshire (1721), the Dormitory at Westminster School (1722–30), General Wade's House in Whitehall (1723) or the Chiswick Villa of 1725–9. That last building is not indeed strictly speaking a Palladian design at all, but a freakish version of buildings by Palladio's pupil, Scamozzi: his Rocca Pisani villa, and Serlio's Odeo Cornaro in Book VII of his *Architettura*.[10]

All this needs to be borne in mind when William Kent's interiors for the old King at Kensington are being evaluated. George and his son had commissioned two definitive Palladian designs in these early years, giving them all the prestige of royal patronage. The Earl of Pembroke had arguably a keener eye for the potential and spirit of Palladio's original buildings than the Earl of Burlington, Kent's patron, ever developed. Burlington and Kent would never produce anything as quintessentially of the new style as Pembroke and Morris's Palladian Bridge at Wilton House, but that would not be built until 1736–7. Kent's Worcester Lodge in Badminton park is the greater achievement; but that came after 1746 and it rises from the ground with Baroque movement, rather than with Palladian calm.[11]

Given that the new King had a proven eye for relatively simple classical buildings and that his German architects could add the correct bead-and-reel, egg-and-dart, water-leaf enrichments to classical orders in a way that no Baroque architect would bother to do, what actually induced King George to employ Kent for those Kensington interiors? The Fine Rooms at Burlington House had been widely admired; the Duke of Chandos had promptly commissioned three major ceilings from Kent for his palatial new house, Canons in Middlesex, and Sir Richard Child, now ennobled as Lord Castlemaine, was employing him to paint *The Hours of the Day* over the Entrance Hall of Wanstead, probably the most talked about building in England for its overweening Palladian design by Colen Campbell.[12] So Lord Burlington had already projected Kent into fashionable esteem while the Kensington commission itself resulted from some careful placing, probably on Burlington's advice, of influential ministers with predilections for classical simplicity.

Criticisms may be levelled against Burlington's talents as an architect; his Dormitory for Westminster School was an awful foreshadowing of the classical good taste that was about to settle like a shroud over English eighteenth-century design.[13] But no one should underrate his ability to infiltrate the right man, or, in Benson's case, the wrong man, into strategic offices. George I's early years saw the expulsion of virtually every architect of genius from the royal service. Lord Burlington is unlikely to have had much trouble persuading the new King to sack Sir Christopher Wren and Sir John Vanbrugh. Their designs would have seemed distastefully florid to a king who had recently been building at Palladian Göhrde. At Kensington it was Sir James Thornhill's turn to be ritually humiliated, and it has to be said that Thornhill, not the wisest of men, made this task easy by abusing the men in the Office of the King's Works who had sponsored his appointment in 1720 as Sergeant Painter.[14] Easily the most talented artist of the times, Thornhill had also recently upset a number of people by launching out as an architect as well as a painter.

It was Thornhill's established right as Sergeant Painter to have first claim to execute a new decorative scheme on a royal palace, so when the Vice Chamberlain, Thomas Coke (of Melbourne Hall, Derbyshire, not of Holkham in Norfolk), asked Thornhill for an estimate, he must have thought that he was secure in asking for a round £800 for one room. Prompted by Burlington, Coke, an amateur architect who had added a severe classical front to his own house, asked Kent for an estimate. Kent's response was £300 if Prussian blue, a cheap paint, was used or £350 using the more expensive ultramarine. Coke and the King now had the luxury of striking a bargain, yet at the same time could enjoy a sense of having exercised good taste by accepting the superior £350 ultramarine estimate.

Thornhill, enraged, immediately offered to work for the same fee; but among his many enemies was the new Surveyor of the King's Works, Sir Thomas Hewett, whose appointment to succeed the wretched Benson, Thornhill had opposed. Hewett now had his revenge. Thornhill's new offer was rejected and, in his usual spiteful and destructive voice, George Vertue, the arts chronicler of these ill-natured and ungrateful years, reported gleefully that 'a mighty mortification fell on Sr James Thornhill', noting as the real villain of the piece Lord Burlington who 'forwarded Mr Kents Interest as much as layd in his power at Court. & strenuously oppos'd Sr James'.[15]

Armed with his folder of Palladio's reconstructions of Roman public baths, Lord Burlington may indeed have tried to exert some influence over Kent's decorative schemes for the interiors of the Palace. But the man with the last word of approval or disapproval on such schemes would have been Sir Thomas Hewett, the leading member of the New Junta for Architecture. He had been appointed Surveyor General of the King's Works to succeed the disgraced Benson in 1719, not as a result of Burlington's influence, but that of the Earl of Sunderland whose library he had designed.[16] Hewett was a talented amateur architect. He had travelled extensively in Italy and was already well disposed towards Kent. Burrel Massingberd had asked him to visit Kent in Rome in 1717 to appraise the ceiling canvas about which the artist had been apprehensive, but the visit had gone well, eased by Kent's present to Sir Thomas of two sketches of heads, not, presumably, those of Attila's scowling face.

Shrewdly homing in on the one artist who had been familiar with the 3rd Earl of Shaftesbury's thinking during the last year of his life in Naples, Sir Thomas had employed Kent's old rival, the Irishman Henry Trench. With his advice and artwork, a garden house was erected at Hewett's Nottinghamshire home, Shireoaks. The description of that building in Vertue's notebooks is highly relevant to what Hewett persuaded Kent to attempt in the Cupola Room at Kensington. Vertue wrote:

> From thence to Sir Tho Hewetts Gardens. Visto's well contriv'd – little greek Tempiatto lin'd with Marbles of Derbyshire, floors sides & Top mixt with other fine rare Italian marbles, being divided into three little roomes. Ceilings painted by Trench – little Cupids on several Angles prettily design'd . . . a bust of Sr Tho. in Marble by Rysbrack.[17]

With three ceilings frescoed by Trench above rooms of brown Derbyshire alabaster that garden pavilion must have been jewel-like. Unhappily not a stone of it survives; but it does seem that in those summer months, when Henry Trench was living in Shaftesbury's Neapolitan villa, the old man would have discussed his vision of a reformed classicism in far more detail with the young talented Irishman than he ever got round to recording in his writings. If that 'greek Tempiatto' is any guide, marble was to be the key; for marble was what Augustus had dealt out lavishly to Rome, and Shaftesbury seems, illogically for a republican, to have envisaged an Augustan age for Whig England. That would explain Kent's fake marble dome for the Cupola Room at Kensington, with the cupids in the angles and the Rysbrack marble; also the painted antique mosaic background to his Ulysses ceiling of the King's Gallery. It would explain too Kent's later bold ventures into marble interiors at Houghton and Holkham, where he would not be working for a monarch on a tight budget rationed out by a suspicious Parliament, but for the real masters of the country, the Whig aristocrats. It would be Sir Robert Walpole at Houghton and Thomas Coke at Holkham who would achieve the architecture vaguely envisaged by Shaftesbury, not the brash, overeager Lord Burlington. But the key figure at this stage was Hewett.

Not much is recorded of him. A *History of Worksop* claims that he came back from Italy with 'a wife, atheism and many eccentricities' and that 'his daughter ran off with a local fortune teller'.[18] It appears that the New Junta for Architecture had, by 1720, a design for a new royal palace drawn up by Alessandro Galilei, a Florentine architect whom they had invited over to England in 1714. As late as 21 February 1720, when he was writing to the Hon. John Molesworth, Hewett was hoping to use this:

> I am not willing that you should dispose of the pallace to anyone without my consent: I have had the Honour to be often with the

> King who is gracious and the best of men; he has the true taste of Architecture and I hope I shall please him. He hath done me the honour to knight me without my desire. I have not yet had an opportunity to show him the Pallace. I hope to live to see you in England again, may I flatter myself it will not be very long before I bring that to pass to your ease and content.[19]

If the King was ever shown Galilei's palace designs they are most unlikely to have interested him.[20] What Sir Thomas had not yet appreciated was the new King's dislike of pomp and circumstance. He took pains to avoid applauding crowds, trumpets and ceremony. With difficulty he was persuaded to boost his thin public image by parading down the Thames to Handel's 'Water Music'.[21] The music he enjoyed, but not the parade. His fondness for Palladian designs was based on the relative simplicity and economy of the Palladian compared with the Baroque. By his Hanoverian past George was cautious over money; only a garden sometimes encouraged him to a lavish gesture, like the Galerie at Herrenhausen, which he had intended for an orangery before his masterful mother transformed it into a ballroom.

There is a second, melancholy letter from Hewett to Molesworth who had retired to Turin. It is dated 12 December 1723. By that time the decoration of the Kensington Palace rooms was well under way and Hewett, not perhaps a very forceful man, was overwhelmed by the realities of cost cutting, officialdom, temperamental artists and public criticism. Quite what relevance the letter has to his relations with William Kent is not clear, but it could be one of disappointment. Molesworth had apparently asked him if the office of Surveyor General was proving onerous:

> I am easy as to my office . . . I must tell you we have no prospect of fine new buildings and, if there were monys and inclinations to build a palace – there are so many weak pretenders, wrong headed mules, that it is impossible to have anything good and of fine taste . . . I made trial of one room at Kensington of the fine Grecian taste [obviously the Cupola Room] which so much fired the quacks, the knaves, the fools, that I was so baited, the work misrepresented to the King, who had seen and approved the design first, and perfectly well executed that I am discouraged to a degree sufficient to spoil any man's genius.

> The worst was my cavillers denied all rules and due proportions. I assure you Art, Geometry, Mathematics are out of fashion here.[22]

This is a fascinating letter as it describes the first reaction of English critics to a very early, if underfunded, experiment of neo-classicism in a high-profile building, a small royal palace, no less. What seems to have hurt Hewett's feelings was the criticism of the proportions of the Cupola Room. Devotees of Palladio usually make a fetish of proportions, losing themselves in their equivalents with musical scales and other pretentious irrelevancies, because the style is so undecorated and dependent upon simple form. But Hewett's real problem was what he first mentions: 'monys and inclinations to build a palace'. Who the 'weak pretenders' and 'wrong headed mules' were is a matter for speculation, but Thornhill and Vertue are likely candidates. Kent is not blamed; 'perfectly well executed' was Hewett's perhaps overgenerous verdict, but it is obvious that the Cupola Room was the one example of 'the fine Grecian taste', so Hewett did not approve the painted ceiling canvases with their stucco surrounds in the other rooms. They were not Grecian at all, but Italian Baroque, executed probably to Lord Burlington's hesitant and ill-considered advice.

It had been the friends of Kent's Italian years who had rallied to his support, regardless of the respective merits of his work and that of Thornhill. Two of the three-man Junta for Architecture were pro-Kent from past experience. The Junta – Hewett, Molesworth and Sir George Markham – had been agitating against the Baroque and for Lord Shaftesbury's new wave of architecture for years. As well as importing Galilei to lend their cause some Italian classical expertise, they also brought over Giacomo Leoni. He was a master stroke as far as King George was concerned. Leoni was a Venetian who had served as architect to George's close relative, the Elector Palatine, and had assisted the Venetian Count Matteo de'Alberti in building a hunting lodge at Schloss Bensberg.[23] Once in England he began producing in five parts an overornately illustrated version of Palladio's *Quattro Libri*.[24]

Hewett had been with Kent in Rome in 1717. Even earlier, Kent had made another good impression when he had been introduced to Molesworth by John Talman in 1709. That was when Talman's party was passing through Florence, where Molesworth was serving as the British envoy. Molesworth was a key figure in the current architectural changeover because he had been a personal friend of the 3rd Earl of Shaftesbury, entertaining him on his last journey down to Naples. That meant that, more than anyone except Henry Trench, Molesworth is likely to have known what manner of stylistic revisions the Earl was proposing when he wrote those later additions to his *Characteristicks*.

With these personal links working in his favour and the King well disposed by his German experience, it is easy to understand how the wrong artistic appointment came to be made. Thornhill would undoubtedly have designed and painted with his usual Baroque richness; but a vague neo-classicism was in the air and Kent gave the impression that he could deliver it. So there is the dismaying possibility that Kensington's interiors are more or less what the junta of taste and the 3rd Earl of Shaftesbury were anticipating. Hewett is also on record as actively disapproving the 'strange Bulky Buildings . . . composed of Towers, breaks, Rustic key stones, etc, out of all manner of proportion and reason' that Vanbrugh was raising.[25]

There are times when simplicity becomes a national fashion, usually coinciding with a period when that nation is short of money and critics can be persuaded to favour cheap solutions. The post-war 1945–60 period was such a time in Britain when Nikolaus Pevsner and his Bauhaus obsession set the tone,[26] and entire cities such as Coventry, Plymouth, Swansea and Liverpool were rebuilt, after the bombing, in a style of drab austerity which has depressed their civic images ever since. Somewhere behind such aesthetic suicides is a lurking puritan conscience and that conscience seems to have been lurking in 1720. Kent was the reverse of puritan in his spirit and inclinations. As a result his aesthetic confusion at working for these patrons at Kensington is apparent when room after room is inspected.

Ideally a tour of the Palace should begin where the present tourist circuit ends, in Queen Mary's apartments – Drawing Room, Bedchamber, Dining Room and Closet – culminating in the grandest, but still very subdued room, the Gallery. Dark with oak-panelled walls, lightened by the homely knick-knacks of blue and white china that Queen Mary collected and admired, this was the quiet domestic Dutch style which Kent would be required to reverse dramatically.

The Queen's Staircase at the end of the sequence was designed by Wren and is equally dark and undemonstrative with its panelled oak. That dignified, dull descent must have come as a challenge to Kent; the old order would need to be replaced by amusing novelty if he was to take this Hewett-given opportunity and make his own mark on royalty. With his redecoration of Wren's King's Staircase on the other side of the Palace he would do just that; but the Staircase was his last commission, painted in 1725–7. First came the Cupola Room (1722), though initially only its ceiling;[27] the decoration of its walls followed a puzzling three years later, in 1725. That delay explains a great deal. Kent would have been, if not exactly reeling from the strain of figure painting in his Psyche–Cupid series at Burlington House, at least very ready to paint something easy for a change. He was engaged at the same time in painting for the cantankerous Duke of Chandos at Canons and his *Leda and the Swan* ceiling there must have given him terrible problems of sexual gymnastics. When he came, at Kensington's King's Gallery in 1727, to paint the escape of Ulysses from Polyphemus by hiding under the belly of a giant ram, he gave up completely and painted Ulysses walking furtively beside a quite small sheep. So what he resorted to at Canons, when he had to paint the sexual coupling of a young woman with a large white bird, defies the imagination.[28] There is a hint in the Duke's correspondence that things were not going well with Leda or the Swan. Writing to Charles Davenant in Genoa he asked what opinion of his talents the Italians had of Mr Kent, 'an English painter who hath studied for these twelve years in Italy'.[29] It could be significant that Chandos was already negotiating to bring an Italian painter, Negotini, over to work in Kent's place at Canons. Davenant's reply has not survived and, perhaps fortunately, Leda was lost when Canons was half-demolished after the Duke's death in 1744.

At Kensington, Hewett was ready with a safe way out that was only minimally figurative. 'Paint', he must have suggested, 'the coffered ceiling of a Roman palace with cupids in the angles as in my garden pavilion.' Kent went eagerly to work. It was an ingenious half-solution. The perspective problems were well within Kent's range and the dark blue and gold octagonal coffering with its false shadows make what is an almost flat ceiling look like a heavy marble dome centred on a big Garter star rather than on the usual classical patera. At the angles Kent painted massive bronze cupids with Prince of Wales feather head-dresses, a typical Kentian camp device. The next question was what to do with the walls and that, after an interval for reflection of several years, is where King George seems to have intervened. In the gardens of Herrenhausen he had indulged himself with sixteen nude lead statues exotically gilded in a surprisingly

1930s effect.[30] It will have taken some time to commission six more golden nudes to give the Cupola Room an authentic air of Neronian decadence, and that would explain the three years' delay. Their white marble niches, the white marble doorways and J.M.Rysbrack's bas-relief of a Roman marriage together with the six busts of Roman emperors, now replacements, would all have taken time to accumulate. They work well with that coffered ceiling, though the impact of the golden nudes is nouveau riche and undeniably a shade vulgar. Vertue analysed them more shrewdly than usual:

> Niches of Marble & pedestals with statues, guilt with burnish'd gold which makes a terrible glaring show, & truly gothic, according to the weakness of the conceptions of the Surveyors. & Controlours of the Kings. Works. Or their private piques.[31]

Vertue seems there to be aiming a thrust at Hewett, the Surveyor, for allowing it all to happen. But what is so laughable about the treatment of the walls are the pilasters. These are not neo-classical, but cut-price versions of the pure Baroque giant order, and instantly detectable as cheap fakes, being mere hollow wooden boxes stuck to the walls and painted, by Kent, to give the impression of fluting. It would be satisfying to blame Benson and Campbell for these clumsy pastiche pilasters because they did carry through the reordering of the state rooms, virtually the only achievement of their fifteen months in office as Surveyor and Deputy. But they had been sacked in 1719, long before Kent got to work, so it does appear as if Kent was personally responsible. The whole effect is the antithesis of the casual classical charm of Palladio's style and harks back to that 'damn'd gusto' of the late seventeenth century that Burlington was so anxious to put behind him, proof that this neo-Palladian project simply had not been thought through and was not done to Burlington's advice. The Cupola Room makes an initial impact on a visitor for perhaps five minutes, and is then seen for what it is: a bad Roman palace stage set. In the house of the governor of a minor Russian province, Latvia for instance, it would not look out of place; but here in a major European capital it represents a sorry falling away from royal Stuart standards of building. Their palace achievements – Greenwich, Winchester, Windsor, even Chelsea, a Stuart hospital for old soldiers – are far more palatial.

There is the problem here of royal bias. Thinly disguised as the House of Windsor, the Hanoverians, who in 1720 pressed Kent into painting this jumble on a low budget, are still on the throne. Where royalty is concerned the English delight in being obsequious, even reverential, when they are not being pruriently spiteful. Modern historians know that the Hanoverian Succession was a case of national treachery to the true royal line, and treachery based on a detestation of Catholics. Now, when a cardinal has a token role in most royal occasions and the Queen can attend Vespers at Westminster Cathedral without causing a stir, it all seems to have been a revolution about nothing, and one for which a considerable price was paid in falling stylistic standards. Visitors wander around Kensington today with their audio guides playing cheerful blasts of eighteenth-century music and mouthing absurdities about the magnificence of the rooms, but with never a word about what a minor cultural disaster Kent's work represents. Cunningly, the visitor's attention is focused on darkened ground-floor rooms where countless glass cases are lit to display Princess Diana's designer frocks.

Kent's two more successful rooms are the Presence Chamber, painted in 1724, and the King's Staircase of 1726–7. In the Presence Chamber, Kent finally ventured where John Talman had urged him to go in 1727.[32] Talman had appraised Kent's talents far more accurately than Burlington had done. Experiences of Grotesque work in Kent's Paris fortnight could have given him the confidence to go ahead, while the absence of any substantial figure painting in Raphaelesque grotesquerie would have been an attraction. Kent took no risks in his ceiling with comic or literary references, but pulled the whole delicately curvaceous complex of urns, winged harpies, sphinxes and fronds together with bold red diagonals that could be interpreted as the Cross of St George, meeting at a roundel where Apollo's chariot is pulled by the Saxon white horse of Hanover. It was all tactfully complimentary and a foretaste of the 'Etruscan' rooms that Robert Adam was to popularise.[33]

Possibly he had learned his limitations the previous year, 1723, on the Privy Chamber ceiling. There he had completed one of those laboured allegorical ovals that Lord Burlington admired, where the canvas is trapped in a thick stucco frame. Hailed in the modern guidebook as 'magnificent', it features Mars, wearing the Garter ribbon, with his arm around Minerva, who represents the Arts and Sciences. This, the guidebook claims, was an allusion to the King and Queen which 'would have been obvious to members of the court'.[34] What would have been more obvious to members of the court was that the King had divorced his wife for adultery in 1694 and shut her up, with a handsome allowance, in the castle of Ahlden, where she would die in 1736. Kent unintentionally complicated the allegory by making Mars, the God of War, look like a buxom woman with an ostrich-feather hat and with soft, plump arms. His Minerva is listless and bored, while one of Kent's angel-genii hovers awkwardly sideways above her head. Hewett is likely to have disapproved of such a non-Grecian decoration and this thoroughly incompetent painting explains why a team of art experts had been brought in earlier to check on Kent's progress only two months after he had begun to paint the Cupola Room and was working on the cherubs in the coving. One complained that 'the boys, masks, mouldings etc' were 'far from being well'. He had 'seen very few worse for such a place'. Another affirmed 'that the said work far from being done in the best manner . . . is not so much as tolerably well perform'd'.[35] It is good to learn that at least Kent's contemporaries were alert to the collapse in artistic standards, but disturbing to find that Kent had made so little progress after those years in Rome; disturbing also that a modern guidebook should feed visitors with sentimental inaccuracies. Bad painting is bad painting no matter who commissioned it; and Kent would certainly not have been paying compliments to the prisoner of Ahlden.

Another Kent oval ceiling piece in the King's Drawing Room, 1722–3, has Jupiter seducing Danaë in a shower of gold. This has none of the incompetence of Mars and Minerva, though Vertue claimed that the gold looked more like snow. It is a thunderously impressive composition, quite one of Kent's best, including all the unpleasant implications of a seductive rape; Danaë's little dog is a charming Kentian irrelevance which he may have added to lighten an ugly episode. These two oval paintings demonstrate that a dysfunctional decorative system was being made fashionable. The surrounds of both canvases are ridiculously complex, distracting attention (fortunately in the case of Mars and Minerva) from the painting itself. But the whole notion that a painting should be permanently framed in stucco and suspended overhead in the most awkward possible viewing position was retrograde. When a Baroque fresco covers an entire ceiling or a wall at eye level it works as spatial enclosure. Here and in the Saloon at Burlington House, where Kent's fussy, predominantly brown coving is being restored, he created a focal central painting and then distracted the eye from it with irrelevant guilloches, Greek key patterns and squiggles. Kent the inspired designer had still to escape from Kent the bad artist and Kent the obedient protégé of an overconfident Lord Burlington.

The most decoratively complex room at Kensington is the King's Gallery. There Kent has tried to apply his successful formula of white, red and gold that he had evolved for the Burlington House Fine Rooms. But this time his solidly architectural gold frames all have paintings hanging in them: big, enjoyable, third-rate canvases, 'workshop of' and 'after the school of'. They are bold enough to fight back against the red walls, which would have flattered them more if they had been white. On the ceiling are seven big canvases illustrating the history of Ulysses. Mention has already been made of Ulysses's walk with a sheep, but none of them is much more competent. Their colouring is rich, but without a connecting theme, and their compositions are static: people face people in Kent's usual failure to create a convincing interaction. The neo-classical, Burlingtonian element in this ambitious cartoon strip lies in the 'mosaic' background painting by an otherwise unknown Spanish artist, Francisco de Valentia, who puts Kent to shame by his effortlessly precise illusion of marble.[36] Valentia reasserts the antique Roman palace impression that Burlington and Hewett seem to have been aiming at. Kent demonstrated how elegantly he could design, when not distracted by theorists, in his set piece of a white and gold pediment over a wind dial above one of his refined white marble chimneypieces.

The one glorious escape from the confines of Hewett's fondness for marble and Burlington's obsession with Roman baths is Kent's theatrical Italian Baroque treatment of the King's Staircase. All along the main flight of black and white marble stairs, which must in their first form have been as dull as the Queen's Staircase at the other end of the Palace, he has painted a balustrade. This is in bad perspective, seen from above instead of from eye level; but looking over it under an arched Ionic colonnade even more uncertain in its perspective is a delightful throng of courtiers and personalities of the King's entourage. Each one has obviously been selected in a pleasant interlude of patronage by the King himself to award his favourites a light-hearted immortality. Because he did not have to paint any of them in motion, and because they are all looking at us rather than relating to each other, they compose perfectly, and the young page boy hanging on to the outside of the balustrade gives them real depth. Peter the Wild Boy from the woods is there, so is the King's dwarf jester, Christian Ulrich Jorry, two Yeomen of the Guard and the King's favourite secretary-bodyguards, the Turks Mustapha and Mehemet. These last two men were not, incidentally, captured in battle by George. They were transferred from the Swedish army, and they both used English expressions in the notes which they wrote for their employer, a further proof of his linguistic range.[37]

A few snatches of Grotesque work appear behind the arches, but most of the background work – gods in niches, sea horses and trophies – is in Kent's favourite colour, brown. The false cupola looking down on the scene is the real mark of Kent's growing confidence in his role as the licensed mischief maker. From four half-circles, four groups of friends chat to each other and cast casual glances downwards. One of those elusive legends that often cling to buildings yet have no firm source relates that Kent painted himself with three friends, one of them being the actress Elizabeth Butler, his mistress. This is one of those stories which ought to be true and there is an artistic oddity to the group which suggests that it might be. All four figures have those unfortunate slit eyes that make so many of Kent's gods, goddesses and nymphs look slightly oriental. The second on the right, next to the lady, is supposed to be a self-portrait. Granted that painting while on one's back and suspended on a scaffold must be testing, but Kent, if this really is a self-portrait, did not flatter himself: he looks fat, cunning and bored. At least it was an amusing idea and most unlikely to have been Burlington's.

What is worrying is that hardly any of the crowd of courtiers lower down, looking through the arches, has the Kentian signature of slit eyes. They are all most attractively painted. Now those horses in Burlington House, where Jupiter is giving his consent to the marriage of Cupid and Psyche, prove that Kent could paint well if he had Ricci's horses to copy. Could he have persuaded an assistant to help him by making careful portrait sketches of each chosen subject, thereby speeding up the work?[38] He painted the King's Staircase straight after the King's Gallery and it is certain, from the signature found during restoration that the highly competent Francisco de Valentia executed all the complex background mosaic work. Was he still around for the Staircase, painting the courtiers or at least outlining them for Kent to fill in? That would explain their normal European eyes. Burlington was obviously not involved because the entire jolly display is purely Baroque in feeling; Kent would have seen several similar stairs in his Roman palaces and Louis Laguerre plays the same trick, though less successfully, in the Saloon at Blenheim, the palace which Burlington, Shaftesbury and Hewett all disapproved of. It looks as if Kent was beginning to please himself. This was his last work at Kensington and it represents quite a journey from that coffered Roman bath vault in the Cupola Room.

It will seem perverse, even disloyal, to conclude this chapter with Thornhill rather than Kent, but it is important not to be tempted in a biography into hagiography. At this stage of his career Kent was lucky rather than talented, part of a movement of national artistic decline, which later he would do much to reverse. Thomas Coke's decision to award the Kensington contract to Kent, not Thornhill, was one of philistine wickedness, a conspiracy in which Kent was a willing accomplice. To appreciate the depth of the iniquity a visit to the Great Hall of Greenwich Palace will explain what Kensington lost but what the Palace could have been given. Thornhill's tremendous paintings at Greenwich put Kent's efforts at Kensington into perspective. If England has any equivalent to Michelangelo's interiors for the Sistine Chapel, it is these Thornhill paintings at Greenwich. Michelangelo brought religious vision and naked physical beauty together in an irresistible combination which deservedly draws the crowds. Thornhill painted the triumphs of a maritime nation in a rich complexity of colour, where his Baroque compositions almost manage to hold together the teeming incidents of battle and joy. The effect is overwhelming and absorbing; but in a time of political correctness when imperial ambitions are frowned upon, it might not catch the public's imagination, even though they are allowed in on a regular basis to marvel at it. Thornhill indulged in none of that gratuitous male nudity which brings the Sistine its permanent fascinated throngs.

He was, nevertheless, the great English painter of his age and of his Protestant, militant society. It was an artistic crime, one from which William Kent unhesitatingly benefited, that the Baroque painter was rejected and Kent's neo-Roman fudge was preferred. It was the stylistic price to be paid for putting the 2nd Electoral Prince of Hanover on the throne of a United, though essentially fissiparous, Kingdom. King George I was the presiding figure, possibly even the ringleader, in a conspiracy to move the country towards an architectural revision which would be described as Palladian, but which might be better described as a cut-price classical simplicity that could pass as Palladian and satisfy the 3rd Earl of Shaftesbury's unspecific call for architectural and artistic change. In 1727, when his stint at Kensington came to an end, Kent had still to prove that his return was much to the benefit of his country, though that cupola over the King's Staircase does suggest that he was beginning to achieve the amused detachment from conventional pomps which would become his strength.

10

The remarkable achievements of an apparent failure

It is in the years immediately after 1725 that the sequences and the narrative of William Kent's career become so complex, so rich in achievements and in stylistic innovations, that the man himself begins to disappear behind the improbabilities. There is such a gap between what contemporary comment and the near illiterate, spluttering flow of his letters reveal about his character and the wide influence his work in those years was to have on the development of English architecture and design, that it is hard to reconcile the shallow jester with the cultural giant.

By 1725 Kent's work for King George I at Kensington was nearing a close, with the suspicion that his best figures, those looking over the balustrade on the King's Staircase, had at least been outlined by the same artist, Francisco de Valentia, who painted the background work on the ceiling of the King's Gallery. Kent had demonstrated to others, and had probably accepted himself, that in oils he was a fourth-rate artist with a modest colour sense, a poor grasp of Baroque composition and a lamentable inability to capture a good portrait likeness. His decorative painting in the Palace had been damned by a committee of experts, and even his patron, the Surveyor, Sir Thomas Hewett, was defensive, clearly disturbed by Kent's essays in 'the fine Grecian taste' and 'discouraged to a degree'.[1]

Yet at this point, the near-failure Kent was just about to enjoy, a ten-year period, to 1735, of plum commissions backed by the prestige of royal appointments – Master Carpenter (1726), Inspector of Paintings in the Royal Palaces (1728), Master Mason and Deputy Surveyor (1735) –

which would make him rich and which would consolidate his three indisputable influences on national design. These would be, first, the establishment of a pattern for the interior decoration of Palladian houses; second, the launch of the Gothick, a revolutionary stylistic movement in an entirely opposite, even confrontational, direction to the Palladian, which he was ostensibly supporting. And, third, there was the subtle development of a landscaping manner which would come to be known and copied across Western Europe as the 'English Garden'.

For comparable achievements Christopher Wren and John Vanbrugh had been knighted. Robert Taylor would become 'Sir' Robert for much less. Such an honour was never even considered for William Kent; and yet he was a royal favourite possessed of an extraordinary social dexterity in dealing between hostile royals and between rival politicians. No sooner had the old King George, his loyal supporter at Kensington, died in 1727, than Kent sidestepped that irrelevant, peppery philistine, George II, and eased his way into the good graces of the real ruler, the new King's wife, Queen Caroline of Ansbach. A key figure in that social campaign must have been Lady Burlington who was one of Queen Caroline's ladies-in-waiting. She was a strong-minded woman who could easily have resented Kent's hold upon her husband's affections and his permanent possession of an apartment in Burlington House, but Kent succeeded in keeping her as his loyal ally and gossip. With the same nimble footwork, Kent would move from providing the décor of an imperial Roman Caesar for one Prime Minister, Sir Robert Walpole, at Houghton Hall in Norfolk, to conjuring up a romantic and original Gothick villa on the banks of the River Mole in Surrey for a later, and far more sophisticated, Prime Minister, Henry Pelham.

All that, and yet Kent the man remains two-dimensional, concealed rather than revealed by the condescension of his few literate friends as a vaguely comical rogue, a butt for notably tedious literary jokes. It is undoubtedly true that Kent revealed more about his nature, his aims and his circumstances during those nine years in Italy than he would ever do in the next twenty-nine years of influence and wealth in England. But a biographer can still worry out, from scraps of comment, snatches of praise and a few irritatingly silly letters, what character lay behind the undoubted genius for improvisation and cheerful friendship.

The obvious source, quarried in almost every account of the period, is George Vertue, whose notebooks outperform, in weird punctuation and odd syntax, Kent at his worst.[2] Vertue is a most suspect authority. There is no evidence that he ever set eyes on Kent or had any personal knowledge of him apart from the one statement that his death resulted from 'high feeding & life & much inaction',[3] a polite indication that Kent was overweight. Otherwise Vertue's sources appear to have been Kent's jealous fellow artists who resented his rapid rise to royal and aristocratic patronage through Lord Burlington's influence. As he admits, 'Mr Kent became Enveyed & admired above all for this noble Lords benefactions to him – & Interest',[4] and that of 'Lady Burlington, whom he had instructed in the Art of drawing & painting in crayons', being 'an Ingenious Man. & of civil & obliging behaviour'.[5]

It is as if, not being personally acquainted with his subject, Vertue had consulted two others, one witness who admired and one who coldly disliked Kent. The admirer considered Kent 'the best architect – this was hard to dispute by proof, but here he stop't not, his genius leading him to decorations, ordering of Gardens, Visto's, Views, prospects. groops of Trees &c'.[6] This was generous enough; 'genius' has been mentioned. But then Vertue quotes the playwright John Gay, admittedly another of Burlington's stable of men likely to succeed in British arts, who 'in his Miscelanies he wonders Kent should go to Rome to study Raphaels works. rather now he should return to Italy. & paint originals, for the Italians to admire & imitate'.[7] Or was that one of Gay's jokes?

It was, above all, money that jaundiced Vertue's assessments: 'Mr Kents payments for his works & drawings especially. were high enough commonly.'[8] Kent received £50 each for the Newton and Stanhope monument drawings for Westminster Abbey, £300 for the work at Kensington Palace: 'he had salarys to the amount of 600 a year its computed, tho' the King G. 2d declared he woud never sit for him for his picture'.[9] Vertue pounces upon that failure to achieve likenesses:

> Another mortification he attempted to paint portraits & succeeded not. especially Hon. Mr Pelham his great patron &c. at last this he could not overcome.[10]

That word 'mortification', not one normally associated with the irrepressible Kent, tolls like a funeral bell through Vertue's gloating list of setbacks. If he is to be believed it was the Duke of Newcastle's refusal to pay Kent more than £100 for all his garden works at Claremont in Surrey '& no ways would better reward him which was no little mortification to Kents mind. and might be the original cause of the mortification in his body of which he died'.[11]

The suggestion that, towards the end of his life, 'some appearance of secret differences in the Burlington Family inclind him to think of takeing lodgings or appartments a little way out of Town which he had fitted up to be there sometimes a retirement', was a parody of the truth. Though how, if there had been a rift with the Burlingtons, he came to be tended 'with great care' at Burlington House, Vertue does not explain. Nor does he explain why Kent, who was a rich man, had taken the lease of a house in Saville Street (modern-day Savile Row), not three minutes walk from Burlington House,[12] if he had wanted to distance himself from his old friend. Instead Vertue hovers around the real truth about Kent: that he was a single man, though affectionately supportive of a mistress and her two children by another man; that he was 'spareing in his way of Expences sober and regular allwayes living with this Noble Lord', and a member of 'St Lukes or Vandykes clubb of Gent & Artists'.[13] For some reason Vertue did not find happy endings satisfying, but he still has to allow Kent, 'Thus sailing thro the wayes of Life well befriended well employd and plentifull incomes he amassd riches and some curious works of art in painting sculpture & printed books.'[14] If he had been honest and fair, that would have been the end point of his assessment of Kent's life.

At the conclusion, however, of all the literary worrying and detective work, there is more to be discovered about William Kent in the irrepressible staffage, the comic-book figures, of his enchantingly rough, immediate sketches than in any amount of Vertue's malice or of Kent's own clumsily delivered words.[15] Through almost all his sketches, underlying the buildings that cry out to be achieved and the threadbare groves that half-reveal them, lies Kent's irreverent animal and human animation, the running commentary of a mocking and unimpressed outsider. There is the celebrated one of the lapdog pissing on Lord Burlington's ankle as Kent, elegantly superior and with hat and cane, discusses planting with him in the grounds of Chiswick villa.[16] In another the rabbits dance by moonlight as Kent sprawls half asleep at the foot of an obelisk.[17] Then there is Kent himself, pissing against an arch, not one of his own designing, apparently, at Chiswick, while that incontinent dog relieves itself by a pine tree.[18] In a fourth a Negro gardener trundles his wheelbarrow while a shepherdess on the other side of a round pond raises her skirts to show her legs.[19] An absurd donkey stands ridiculing the grandiose triumphal arch that Kent has been asked to design for Holkham.[20] In another Kent pats Alexander Pope reassuringly on the shoulder as a sacrificial altar, in the grounds of Pope's rather suburban but very aspirant villa, fumes and a naked goddess attended by mermaids descends from the foot of a rainbow.[21] The literary and garden historian John Dixon Hunt believes that a sketch of an Ionic rotunda with an animated game of bowls in the foreground of another playful sketch cannot be a view of the Temple of Ancient Virtue at Stowe because 'there never was as large an area as this in the Elysian Fields, nor does the lie of the land encourage its use as a bowling green as shown in this drawing'.[22] Hunt can never have played boules over rough ground in France. It is of the essence of a Kentian Arcadia that they are for pleasure and relaxation. Who else but the jolly realist Kent would actually illustrate two naked bathers enjoying a cold bath by a temple, never built, for Chatsworth?[23] Cold baths were a standard feature in eighteenth-century parks and the consequent nudity must have been commonplace. Henry Hoare splashed about with friends in the Grotto of the Nymph at Stourhead to the music of French horns.[24] Only William Kent illustrates the practice because he was a rare, normal, uninhibited artist in an artificial age of formal manners yearning for informal gardens.

The message of Kent's staffage is one that comes across more clumsily in the letters which he seems to have been none too eager to write. Either the educational standard of Bridlington Grammar School, up in that monkish gatehouse, was very low or Kent was dyslexic. But something of that bumbling integrity is still conveyed: an honest, ordinary human being in a society that was generally pacing itself admiringly in front of a mirror. To write a letter to the rigidly devout and earnestly proselytising Countess of Huntingdon, the founder of a popular religious sect, stating 'But I never will have a good opinion of over-religious people' must have been a cheeky challenge rather than an uninformed faux pas.[25] The same letter reveals something of his closeness to the Pelhams, for whom he had built Gothick Esher Place:

> I have been much concerned about the loss of my very good friends, Mr Pelham's two sons. Lady Katherine fell ill the same way immediately after, but is recovered.[26]

Those sons were only young boys when they died, leaving Pelham with no male heirs. But Kent, with his irreverent sense of fun and facility for quick sketches of naughty animals, was the kind of man who could relate readily to children and really think of them as his 'very good friends' – something of a J. M. Barrie complex. In his will, Kent would leave Lady Catherine, the boys' sister, 'the head of Edward the sixth', the painting of another boy who died young, as a memento of that shared sorrow.[27] Kent's will is full of such thoughtful gifts to friends: 'The Night piece Nativity after Corregio' to Lady Burlington, 'the School of Athens after Raphael' for Henry Pelham, 'to Ferdinando Fairfax', his favourite drinking companion, 'my yellow siena Table inlaid the Boarder white Fret'.[28] Each of the Burlingtons is remembered with some choice item from Kent's rich collection, yet all the sour George Vertue could write about the bequests in his notebooks was:

> But to his noble Lord and his Lady – in the end, their wanted in his Will some kind and generous remembrances of gratitude, as certainly was his duty (but left unmentioned).[29]

As if William Kent, the Bridlington boy wonder, should have left some substantial sum of money to one of the richest men in England, a lord who had been lodging him as a valued friend and employee for the last twenty-nine years, rent free. In another of his character assassinations, Vertue claimed that, while in Rome, Burlington had abandoned his previous favourite artist, the Frenchman Louis Goupy, and 'took into his favour other painters of this nation, Mr French [that Dublin lisp strikes again] & more especially <a Countryman of his> Mr Kent – a Yorkshireman there on his studies. who so far engrossd his Lordship favours – by merrit or cunning – which dislodgd Mr Goupy'.[30]

There are implications in the phrase 'merrit or cunning', and obviously the most valuable evidence as to the relationship between Lord Burlington and Kent would be letters from Burlington himself. He had presumably been Kent's loyal friend, ever since that autumn of 1714 when Kent is assumed, on no evidence, to have cheered the young Earl on his fever-smitten sickbed in Rome. But Burlington's passion was the collection, not of handsome youths for venial purposes, but of men of genius who would enrich the nation: men such as Alexander Pope, John Gay, George Handel and William Kent. He was an aristocrat and not inclined to reveal emotional confidences, so Kent, living often in his house, would have received very few letters from him. The following letter, from Burlington to Pope, dated 2 November 1729, will give some notion of the mood of a typical Burlington reply:

> enclosed I send you the paper which I signed with that pleasure, that I shall always take, in every thing where I can be of the least use to you. I am very sorry to find your cold continues, I hope you keep warm, which I take to be the only remedy in this dismal season. I intend to call upon you in a day or two, and will have more leasure, than I can have now, for both dinner and company wait for me. I am dear Sir your most affecte
>
> humble servant
>
> Burlington.
>
> Kent is much your servant. pray my sincere compliments to Mrs Pope.[31]

Not much revelation there, but a very large proportion of the letters that an influential lord like Burlington received must have been requests for favours. Pope, for all his comfortable circumstances, was the most appalling scrounger and ingratiating creep. No admirer of Pope's poetry should ever read his letters: they are disenchanting.

They are, however, of great service on a moral matter. Pope was a virulent homophobe. He had outed the relationship between Addison and Steele[32] and poured unforgivably venomous verse over the head of Queen Caroline's exquisite confidant and Sir Robert Walpole's political ally, Lord Hervey, for being openly in love with the 1st Lord Ilchester, Stephen Fox:

> Yet let me flap this Bug with gilded wings,
> That painted Child of Dirt, that stinks and stings;[33]

and so on, in a paroxysm of loathing for indeterminacy of gender. If there had been any smack of homosexuality in the relationship between Burlington and Kent then Pope would have detected it, reacted with venom and dropped Kent like a shot. It is possible that, when Kent was a young man with his fortune to make, there had been some emotional attachment between him and the sexually ambivalent John Talman, who had persuaded him away to Italy. But that had been many years back and now Pope had a positive relish for Kent's company, the firmest possible moral certification that Kent was normally sexed. His relationship with his Earl was one, on both sides, of affectionate, thoughtful convenience, a normal attraction of opposite types.

A typical Kent letter to Burlington, one written on 28 November 1738,[34] may appear to be a disjointed chaos of bad syntax, execrable spelling and cheerful gossip, but it is most revealing of Kent's nature and status. In the first few lines:

> My Lord, – I received yours, am sorry to here you had so bad a cold, io spero che la purgatzoni has carryd all of before this time – Jack Campbell and I have been to see how the mighty works go on at Euston, whe came back last Sunday seven night with Mr Pelham as for news I believe you have more in the countery then I find here –

he has asserted his impudent familiarity with a reference to constipation. Does the long-nosed Burlington of those portraits look like a man who welcomes jokes about his bowel movements? From Kent he obviously does. The snatch of Italian keeps up the Signior image which Kent obviously relishes. Then come three tremendous name droppings, all very casual. He has come back from Euston, the Duke of Grafton's house, with 'Jack', the next Duke of Argyll and the key to Whig influence in Scotland, with Mr Pelham, the next Prime Minister but one. It was hard to beat that for social status or for influence in garden design in a Whig-dominated England of 1738. Euston has one of Kent's first hunched-pediment, Palladian pavilions; Mr Pelham's Esher had, before suburban sprawl destroyed it, a Kent garden which was probably even more beautiful than that at Rousham, which, happily, survives. A little later in the letter the owner of Rousham, General Dormer, is mentioned. That old war hero had inherited Rousham a year before, in 1737. Jolly companionship and profitable design contracts were apparently closely linked in Kent's social life.

The letter drops abruptly down to the hard-drinking, food-guzzling but art-loving and bronze-collecting circle of Kent's regular cronies: 'Byron & nando mark & Mr Mills & myself'. They meet to play whist every week and need no introduction as they are Burlington's cronies also. After a garbled compliment to the difficult and dominating Lady

Burlington, Alexander Pope lurches into the text. Pope, the translator of Homer and the most celebrated literary figure in Britain at that time, seems to have been suffering from a hangover and craving forlornly for William Kent's company:

> had not seen Pope but once this two months before last Sunday morning & he came to town the night before the next morning he came before I was up it had raind all night & rain'd when he came I would not get up & sent him away to disturb some body else – he came back and sayd could meet with nobody, I got drest & went with him to Richarsons & had great diversion he shew'd three pictures of Lord Baulingbrok one for himself for Pope, another Pope in a mourning gown with a strange view of the garden to shew the obelisk as in memory to his mothers Death, the allegory seem'd odde to me.

If anything is to be made of this odd episode it is that William Kent had made himself important to some very important people, Tory as well as Whig. Henry St John, Viscount Bolingbroke, had been the white hope of the Tories before the debacle of 1714 and the Hanoverian succession. The fact that Alexander Pope was a Catholic clinging desperately to the friendship and patronage of Lord Burlington, who was a Whig, with, apparent, secret Jacobite sympathies, is a useful reminder of how various were political loyalties at this period and how ambivalent an artist like Kent had to be to prosper.

But clearly, if Kent is reporting truthfully, and his account does ring true, he and Pope were close friends and Kent was the more dominant. After further chat about General Dormer buying a Giovanni di Bologna bronze, the letter leaps back to Pope again:

> my service to mr Bethell and tell him his friend Pope is the greatest Glutton I know, he now talk of the many good things he can make, he told me of a soupe that must be seven hours a making he dine'd with mr Murray & Lady betty & was very drunk last Sunday night he says if he comes to town he'll teach him how to live & leave of his rosted apples & water.

How much of this is truth and how much a joking fantasy is arguable, but it is the authentic voice of Kent and clears up one of the general misunderstandings about his domestic arrangements. He had an apartment in Burlington House for occasional sleepovers, but Pope is most unlikely to have been turned away on a wet morning from a great London town house. Kent was reasonably wealthy. He died, according to Vertue, worth £10,000, and he had his own house in Saville Street, but that was always rented out in his lifetime. So where did Pope come, downcast and beseeching company? Did he keep a studio base and a bachelor's pad in the mews? His friend Nando Fairfax lived next door, so was that where the friends sometimes met for their weekly game of whist, and where Kent cooked his mutton steak, probably to an Italian recipe? The steaks were so good that Pope tried to induce Burlington to dine with him by promising 'a mutton steak in the manner of that great master. Signior Kent'.[35]

It is unlikely that Kent's actress mistress, Elizabeth Butler, and her two children, George and Elizabeth, lived there. It would have been functionally convenient for Kent to be a bachelor with one servant. His will leaves 'unto my servant who shall be living with me at the time of my decease ten pounds';[36] so they came and they went. Elizabeth Butler lived in the parish of St Paul's, Covent Garden and, while Kent was affectionately concerned with her two children, his will mentions them after his sister Esther Pearson in Bridlington and he made Esther's three children his residuary legatees. Actresses do tend to live unconventional lives and that would explain why Kent never made an honest woman of Elizabeth. The detached status would have suited his lifestyle admirably. Lord Burlington would have been more important to him than Elizabeth Butler.

There is another letter in the Chatsworth collection from Kent to Burlington which does touch upon the serious side of their relationship very movingly, but it stands isolated and, as far as we know, unanswered, though Burlington valued it and kept it, as he kept Kent's more boisterous letters. It is dated 16 November 1732 and is full of melancholy reflective passages, quite unlike the usual Kent style: 'your building at Chiswick is very pretty & yr obelisk looks well I lay there the other night but though I love it, was too malancoly for want of you I wish to see'.[37] Does that explain the sketch of Kent asleep at the foot of the obelisk with the rabbits dancing? Pope might have been suspicious if he could have read that. Kent had recommended a servant to Burlington:

> the person I mention to you for a servant in your house is such a one, that I don't know but by people loveing and living with them may in time think the same way, as I flatter myself I do with you.

There is no more revealing comment on their relationship anywhere else in writing of the period. Between them they had, for better or for worse, changed England's artistic direction.

That unexpectedly warm and sensitive mention of people 'loveing and living' together, in a letter that Burlington carefully preserved, is a reminder of Burlington's need for emotional support in a life that was not all domestic roses. His wife, Lady Dorothy, flaunted her affair at court with the Duke of Grafton. Her own uncle described her as 'the wickedest, mischievous jade upon earth' who went around 'imposing upon her husband and exposing him only to show her own power'.[38] That wilfulness led to tragic consequences when she arranged for their favourite daughter's marriage to the son and heir of her lover, Grafton. Within less than a year Lord Euston's ill treatment resulted in their daughter's death and talk of Burlington challenging Euston to a duel of honour. So Kent was probably the friend and confidant to whom an apparently aloof and reserved aristocrat turned for cheerful male company, while Kent turned to him for praise and direction.

Most of Pope's letters about Kent are foolish, tedious spoofs ten times longer than they should have been; but there are a few glimpses in them of an uncertain, self-doubting figure behind the steak cook, the wine connoisseur and the bubbling enthusiast of 'a hundred things that cannot be writ'.[39] Timidity and modesty are not the qualities that Kent's portraits or his creations convey, but they may explain the curious absence of anecdotes about the man. Perhaps Pope is right and Kent was, behind the laughter and the badinage, an uncertain soul, given to self-doubt and needing the dynamism of Burlington and the sharp wit of Pope for support. There is another report on his nature from the same observant writer in a letter of 27 November 1736, to Burlington again:

> The Signior is in perfect tranquillity, enjoying his own Being, & is become a happy but plumper copy of General Dormer. In sweetness of manners he is allowed on all hands to be a meer Ludovico Dolce . . . I go frequently to him, not only thro' the affection I bear him, &

> the Respect I pay to his Genius, but in good earnest to learn what I can & as often as I can, of yourself & my Lady.[40]

That last ingratiating line was very Pope, but otherwise the poet is offering quite a new angle on Kent. Then again, in 1738, Pope was writing to Burlington to report Kent in another trauma of doubt: 'I have seen Kent, & endeavour'd to comfort him, under all his Calumniators & afflictions, with the representation, *That All Great genius's have & do suffer the like*'.[41] How consoling Kent found this aphorism is not known and it has to be observed that, if Pope spent some minutes building his friend up, then he spent several hours putting him down. Pope's modern admirers will not accept the criticism that the poet's sense of humour was laboured and dull. Where literary criticism of the eighteenth century is involved virtually anything tedious and unkind can be passed off as wit. In retrospect it is clear that Pope used Kent as a running joke of obesity and idleness to keep the Burlington family amused and to assert his own intellectual superiority.

On 29 October 1738, Pope wrote to Lady Burlington a mock-heroic proposal of ponderously prolonged wit proposing that Kent should be made vicar of Eyam, a Derbyshire living with £1500 a year, and in Lady Burlington's gift.[42] Kent's actual name was reserved to the very end of the letter. Before that Pope had listed his qualities as a candidate: a 'Pontifical Dignity', 'Learned', but not 'courteous', 'eloquent', but not 'courtly', 'wellbred', but not 'bookish', possessed of 'a good stomach' as well as a 'goodtaste', independent and truthful. Veering all the time towards an appreciation of Kent's real qualities, Pope described him as a conservative, 'one who hath born Testimony to the Truth, in the face of Kings, Queens & Potentates . . . by no means a Respecter of Persons, but using Sharp Speeches to the Greatest'. He continued:

> I think your Ladyship begins to find the Excellent Person at whom I point, (or rather to *Smoke* him, for he is very hot, & very fat)
>
> Of Size that may a Pulpit fill,
> Tho more inclining to Sit still.

Still labouring away at his three-page-long joke, Pope continued:

> nor do I know any Motive he could have to accept of the Living, save to get into a Soft Pulpit, where is a Soft Cushion, to lay his Soft

> Hand, & rest his tender Tail, from the Fatigues of a Horse, that now afflicts his Soul, moves his Entrails (especially after dinner) & troubles all the Bones within him.

It is salutary to be reminded sometimes what bores some distinguished literary figures could become when surrounded by polite flatterers. Apparently Pope had asked Kent to call on him two or three times and Kent had claimed fatigue. This was the poet's riposte.

His other comic broadside was equally long-winded. It took the form of a bogus petition signed by the entire Boyle family and written in mock-legal jargon; its date is somewhere around 1741 when Kent was urging the felling of one of those trees growing ridiculously close to the garden front of the Chiswick Villa.[43] Its destruction, so the petition ran, was 'by the Instigation of Sathan, & of William Kent, his agent and Attorney, conspiring thereunto, devised and plotted', and there was much would-be comical, repetition. Finally, as the peak of the jest:

> We, Your Honour's humble Petitioners who have many years known, accustomed & frequented the said Tree, sitten, reposed or disported under the Shade thereof yea and seen the said William Kent, the Agent & Attorney of the said Sathan, solace himself with Syllabubs, Damsels, and other Benefits of nature under the said Tree, do

to cut the joke short, pray 'that the said Tree may remain'. Passages from this petition are usually quoted to illustrate what good company Kent must have been with his syllabubs and damsels, and how charmed the Burlington circle was with his fun and good fellowship.

What the petition really reveals is how necessary it was for that idle, giggling group of aristocratic wasters to reduce to a lazy, fat joke the disruptive force that Kent must have exercised in a most self-satisfied and intellectually sterile period of English cultural life. Its literary idols all, except for the exile Swift, who was, understandably, going mad in Georgian Ireland, had feet of clay. The main stylistic projection in architecture, the Palladian, was the revival of a revival, and poetry had been reduced to heroic couplet versification. The Romantic rebellion against it all was entirely overdue. An arid mannerism and simpering confidence had taken over the nation under the name of Augustanism, a Roman charade, an unscholarly groping after neo-classicism which in a time of national prosperity was soon to produce some of the most uninspired classical building, domestic and public, since the Renaissance. It is no wonder that Kent, the irreverent, should seem a refreshing rebel; and no wonder that, as subsequent chapters will illustrate, he would be able to bring, if not a gale of creativity to his smug contemporaries, at least a breath, two breaths in fact, of fresh air and artistic revolution, one to English architecture and one to English landscape gardening.

In Britain the word 'Georgian' has only to be spoken or written for an unmerited reverence to seize listeners and readers alike. It demarcates a sexless zone beyond normal criticism. At one lecture to the Georgian Group – Patron at that time the Queen Mother, now Prince Charles – the subject was Horace Walpole, who seems to concentrate in the minds of many Georgians the porcelain, simpering charm of that period. The theme of the lecture, soundly supported by Walpole's own, now published, but little read, writings, was that the man was a rogue who had stolen much of the credit from several superior contemporaries, William Kent among them, for the Gothick revival. That was bad enough. But when Walpole's own words were quoted to prove that he had enjoyed a romantic, gay love affair for several years with the 9th Earl of Lincoln, Henry Pelham's son-in-law, a number of ladies walked out in protest. It was not just a matter of 'No sex please, we're Georgians', but also one of 'let us have no sharp realistic standards of appreciation of the true, coarse tone of the period'.

That puritanical reverence for all things Georgian, whether poetry, prose, politics, painting or architecture, is the blight that still lies heavily on eighteenth-century studies here and in America. William Kent was an outsider in his own times and a great man for that reason. Consideration of Kent should never be hindered by 'Georgian' preconceptions; and with wary, open minds it will be appropriate to consider in the next chapter what influences really lay behind the Palladian Revival and the 'English Garden', when Alexander Pope will feature again, caught up in the creative confusions of his friend Lord Burlington.

11

Across the Thames a princess creates a Rococo moment

Because his reign was short, from 1714 to 1727, and because he was quite old, a middle-aged fifty-four, when he came to his uneasy throne, it is not often noticed that the reign of George I was an enchanting Ruritanian romp.[1] It was a rare time of peace in Europe. King George and the Regent of France were first cousins and that allowed the Hanoverians to conduct relatively harmless family wars in and around their gimcrack London palaces for the entertainment of their fascinated subjects. For more than seventy years England had not been able to enjoy the emotional soap opera of a real royal family. Charles II had only produced bastards. James II had been thrown out basically because his second wife had produced a son, threatening a Catholic succession. William of Orange was homosexual; and all poor Queen Anne's children had died very young. So to have, with their new invited German monarch, his son George Augustus, a brusque, courageous, blue-eyed Prince of Wales, with a buxom, blonde Princess Caroline, his wife, producing children at reasonably regular intervals – Frederick (1707), Anne (1709), Amelia (1713), George William (1717), William Augustus (1721), Mary (1723) and Louisa (1724) – was an emotional treat for the loyal at heart. A monarch is expected to be fertile and King George I, who had shut his wife up in prison for life, and tacitly permitted the murder of her Swedish lover, needed all the domestic bliss his son and daughter-in-law could provide as a distraction from his own marital inadequacies.

In 1717, four years into a hitherto boring reign from a social point of view, a satisfyingly dramatic royal row broke out which was to focus social attention upon those pretty reaches of the Thames around Lord Burlington's Chiswick, and thrust William Kent into the patronage and the powerful influence of Caroline, Princess of Wales. Like most future Hanoverian squabbles it began over trivia and could easily have been avoided. Little George William was the Princess's next child to be born after a baby that had died at birth in 1716. He was, therefore, doubly precious for that reason and trebly precious for having been born in England, not Hanover. The proud father chose the King and the King's brother, Ernst August, to be godfathers. But the King, for political reasons, ordered that Ernst August, Duke of York and Albany, Earl of Ulster and ruling Prince-Bishop of Osnabrück, should step aside and an Englishman, the Lord Chamberlain, the Duke of Newcastle, should take his place. This enraged Prince George, who had proved on the battlefield of Oudenarde, fighting for Marlborough in the Hanoverian cavalry, that he could get very cross indeed, cutting and slashing away with the best of them.

After the christening ceremony he rushed up to Newcastle, stomped on his toes and shouted, in his bad English: 'Rascal, I find you out!' Or so he claimed he had said afterwards.[2] Newcastle, a loyal, sensitive soul, thought that he had been challenged to a duel by the heir to the throne, and hurried off to the King for protection. A deputation of peacemakers found Prince George defiant, whereupon his father put him under close arrest in his chambers, then banished him to St James's Palace. The Princess Caroline was to be allowed to remain with her children only if she cut off all communication with her husband. Though still weak from childbirth, Caroline stoutly refused, declaring that her children were not worth a grain of sand compared with her beloved husband. So she too was exiled to St James's, leaving her children weeping and the very young baby robbed of a mother's care. Caroline was an excellent, attentive mother who spanked her children and had them inoculated against smallpox.[3]

That was the start of a permanent political divide. The Prince and Princess set up house, minus their children, in Leicester Square, entertained lavishly with amusing masked balls and deliberately courted support from all the disenchanted and disaffected. Caroline 'loved to see odd persons' and particularly enjoyed the company of Jonathan Swift: 'having sent for a Wild Boy from Germany, [she] had a curiosity to see a wild dean from Ireland'.[4] The King disliked putting himself about socially, but now in self-defence, nervously aware that the English would not tolerate unpopular rulers, he had to take large parties to the opera in the evenings and chat genially at courts.

Worse was to come. The Princess was forbidden even to see her daughters without a chaperone. The poor children complained that they were orphans and that their grandfather did not visit them because he did not love them. That forced the King to spend an hour with them every day. Deprived of his mother's milk, the baby fell into a decline. Too late he was sent to Leicester House, only to die of a convulsion in his mother's arms. The country looked on in amazement, as well it might.

To focus social life more clearly upon themselves the Prince and Princess moved in the summer of 1718 into the exiled Duke of Ormonde's confiscated house, Richmond Lodge, in Richmond Old Park, across the Thames from Syon House.[5] Socially and stylistically it was a turning point. This was the time when England could so easily have gone Rococo like France. In 1719 Jean Antoine Watteau was briefly in London; the world of fashion moved up the Thames to share in Prince George's sudden enthusiasm for fox hunting. There were race meetings with royal prizes of saddles and boat races on the river. That long reach of the Thames opposite Syon had been laid out by Ormonde as a terrace, planted with trees. This served as a grandstand for the races and for concerts of water music in the evenings, the playing acoustically enhanced by the river itself. Flotillas of boats rowed fashionable London up to enjoy the spectacle. It was a perfect realisation in England of the pastoral idylls of Watteau and Boucher. At Hampton Court the old King walked his gardens alone and gave a few dull dinner parties in the evenings.

This was Princess Caroline's moment and it would in time become William Kent's opportunity. The concentration of nobility, gentry and market gardeners living along this stretch of the Thames was impressive. For his neighbours on one bank of the river or the other Lord Burlington at Chiswick had the Duke of Shrewsbury, the Duke of Argyll, Lady Rochester, Lord Percival, Mr Stonor, Lord Winchelsea, Sir Godfrey Kneller, the Duchess of Hamilton, the Earls of Radnor, Islay and Strafford. As the estate agents say today: 'Location! Location! Location!' Small wonder that Sir Robert Walpole contrived to get himself appointed as Ranger of Richmond Park, in which office he was required to meet the Prince of Wales or the King at the Park Gate when royalty came to hunt, and he could wear a green and gold uniform with the Ranger's cap on his head and the leash across his shoulders. It was at Richmond, in an early *entente cordiale*, that he entertained the Chief Minister of France, Cardinal Fleury: France again and the Rococo moment.

Lord Burlington's name appears rarely in letters of the period, which is curious considering his wealth and influence in the north of England. It seems he was not a sociable figure, and for those few strategic months of high fashion on the Thames in 1719 he was absent, scouring the Veneto for Palladio's designs of bath houses and snatching Kent up for a headlong return journey. It was a bad time to be away. The defiant Prince and Princess of Wales had moved out to Richmond for their second summer season in late May and Caroline, appreciating the drawing power of a well-sited park, handy for the capital, called a garden conference. Alexander Pope was one of those invited. From his letter describing it, the proceedings reached no precise conclusion, but there are fascinating hints that garden design, at that time dominated by the harsh but lively geometries of Charles Bridgeman, with his angular groves, long, decisive avenues and amphitheatres of earth or tree planting, was edging towards more informal effects. Pope, for one, despised topiary but was otherwise Bridgemanic.

Away in Italy and Paris, Burlington and Kent had missed out on a seminal occasion, though Pope would have been able to bring them up to date in garden trends when they finally returned in November. His letter to Lord Bathurst of 13 September 1719 needs to be quoted at length because Burlington had, before he left for Italy, laid out an old-fashioned garden behind the old house at Chiswick at exactly the wrong time for such tired formalism. He and Kent would need to think and to act fast if they hoped to be leaders in garden fashion. As for a new house at Chiswick, how would an austere neo-classical design, such as he had been hunting down in Italy, work if England was about to follow France in pastoral revelry, informal entertainments and Rococo ornament?

This is the relevant section of Pope's letter describing the Princess Caroline's garden conference:

> That this Letter be all of a piece, I'll fill the rest with an account of a consultation lately held in my neighbourhood, about designing a princely garden. Several Criticks were of several opinions: One declar'd

he would not have too much Art in it; for my notion (said he) of gardening is, that it is only sweeping Nature: Another told them that Gravel walks were not of a good taste, for all of the finest abroad were of loose sand: A third advis'd peremptorily there should not be one Lyme-tree in the whole plantation; a fourth made the same exclusive clause extend to Horse-chestnuts, which he affirm'd not to be Trees, but Weeds; Dutch Elms were condemn'd by a fifth; and thus about half the Trees were proscrib'd, contrary to the Paradise of God's own planting, which is expressly said to be planted with all trees. There were some who cou'd not bear Ever-greens, and call'd them Never-greens; some, who were angry at them only when cut into shapes, and gave the modern Gard'ners the name of Ever-green Taylors; some who had no dislike to Cones and Cubes, but wou'd have 'em cut in Forest-trees; and some who were in a passion against any thing in shape, even against clipt hedges, which they call'd green walls. These (my Lord) are our Men of Taste, who pretend to prove it by tasting little or nothing. Sure such a Taste is like such a stomach, not a good one, but a weak one. We have the same sort of Critics in poetry; one is fond of nothing but Heroicks, another cannot relish Tragedies, another hates Pastorals, all little Wits delight in Epigrams. Will you give me leave to add, there are the same in Divinity? Where many leading Critics are for rooting up more than they plant, and would leave the Lord's Vineyard either very thinly furnish'd, or very oddly trimm'd.[6]

The striking feature of this account, elegantly as it is written, is Pope's own surprising reluctance to take sides or to put forward anything positive. He was still of Charles Bridgeman's party at this time and would soon, in 1726, be begging a design and a workforce from Bridgeman, who was working for the Princess at Richmond. The men would create a little amphitheatre in Pope's five-acre plot at Twickenham. When arguments are being put, urging that by his poetry Pope moved English garden design forward to more natural and relaxed solutions, his cautious neutrality in September 1719 should be remembered. That vague phrase that gardening 'is only sweeping Nature', spoken by someone who 'would not have too much Art in it', was, according to Warburton who was writing much later in 1751, a quotation from Sir Thomas Hanmer, which is hardly helpful.

It might appear that a case is being made, on very little evidence, for these Richmond garden and river fêtes as being a potential Rococo turning point for a country which would eventually give the style a cold and hesitant welcome. In which case John Rocque's 'VEUE de la Maison ROYALE de RICHMOND, du coté de la Tamise a 3 lievres de LONDRES', drawn by Chatelain, should be studied.[7] Taken from the north or Syon bank of the river, it illustrates the modest Richmond Lodge behind a park enriched by Kent's Rotunda and several lesser garden buildings. More prominently on the Syon bank, drawn in rich detail, a whole cast of gentlefolk, copied from Watteau's *Embarkation for the Island of Cythera*, is preparing to ferry over to Richmond, which is substituting for Cythera, Venus's island of love. The view was drawn before 1739, but the association between the celebrated painting by a genius of the French Rococo and Kent's Richmond, essentially the creation of his patron, Princess Caroline, suggests how close the foreign style came to crossing the Channel. Richmond should have been Kent's launch pad for Rococo informalities, but Burlington's obsessions at Chiswick will explain why that way in garden design would never be confidently taken.

As for the poor little royal children, their bereft Princess mother and their wicked grandpapa, it was now that Princess Caroline and Sir Robert Walpole forged an alliance of both convenience and practical affinity. Walpole and his ministers pressed the grumpy and reluctant old King to a graceless semi-reconciliation. Walpole reported 'that the *King* was very rough with the *Princess* – chid her very severely in a cruel Way' when they met in private in 'a little Closet, where they stayed an Hour and ten Minutes'.[8] But with her shrewd eye for the realities of power, the 'Princess came out transported at the *King's* mighty kind Reception, and told the Doctors and Everybody how mighty kind he had been to her'.[9] Caroline was a very determined woman. In some ways she would become as strong and as shaping an influence upon William Kent's career and stylistic ventures as Lord Burlington. It might be argued that she was the patron who pushed Kent firmly towards both Gothick experiment and a more natural style of landscape gardening. That would leave Burlington as her opposite influence, encouraging his friend equally firmly towards Palladian rather than Rococo disciplines of design: to a dry copying of scholarly details of dead architecture rather than to the lively invention and figurative forms of the Rococo. Kent's career owed everything to

Burlington's preferment, but he paid the price by a severe restriction of his creativity.

This two-way tug of styles between Caroline and Burlington had national consequences and it makes the Princess's intellectual background most relevant to Kent's artistic development. She was a modern woman of her times, a bluestocking who, being an orphan, had been educated at the court of her guardian, the Queen of Prussia, by the philosopher Gottfried Wilhelm Leibniz. More earthy and practical than most of his kind, Leibniz invented a calculating machine and the binary system of numeration. Of far more relevance to Caroline was his deep interest in history and the historical authenticity of the Hanoverian House of Guelph. In 1676 he did scholarly research for the Duke of Braunschweig-Lüneburg to develop arguments supporting the right of the Guelphs to succeed to the throne of Great Britain. Later, when Ernst August, father of the future King George I, was pressing to be made one of the Electors of the Empire he made Leibniz the Historian to the House and ennobled him as Hofrat. So convincing was Leibniz's thesis on the origins of the Guelphs from the noble Italian princely House of Este, that in 1692 Ernst August was solemnly awarded his Electoral Cap. All of which explains why Caroline, expecting her not very clever husband to be the next King of England, had a healthy respect for the supportive role that history could play in shoring up an uncertain claim to a throne. Leibniz's experience would have taught her that there is a persuasive romance to historical associations, and at some point she must have discussed this notion with William Kent. It would bear architectural fruit in 1730.

As well as being a romantic historian, Leibniz was loftily apart from the theological disputes of Catholicism and Protestantism, working for the spread of Christianity by the merging of its two great branches. His teaching on this also rubbed off on to Caroline, sending her into the shadowy regions of universalism, which is another way of saying that she felt superior to all revealed religions and had no time at all for an infallible Bible as a spiritual guide. Nature as a revelation of Creation had more appeal to her. Nothing that we know about her – and from the memoirs of her platonic lover and devoted companion, Lord Hervey, we know a great deal – is as relevant to her aims in gardening and her subsequent direction of Kent's receptive mind, as a passage in the diary of the courtier and aspirant politician Lord Egmont. Again it deserves to be quoted at length for the light it throws, not only on Caroline, but on the underlying roughness of the times. Egmont had met her on the evening of 31 December 1734, half by accident:

> I told her flatterers were fools, for generally Princes see through it. 'True', said she, 'and therefore it must be done very gently and fine.' Soon after which Sir John Rushout telling her that we owe our best taste of gardening to her, she replied. 'Yes, indeed, I think I may say that I have introduced that, in helping nature, not losing it in art.' It were too long to write the rest of the conversation. I dined at home.
>
> This day a soldier was hanged for murder near Somerset House; the wretch died drunk and blaspheming.[10]

It is infuriating that Egmont was to record for us no more of that fascinating conversation on natural gardens. The letter was written fifteen years after that inconclusive garden conference of Pope's report. But in those fifteen years enough had been happening under Queen Caroline's control at Richmond to indicate the direction of her taste and to explain, as Kent was busily employed in Caroline's Richmond, Burlington's Chiswick and Pope's five acres at Twickenham, the direction of Kent's garden thinking. In a tight, insular society the lead given by royalty is more often the key than is usually admitted. In our own times few critics have been able to resist a cheap sneer at Prince Charles's ideal village at Poundbury, outside Dorchester. Yet if we consider the new suburban developments around urban centres, those where middle-class money needs to be attracted, it is remarkable how many rather less subtle, but still obvious children of Poundbury have been going up, with exactly the same attention to variety of pastiche and individuality of profile.

What would be valuable would be some comment from Burlington upon the direction which Caroline was giving to his protégé. Nothing is recorded, but he could well have reacted with alarm when Kent would begin to show a more lively interest in the historical remains of English history than those of antique Rome. A pro-Roman demonstration of architecture would be required and with the villa at Chiswick, built between 1725 and 1726, a very robust demonstration was delivered.

12

Burlington's neo-classical counterattack at Chiswick

Returning from the Rococo festivities on the south bank of the Thames, recounted in the previous chapter, to 1719 and the north bank of the river, Lord Burlington was in a predicament there, one largely of his own creation. Being a driven, obstinate man he was only half-intelligent enough to appreciate his problem. It is no accident that, though Burlington was one of the most influential figures in English architectural history, the only substantial biography of him is written in French[1] and Rudolf Wittkower, his most engaged analyst, died without writing the English biography that was promised.

Burlington left no clear written testament as to what he was trying to do stylistically, probably because he was not very sure himself. He launched a successful Palladian revival, a thirty- or forty-year period of generally dull, classical buildings that the nation has had to make the best of and claim to admire, because, that being its heritage from the first half of the eighteenth century, there is little or no alternative. But Burlington was, on the evidence of what he and Kent put together in the Villa at Chiswick, not intending a Palladian revival at all. Fired, in a vague, uncertain way, by the Earl of Shaftesbury's call for a national revival of culture and the arts, Burlington was fumbling towards an antique Roman authenticity, a neo-classicism without the archaeological scholarship to support it. Those French-style entertainments of Princess Caroline across the river, popular and Arcadian as they were, had no authentic classical base, only the Duke of Ormonde's pleasant, Anglo-Dutch Richmond Lodge.

The royal emphasis was focusing on gardens, not buildings, and on semi-natural gardens, wildernesses of winding paths, and a tree-lined terrace overlooking, not a straight canal, but a big, natural river. Burlington needed to make a gesture quickly, and a bold one. His predicament was that, where gardens were concerned he had already shot his bolt. Starting in 1716, before his second Italian visit, he had laid out a thoroughly old-fashioned *patte d'oie*, a formal goose foot of three dead straight avenues running through walls of greenery to terminate on three garden buildings.[2] First came the Pagan Building, a handsome, domed pavilion, probably by Burlington's initially favoured architect, James Gibbs, whom the Earl now rejected. Then in 1717 Burlington, with the help of his new favourite, Colen Campbell, designed the Bagnio, a cold bath, in what he must have hoped was an antique Roman style, but which was, through Campbell's influence, an attractive jumble of Palladian motifs. Last of all, to conclude the right-hand avenue, was the Rustic Arch. The foolishness of this goose foot was that it centred upon nothing, not on the old Chiswick House, but upon a vacant plot a little to the west of it. To compound that error Burlington would, between 1725 and 1726, build his new Villa even further to the west, facing, a few yards away, into The Grove, a dense thicket. A starting point for the trio of avenues would eventually be created by a 'Link Building' connecting the House and the Villa in a style different from both. So, by 1719, when Burlington returned from Italy with Kent, who had neither designed nor built anything in his life, and a bundle of Palladio's conjectural reconstructions of Roman baths, the complex at Chiswick consisted of a new, but already dated, garden in the wrong place, near a big, old-fashioned house. It was hardly the launch pad for a revival of Roman grandeur. Meanwhile, upriver, young royalty had completely outpointed the naturally stiff and unsociable Earl, just by being relaxed, cheerful and, in the continental sense, modern.

William Kent has to take some blame for what happened next in the 'architecture by numbers' design of the new Villa. To be fair to him, he was wildly busy during its period of construction. He was designing interiors between 1724 and 1725 at Ditchley House, Oxfordshire, for Lord Lichfield, which are the logical perfection of that refrigerated Roman style he and Burlington had tried out in the Fine Rooms of Burlington House. At the same crowded time he was decorating Raynham Hall in Norfolk (1725–31) so impressively that Sir Robert Walpole felt obliged to let him decorate his own tremendous new palace at Houghton, because the owner of Raynham, Viscount Townshend, was Walpole's chief rival in the Norfolk gentry stakes. So Houghton had to be more outrageously grand than Raynham. Kent had the knack of running with the hare and hunting with the hounds. Understandably, therefore, he could have had only half his attention fixed upon the new Chiswick. As a result the Villa has ended up a most interesting building, full of design errors, put together by two amateurs, neither convincingly antique Roman nor authentically Palladian, which is a fair description of English architecture until a combination of Robert Adam and some archaeological research brought in a rather more authentic neo-classicism after 1760. Kent really was an opportunist; he had more talent than principles and, like all opportunists, he cut corners.

No one should judge Chiswick Villa without first contriving a visit to what it might have been, to Colen Campbell's Mereworth Castle among the truly Arcadian apple orchards of Kent. Mereworth is the design that Burlington was offered and rejected, apparently because it was wholeheartedly Palladian, a brilliantly confident, if dysfunctional, English essay on Palladio's Villa Capra or Rotunda, just outside Vicenza. Campbell drew the design for Burlington, but the Earl, under Kent's jealous influence, rejected it. Campbell's star was waning, so he took it to the Earl of Westmorland who built it at Mereworth.[3] Though not often open to the public, Mereworth is very rewarding with its battery of expensive porticoes set up above a dry moat and its steep dome topped, as Western domes should be topped, with a cupola. Fixated upon those Roman bath plans, Burlington would insist upon shallow, almost Byzantine domes with no satisfying cupola crown.[4] They give his Chiswick a topping like that of an overlarge mushroom; they would wreck his designs for a new Parliament building, and there has to be a suspicion that Kent also favoured them. Kent's most successful building, the Worcester Lodge at Badminton, a masterpiece of rising, energetic power, is still crowned by a shallow, bald pate: a Roman bath dome.

Given that the exterior of the Villa never recovers from Burlington's insistence on an alien topping, those big Diocletian windows in the octagonal drum of the dome do light the Saloon inside much better than the central apartments of either Mereworth or Palladio's Rotunda are lit. Yet the Earl and Kent got the idea from a Palladio design for a square tower to the Villa Valmarana at Vigardolo.[5] But then, in the cut-and-paste process, the Earl's search turned to Scamozzi. The entrance front of the Villa is a composite of two designs by Vincenzo Scamozzi, one for his Villa Molini, the other for the Villa Rocca Pisani.[6] Burlington's precedent there would have been Inigo Jones who knew Scamozzi personally, but never met his master, Palladio. Wilton House and the Whitehall Banqueting House are both more Scamozzi than Palladio, but subsequent reverence for the older architect has resulted in Scamozzi never being given his due.

All Chiswick's exterior effects, apart from its pompously complex stairs, are staccato: its windows are cut independently of each other, isolated incident on bare walls. This is the antique effect which indicates that it was Burlington who pressed Kent into those staccato features that make the Entrance Hall at Ditchley so austere and Roman in suggestion, with Corinthian columns and pediments dramatising doors and niches. It is possible to sense the Rococo-inclined Kent rebelling against that discipline with rich swags, wreaths, busts and a full display of architectural ornaments on the cornices in both Ditchley and Chiswick. Later he would find other stylistic escape routes.

Not one of the Villa's four façades can be taken for granted. On the garden front facing that thicket, Palladio came back into play with a near exact copy of the Villa Valmarana's own rear elevation[7] of three recessed Serlian windows and round-headed niches, though Burlington added a second grandiloquent staircase for anyone anxious to walk in that thicket. The obelisk chimneys, which smoked badly and stick up like absurd hare's ears on that otherwise chaste roofline, should be one of Kent's better jokes, but in fact a drawing for them in Burlington's own hand exists and their source is again Scamozzi.[8]

It is in the interiors of the Villa that Kent, the irrepressibly decorative and disrespectful, comes into his own. The exterior must be all Burlington; it is a building as uncomfortable and unreal as all those monuments in country churches to local lords wearing Roman togas and full-bottomed wigs. Who was it who said 'A wig gives a Gentleman all the gravity of a water spaniel'? The Chiswick Villa was proposing a similar absurd gravitas for a gentleman's house; and the aristocracy would spend the next forty years trying to accommodate the proposition. Kent would have the wit to offer a more consciously English, historically associative alternative at Esher Place, but that was still five years ahead. At Chiswick he was as guilty as his friend, though that dog pissing on Burlington's leg was hardly a vote of confidence in the project.

To enjoy the best and the worst of the Villa's extraordinary interiors, one of London's most extreme visual pleasures, they should be experienced in bright sunshine before the visitor hurries out to absorb the more creative complexities surviving from Kent's gardens. Decorative schemes that just about work in a large room space like the Entrance Hall at Ditchley or the vast Stone Hall at Houghton, both of which were virtually contemporary, are an embarrassment in the miniature apartments of Chiswick. But once the 'Grand Hotel' central axis and the 'whore's boudoir' romps of the side rooms have been accepted the sequence of rooms opening tightly, one into another with no intermission of corridors, is memorable.

In the Cupola Room at Kensington Palace the coffered ceiling was only painted. Here, much closer to eye level in the central Saloon, it has been realised in three-dimensional plaster with every Roman bath detail brightly lit by those Diocletian windows. Very few plans and directions for the interiors by Kent have survived and the 'Preliminary section' by him for the 'Domed Saloon',[9] published in his *The Designs of Inigo Jones* of 1727, may explain why. It is very naughty. Two naked nymphs loll in Michelangelesque attitudes on the door pediment. The three paintings above in ornate, swagged frames illustrate, on the left, a naked nymph on a rock being supported, or assaulted, by naked tritons; on the right, a naked woman sitting on a bank, clutching her breast and regarding thoughtfully an equally naked man whose head is propped sleepily on his arm. All five classical figures in the central painting are fully clothed. To make up for this the lunettes between the Diocletian windows feature, on the left, a naked Leda being seduced from the front by a swan and, on the right, a naked girl on a couch looking out over a landscape. Poor Kent! If only his full-scale frescoes could have been as lively and licentious as these miniatures his reputation would have been made.

Is it possible that Burlington planned this Villa, attached to its main house by obscure doors and the long sequence of the Link Building, as a bachelor pad for riotous purposes? It has no main stairs for women to descend in wide skirts and no room where dancing could have taken place. The Red and the Blue Velvet Rooms have all the ambience of a French bordello. Or were the original interior designs one of Kent's many visual jokes? That seems more likely, though the whole concept of the Villa as developed here was one of a self-indulgent connoisseur's isolation from something or someone. Again the difficulty of writing a convincing biography of Burlington is underlined. Considering their impact on English cultural society he and Kent both kept themselves out of the light of comment and anecdote. It should be noted, however, that all those nudes were women and that Kent had found stimulating subjects to paint from the lewd love life of the Gods as related by Ovid in his *Metamorphoses*. Kent owned an Italian version of this in manuscript.[10]

After the Saloon, which still has a few oversized paintings of full-breasted women and a loyal copy of King Charles I with his family, the Red and Blue Velvet Rooms should be left for later. The Villa's most stunning and influential interior lies straight ahead. This is the Gallery where the staccato details of doors, windows, columns and picture frames are so richly elaborated and gilded, and the deep beams of the painted ceiling are so near the eye, that there is not enough bare wall surface for the projection of antique solemnity to be conveyed and very little room for furniture or even for people. Yet Nero's Golden House could have been much like this. The apses with their gilded coffering, the statues in their niches and the vistas through the three roomlets are spatially exhilarating. It is small wonder that Robert Adam would seize upon the same devices again and again,[11] and that in Thomas Coke's palatial Holkham Hall the sequence would be repeated. Virtually every architectural detail relates to an authority. The ground plan is from Palladio's Villa Valmarana again; the richly unsuitable ceiling is from Inigo Jones's bedchamber for Queen Henrietta Maria at the Queen's House in Greenwich. Two of Kent's jokes are there to be relished: the woman in the Circular Closet who is looking up apprehensively at her towering headdress of golden raffle leaves, and the sumptuous Corinthian cornice that suddenly comes to a stop because the Serlian window is in the way. The first joke is of pure Rococo exuberance, the second sheer incompetence.

Is this serious architecture? What could anyone do in such a space except look at art, and there is not even much wall area for that. One vigorous pirouette and a dancer would hit a wall. But the excitement of the place is how few steps are needed to change the décor totally. The Gallery has a kind of millionaire's chastity, the Red Velvet and Blue Velvet Rooms are defiantly impure yet without the slightest hint of a

Sir Francis Dashwood Hellfire Club; they are simply self-indulgent. In the Red Velvet Room, Kent's ceiling painting repeats the uneasy perspectives and toppling male nude of the Burlington House Fine Rooms and San Giuliano in Rome. In the Blue Velvet Room, crushed by Burlington's criminally overscaled ceiling brackets,[12] Kent has reused some sketch of the Virgin Mary that he made on his travels and cast her as the 'Spirit of Architecture', one of his very worst efforts. She and her three cherubs are sliding down a metal pipe balanced on a cloud. Grotesque work on golden dots fills the lesser spaces and must have taken days to execute. A word of grateful praise must be given to English Heritage for its courage in restoring these rooms to their nouveau riche, expensive look of 1727. The National Trust would never have had the nerve, and would have insisted on everything looking modishly distressed. English Heritage got it disturbingly right.

Whether Kent and Burlington got it right is another question. Should a heavy French-style ceiling of 1630 be put on top of a miniature bath house for the Emperor Nero? The Villa attracted attention in its day, much of it mocking, like Lord Hervey's memorable joke that it was 'too small to inhabit, and too large to hang on one's watch [chain]'.[13] Hervey also wrote that the Samoyed people of north-eastern Russia, 'a short, ugly species, hardly humanised in their form & not more civilised in their manners . . . live in a chilled climate where light & warmth are as great strangers as in a house of Ld. Burlington's building'.[14] Hervey's dislike of Burlington would explain his contempt for Kent. His other comment on the Villa at Chiswick was the reworking of the 50th Epigram in Martial's 12th Book:

> Possess'd of one great hall for state,
> Without a place to sleep or eat;
> How well you build let flattery tell,
> And all mankind how ill you dwell![15]

There again, Hervey was mocking some very real defects in the Villa's planning and conception.

For a house devised in a spirit of historic scholarship it only occasionally evokes its targeted period; in the three centuries since it was built it has acquired no magic, no legendary associations. When Burlington was living in it he held no famous masquerades, no Venetian carnivals in its gardens. It seems an entirely selfish house for a connoisseur. Hervey may have summed it up accurately.

It could be suggested tentatively that, in the third decade of the eighteenth century, when England had a choice of stylistic directions: the Rococo of the Continent or the revived Palladian of its own Stuart past, the wrong road was taken. The Villa at Chiswick was a signpost pointing to a dead end, to a road already travelled by more creative, less inhibited architects. If William Kent spent much time on it, then it was time ill spent.

13

Chiswick – the garden as a learning experience

From the golden, autumnal profusion of sketches that Kent made, in pen and flattering brown wash, for the garden at Chiswick it is evident that he spent more time and thought over these grounds than over any other garden with which he was associated. Yet Chiswick is in no way a real Kent garden. It was Lord Burlington's creation with occasional passages of Kent coming to the rescue: the perfect matching twin to the Villa that fronts it. They are both self-indulgent Burlingtonian ventures with febrile, often ill-judged, Kentian enrichments. The Villa and its garden were the price Kent paid his patron-friend for all his awesome initial contacts: a king, queen and several dukes, and his rapid promotions in the royal service.

Where architecture and garden design were concerned both men were amateurs, feeling their way by trial and error; but they were amateurs coming from opposing theoretical backgrounds. Burlington had been lightly brainwashed by Colen Campbell, who had probably never been near Italy, into a hazy vision of a noble Roman simplicity towards which he had to strive. For Burlington a garden was a long, straight avenue of greenery with a classical building at the end of it, and there is no evidence that he ever advanced from that. Kent, with his natural, high-camp tendencies, would, all his life, yearn after interiors in Rome's contemporary Baroque. That gave him no helpful leads on gardens. With a confused memory of jumbles of exciting stone features on hillsides he had to work out an appropriate English version of them that would escape Burlington's telescopic obsessions, just as, in the Villa, he had tarted up the ceilings and multiplied the classical enrichments to enliven Burlington's correct detailing.

The two men should have quarrelled and gone their separate ways within a year or two of their return to London, but they never did. Something, an awareness perhaps that they were both flying by the seat of their pants, two confidence tricksters carrying a whole wealthy, rather ignorant, aristocracy along with them, kept them together. Someone who could throw off those cheerful, seductive sketches must have made the sun shine every morning. With his long, solemn face, Burlington may have needed Kent more than Kent needed Burlington; but the Whig establishment needed them both even more to add a senatorial majesty to the constitutional hijack they had pulled off in 1714. Nevertheless, in the 1720s and 1730s, when Chiswick's grounds were being shaped and then reshaped, upon whims with no overall planning, Burlington was in charge; he was the master and Kent was still his man.

There is all the evidence of the improbable success of his Palladian revival to prove that Burlington was a very determined, influential figure, a formidable, top-ranking aristocrat posing, without a scrap of training, as a professional architect and arbiter of taste. But there is not much to prove that he was notably intelligent in his artistic judgement. To encourage the arts in England he had brought back from Italy a bad sculptor, Guelfi, a bad and quarrelsome composer, Buononcini, and a bad painter, William Kent: hardly a dazzling record of patronage. As for the architecture which he reintroduced, the jury is still out on Colen Campbell and the generally lifeless, nervously rule-bound Palladianism that he proposed and England tamely accepted. How many Campbell houses, apart from Mereworth, which is virtually a copy, capture either the relaxed charm and lively invention of a Palladio original, or come anywhere near to suggesting an Antique Roman authority? With Chiswick, gardens were in danger of going the same way as all those Burlingtonian initiatives in architecture, sculpture and music. To say that Kent came to the rescue there would be premature; rescue would take time and experiment; but at least Kent was able to see what was going wrong. A minus, in that sense, was a plus.

There are three Chiswick gardens: the first, and in some ways the most important, was Kent's projection of it on paper in those enchanting sketches. He had the perfect vision in those, even if he could not realise that vision on the ground. The second Chiswick was that tight criss-cross of alleyways that Burlington imposed and that Rocque captured in his *Engraved Survey* of 1736, for garden historians to wonder at and wrangle over. Last of all is the Chiswick garden that has survived today: a London lung, a public open space, not revered and nurtured like the manicured gardens around stately homes that are open for a fee, but a pleasant, battered area of warning notices, frisby throwing, ice-cream eating, squalid toilets and sunbathing on rough lawns.

For someone familiar with the Rocque survey a visit to the real Chiswick will come as a surprise. There are no intervening spaces on Rocque; feature is piled upon feature, all compressed and jostling together, so Chiswick looks on paper like a major estate when, in fact, it is a modest, almost suburban affair, a five-minute walk from one end of it to the other. But Rocque does capture Burlington's thoroughly old-fashioned, seventeenth-century obsession with avenues, not only that first misaligned *patte d'oie*, but four systems in all, slammed down and interlocking on that limited area. From left to right and working from Rocque's baseline upwards, there are the two avenues and a terrace based on the Obelisk with the Roman Marriage sculpture at the Burlington Lane entrance. When the left hand of those two avenues reaches the bridge over the New River it becomes a member of a new goose foot facing south-west. Then there is the grand, original *patte d'oie* with its three building terminals. It is probably a little unfair to blame its misalignment on Lord Burlington as the 1689 Kip and Knyff view of the old house shows its central avenue already in place, though very recently planted; Burlington must have decided to adapt his father's planting rather than begin afresh. Last of the four is the avenue running from the stables past the Orangery to the Doric Column at the centre of six radiating paths. Virtually every triangular or rectangular interstice between these straight avenues was, in 1736, thickly planted with trees. Chiswick was a miniature French forest garden of the seventeenth century with classical buildings at the focal points. Winding footpaths were cut through almost every boscage except The Grove, but the scale of the garden was so diminutive that few of these sinuous footpaths for ladies' recreation would have been even a hundred yards long.

To complicate these strictly angular complexities still further, it should be remembered that the garden area below the New River was only added by Burlington's land purchases of 1726 and 1727. The original garden ended at the Bollo Brook, as the New River was then called, so that first grand *patte d'oie* included everything. This explains the extreme linear compression of features along what was the upper bank of the Brook and the garden's original boundary. It was a flat area of land with no views of the Thames and no interesting irregularities. If Charles Bridgeman was called in for advice and ideas, as seems likely, he will have added the two little pools, apsidal- and exedral-ended, with the Ionic Temple and Amphitheatre squashed between them, in a desperate effort to liven up a very dull garden.

After the land purchase had permitted some extension, Burlington predictably planted more avenues and dammed the Bollo Brook to make a straight Canal. This left the two little pools looking redundant alongside the much bigger Canal. Then the Ionic Temple had to be given a back porch to make it look out across the Canal instead of presenting a windowless backside to what was now a major feature of parade. At this confused moment Kent seems to have felt confident enough to intervene. Dates for the various additions to the garden are hard to pin down; but presuming, as seems reasonable, that the Canal would have been dug along the line of the Bollo Brook in 1728, the year after the last land purchase of 1727, in that same year, 1728, Kent, out of loyalty and also because of his genuine interest in antiquity, is bound to have read the proofs of a slim volume, *The Villas of the Ancients Illustrated*. This was written by Robert Castell, but its publication in 1729 had been paid for by Burlington as part of his obsessive determination to revive Augustan manners, not just in houses, but in the gardens appropriate to those houses.

The entire Castell episode is both mysterious and shocking. Apart from the obvious facts that he was ambitious, scholarly and had a high critical intelligence, very little is known about the man except that he had an educated wife, several children and that he was 'born to a competent estate'.[1] He was anxious to publish a translation of the works of Vitruvius, probably as a follow-up to the interest that had been raised by the various volumes of Campbell's *Vitruvius Britannicus*. As a trial publication before this major venture, on 1 February 1727 he had proposed a short volume on a subject which Vitruvius 'had been least curious to explain': Pliny's account of his villas at Laurentinum and Tuscum.[2] This would test the public's interest, come out by subscription and offer as a special inducement 'Remarks on . . . Gardens and &c of the Ancients'.[3]

Kent must have been well informed on the project because on 11 November 1727, William Aikman, a minor painter in Burlington's circle, wrote to Sir John Clerk of Penicuik to warn him that Clerk's son James would be wasting his time translating Vitruvius because 'Mr Kent assures me the Vitruvius is already undertaken by the author of Pliny's Gardens and is pretty advanced so as Proposals are to come out this winter',[4] which gives at least the impression that Burlington was behind both Castell's ventures: the Villas and the complete Vitruvius.

In 1728 a definite proposal came out for Castell's *Works of Vitruvius* with 'proper notes', using 'by his Lordships special favour' illustrations by Palladio and Pirro Ligorio in Burlington's library together with 'the Remarks of Mr Inigo Jones, the Vitruvius of his Age, on the Italian version of the Author, by Daniel Barbaro'.[5] But on 18 June disaster struck. Robert Castell was committed to the Fleet Prison for a debt of £400 and, to compound his troubles beyond remedy, the new Warder of the Fleet, Thomas Bambridge, demanded a bond of £4000 security. Castell reacted honourably to this legal blackmail, 'resolving not to injure further his family or his creditors', and refused the demand.[6] Bambridge consigned him to a 'sponging house' where there was a case of smallpox and on 12 December 1728 Castell died of that disease.

This, perhaps surprisingly, caused a national scandal. On 25 February 1729 a House of Commons committee was set up to enquire into the state of prisons and Castell's death was a subject in the committe's first report of 20 March 1729. Bambridge was tried for the murder of Castell but acquitted on 22 May 1729. The dead man's widow appealed, but a year later, on 26 January 1730, Bambridge was acquitted again. Meanwhile Castell's *Villas of the Ancients* had been published on 5 July 1729 as a charitable venture for the relief of his widow and orphaned children with 117 subscribers, many of them members of the parliamentary committee, for the 133 copies. Such was the interest nationally that the book went through three editions and Stephen Switzer was jealous enough to insist, in his 1742 *An Appendage to Ichnographia Rustica*, that his original 1718 *Ichnographia* had influenced Castell.

The puzzle where Burlington and Kent are concerned is why they took no steps to rescue Castell from the Fleet Prison. Was he killed off before they could make a move? Whatever the reason his manuscript of the Vitruvius translation with its notes has never been found and Burlington does not come out well from the incident.

In its limited range Castell's book is most impressive. His scholarly exegesis of Pliny's descriptions of the gardens around his two villas, Laurentinum on the seashore near Rome and Tuscum up in the Apennines, is thorough, which will have made his conclusions all the more convincing and unwelcome to Burlington, who would have been expecting to read that Roman gardens were formal affairs of many orderly straight lines, like Chiswick. Instead, Castell picked up Sir William Temple's earlier speculations on the 'Sharawadgi',[7] or asymmetrical, beauties of Chinese gardens and claimed that the Romans had discovered them first and valued them highly. In Pliny's gardens Castell believed that two design approaches, one strictly formal, one entirely natural, had been combined to create a third:

> whose Beauty consisted in a close Imitation of Nature; where, tho' the Parts are disposed with the greatest Art, the Irregularity is still preserved; so that their Manner may not improperly be said to be an artful Confusion, where there is no Appearance of that Skill which is made use of, their *Rocks*, *Cascades*, and *Trees*, bearing their natural Forms.[8]

To express this '*Imitatio Ruris*' fully a garden had 'to be well stockt with Trees and Water; which last we may suppose took its seeming natural Course through the rougher Parts of the Garden, and in the regular appeared in a more artful Disposition',[9] which sounds like an anticipation of the landscaping of Capability Brown, post-1751, when he launched out on his professional career, yet the date is only 1728.

The whole emphasis of Castell's interpretation is a prescient Romantic appreciation of wild natural scenery. At Laurentinum one of the charms of the villa is that the breaking of waves on the shore can be heard in the sleeping quarters; while at Tuscum 'You would take great Delight, in viewing the Country from the top of the Mountain; for it would not appear as real land, but as an exquisite Painting'.[10] So not only does Pliny–Castell anticipate the Picturesque painterly qualities of nature, but this revolutionary little book leaps the fence and finds all Nature a garden in 1728, a discovery which Horace Walpole, publishing his *The History of the Modern Taste in Gardening* in 1771, credited to William Kent.[11] Castell is quite explicit. The *Gestatio* at Tuscum, 'in the form of a *Circus*', is fenced in by a wall hidden behind box hedges:

From thence you have the View of a Meadow not less beautiful by Nature, than these the fore-mentioned Works of Art: then you see Fields, with many Meadows and Shrubs.[12]

This emphasis upon visual escape from the garden to more natural and even superior scenery outside, comes up again and again, only the ha-ha is missing:

Not far from the Bath are Stairs that lead to the *Cryptoporticus*, after you have passed three Diaetae [ordinary living rooms]; one of which looks into the little *Area*, with Plane-Trees, another to the Meadows, and the other has a Prospect of the Vineyards, and several other Parts of the Country . . . this Summer *Cryptoporticus* being placed aloft, does not only see, but seems to touch the Vineyards.[13]

For Pliny, the glory of his Tuscum villa was its natural situation. 'Imagine to yourself', he writes enthusiastically:

a vast Amphitheatre, which only the Hand of Nature herself could form; being a wide extended plain surrounded with Mountains: whose Tops are cover'd with lofty ancient Woods; which give opportunity to frequent and various sorts of Hunting. From thence the Under-woods descend with the Mountains.[14]

Not everything in Tuscum was outward looking. The chief interior delight of its garden lay in subtle effects of falling water:

Out of the *Stibadium*, the Water flows from several small Pipes, as if pressed out by the Weight of what lies on it, and is receiv'd and contained in a Bason, so artfully order'd, that tho' full, it does not run over . . . against the *Stibadium* is a Fountain that casts forth and receives Water, which being play'd up to a great height falls into it again and runs off through Drains that are join'd to it.[15]

Castell printed Pliny's Latin text in parallel columns to his English translation, so his authority was undeniable. A truly Roman garden should have wide views out over natural meadows and cultivation. Within its bounds there should be effects of tumbling waters. It says something for the genial partnership of Kent and Burlington that, while Burlington ignored the implications of Castell's text and leapt eagerly upon the pronounced formal avenues and exedra of Castell's detailed illustrations, he allowed Kent to pick up that delight in views, natural waters and complex cascading fountains. On his plans Castell had actually indicated these areas of *Imitatio Ruris* pictorially with little twisted trees and winding rivers, so there was no avoiding the message. In one area of Chiswick, The Grove, Burlington cut out a splendidly formal avenue and followed Kent's exquisite design for the statues at its exedral head.[16] In another area Kent was allowed to create an artificial terrace from which to view the Thames and build upon it a disastrously complex water feature. That geometrical canal so recently dug out to receive the waters of the Bollo was naturalised to give Chiswick, so near and yet so far from the banks of the Thames, its own miniature Thames. Finally the sector between the Villa and this new river was cleared of its topiary maze and laid out in what is usually claimed to be Kent's very first essay in 'artful Confusion', that 'close Imitation of Nature' that Castell–Pliny had urged and which would soon be perfected by Kent at Esher and at Stowe.

Perfection, however, was not achieved at Chiswick. The New River has a few token irregularities in its banks, but its main course is still canal-like. Earth removed when it was being dug out was piled up to create an awkward artificial bank that never feels natural and that has long ago lost its always limited views of the distant Thames. But Kent's real mistake was the Cascade. He drew more sketches for this than for any other single feature at Chiswick,[17] but at this stage in his career he had not taken in Pope's exordium: 'in all let Nature never be forgot'. His Cascade was and remains a mistake. It is in the wrong place, it looks unnatural and it has never worked properly.

Kent's concept was theatrical but the hydraulics behind it were hopeless. His aim was to dramatise the carriage approach to the Villa from the Burlington Lane Gate. The drive runs along in the shadow of that artificial terrace and then, as it breaks out on the left with a view of the head of the New River and the Villa half-seen through a few trees, Kent planned on the right that there would be the roar of the cataract tumbling down from the grotto openings of rough rock to create a water splash across the drive before falling down through another storey of grotto arches into the New River. That was the idea. The reality was that Kent had created a small, hidden reservoir up at the top end of the terrace.

Water had to be pumped up into this by hand. It could never have looked natural as the water emerged up in the air out of the end of the terrace and it only produced a flow lasting for a minute or two. In 1743 Charlotte Boyle described its performance to her mother: 'I was on Saturday to see the Chain pump work up the spring, the water comes into the river very fast, but it dry's up in a minute.'[18]

When an important guest was expected one servant must have been posted at the Burlington Lane Gate end of the terrace to signal to another standing at the Cascade as the carriage swept in from the road. Then, with luck, the waters would be released and by the time the carriage reached the head of the New River there would be an impressive flow from the upper grotto arch, the carriage would splash through it and, by the time the water from the reservoir was exhausted, the carriage would have arrived in the forecourt of the Villa. Heath Robinson never invented anything more unreliable or more ridiculous. Even today the Cascade is proving impractical. An extensive and not altogether happy programme of restoration was carried through a few years ago by the local authorities and their commemorative plaque claims that, now electricity has taken over the pumping function, the problem has been solved. However, the Cascade is still as dry as a bone.

Even if it had worked the water would have been flowing in the wrong direction, away from the Thames, not towards it. A simple and more reliable cataract could have been created by damming up the Bollo Brook and letting it tumble down a two-foot drop without the need for pumps. It would have been interesting to have eavesdropped on the conversations between Burlington and Kent the first time the Cascade malfunctioned. That exchange of views might explain why Lord Burlington, whose cash flow was as unreliable as the Cascade, never risked money on the sensitive schemes for water gardens further up the New River which Kent had sketched out for him.[19]

Poor Kent, with the best of Castellian intentions, had made every possible mistake, but the impressive feature about this comic episode is that he learnt from his errors. His friend Pope had been perfectly correct in urging awareness of the possibilities of any given site. In flat, well-watered Chiswick those water gardens that Kent went on to sketch would have been the ideal solution. The actual idea of running a carriage drive on a shelf between two waterfalls was dramatic and inspired – if only it had been laid out on some steeply sloping hillside. The trouble was that

Middlesex is not the Apennines. But those impressive grotto mouths which Kent drew so industriously would work perfectly some fifteen years later when he applied them to the gentle slopes of Venus's Vale at Rousham. Chiswick's importance was that it was a harsh learning experience. It has to be hoped that, after the carriage of an important visitor had driven past a completely waterless cataract, or even been doused in the first rush of a delayed water release, Kent and his patron would have the grace to smile sheepishly.

There was, and still is, that second Chiswick, the vision on paper: an invaluable record of Kent's creative mind being applied, possibly for the first time, to the possible relationships between trees, sculpture, small buildings and water features. It is treasured away at Chatsworth and it is in these sketches that the concept of the English Arcadian Garden can be traced in one witty improvisation after another. They are only readily accessible today in John Harris's invaluable book, the catalogue for an exhibition held in Montreal in 1994, and in Pittsburgh and London in 1995.[20] Large reproductions of them should be hung upon the walls of the café-restaurant in Chiswick's grounds, where they might inspire the appropriate authorities to be more restorative in their responses to the surviving hedges, paths and thickets of the place.

If we were fortunate enough to have the sketches and maquettes that Michelangelo must have made in preparation for his *David* or Shakespeare's commonplace book for the years of his great tragedies, how revered and informative they would be. But it is no exaggeration to rate these Kent sketches as highly. In revealing freshness of detail they preserve the origins of a new way of looking at the English landscape through the eyes of historicist fantasy. In one wonderful piece of nonsense Kent was proposing to top that outrageous Cascade with a two-storey octagonal temple, perhaps a lodging for a permanent sluice keeper and pumper![21] In another a Negro brings drinks, three dogs scamper and a lady curtseys before a delicious composition of one term-studded corner of the Exedra seen in front of the Ionic Temple's portico with thin young trees providing a veil.[22] It is enough to send one off to see if the vista still survives; and the wonder is that it does, though a fence has been added to stop people drowning themselves in the Orange Tree Garden pool, and the stone lion has been moved. Kent drew Georgian England as the average twenty-first-century Georgian enthusiast likes to envisage it.

The essence of a future Kent parkscape would be glimpses of classical order in miniature seen through a curtain of foliage. As a bonus there would be Plinian vistas ranged beyond. One pen and wash study has what would become the Temple of British Worthies at Stowe sited here in Chiswick.[23] Another shows an infinitely more satisfying, faintly pencilled exedra close to that which would finally be set up in Chiswick's grounds.[24] What Kent was proposing was not so much the murder of the formal garden as a poetic way of retaining the classical resonances of it while gently removing its formality. The breadth of Burlington's sensibility is demonstrated by the fact that he allowed Kent to get on with it, while ravaging his own bank account in the process.

It would be unscholarly and mean spirited to leave this chapter without asking several pertinent questions. Would all this visual experiment, these Chiswick delights and disasters, have taken place if that obscure classical scholar Robert Castell had not been paid by Lord Burlington to deliver a message which Burlington would rather not have published? Were the implications of Roman literature relating to natural scenery and consequent garden design so inevitable that they would have come out in any case? Would Kent have had the natural perception to 'leap the fence' without being pushed over it by Castell? Why was it the unknown Castell and not the famous classical scholar and poet Alexander Pope who made the point so tellingly and with such irresistible plans and illustrations? Was the entire Georgian devotion to the ritual of the cold bath a shamefaced response to what Castell made absolutely clear: that the most important rooms in any big Roman villa were the bathrooms? If an English lord really wanted to be Augustan in his lifestyle he would have to bathe often and in company for preference. Lord Burlington may have been disturbed by the moral implications of what he had paid Robert Castell to publish and left him, the man who first printed the idea of an English Arcadian Garden, to die of smallpox in a debtors' prison.

14
From antique brilliance to sumptuous decadence

In 1725 Kent was riding very high indeed. If the dates attributed to his commissions are to be believed – and they do vary widely – he was at one and the same time engaged in decorating for the old King George I at Kensington, for the Duke of Chandos at Canons, Lord Burlington at Chiswick, the Earl of Lichfield at Ditchley and Viscount Townshend at Raynham. So, with a viscount, an earl or two, a duke and the King himself, all eager to employ him, how much higher could he go? The answer is simple: to be asked to decorate, not some enlarged town house like Kensington Palace, but a real palace for the real ruler, the Grand Vizier, the 'Great Man', as he was deferentially referred to, Sir Robert Walpole, already four years into his twenty-year term as First Lord of the Treasury. That was the crowning accolade; and it was just about to come Kent's way by his usual contriving.

Five, and then six, commissions, all being worked upon at once may appear an impossible burden for one man. But these were not for Kent the garden designer nor Kent the architect; they were for Kent the interior decorator, which explains the uncertainty over dates. His work at Raynham in Norfolk, for instance, is dated to about 1731 by Margaret Jourdain, but by Christopher Hussey to about 1727, by Howard Colvin to 1728–9, and by Michael Wilson to 1725–32, and they are all likely to be correct. Anyone who has endured the painful experience of having a house redecorated will have some woeful anecdote to tell of workmen who did not turn up on the expected day, of special paints or materials that failed to arrive, of misadventures with the weather, or dreadful discoveries of dry rot. If we recall how long Kent kept Sir John Chester of Chicheley Hall waiting for a canvas not much longer than its title, *Herse and her Sisters a sacrificing to Flora, and Mercury a flying when he fell in love with her*, the apparent disparity in the dating becomes instead an accuracy of record.

As an interior decorator Kent's first duty would be to liaise with the master and the mistress of the house and then to employ and manipulate someone more experienced and practical than himself to turn his amusing, rough sketches into precise, measured designs. Most of Kent's ceilings are canvases which he will have painted in a studio and later had hoisted into position. Only rarely, as on the Kensington staircase, did he and his assistant paint directly on to a plaster surface. Then would come all the trying, day-to-day, business of cajoling, ranting and treating the craftsmen, joiners in particular, but also metal workers and fabric importers, into an understanding and a deadline. This raises the interesting question: where was Kent's studio or workshop? Had he commandeered a stable loft at Burlington House, or did his house in Saville Street, usually rented out, have convenient mews buildings? Somehow it seems unlikely that Kent ever kept a horse and carriage or employed a coachman and a stable boy, so there may have been ample spare premises at the back.

Pope, who was invariably spiteful about everyone except his immediate benefactors, implies that Kent drank readily, if not excessively. Sir Thomas Robinson, who was an admirer of Kent's garden designs and interior effects, states confidently:

> The Signior, as he was call'd, often gave his orders when he was full of claret [which from the context could hardly have been at the dinner table, and suggests therefore an all-day intake of alcohol], and he did not perhaps see the work for several months after; he had indeed a pretty concise tho' arbitrary manner to set all right, for he would order, without consulting his employers, three or four hundred pounds of work or more to be pull'd down, and then correct the plan and bring it to what it ought to have been at first.[1]

This was anecdotal but quite plausible. That bequest in Kent's will of 'the Busto of Michel Angelo with wooden term' to Mr Thomas Ripley, who had worked with him or for him, sounds like a grateful remembrance to the skilled draughtsman and master builder who had helped Kent out at Raynham. But when that cornice in the gallery at Chiswick ended up two feet high and in the wrong place, Henry Flitcroft, Lord Burlington's new young draughtsman, had sounded no warning bells. This could explain why Flitcroft was not mentioned in the will. No bustos for a young man who had left Kent looking foolish. All of which bumbling and improvisation leaves the question open: why was the English Establishment, and ultimately Robert Walpole at its pinnacle, so ready to engage with this cheerful opportunist? Burlington had obviously enabled him to get his foot in the door, but why, subsequently, was that door left so wide open? The explanation is that Kent had contrived, from very early on, to associate his name closely with one brilliant gimmick, a secret weapon of persuasion perfectly shaped to have everyone, from the old German King downwards and brash, worldly Sir Robert Walpole in particular, clamouring for the Kentian touch.

If we consider, for a moment, what Kent's name is automatically associated with today, the answer is obvious. We do not describe a garden layout as 'Kentian', nor any style of architecture as 'Kentian', though Kent did design some notable gardens and buildings. But when we see a piece of gilded furniture, designed in a chunky, unashamedly figurative Baroque, a set piece of highly skilled softwood carving, every amateur connoisseur recognises it as 'Kentian'.[2] So confidently, indeed, that it comes as a shock when touring splendid Roman palaces like the Pamphilj and the Doria Pamphilj or, if an introduction has been acquired, the Quirinale, to find 'Kentian' side tables, thrones and chairs that must have been made before Kent was even born, certainly before he arrived in Italy in 1709.

A misplaced feeling of patriotism seems to have made some authorities reluctant to admit Kent's open plagiarism. Margaret Jourdain, usually so sound in her judgement, writes grudgingly that Kent's furniture at Houghton and Chiswick 'shows some slight influence of Venetian work of the sixteenth century',[3] even though he had spent nine years in Rome and fewer than nine weeks in Venice.[4] It was that natural nostalgia of Roman aristocrats, many of whom claimed senatorial descent, for the Imperial Rome of the Caesars, that made the figurative motifs of their chairs and tables so appealing to the English nobility, at a time when they were trying to award themselves Britannic togas and to be sculpted wearing them on their funeral monuments.

With their fat, naked babies, almost life-size, their fiercely taloned eagles, sexually ambiguous harpies and roaring lions, Kent's theatrical creations bowled the English aristocracy over on sight. Dangling swags of fruit and flowers hang between the legs of settees. Fish scales, a device copied from Nicholas Pineau, acanthus scrolls, satyr masks and husks infest the legs themselves. Not only were they covetable museum pieces to be bequeathed reverently to a son or daughter, but they, more than any of Kent's other decorative devices, his chimneypieces, overmantels or mirrors, must have struck the naive English as having a convincingly antique and authentic Roman air, such a change from the spindly, upright propriety of Carolean furniture. It is significant that the golden dolphin side tables and the sphinx-supported tables that Kent delivered for the Cupola Room at Kensington no longer rest there. The royals have spirited them away to Windsor, just as the Devonshires have taken some of Chiswick's best side tables away to Chatsworth, because such furniture automatically declares the room in which it stands as being one of superior magnificence. Kentian furniture is not for use; it does not encourage lounging. As Sir William Chambers pointed out: 'A hall or saloon large enough to receive company of sixty or one hundred persons can be furnished adequately with six or eight chairs and a couple of tables.'[5] On formal occasions Georgians stood up; good furniture was to be looked at, not sat upon, hence one Kentian chair to ten well-bred Georgian gentry.

Kent would never, of course, have carved a single, plump-cheeked cherub or heavy garland himself. The designs which he imposed upon firms like Turner, Hill and Pitter in the Strand and upon cabinet makers like James Moore and Thomas Roberts, must have caused consternation when they were delivered, occasioning a frantic quest for experienced Italian wood carvers. Pyne's *Royal Residences* shows, in its illustrations of Kensington Palace, couchant sphinxes supporting a marble slab in the Dining Room and four similar supports in the Cupola Room, with yet another such table in the Queen's Bedroom.[6] Jourdain, who was writing in 1948, a year of the Pevsnerian ascendancy and Bauhaus values, remarks apologetically that 'Kent's furniture is overweighted by ornament', but 'these qualities were in demand'.[7] She supposes that Guelfi may have done much of the carving; an interesting suggestion as he certainly carved the cherubs over the doors in the Fine Rooms at Burlington House. Perhaps we exaggerate his artistic status and he was basically a skilled craftsman like the stuccodores Artari and Vassalli, who were working here at the same time. One staggering piece of furniture in Houghton has birds in cages carved within its frail legs. The curious thing about this fashion is that nothing could be more remote from the severe Roman antiquity that Lord Burlington was aiming to suggest. Kent was actually bringing the Baroque, that European stylistic episode which England never really noticed, in by the back door during just those decades when states like France, Germany and Kent's Italy were easing into the more refined and delicate Rococo. It was the price of being an insular power, defended by the Channel from both military invasion and current continental high fashion. Kent's design career would be spent either trying to accord Inigo Jones with the Baroque or finding substitutes for the Rococo fashions he was missing.

There is a striking antithesis between Kent's career as a garden designer and his career as an interior decorator. Beginning with the garden at Chiswick, Kent made all his errors early, before he had fully worked out an Arcadian vision. With his interiors, however, he had, early on, contrived an acceptable eighteenth-century compromise with a real Roman Antique style. He began confident, assured and restrained at Ditchley and collapsed afterwards, especially at Houghton, into the temptations of decorative excess, what the 2nd Earl of Oxford, admittedly a cantankerous old wretch, described as 'neither magnificent nor beautiful . . . a very great expenses without either judgement or taste'.[8] One of the central questions of this book must be whether Lord Oxford's judgement was a fair one, but it is not easily answered.

The commission to decorate the reception rooms of Ditchley, the next-door park to Blenheim, for George Lee, the Jacobite Earl of Lichfield, between 1724 and 1725 was Kent's first country house opportunity and he took it brilliantly. Burlington had brought him back from Italy expressly to devise a new 'gusto' that would satisfy the dead Earl of Shaftesbury's appeal for a senatorial style, one that would convey ancient Rome in an acceptable contemporary idiom. In the Entrance Hall at Ditchley, Kent delivered exactly that, a space that was ordered, symmetrical and grand, yet with more than a touch of raw pagan richness: beast-head masks and reminders of all the old gods. The house is now a very superior conference centre, only rarely open to the general public and consequently not as well known as it should be. That descriptive term 'house on the cusp' – one between two styles – may be overused, but Ditchley truly deserves it. Kent was an integral part in the change in Ditchley's interiors from a laboured Baroque to whatever it was that the ardent amateur Burlington was attempting to project. If only Burlington could have controlled his itch to interfere and reined back his paid spy and amanuensis, Henry Flitcroft, Ditchley might have had a suite of reception rooms that would have anticipated the neo-classicism of Robert Adam by thirty-four years and set the whole country on a style of interior decoration infinitely more rewarding than the warmed-up Inigo Jones style which Burlington foolishly decided to champion and that Flitcroft practised in his second-hand pastiche.

It was here at Ditchley that Lord Burlington's grand project faltered. He had the new style that he was looking for in his grasp, or at least in William Kent's grasp, and he let it escape him. Exactly what happened is not recorded. Perhaps the preparation for the book, *Some Designs of Inigo Jones*, on which he and Flitcroft were working for publication in 1727, had persuaded him that a simple revival of Jones's Caroline classicism would be more suitable, more patriotic, than the Roman revival he had originally considered. That seems most likely as the other reception rooms at Ditchley on which Kent and Flitcroft worked are tame Caroline affairs with just the occasional flash of Kentian invention: Medusa heads writhing with snakes in the frieze of the Drawing Room, and an obvious Kentian overmantel in the Velvet Room. It is, of course, possible that the Earl of Lichfield became uneasy when he saw what Kent had delivered in his Hall. Whatever the cause, this house was not only on the cusp between Baroque and Palladian, it was on the cusp of Roman Antique and Caroline revival.

James Gibbs originally designed the house, but Francis Smith had actually presided over its erection between 1720 and 1722.[9] Smith was a man who usually made his country seats look as much like a row of houses on a town square as possible. Consequently Ditchley has an impressive but unfinished appearance with a bare, straight roofline above rows and rows of windows. Gibbs had proposed a pediment and four roof cupolas, as at Houghton, but Smith dismissed these as unworthy frivolities. A statue of Loyalty in senator's dress does, however, confront another of Fame with her trumpet on that flat, unsatisfying attic line. This uninventive Baroque central block makes a reluctant move in a Palladian direction with quadrant arms leading to two substantial seven-bay pavilions. It was upon the interiors of this irresolute complexity that Kent was required to impose a style suggestive of Roman antiquity.

A staccato order of disciplined features, three to each side and ranged in three tiers, prevails, their stone colour standing out in bold contrast against the twilight dark of the bistre painted walls. Underneath these individual decorative events runs a wicked Kentian subtext of beast heads. Lion-head masks suspend lamps on long chains; if two thick swags of carving meet they are seized by the teeth of a snarling lion, and where, over his chimneypiece, Kent usually designs a nymph's head or some mythical scene, here on the Hall's chimneypiece is a sinisterly distorted mask which resolves, on close inspection, into the pelt of a flayed lion as worn by Hercules over his shoulders. It imparts an authentic cruelty; in his nine Roman years Kent had noticed the savagery behind the imperial façades. Where Robert Adam was to reach out to neo-classicism in shallow relief, Kent worked by bold projection. Every feature upon the walls, the pediments in particular, is actively three-dimensional, lending the room an exterior air as in an open atrium. Uppermost are circular plaster reliefs, from the Arch of Constantine in the Forum, men and horses alternating with solemn sacrifices to the gods in the rectangular ones. Busts of worthies on projecting brackets are sited over the minor doors and Kent's two insipid paintings of the loves of Venus and Diana on the lowest tier. The principal doors and the niches for statues are treated as columned tabernacles and on their pediments female pairs of the Arts and Sciences lounge in Michelangelesque attitudes.

All this Roman order was refurbished in the 1930s by a wealthy American couple, Ronald and Nancy Tree; so the gold leaf of the telescopes, measuring rules, lyres and books of these reclining white women is more than a little suspect. But, bearing in mind those golden statues in the Cupola Room at Kensington, if the colouring is not Kent's original idea then it ought to be. Eventually, Ronald Tree, by assiduous fox hunting, got accepted as a Conservative candidate and was elected to Parliament. He wrote retrospectively: 'The clouds of war were gathering but they failed to dim the delights of Ditchley, which we dared to dream would be eternal.'[10] When the storm did break and the Blitz was raining bombs down on London, Winston Churchill had retired to Ditchley on the dangerous nights of full moon for fourteen weekends of peace and tranquillity, very different to the pre-war Ditchley he had known, when Oliver Messel set up a marquee for a ball and decorated it with Negro heads wearing feathered hats and ropes of pearls – pure Kent-style campery.[11] Ditchley's interiors do seem to smack of decadence, of Caligula rather than Augustus.

Kent seems to have sniffed that scent of playful corruption when he first arrived at the half-completed house and found the master stuccodores, Giuseppe Artari, Francesco Serena and Francesco Vassalli, indulging their fantasies without restraint in the Dining Room (now the Saloon), the next room through after the Hall. Their stucco work is shallow and flowing, quite unlike what Kent went on to design. Their cherubs embrace each other cheerfully, wyvern beasts with long curly tails twist among the scroll work and there are masks everywhere, flanking the chimneypiece and even embroidered on Minerva's skirt in one of the panels. Kent borrowed the masks but imposed his quite different order upon the Hall. None of the staccato features on his walls touches any other feature, but in the room next door every feature is connected. Lord Burlington's watchful spy, Henry Flitcroft, may have kept Kent in that disciplined mood of decoration. Flitcroft's reports back to Burlington may have brought him down to Ditchley to persuade either Kent or Lord Lichfield to give up the Roman Antique and make a disastrous switch in subsequent rooms to the white-and-gold work with broken pediments, shallow wreaths and palms that Inigo Jones and his pupil, John Webb, had established in the Caroline rooms of Wilton House some eighty years before.

There was a certain curious parallelism between Kent and Flitcroft's relationships with Burlington. It is always assumed that Kent became the Earl's friend during those long weeks of a Roman winter when Burlington was lying in bed, sick with a fever. Flitcroft became close to Burlington when, as a young carpenter, he fell from scaffolding in Burlington House and broke his leg.[12] While he was being nursed back to health by his considerate and kindly employer, Burlington discovered Flitcroft's talent for drawing, engaged him to realise his schemes and advanced him to government posts as a reward. Flitcroft went on to an active but unremarkable career as an architect of churches, country and town houses. At Ditchley he is recorded as being paid 'for designing 2 sorts of table frames', which Hussey believes is a reference to the Kent-style settees and side tables in the Hall.[13]

In contrast with these pieces of furniture, which have a token show of claw feet and scallop shells, the Drawing Room has two side tables that could be plausibly ranked as the finest examples of Kent's furniture to have survived anywhere in Britain. Their presence in Ditchley is accidental; they were given to one of the Trees' sons by his aunt who owned

Mereworth Castle,[14] but they deserve mention for their quite astonishing excellence and delightful finish. The eagles have a superb arrogant and heraldic grace; their clawed feet rest upon heaps of robustly carved shells and, most perfectionist detail of all, the bases upon which they stand have been covered with the representation of infinite grains of sand. If anything could raise Kent's reputation among the aristocracy it would have been upon pieces like these two. They are not tables but artworks, sculpture to rank with the finest carving of Grinling Gibbons, and if they were made for Mereworth they would have been designed very early in his career.

Apart from these unique tables, where Kent's and Flitcroft's work has survived later Rococo and Chinoiserie additions, in the Drawing Room, Tapestry Room and State Bedroom, they were settling down into that predictable, chunky Baroque of boldly moulded shells in broken pediments set over any feature, overmantel or family portrait that required emphasis. Sometimes a nymph's or an eagle's head takes the place of the shell cliché. Palms and garlands are always symmetrically paired. Henry Cheere's white marble chimneypieces have a feeling of Inigo Jones's discreet order about them, and it is no accident that the ubiquitous Flitcroft was, at this period, drawing, under Burlington's patronage, the illustrations for Kent's book, *The Designs of Inigo Jones*. At Ditchley, Burlington still had his hands on the levers and he was behaving like a nervous amateur. Kent needed to get away.

Working for a Jacobite sympathiser was not, however, a tactically clever move in the late 1720s, and Kent's contemporary involvement with the redecoration of Raynham Hall in Norfolk for Viscount Charles (Turnip) Townshend was a shrewd step sideways, back into the Whig elite. It meant that he would be working for the one man whom Sir Robert Walpole always felt he had to outpoint, his brother-in-law. The Townshends had been high ranking in the East Anglian hierarchy when the Walpoles had been mere squires of Houghton. Even when Sir Robert had made himself securely First Lord of the Treasury and First Minister by restoring financial stability after the bursting of the South Sea Bubble in 1720, Charles Townshend was, as Secretary of State for the South with responsibility for foreign affairs, still Walpole's political partner and almost equal. To seal their long-standing alliance Townshend had taken, as his second wife, Walpole's sister, but underlying tensions remained. Walpole had a bawdy sense of humour and a great gift for tactical friendships, but Townshend was, according to Lord Hervey, 'rash in his undertakings, violent in his proceedings, haughty in his carriage, brutal in his expressions . . . so captious that he would often take offence where nobody meant to give it'.[15]

Passions had been simmering over a treaty Townshend had concluded with the old enemy, France, but the final rupture came one evening at Windsor when Queen Caroline asked Townshend where he had dined that day. When he replied 'at home with Lord and Lady Trevor', Sir Robert put in smilingly, 'My Lord, Madam, I think is grown coquet from a long widowhood, and has some design upon Lady Trevor's virtue.'[16] As Lady Trevor was not only renowned for her strict life and conversation, but had 'the most virtuous forbidding countenance that natural ugliness, age, and smallpox ever compounded',[17] this was meant as a joke. But Townshend was furious, declared that he had neither the constitution, the purse nor the conscience to indulge in 'follies and immoralities that are hardly excusable when youth and idleness makes us most liable to such temptations'.[18] His voice trembled, his face went pale and every limb shook with passion. But Sir Robert, who never lost his temper, just smiled again and said mildly, 'What, my Lord, all this for Lady Trevor?'[19] The Queen was embarrassed and immediately changed the subject, but there was never a real reconciliation.

It was typical of Kent that he could turn their hostility to his advantage and serve in succession two such bitter enemies. Their houses were integral to their rivalry. The foundation stone of Sir Robert's Houghton was laid in 1722 and, as Hervey noticed,

> Lord Townshed looked upon his own seat at Raynham as the metropolis of Norfolk, was proud of the superiority, and considered every stone that augmented the splendour of Houghton as a diminution of the grandeur of Raynham.[20]

Kent began the redecoration of Raynham in 1725 and the long campaign of decoration at Houghton in 1726, very much to his own profit. So he must have known exactly what the situation was and how to manipulate it.

Raynham has a very complex building history and its middle section was reputed, on no sure evidence, to have been designed by Inigo Jones. Kent was not, therefore, free to design afresh, and he was working for a difficult employer. At Houghton, in contrast, he would have a whole new palace, half-Gibbs, half-Campbell, to decorate with a virtually unlimited budget and a patron of wit, charm and gross appetites to satisfy. Houghton was to be far and away Kent's most important commission, work designed with the eyes of the nation upon him and executed free at last from the moderating influences of Lord Burlington and his spies. It is interesting, therefore, how many critics of the past and the present tend to find Raynham more acceptable. The lake at Raynham pleased both Lord Hervey and Lord Oxford; Houghton was waterless, the house being supplied from a very deep well. While rapturing on about Raynham's park neither Hervey nor Oxford had a good word to say about Kent's refurbishing of the house. 'The rooms are fitted up by Mr Kent', Lord Oxford began,

> and consequently there is a great deal of gilding; very clumsy over-charged chimney pieces to the great waste of fine marble. Kent has parted the dining room to make a sort of buffet, by the arch of Severus; surely a most preposterous thing to introduce a building in a room, which was designed to stand in the street.[21]

In a letter of 21 July 1731 to Prince Frederick, Lord Hervey was equally dismissive: 'Kent, gilding and expense can add nothing to the house. It is not the worse for his having seen Houghton, though I believe he is. For if he had liked that house less I fancy he had liked the Master better'; this cryptic comment concluded with 'ce cy est seulement entre nous'.[22] In typical Hervey fashion he was keeping in with both the Prince and his parents.

Today, Raynham Hall is best enjoyed as a nervous anticipation for much richer interiors at Houghton, a light, civilised, unpretentious place. The Entrance Hall is now confidently attributed to Thomas Ripley by it owners (though not by Howard Colvin). Intensely rectangular, it has a giant Ionic order and a cornice that seems preparing to support a gallery yet never achieves one. The ceiling and the detail are Jonesian. Kent's stairs are a clear try out for Houghton with golden figures of helmeted goddesses, a nude Hercules, urns, wreaths and drops on a bistre background, antique in impact and amateurish. The buffet that Lord Oxford condemned is the merest shadow of the glorious marble version that Kent was able to create at Houghton. Easily the most memorable interior at Raynham is the Belisarius Room where Kent painted Fame lauding Alexander Pope in the centre of the most outrageously heavy plaster wreath in Britain. Experts insist that this prodigy must be of the seventeenth century as each flower is individually moulded; but if Kent did not actually design it he clearly loved it and it would be satisfying to attribute it to his mischievous creativity.

At Houghton there is a better case for attributing a feature to Kentian mischief: those four tea-cosy domes that soften and enliven the stern geometry of the central block. Campbell had proposed four angular pavilions, harsh and geometrically Palladian. Everyone knew about them because he had published the design in his *Vitruvius Britannicus*. So what, or more accurately who, persuaded Sir Robert to scrap them for the cheerful Baroque comforters? As John Harris has explained, there are many of James Gibbs's Italian touches to Houghton's window architraves and those domes are pure Gibbs.[23] But who was the insidious Baroque infiltrator? It cannot be proven, but Kent had just come from decorating Ditchley, a wilfully unfinished Gibbs house with a long, harsh roofline unrelieved even by the slope of leads. Yet Gibbs's plans clearly called for two lively domes to enhance the roofline. Did Kent put a word into Sir Robert's ear and urge the switch to four domes? It would certainly have been Kent's Baroque preference and there seems to have been a hostility between Kent and Campbell, with the latter falling out of Burlington's favour once Kent was back in England. Whatever strings were pulled the domes are happily un-English and extrovert. Christopher Hussey bewailed the lack of drums but drums would have made the whole palace look like an upturned footstool.[24]

As it is, Houghton makes a tremendous statement for all its cross of styles. If the English were not to follow on from Vanbrugh's intensely individual castellated Baroque, at least they now had, from their Prime Minister if not from their King, a great house by any continental standard and one easily copied. It sits there serenely in its dull green park, the wide wings of its side pavilions swooping out in the wrong, or garden, direction, its entrance front in faintly golden Whitby limestone, able to impress without the support of wings; the poor relation stable block in crumbling, dark-brown Snettisham carstone with red-brick interior walls is set irrelevantly a hundred yards away for inconvenience. It was a house that even Walpole's enemies had to acknowledge as a national statement. As Lord Oxford spluttered crossly: 'Some admire it because it belongs to the first Minister; others envy it because it is his, and consequently rail at it.'[25] Oxford proceeded to rail, exposing his own poor judgement, enviously listing its paintings, its Laocoön, its Stone Hall ('very dark'), its lantern ('very ugly'), the Gladiator ('very ill-placed'), the State Bedroom ('very indifferent') and added, 'the design is Kent's, which is no addition to it'.[26]

Lord Hervey, the third party in the team – of Walpole, Hervey and Queen Caroline – which controlled the irascible King George II and virtually ran the country, could afford to be more honest. He thought the ceiling of the Stone Hall 'the best executed of anything I ever saw in stucco in any country', and Kent's gold-on-bistre staircase 'the gayest, cheerfulest and prettiest thing I ever saw; some very beautiful heresies in the particulars, and the result of the whole more charming than any bigotry I ever saw'.[27] And Hervey, it should be remembered, disliked Kent for his good relations with the Queen, Hervey's platonic mistress. He ended his letter of description to Prince Frederick with:

> In short, I think his [Walpole's] house has all the beauties of regularity without the inconveniences; and wherever he has deviated from the established religion of the architect's [Campbell's Palladianism] I believe Your Royal Highness would say he had found his account in being a libertine.[28]

Hervey's descriptive writing is usually rewardingly gnomic.

Despite his eminence and his twenty-year reign, few historians have been able to understand Sir Robert, the creator of this pattern for future designers; and as usual William Kent has left not a word of record to explain the long labour for his greatest patron. Writers pick up Walpole's cynical 'Every man has his price', or his despairing words to Henry Pelham, his closest political friend: 'When you have the same experience of mankind as myself you will go near to hate the human species.'[29] His physical appearance is only remembered through Queen Caroline's inability to believe that his mistress, and later second wife, Maria Skerrett, could ever have loved him: 'that poor man – avec ce gros corps, ces jambs enflée, et ce vilain ventre'.[30] But if we forget for a moment the great beer belly and the earthy humour, there was another Walpole, one recalled in Lady Mary Wortley Montagu's love-lorn poem:

These were the lively eyes and rosey hue
Of Robin's face, when Robin first I knew,
The gay companion and the favourite guest,
Loved without awe, and without views caressed.
His cheerful smile and honest open look
Added new graces to the truths he spoke.
Then every man found something to commend,
The pleasant neighbour and the worthy friend;
The gen'rous master of a private house,
The tender father and indulgent spouse.[31]

While, to use Sir Robert's own words, there is the self-confessed simple countryman writing to a friend to urge the attractions of Houghton in 1743:

> This place affords no news, no subject of amusement and entertainment to a fine Gentleman. Men of wit and pleasure about town understand not the language, nor taste the charms of the inanimate world: my flatterers here are all mutes, the Oaks and Beeches and the Chestnuts seem to contend which shall best please the Lord of the Manor, they will not lie.[32]

And in the same letter, here is the art lover confessing his pleasure in his paintings:

> Within doors we come a little nearer to real life and admire upon the almost speaking Canvas, all the airs and graces which the proudest of town ladies can boast, with these I am satisfied as they gratify me with all I wish and all I want, and expect nothing in return which I am not able to give.[33]

This is a more plausible picture of the man who virtually bankrupted himself urging William Kent in room after room to provide new delights, more surprises, further excesses of marble, velvet, gilded plaster, lolling beauties, romping cherubs and muscular athletes. It was Vertue who noted the sheer unpredictable variety of Houghton's interiors once that orderly and, save for the domes, predictable exterior had been penetrated. Spaces that were 'all finely adorned and furnished with great variety, rich furniture, carving, gilding, marble and stucco works – every room in a different manner'.[34]

A house by Robert Adam has a stylistic sequence, variously yet artistically connected. Here in a Kent house where, marvellously, everything except the paintings has been retained, there is little to connect one room stylistically with another: Inigo Jones, Italian Baroque, Upholsterer's Heaven, all surge together. The seduction of Kent's style lies in an overt vulgarity and enjoyable richness of textures and colours which confuse any normal aesthetic judgement. Many doors, windows and cornices are recognisably Palladian, but the combined effect is not Palladian in any sense; it is what used to be called 'Curzon Street Baroque'.[35] Between them, Sir Robert and Kent threw good taste to the winds: 'Want a bed?' 'Spend £1000 on it.' 'Will that cover the lot?' 'No, only the curtains!' And still today we marvel at the bed, in Kent's favourite green velvet, much bedizened with gold and with the shell motif to end all shell motifs rising above it, almost to ceiling level. It catches the essence of Kent: invention and good taste pushed past their barriers into high campery. In a house of so many aesthetic outrages it is hard to know where to begin, but now that the entrance stairs have been demolished to save money, the beginning has to be in the basement, the 'Rustic'.

Long, low, ill lit and well heated with four fireplaces, it was from here that England was ruled. Every November, Sir Robert and his friends gathered for two weeks, with another week in July, to hunt, drink, eat and prepare for government. They were friends, not cronies, for Walpole had a huge talent for friendship and forgiveness: it was the secret of his political reign. The invaluable, though never completely reliable, Lord Hervey describes the sessions:

> Our company at Houghton swelled at last into so numerous a body that we used to sit down to dinner a snug little party of about thirty odd, up to the chin in beef, venison, geese, turkeys etc.; and generally over the chin in claret, strong beer and punch. We had Lords spiritual and temporal, besides commoners, parsons and freeholders innumerable. In public we drank loyal healths, talked of the times and cultivated popularity: in private we drew plans and cultivated the country.[36]

The atmosphere of those 'Norfolk Congresses', as Walpole called them, still lingers in the shadows of the Rustic with its glaring white nudities, not of Apollo or Daphne, but David and Goliath. Then comes the strangest of all Houghton's oddities. The Earl of Pembroke had given Walpole that famous statue in bronze of the Gladiator which Inigo Jones had set in the middle of The Grove at the end of the main axis of Wilton Garden: a rare gift indeed.[37] But to display it as dramatically as it deserved Kent devised a massive stone plinth on four columns entirely filling the well of the dark stairs up to the main floor. In the shadows Kent's gold-on-bistre shepherds, gods, scrolls and urns catch faintly what light there is. Was Kent remembering relics of Roman frescoes half-seen in the cavernous excavations of Nero's Golden House in Rome? On this plinth stands the Gladiator, presenting his bronze rump shamelessly to everyone climbing the stairs. It is Houghton at its most theatrical, and the Stone Hall, which the Gladiator threatens through an open door, is also pure theatre.

This is enormous and very cold, a grey Imperium of Caesar statues: Trajan, Commodus, Septimius Severus, line the walls with Sir Robert, in defiant immodesty, taking his place alongside Marcus Aurelius. The Laocoön cannot compete with the Gladiator, but there is a lovely Rysbrack plaque of Sacrifice to Diana to set up a hunting theme that rivals the imperial show. Huge park vistas of typical Norfolk nothingness can be seen through the windows. There are pairs of sexual-looking sphinxes in the corners and, the one possible false touch, there are caryatid women with pots on their heads. A gallery runs all the way around the Hall and above that, completely out of character yet exquisitely cheering, is Artari's gambol of cherubs in their naughtily playful race around a billowing cloudscape. If he had designed nothing but the Stone Hall and then dropped dead, William Kent would still deserve to be remembered.

Foolish, spiteful Horace Walpole, Sir Robert's son, claimed that his father, mistrusting Kent's skills as an architect, had restricted him to monochrome effects on the Stone Hall.[38] This is manifestly untrue. In every room of state opening off from the Stone Hall there is a new surge of colour, rarely in any coordinated scheme, but with pinks, greens, light blues as well as all the tobacco-stained creams and golds of Kent's standard 'Fine Rooms' display. Everyone will have a different favourite or quite possibly find them all indigestible; but this is the house to visit to find that the English eighteenth century, in its first half at least, was not necessarily tasteful or refined, but challenging and over the top. Robert Adam and Henry Holland would come later and extreme elegance would set in, but the 1720s and the 1730s were William Kent's decades of a last-ditch, experimental Baroque, haunted by the protests of Inigo Jones and, one suspects, the more audible complaints of Lord Burlington, though he had done little to contain Kent's exuberance at Chiswick. Here at Houghton Sir Robert and Kent were aesthetic soul mates and the Marble Parlour, the State Bedroom and the Saloon must contend for the title of 'Most impossibly Fine'.

The Saloon has the wildest menagerie of Kentian Baroque furniture, the Marble Parlour explores space more excitingly than any other room with the two vaulted caverns of its marble buffet in that half-purple Plymouth stone and Rysbrack's second masterpiece, his Roman Sacrifice. But the State Bedroom has one surprise that visitors, hypnotised by that green bed, might miss. Overhead is slung a Kent painting of Aurora composed around some daring perspectives that almost succeed, while Aurora herself offers a show of legs, half-revealed breast and coy sexuality that verges on the edge of soft pornography. The bed, Aurora and the tapestries of Venus and Adonis are clearly intended as an outright assault on the libido. Was the Duke of Lorraine, who spent a night or two there, carried away by it all?

For elegance after so much gilded smut, the Cabinet Room bears the palm, with one of Kent's very best towers of combined chimneypiece and soaring overmantel. As usual a broken pediment tops it all, with not one but two shell centrepieces and a nymph's head. The painting is not the original canvas. It is customary to wring the hands over the 3rd Earl's sale of most of his grandfather's pictures to the Empress Catherine of Russia. In fact the Cholmondeleys who succeeded Horace Walpole, the hapless 4th Earl, who never even lived in the house, have brought in some very fine and appropriate paintings. A cursory viewing of the ex-Walpole paintings, now hanging in the Hermitage, suggests that they were an average collection bought, as it were, by the yard from dealers by Sir Robert who never had the time to visit Italy and was satisfied by buxom women like Aurora.

Houghton's importance was for its own time, rather than for ours. We are merely appreciative or disturbed visitors. For its contemporaries it was a template and a statement of national pride. A Norfolk squire had shown the aristocracy something to aim at. With its subtle reservations, Sir Thomas

Robinson's judgement on the house after a long stay there at one of those notorious Congresses should be given the last word:

> It is the best house in the world for its size, capable of the greatest reception for company and the most convenient State apartments, very noble, especially the hall and saloon. The finishing of the inside is, I think, a pattern for all great houses that may hereafter be built; the vast quantity of mahogany, all the doors, window-shutters, the best staircase being entirely of that wood; the finest chimnies of statuary and other fine marbles; the ceilings in the modern taste by Italians, painted by Mr Kent and finely gilt; the furniture of the richest tapestry etc; the pictures hung on Genoa velvet and damask; this one article is the price of a good house, for in one drawing-room there are to the value of £3,000; in short the whole expense of this plan must be a prodigious sum, and, I think, all done in a fine taste . . . We were generally between 20 and 30 at two tables, and as much cheerfulness and good nature as I ever saw when the company was so numerous. [There] were only two ladies.[39]

It is Robinson's last sentence, that mention of 'only two ladies' to twenty-eight men which explains Houghton's contentious image and qualifies Kent's achievement. It is a man's house, rich and crowded with individual beauties, but no one would ever describe it as 'refined'.

15

Queen Caroline and a landscape on the cusp at Richmond Lodge

William Kent may have left a very meagre literary record of his thoughts and opinions, but he has left a remarkable trail of evidence testifying to his social dexterity and stylistic ambivalence. It is typical of his career that, while he was working at Houghton in an all-male environment to produce interiors of macho luxury, he was also being employed by Queen Caroline at Richmond Lodge, after 1727, to devise garden buildings of an imaginative fancy which can be fairly described as feminine. There would be essentially two elements to the developing Arcadian Garden: idealised natural landscapes and exotic garden pavilions with which to diversify these grounds. It was around Richmond Lodge, and to the Queen's direction, that Kent's playful, yet at the same time richly iconographic, garden buildings captured the attention of the nation in a way that Sir John Vanbrugh's earlier and ponderously splendid garden structures at Castle Howard had never done.[1] Royal approval and the modest expense of quite small buildings made an irresistible combination. All that was needed now was that second element, the idealised landscape of softly natural lawns and treescapes to contain these eclectic temples; but that second element was never perfected at Richmond, for various royal reasons.

Once she had become Queen with a substantial allowance at her disposal, Caroline borrowed Kent from Burlington. To have become Queen Caroline's architect for at least five garden pavilions in her Richmond Park, two of them – the Hermitage of 1732 and Merlin's Cave of 1735 – nationally celebrated and vigorously debated in polite journals, there must surely have been some quite intimate meeting of sympathetic minds. Those two principal buildings were unusual and they were the frames for a complex iconography that can reasonably be described as 'philosophical'. Because they aroused great interest they were widely imitated across the nation. There is, nevertheless, no record of how the Queen and her architect met, how Kent was directed or what Caroline, a very shrewd, highly-educated woman, thought of him. For a career in the eye of publicity and envy there are amazingly few anecdotes about Kent. Behind a screen of superficial good humour he was the invisible designer.

Only his sketches tell something of what gossip fails to reveal. He must have received some royal audience and congratulations for the theatrical magnificence of his Baroque Triumphal Arch.[2] He had designed this in order to dramatise the entrance on horseback into Westminster Hall of the King's Champion when he threw down a gauntlet at George and Caroline's Coronation Banquet on 11 October 1727. Four giant caryatids, one bare-breasted, and all thirty feet tall, representing Prosperity, Learning, Unity and the Arts, supported Fame, Neptune and Britannia on a pedimented Ionic entablature. Queen Caroline loved symbolism. In addition to her commissions for Kent, Caroline, in an act of admirably firm patronage, employed and tamed the geometrically inclined Charles Bridgeman. Between them Kent and Bridgeman created a garden-park at Richmond seductively different from Bridgeman's usual axial layouts of straight lines and circles. Caroline and Kent were presumably jointly responsible for the change in Bridgeman's method of design.[3]

Queen Caroline cannot, however, take all the credit for innovations in the direction of natural lines and wandering ways. In England, from the start of the eighteenth century, a mood of pastoral, Arcadian, and ultimately of Rococo, garden designs had been building up. Alexander Pope's *Pastorals* had been published in 1709. They are the reflections of Alexis, a shepherd boy and entirely Theocritan; so they inspired a fashion whereby entire parks were transformed to evoke an ideal vision of the ancient world. Addison's *Spectator* articles of 1712 had suggested persuasively that an entire estate could serve as a natural garden.[4] Stephen Switzer published his *The Nobleman, Gentleman, and Gardener's Recreation* in 1715, developing Addison's ideas more practically. His 1718 *Ichnographia Rustica* carried them further with attractive plans of vast garden-parks threaded by sinuous carriageways and studded with lakes and coppices.[5] He was a trained and professional gardener, and when he quoted from Pope's *Windsor Forest*, which celebrates a park well known, royal and natural, the poet and the professional were uniting significantly. Princess Caroline's 'Conference of Garden Lords' the following year had been a shrewd step further. From Leibniz she had learnt to look ahead to a new age.

The taming of Bridgeman is harder to trace in exact chronology, but some of the steps can be read from the 1734 Rocque plan of royal Richmond. The park was most unusual: well over half of it consisted of ordinary hedged farm fields, which had been left to provide partridge shoots for the permanently warlike King. George II was the last English king to have actually fought on a truly dangerous battlefield. His horse had been shot from under him at Oudenarde, and the general who was helping him to a new mount had been killed at his side. On the field of Dettingen, George was fearless, even ferocious, under fire. So those partridge fields were a social safety valve where he could blast away safely and give his wife time for civilised conversation with the diminutive, pretty and very witty Lord Hervey.

Hervey and the Queen were inseparable, a remarkable and completely sincere platonic relationship. That she should have accorded so closely with a man of such a civilised bisexual sensibility is the best proof of her own intelligence, as it is, conversely, of her husband George's trusting affection for her. They were a perfectly balanced trio; a typical entry from a Hervey letter to his lover, Stephen Fox, 'mon bien aimé', runs:

> The Court hunted again yesterday. I had the good fortune to be too late, and to be shut out of the park; for the ways of Richmond on those days are like the ways of Heaven – 'strait is the gate and few there be that enter thereat'. The King had no sport, and consequently a great deal of pleasure; for he was back again by twelve a clock, to the great satisfaction of his heart and ease of his derrière. I ride as usual every morning with the Queen; but Lord Halifax has taken it into his head of late two or three times to se fourrer dans la partie, et m'ennuye à me faire pleurer.[6]

In hunts across Richmond Park, upriver behind Richmond town, Hervey 'never saw the hounds but rode as usual the whole time by the Queen's chaise'.[7] Court life was conducted very much out in the parks and

(*Above left*) William Kent's father, William Cant, a prosperous Bridlington Old Town joiner, built this house for his family at 45 High Street in 1693. His son was born here and left the house to his niece's family. (*Above right*) Ogee arches of the Decorated Gothic period on the west front of Bridlington Priory which stands across The Green from Kent's schoolroom in The Bale, the Priory's 1388 Gatehouse.

Kent was given fifteen golden scudi by the congregation of San Giuliano dei Fiamminghi in the Via del Sudario, Rome for painting this *Apotheosis of St Julian* in 1717.

Kent's masterstroke in presentation was to introduce to the English aristocracy the fashion he had observed in Rome for 'Antique Imperial' furniture featuring eagles and various beasts, usually gilded and supporting heavy table tops.

Kent devised his 1733 Gothick inventions at Esher Place around the existing fifteenth-century Waynflete Tower. Now only the Tower survives in a suburban housing estate.

The Temple of Venus at Stowe (1731) was originally decorated with raunchy episodes from *The Faerie Queene* to serve as an Arcadian bordello.

Set on an island in the lake at Stowe, Kent's memorial to Congreve exemplifies its creator's whimsical, figurative and un-Palladian inclinations.

The conventional classicism of Kent's 1734 Temple of Ancient Virtue can be seen across the river of the Elysian Fields from his far more inventive exedra of British Worthies.

J. M. Rysbrack's 1733 monument in Blenheim Chapel to the great Duke of Marlborough was designed by Kent with his typical touches of humour and physicality.

More like an institution than a house, Holkham Hall (1734-65), seen here on its garden front, recycles an early Kent design for the Horse Guards Parade in Whitehall.

In the Marble Hall at Holkham Kent fused the Antique Roman with the Baroque in an interior which would have been even more theatrical with its statue of Jupiter.

The head of the Jupiter statue, bought during Coke's Grand Tour in 1717 and now kept in store, which should stand at the foot of the stairs in Holkham's Marble Hall.

In the 1730s Kent softened the lines of Bridgeman's round pond at Claremont, Surrey and added the Belisle Temple for the Duke of Newcastle's dab fishing.

With the Praeneste Arcade (1738-41), seen here from Venus Vale, Kent shaped an atmospheric viewing loggia to the natural folds of a hill above the river at Rousham, Oxfordshire.

The Gothick Mill at Rousham was created by Kent around an existing cottage to extend and enliven, together with an eyecatcher, the views from Rousham Gardens.

The Temple at Euston Hall, Suffolk was designed by Kent in 1746 for the Duke of Grafton, Lady Burlington's lover, and recalls the lost Bagnio at Carlton House.

In his posthumous Worcester Lodge for Badminton Park (completed 1750), Kent achieved the ultimate park marker, animating Palladian forms with Baroque thrust and power.

gardens, which could explain why so little was spent on modest royal houses like Richmond Lodge. English palaces were small by continental standards and offered scant privacy. As the Lord Halifax episode illustrates, social life could best be conducted out in the landscape where company could be selected and privacy assured. That explains the way Queen Caroline had shaped her grounds. The retained fields were sliced across by five straight avenues of chestnut trees for the most part, relics of the essentially dull gardens that George London had laid out for Ormonde.[8] In striking contrast with these seventeenth-century features were Caroline's Wildernesses, not just one, but five of them, three linked together near the Lodge, and all providing woodland walks for unobserved trysts and conversations secure from eavesdroppers. These, together with the game fields, came close to creating a *ferme ornée* years before Philip Southcote's famous ornamental farm, begun in 1734 at Woburn, near Chertsey in Surrey.[9] That will be what Caroline meant when she spoke to Egmont of 'helping Nature, not losing it in art'.

She had restricted Bridgeman to laying out these gentle, informal woods and to planting an Elm Amphitheatre instead of his usual intrusive, military-style, serried ranks or 'platoons' of trees.[10] Garden geometry was not, however, entirely ruled out. He was allowed to plant a Diagonal Wood and one of his trademark stepped clearings. The Duck Pond was rectangular and a straight Canal was dug from Richmond Lodge down to the Thames. Two old-fashioned viewing mounts were raised and Caroline extended the Duke of Ormonde's riverside terrace all the way down to Kew Green, where she bought more land and built a modest Queen's House with the generous £100,000 a year that Sir Robert Walpole had persuaded Parliament to vote her after the 1727 Coronation. The Queen's part in the bargain was to learn from Lord Hervey precisely which measures Walpole wanted the King to approve and then to use her influence on her husband to make sure that he did approve them. She was well paid for her role in the political arrangement and she spent a considerable portion of what she earned on William Kent, whom she had taken, as by the royal prerogative, from his work at Chiswick and Houghton. It was what the Queen actually paid Kent to design that made the works at Richmond Lodge so influential.

The Lodge itself suffered from damp and its walls were so thin that conversations in one bedroom could be heard in another. Apparently, an amateur, the Earl of Ranelagh, had superintended the construction for his friend the Duke of Ormonde.[11] The Queen might, therefore, have been expected to improve or even rebuild the Lodge. Instead she spent everything on the grounds. There was already the Duke's Summerhouse on the Thames bank, little more than a seat, but under Kent's direction another five garden buildings were raised in and around the Queen's Wildernesses, so the entire mood of life at Richmond was al fresco. A handsome Dairy for the Queen to play at being a milkmaid was constructed at the head of the new Canal. At its bottom end, where the Canal reached the river, Kent built a domed circular Temple on a mount and designed an altar for it. There was an elegantly refined Queen's Pavilion, hidden away in the woods.[12] Then Kent created the first of those two much more ambitious and iconic garden buildings that would initially catch the mockery of the press, but soon seize the admiration and curiosity of the whole country.

The first of these, proposed in 1729, built and ready for occupation, or, more accurately, for public display, by 1731, was the Hermitage down by the Diagonal Wood in the north of the grounds near Kew Green.[13] In the mid-1730s Kent would be designing temples for Viscount Cobham at Stowe intended as political propaganda against the regime of Sir Robert Walpole, but here at Richmond the Queen projected the garden building as a celebration of national success in new science and new philosophy, a kind of miniature pantheon to the nation's worthies. Because of the Hermitage's innovative importance it would be satisfying to have some record from Hervey of the Queen's meetings with Kent when the project was discussed, but because Hervey took strongly against Kent, jealously sensing a rival for the Queen's attention and intellectual stimulation, we only have one of his malicious little anecdotes. The Queen happened to mention that a hostile magazine, *The Craftsman*, had abused one of Kent's garden buildings. 'I am very glad of it', interrupted the King, 'you deserve to be abused for such silly childish stuff, and it is the first time I ever knew the scoundrel to be in the right.'[14] But then the King was notoriously a bad-tempered philistine who prided himself on his contempt for literature, poets and painters. Kent would have been left in no doubt of his monarch's dislike of his work.

Fortunately Pope, being an enthusiast for gardens of incident, naturally disagreed and wrote a humorous defence of the Hermitage project. But Kent seems to have crumbled under the criticism and lost heart. So Pope wrote to Burlington on 6 November 1732:

> Pray lay your commands upon Kent, to send you the Short Dialogue I writ on his behalf, between the General [Dormer of Rousham] & myself, shewing the cause why nobody takes notice of him when they speak of the Hermitage. He is modest & afraid to give offence, so has kept it in his pocket, nor even dared to shew it to the General, by which means my Wit is lost in obscurity.[15]

The last line betrays Pope's selfish interest in the case, but what is revealing and unexpected is that Kent was modest and afraid to give offence.

Lady Burlington, who was one of the Queen's ladies-in-waiting and on good terms with Kent, probably effected an introduction between Princess and architect, and as usual one of Kent's sketches tells something of how Caroline was charmed into awarding a commission. There is a detailed pen and ink and sepia wash drawing by Kent showing the Richmond Hermitage framed by trees that are far more deciduous and substantial than Kent's usual spindly conifers.[16] At this point in the early 1730s, Kent has not yet developed his touch for smooth, natural lawns. Instead, a miniature Bridgmannick amphitheatre of two grass steps supports the building. At the foot of these steps is a staffage that will have delighted a Queen who had already proved herself susceptible to the flattering charms of the safely effeminate Hervey. A muscular satyr kneels, devoutly kissing the hand of the patroness of the Hermitage, who is a well-dressed shepherdess, complete with crook and bonnet. It is obviously meant to be the Queen herself, playing out a Marie Antoinette foreshadowing, delicately caught up in those Arcadian fantasies that Kent, more effectively than any of his contemporaries, was launching upon the nation with this royal blessing. So Kent was a charmer of ladies, able to gratify the suppressed longings of an absurdly formal society for escape into classical legend and medieval myth, away from their powdered wigs, their desperately mannered verse and their sharp class distinctions.

A hermitage is usually thought of as a Gothick relic, but Kent and Caroline were not yet in their Gothick phase with Merlin's Cave; that would come four years later, after Kent had created Gothick Esher Place and perfected its Arcadian landscape for Henry Pelham. Kent drew a classical Hermitage with Pan's pipes in the pediment and 'Arcadia' inscribed over its central doorway. It had three entrances, as if for three separate hermits, and the structure appeared to have grown under a weight of rugged rocks, though its doorways were guarded by gilded ironwork. Inside was not a lady's retiring room, but a reminder to the nation of the new science of Isaac Newton and, more personally for the Queen, a reminder of the new Natural Philosophy of her old teacher Leibniz, with whom she had continued to correspond until his death in 1716. Alert, however, to the need to flatter English pride she placed busts, not of Leibniz, but of lesser English philosophers, Samuel Clarke and William Wollaston, on one side of the chamber, balanced on the other side by busts of Newton and of John Locke. Robert Boyle's bust stood in the middle as being both a scientist and a philosopher.

It was the kind of symbolic device that perhaps only a foreign German Queen would have been educated and serious enough to have devised, though quite why the pantheon should have taken the form of a ruined Hermitage is not clear, unless it was one of Kent's whimsicalities. What matters is that it caught the popular imagination and there was a clamour for tickets to view it. In future not many major garden developments could do without a hermitage among its garden buildings. The Queen and Kent had set a fashion for the next thirty years, not just in hermitages, but in a scatter of small, imaginatively stimulating pavilions carefully disposed in a contrived, apparently natural, picturesque landscape. The surge of interest in such eclectic buildings would soon be followed up in 1735 with the Kent–Caroline team's even more sensational and iconic Merlin's Cave, built a hundred yards to the south of the Hermitage. So was it here, in the grounds of Richmond Lodge, between 1729 and 1735, that the Arcadian Garden, or *Jardin Anglais*, so widely admired and copied on the Continent, was actually born? Were the garden buildings the important element in the concept rather than the picturesque, idealised landscape?

It is reasonable to assume that Kent himself was able to charm the Queen into funding his garden buildings, converting her from the strictly formal Versailles style of garden layout, which she had been accustomed to admire at Herrenhausen in Hanover, with its massive formal parterres and its long axial vista to a giant fountain spouting in a circular grove, all geometrical in essence.[17] But it would have been Caroline herself who proposed the iconography of the two main pavilions with their praise of national genius and their political propaganda. Kent's buildings have unfortunately all been swept away, most of them by the vandalism of Capability Brown who may have destroyed more fine Arcadian gardens than he ever laid out himself in his own distinctive style of vacant elegance. Our best record of the Queen's Richmond in its Kentian prime is supplied by three vignettes at the foot of Rocque's 1736 edition of his Richmond Gardens plan.

In all three views, of Hermitage, Dairy and Merlin's Cave, the gardens are alive with elegantly dressed strollers, a reminder that it was by opening their grounds to the polite public that royalty and the aristocracy retained a firm hold on the general affections and appreciation of the country at large. Tickets for entry to Richmond were not only eagerly sought, but were readily supplied. Six couples stand in the Wilderness glade admiring the theatrically ruinous Hermitage and another couple have just emerged from viewing its monument to national science and philosophy. The Queen's Dairy is far more formal in its position at the centre of an exedra of clipped hedges, with Bridgeman's green terraces sharply defined as if by a cutting instrument. The Dairy is anything but relaxed in style. It is a handsome pedimented, classical temple with a Venetian-style, tripartite entrance and heavy rustication in the older Gibbsian manner, a preparation for the delicate porcelain milk dishes within. One man is fishing in the Canal and six groups, all well dressed, are strolling through the young woodland and over the trimly cropped turf.

Bridgeman's geometrical lines at the head of the Canal, like his precisely cut banks to the Duck Pond and the stepped green terraces to the mount with Kent's circular Temple seen on the Chatelain view, are a reminder of the limitations of the Richmond grounds. Kent has been able to lavish them with garden buildings, but not with the natural looking lawns which he would be laying out around the grounds at Esher Place and in the Elysian Fields at Stowe in the mid-1730s. Richmond was innovative, but not a final solution to the Arcadian Garden, rather a garden on the cusp from Bridgeman's semi-formal styling to the true *Jardin Anglais*.

16

Twickenham – a real garden designer and a poet who claimed to be one

From what John Rocque's plans and vignettes reveal it is evident that Queen Caroline's Richmond Park had still not achieved the final formula of an entire park treated as a landscape painting, only multiple garden buildings in multiple separate wildernesses. But who had inspired a princess from formal Herrenhausen to venture as far as she did, and who would inspire the next stage to the complete picturesque Arcadian Garden?

It would be surprising if the answer did not lie just across the Thames in the village of Twickenham. In the years after Caroline's 1719 'Conference of Garden Lords', Twickenham and its environs could boast, in addition to the usual amateur garden enthusiasts who make nursery gardens a paying business, five of the biggest names in garden history: Lord Burlington, William Kent, Robert Castell, Alexander Pope and Batty Langley. But before weighing up their influence on the Queen it will be helpful to remember how this dualism in the evolution of the final Arcadian Garden has led two of our most distinguished living garden historians, Mavis Batey and John Dixon Hunt, to quite different conclusions on the sources, and not just the sources, but even the nature of the Arcadian Garden movement. One conclusion can be described as literary, a belief that poetry can shape garden design. The other can be summarised as painterly or 'travel-wise': the theory that paintings by artists like Francesco Albani, Claude Lorraine or the Poussins, brought back from Italy as mementos of gardens enjoyed on a Grand Tour, were copied by their owners in their parkscapes.

Mavis Batey, former President of the Garden History Society and a frequent contributor to its journal, has written a persuasive book, *Alexander Pope: The Poet and the Landscape.*[1] It is slim, illustrated with evocative photographs, and has whole pages of Pope's poetry set alongside garden scenes which, in her analysis, were inspired by the lines across the page, passages like:

> He gains all points, who pleasingly confounds,
> Surprises, varies and conceals the bounds.
> Consult the genius of the place in all;
> That tells the waters or to rise, or fall,
> Or helps the ambitious hill the heavens to scale,
> Or scoops in circling theatres the vale.[2]

Such lines are indeed a convincing summary in rhyme of what Charles Bridgeman did at Claremont in Surrey, Amesbury in Wiltshire and at Eastbury in Dorset. He would detect a latent geometry in an existing natural topography and then harden and emphasise it with avenues and planting, or quite literally 'scoop' it out, by earthworks.

It is important to think carefully about her theory. When an eighteenth-century garden designer read lines like:

> The darksome pines that o'er yon rocks reclin'd
> Wave high, and murmur to the hollow wind,
> The wand'ring streams that shine between the hills,
> The grots that echo to the tinkling rills,[3]

would he, or she, then plan and plant a park in imitation as Charles Hamilton did in some reaches of his garden-park at Painshill, Surrey, between 1738 and 1773? Is it possible that some poems written at this period resulted directly in landscape gardens? Mavis Batey believes that it could and that they did. These new gardens, she maintains, were direct responses to literature; Pope could write, others would then plant.

John Dixon Hunt, who in much of his writing takes literary influences very seriously, believes differently.[4] He argues that it was simply Kent's nine years' experience of Italian gardens with all their rich display of garden buildings, stone exedra, statuary and urns, that gave him the drive to furnish English gardens with the same grottoes, fountains and devices. The Italians' aim had not been to imitate or perfect Nature, but to create variety, an enriched landscape of surprises. Hunt traces this Italian style back

> to Aristotle's *Rhetoric*, which notes how the human mind delights in change, and to all the Christian recognition of God's essential goodness and optimism which fathered 'unspeakable riches' . . . Variety was pleasant in and for itself.[5]

In support of Hunt's reasoning are famous Italian gardens like that at the Villa Garzoni at Collodi, Bomarzo and particularly the Boboli Gardens in Florence, the one garden that almost all Grand Tourists would have seen. The essence of these is not their subtle arrangement of trees, sloping lawns and lakes. They were not meant idly to flatter the eye of someone bowling along in a fast carriage. At every few paces of a walk they delight with lewd or lovely statues, the mouths of stone monsters, pavilions by round pools, grottoes of frosted stonework, garden seats supported by tritons or tumbling cascades. They entertain as well as delight. It is rarely stated, but most ambitious English gardens of this period functioned for sexual release in a repressed society. They offered mild horticultural pornography, just like their bolder Italian models. Statues of nude, athletic men and attractive young women, catamites like Hadrian's lover, Antinous, and hermaphrodites are scattered discreetly near cold baths for personal nudity and pavilions for private retirement.

Horace Walpole accords roughly with Hunt, but considers these English gardens to be copies, not of actual Italian gardens, but imitations of the paintings of Francesco Albani (sometimes known as Albano). Walpole thought the grounds of Stowe pure 'Albano': 'I do like that Albano glut of buildings, let them be ever so much condemned',[6] and finds that they offer 'more beauties of light, shade and buildings than any of Albano's I ever saw'.[7] Significantly, in that last quotation, Walpole considers effects of light and shade as important as the garden buildings. So he had already analysed the dual aspect of these new gardens by 1751: composition on the one hand, historical resonance on the other. Incidentally, Walpole, writing in his much-quoted though sometimes very partial and unreliable *The History of the Modern Taste in Gardening*, had realised the important transitional nature of Queen Caroline and Bridgeman's work at Richmond Lodge:

> he [Bridgeman] ventured farther, and in the royal garden at Richmond dared to introduce cultivated fields, and even morsels of a forest appearance, by the sides of those endless and tiresome walks, that stretched out of one another without intermission.[8]

When, however, Walpole comes to the authors of the great garden advance, he has time for only two of the five potent figures listed earlier: Kent and Pope. Yet the one man of the five who boldly criticises the flaws in the Caroline–Bridgeman–Kent gardens and who puts his finger upon precisely the weakest point in Bridgeman's gardens is Batty Langley. He was a hands-on, practical nurseryman, a bold innovator and the inventor of the 'arti-natural' style;[9] yet he is usually dismissed as an amiable eccentric, on the fringes of style. In fact, if his lavishly produced *New Principles of Gardening*, published in 1728, is thoughtfully evaluated and the glib generalisations in Walpole's *History* are treated with caution, then Langley emerges as the true early mover and shaper of garden design. Abler, or more ruthless, self-publicists like Alexander Pope, his fellow Twickenham resident, have put Langley's writings and influence into undeserved neglect.[10]

The trouble with Batty Langley is that he does not emerge from contemporary sources as a very gentlemanly figure, and garden historians, by the nature of their studies, tend to drift inadvertently into snobbery. There is the curious problem of his Christian name. How does one react respectfully to a garden designer called 'Batty'? If his father, Daniel Langley, a Twickenham gardener, had christened him Bartholomew, he would have been taken far more seriously. Then Batty, as he has to be called, was an ardent and committed Freemason, and academics tend to curl their lips instinctively at any mention of that great and influential order as if it were equivalent to the Mafia.

A further black mark against Batty, the prolific author of architectural textbooks and guides for provincial builders, is his writing style. He opens his *New Principles* in an honest, but tactically unwise, aggressive, self-confident manner that automatically grates, even though it has a measure of truth: 'Our gardens are much the worst of any in the world, some few excepted . . . Nor is there anything more shocking than a stiff, regular garden.'[11] He was blowing the first loud and clear blast of the trumpet against the monstrous regiment of formal Franco-Dutch style gardens that had prevailed in England since 1660. It was a very brave thing to do, and his book was no ill-printed pamphlet, but a richly illustrated folio, teeming, not only with controversial ideas, but with many fold-out plans and drawings to point up those ideas. He attacked George London and Henry Wise by name, men whose Brompton Park nurseries had dominated royal and aristocratic garden design since 1682;[12] and his attack was unequivocally aesthetic. Langley wrote against 'that regular, stiff and stuft up Manner', against gardens 'crowded with Evergreens, more in the aspect of a *Nursery* than a *Garden of Pleasure*'.[13] He was writing to the detriment of his own profits when he sneered at 'trifling flower knots, Parterres of Cut Work, Embroidery, and Wildernesses of Evergreens'.[14] Such garden features would have included the bedding plants and shrubs on which a nursery garden's profits depended, so Langley was taking risks. He had a clearly stated vision of the type of garden that was required to replace the formal Franco-Dutch layouts. 'The pleasure of a garden', he wrote in that fierce introduction, 'depends on the variety of its parts . . . so as to have a continuous series of *Harmonious Objects*, that will present new and delightful Scenes to our View at every step we take, which regular gardens are incapable of doing.'[15] That was almost exactly what Hunt urges as the compelling impulse behind the emergent Arcadian Garden: variety and surprise. Where a garden is laid out in the Franco-Dutch manner to be viewed from a terrace as one complete geometry, expressive of landed power, there can be no element of surprise, only one of order.

Langley's daring was not limited to the slighting of London and Wise. He attacked Queen Caroline and King George's Richmond Lodge gardens explicitly, following that up with a point-by-point attack on what Bridgeman had been doing: setting garden pavilions up on unnaturally terraced elevations, laying out step-gardens, and planting trees in unnatural straight lines. He stated boldly that, the 'fine Terrace Walk of his Majesty's Royal Palace of Hampton Court . . . being naked of shade is thereby useless when the sun shines, as is also his Royal Majesty's at Richmond next the river'.[16] Then his assault narrows in upon Bridgeman and the trick of multi-terracing that Kent had picked up from Bridgeman. 'Never', he ordered, 'break their slopes into many Angles that their native Beauty is destroy'd', or on the Mount, 'you shall have its slope which should be entire from top to bottom, broken into three, if not four small trifling ones . . . so that instead of having one *grand slope* only with an easy Ascent, you have three or four small ones that are *poor and trifling*.'[17] That was exactly what Bridgeman, or Kent, had done to the Mount which supported the circular Temple at Richmond.

Langley nagged away at his obsession:

> And the only reason why they are made in this Stair or Step like manner, is first to shew their Dexterity of Hand, without considering the ill Effect and lastly to imitate those grand *Amphitheatrical Buildings* used by the Ancients.[18]

This was a shrewd jab at Bridgeman's favourite garden feature, the amphitheatre; and there is much more:

> In this Low mean manner I find some slopes made at the head of his Majesty's Canal and Mount next the Thames at Richmond. Which Canal is much *too narrow* for its length: I also find the Plantations of *Forest Trees* on each side thereof, *not only broken in the middle* without Reason for so doing, but stiff and regular in their Situations, without any Regard to that beautiful Order which Nature observes in all such rural Operations.[19]

As if criticism spattered over a royal garden were not enough, Langley continued: 'I observe the like *Error* in the *Slopes* of the Garden of the *Honourable* Mrs Howard at *Twickenham* [Marble Hill], being view'd at the River Thames, and the same at General Biffet's Amphitheatre (as call'd by its Architect) in his garden at the same town.'[20]

What Langley did not criticise as old-fashioned, even though it was dug in 1726 before his book came out, was the little stepped amphitheatre which Pope, the self-proclaimed garden innovator, coaxed Bridgeman's men to dig and turf for him in his small garden as a base for the Obelisk he was to raise in memory of his mother after her death in 1733. The Obelisk served as the visual focus to his overwritten and probably overpraised layout. Kent was saved from criticism by timing. His Hermitage sketch for the Queen, with its Bridgmannick 'stair' or 'step' setting, was drawn in 1729. But the dates mean that both Kent and Pope were lagging behind the aesthetic perceptions of the nurseryman in their own area; Langley could have supplied the missing element which would have made the grounds at Richmond Lodge the first true Arcadian Garden. He came to a perception of the natural Arcadian landscape garden before Kent, though Kent, unlike Pope, was quick to take Langley's perception on board at Esher and in Stowe's Elysian Fields.

As an assiduous cultivator of the aristocracy, Pope is most unlikely to have had much time for the strident Batty Langley, even though he probably patronised Langley's nursery garden every spring for new plants. There is no trace of Langley's arti-natural mazes in the gradual, relaxed curves of the paths that thread the shrubbery on either side of the central axis of his garden from the Villa to the Obelisk. Those paths do lead occasionally to circular clearings, but if Langley's directions had been followed the clearings would have had features of interest. These may well have set Queen Caroline's mind working on exotic garden buildings in 1729, a year after the book came out, but it was the mazes which Langley designed so liberally that are most likely to have caught the Queen's fancy. The book's frontispiece opens out to offer four intricately curved and convoluted labyrinths for readers to choose from and to copy. It is easy to imagine the strong-willed, enthusiastic Queen poring over them and deciding not to choose one but to have all four set up in various quarters of her extensive grounds, as in fact versions of them were. Pope would not have been impressed, but what about Kent?

This raises a question which is, however, unlikely ever to be answered: did Kent and Langley know each other and exchange views on gardens and architecture, the Gothick in particular? While there is no scrap of evidence that they ever met, probability suggests that they must have done. Given a population for Twickenham of less than a thousand and the Langley nursery as the chief garden emporium of the village, would Kent, cheerful and friendly by nature, have been able to avoid some meetings with the owner of the nursery when Kent himself was advising on both the Queen's garden at nearby Richmond and at Pope's garden in Twickenham village itself? In 1728 Langley had just completed laying out, presumably with some of the arti-natural curls and twists urged in the book, the gardens of Thomas Vernon, the MP at Twickenham Park. Vernon was the brother-in-law of John Aislabie, who laid out the gardens at Studley Royal near Ripon, possibly the most beautiful garden of the entire eighteenth century, the one real competitor to Stourhead for that title. Surely Kent would have been interested in quizzing his garden supplier? Even if he had not met him in person, Kent would have known and read Langley's sumptuously illustrated and controversial book.

That speculation leads to another. At Esher in 1730, Kent would be the first confident practitioner of a revived, unscholarly, but lively Gothick architecture. Langley would be the first to publish, in 1741–2 and 1747, an introduction to Gothic architecture, handsomely illustrated, as usual with a Langley book, by his brother Thomas. Was that entirely a coincidence? Langley, a Freemason and ardent admirer of Nicholas Hawksmoor's Gothic experiments, is more likely than Kent, with his continental Roman background, to have pioneered the Gothick. Might Langley have influenced Kent not only with the idea of creating smooth, natural-looking lawns but also with the Gothick? There is no final answer. But the coincidences make it seem very probable. In both cases, garden and house, Langley had the concepts, while Kent delivered the realisation of those concepts.

With Kent and Pope, of course, there are no uncertainties about relationships. They were excellent good friends and that skilful cadger Pope often dunned Kent for a design, for his recipe for mutton steak, or for someone amusing with whom to drink. The problem with their relationship is whether there was ever a two-way flow of influence between them on the making of gardens. Modern critical scholarship on Pope has inclined to hagiography, his voluminous output of verse, his letters and accounts of admirers like Joseph Spence proving rich quarry for thesis writers, cultural historians and biographers.[21] To set against this generally admiring analysis of his struggle against physical disability and religious prejudice, the Revd George Gilfillan's trenchant summary of his character, published in 1856, should be taken into account:

> He was a spoiled child, a small self-tormentor, – full to bursting with petty spites, mean animosities, and unfounded jealousies. While he sought, with the fury of a pampered slave, to trample on those authors that were beneath him in rank or in popularity, he could on all occasions fawn with the sycophancy of a eunuch upon the noble, the rich, and the powerful.[22]

Hardly a flattering description, but one worth bearing in mind when considering his relations with and written comments on William Kent, who, it should be noted, handled the poet with almost contemptuous ease, mocking or ignoring him in his petulant fits.

If we are honest, Pope's poetry today is very much an acquired taste, and one easier to acquire for readers who are themselves naturally vengeful, unforgiving and point scoring. He wrote condescendingly, putting the world and his rivals in their place with jingling aphorisms, which now and then break through, almost by accident, into a couplet of poetry rather than mere verse. His modern critics tend to pour a honeyed sympathy upon him because he was only four feet tall and undoubtedly gallant in his crippled adversity. But his life was a struggle and he wrote, consequently, with a huge bias in his own favour, so his claims for garden design and all the success of his own garden at Twickenham are suspect. He could never be described as a naturally generous person or a strictly honest one.

It is not regarding his reputation in his own lifetime too favourably to say that it stood almost as high as Shakespeare's does with us today. Eighteenth-century England's self-identification with classical Rome was something that began as a pose and ended up very close to a certifiable psychological delusion. Pope's competent but dull translations of Homer's *Iliad* and *Odyssey* gave the educated classes of the nation profound satisfaction. Until the Romantics came to the rescue, the ridiculous blight of the heroic couplet would lie upon English creative writing. It was believed to be classical, or in some unfathomable way the equivalent of the classical method of writing poetry, even though Latin poetry does not rely on rhyme at all, but on a highly complex system of scansion entirely inapplicable to the stresses of English. Poetry was not the only art to fall under this classical obsession. Architecture, which could have been released and revived if Vanbrugh's wild Baroque lead had been followed, became obsessed with the correct application of classical orders and remained trapped within worn-out models of supposed good taste until the Gothic Revival and the subsequent earthquake of uninhibited Victorian eclecticism took over; by which time any true national sequence of architectural development would have been lost forever.

To his lasting credit, Kent was foremost in that break away from the tyranny of classicism, but because Pope was such a dyed-in-the-wool classical revivalist, Kent's close friendship with him, particularly in garden matters, is suspect. As England in its insular wilfulness was beginning to rebel against formal gardens, an almost equally unhelpful heresy was developing. This was the notion that the closer a garden approached to a natural condition the more superior was that garden's aesthetic. It was a ridiculous polarisation and one implicit in Pope's vapid heroic couplets:

> First follow Nature, and your judgement frame
> By her just standard, which is still the same:

Unerring NATURE, still divinely bright
One clear, unchanged, and universal light,
Life, force, and beauty, must to all impart,
At once the source, and end, and test of art.[23]

A garden is, of its essence, unnatural, but it will manipulate natural forms, as in the recent fad for wild-flower meadows, which are only deliciously spurious concentrations of flowers and grasses, all of which can be described as 'natural', though not in their contrived association. The word 'Nature' resounds repetitively throughout Pope's long 'Essays': on Man, on Criticism and on Moral matters. If we substitute for the word 'Nature', wherever it occurs, the word 'Opinion', although the scansion would falter the sense will not change radically.

Pope's Twickenham garden was often visited in his lifetime, a combination of Anne Hathaway's Cottage and Shakespeare's Birthplace, a tourist trap closely associated with a national treasure.[24] It was even more visited after his death, when his old gardener, John Searle, wrote a guidebook to it, with a map, which differs significantly from the sketch map which Pope himself had drawn in the positioning of the Shell Temple and the Mount.[25] It was an ingenious space carved from bushes of unspecified varieties. Rising up from his cellar the main axial line ran past the Shell Temple, the Mount and the Grove, or Quincunx, to the round Bowling Green, a second Grove and lastly the Obelisk. Paths wandered on either side off this axis through the bushes to little clearings. There were sufficient general similarities between Pope's layout and the garden which Kent would design for the Prince of Wales in 1735 at Carlton House for Horace Walpole to make much of Kent's debt to Pope. But Pope's debt to Kent was more direct: it was the enchanting fantasy drawing that Kent made of himself with his arm upon Pope's shoulder, standing in Pope's garden with Pope's dog Bounce. The two men are looking up at one of the most elaborate, expensive and ingenious domed garden temples ever erected in England. It is an octagon and the eight blocked Corinthian columns that support the dome must have been shaped by a sophisticated industrial process of steam compression so that each one bows symmetrically outwards. Obviously the Temple could never have existed in the form which Kent playfully drew. Nor was there ever a big bowl on tripod legs with a large live fish in it, any more than a naked goddess on a shell supported by tritons was ever accustomed to visit Twickenham of an afternoon. The scene, with its arching rainbow, was a Kent capriccio which Pope enthusiasts have chosen to consider an authentic mark of their hero's genius. Absurdly, Pope holds a Claude Glass for long-distance views.

Pope's cellar, which he called his 'Grotto' or 'Egeria', did have a real existence. Pope was as much a natural scientist as a poet. His cellar walls were encrusted with a confused geological display of mineral specimens, and his axial garden was an attempt to demonstrate optical effects by narrowing vistas and applying dark or light evergreens to achieve illusions of size. By plastering broken bits of mirror glass in among the geological specimens he was able to achieve freakish effects of light, reflected partly from his front garden running down to the river, partly from an alabaster lamp. As part of his presentation of himself as the great poet, he sometimes interviewed people whom he wanted to impress, like Lord Bolingbroke, in the shadows of this cellar, with sound effects of dripping water. With his big head, large, sensitive eyes, melodious voice and dwarfish stature it must have been a memorable performance.

Kent obviously gained by his association with one so nationally famous, but the two men never took each other too seriously. Pope wrote his elaborate skits on Kent's obesity and idleness, while Kent had a running joke with Burlington about Pope's greed and excessive wine bibbing. It is unlikely that any passage of Pope's didactic verse made as direct an impact upon Kent's garden sensibilities as Batty Langley's sincerely felt

> What a Shame it is, to destroy a noble Oak of two or three Hundred Years' Growth, that always produces a pleasant Shade and graceful Aspect, for the sake of making a *trifling Grass Plot* or *Flower Knot* regular. Those great beauties of Nature, Hills and Valleys, were always levelled at very great Expense to complete their Regularity, or otherwise I may justly say, the *total ruin of the Gardens*. And their Basins, Canals, and other *Pieces of Water*, had always a very *mean Latitude* to their Length, as well as *improper Figures* broke into many Angles which destroy the beauty of fine Water.[26]

The difference between Langley's writing and Kent's practice was, however, almost absolute. Langley never once, in all those impressive 'arti-natural' plans, drew a lake, pond or canal with natural-looking banks. He, or his brother Thomas, always chose geometrical shapes. When he declared 'what a great pity it is that *Gentlemen* should be then led on for want of being furnished with Designs that are *truly Grand and Noble*, after *Nature's own Manner*',[27] the designs that he presented were, as he described them himself, not 'Natural', but 'Arti-Natural'.[28] It would be left to Kent to produce the supremely clever artifice: gardens that really looked like Nature even though they were subtly contrived compositions.

But for all this show of Nature, Kent was never able to break away, or even wanted to break away, from his century's love affair with classicism. All his landscape gardens were Arcadias with classical trimmings. As Horace Walpole wrote, intending a compliment: 'We owe the restoration of Greece and the diffusion of architecture to his skill in landscape';[29] as if the real Greek Arkadia could ever be recreated among England's lush green meadows and billowing deciduous woodlands. Geographical awareness was still in its infancy when Walpole wrote of Greece restored. Walpole rattles on about evocations of Tempe and Daphne:

> If Stowe had but half so many buildings as it has, there would be too many; but that profusion, that glut, enriches and makes it look like a fine landscape of Albano; one figures one's self in Tempe or Daphne,[30]

not realising that Tempe was a grand, stony wilderness and that Daphne was in Syria. He and Kent were caught up, like all their contemporaries, in this illusion of classicism revived. It was an 'Augustan' era that the Emperor Augustus would never have recognised: Tempe and Daphne evoked in the entirely inappropriate settings of lush woodland and fertile water meadows, men in tights and powdered white wigs imagining that they had achieved a Roman dignity. Every age of history seems to need its grand illusions for support: a Marxist paradise, a thousand-year Reich, a League of Nations. That Augustan illusion had the happy accidental effect of leading Kent on to create Arcadias that were neither natural nor like Arcady, but lovely composites of idealised English landscape liberally scattered with architectural evocations of past history. As he fumbled his way to that near perfection he had been helped, to varying degrees, by Lord Burlington, Charles Bridgeman, Robert Castell, Queen Caroline, Alexander Pope and Batty Langley. Now for the last stage he would need the friendship and the encouragement of a man who would soon become First Lord of the Treasury – not the present holder of that post, Sir Robert Walpole, but Henry Pelham.

17

First for a prime minister and then for a queen – a forgotten Gothick revival

When the reputation of a house like Esher Place is considered, one of the three most revolutionary buildings of the English eighteenth century, the power of the written word and the impotence of silence becomes, if not frightening, deeply frustrating. Its designer, William Kent, was on the edge of illiteracy. Henry Pelham, who took the risk of commissioning it, was too busy playing politics and then ruling as a successful Prime Minister to write up his achievement. Yet Esher was built, innovative and confident, around the core of Bishop Waynflete's 1480 Gate Tower, and was complete as early as 1733. Not only did it have a firm pattern of overtly Gothic fenestration, its reception rooms had a flexible ground plan with four octagonal and one apsidal-ended room. The tyranny of the rectangle was decisively broken there, and what enabled it to be broken was the bold staccato of three-storey canted bays projecting dramatically into its entrance court. Long before Sir Robert Taylor's supposedly pioneering canted bays of 1755 at Harleyford Manor on the Thames,[1] Kent had flooded the rooms of Esher with light from three sides by designing at each end bays that copied the two original Gothic bays from Waynflete's Tower in the centre. At Esher an actual battle of styles was fought out on one single façade, with the structural freedom of the Gothic style liberating a country house functionally from the small windows and the flat elevations which Palladianism had inherited from the Veneto where light and heat were enemies to be guarded against. With its grudging sunshine, England is a natural bay-window country, or was until plate glass was invented. At Esher, Kent reminded us of the bay and its practical light effects.

If all these remarkable features, combined in a grand nine-bay country house, had been designed for some obscure eccentric, living hidden away on the Welsh borders of Shropshire, it would not have been surprising if awareness of its experimental nature and stylistic importance had been confined to a few disapproving neighbours. But Esher Place was unremarked and ignored even though it was built in an area of fashionable retreat a few miles, an evening carriage ride, from the centre of London. Kent was working for the royal family and the Prime Minister; Henry Pelham was a powerful politician, the friend of Sir Robert Walpole, the brother of the Duke of Newcastle and, after 1743, himself a notably successful and popular Prime Minister for eleven years. During those eleven years Gothick Esher Place would have been a centre of entertainment and influence: the premier's weekend house and one of the best known houses in Britain. Yet, because no one wrote about it no one seems to have noticed its significance; consequently it had very little significance. Publicity is all. Because neither Kent nor Pelham wrote to draw attention to what they had done – which was to launch the Gothic Revival with the first serious counterstroke to classicism since the Renaissance – no one has ever given Esher the credit it deserves.

As recently as 1900, when a usually intelligent historian, H. Avray Tipping, was writing up Esher for *Country Life*, he commented:

> Kent was an excellent exponent of the landscape school, but his architecture was almost uniformly bad, and it is melancholy to reflect that Pelham employed him to insert pseudo-Gothic windows which may now be seen in the fifteenth-century tower.[2]

A revolution lay under Tipping's nose and all he could do was reject it. As a result of this philistine ignorance and the absence of contemporary written reaction, most of Kent's work was pulled down, a dull replacement was built on the site of Kent's Belvedere Tower and the building lots of suburbia covered Kent's inspired, earliest and probably best, landscape layout. Waynflete's Gate Tower survives, with Kent's 'pseudo-Gothic windows', actually a delightful geometry of quatrefoils with ogee memories of Bridlington Priory's west front in the tripartite windows, but nothing else except an urn and a few garden scraps of stone.

All the credit for the Gothic Revival has gone to Horace Walpole, Sir Robert's youngest son, for his indecisive, ramshackle but charming house, Strawberry Hill in Twickenham.[3] It was not even begun around the core of a run-down cottage, Chopp'd-Straw-Hall, until 1749, a clear sixteen years after Esher Place was completed. There would be at least six years of hesitant additions before Strawberry could be described as a Gothic house, but Strawberry was written up at every stage of its building. Walpole devoted his life to studying genuine medieval Gothic architecture, building his reputation as the author of the Revival and denigrating his rivals, Kent included, even though he appreciated Kent's gardens more than anyone.

Walpole wrote with a brilliant journalistic facility and an unscrupulous disregard for the truth. His style is limpid and he had a gift for the memorable phrase. Because Walpole wrote that Kent 'leaped the fence, and saw that all nature was a garden', most readers believe that gross and largely unhelpful generalisation because he followed it with

> He felt the delicious contrast of hill and valley changing imperceptibly into each other, tasted the beauty of the gentle swell, or concave swoop, and remarked how loose groves crowned an easy eminence with happy ornament, and while they called in the distant view between their graceful stems, removed and extended the perspective by delusive comparison.[4]

Lesser writers have been trying to play those tricks with bogus optical cant ever since. If only Walpole could have applied his spurious scientific jargon to the house Kent built at Esher as well as to the garden he had laid out around it. The concern of this chapter is not that the writing of England's political history in the eighteenth century has still not recovered from the spin which Walpole gave to it, with his Whig theory of constitutional growth. Rather, it is to give Kent and Henry Pelham their due: Kent as an imaginative designer, Pelham as an inspired patron. Walpole, the darling of all Georgians for the treasure of the letters which he wrote, carefully retrieved and ordered for posthumous immortality, deserves to be recognised as a devious charmer and unscrupulous manipulator of facts, stylistic as well as political. Esher was Kent's most important house and his most successful garden. Both are lost but they deserve a memorial.

About Walpole's talent for words there must be no uncertainty. When he wished to be fair – and his own reputation for innovation was not under threat – he could write like an angel, or more accurately, like the garden correspondent of a Sunday colour supplement. In Walpole's lyrical prose Esher's garden survives in all its Rococo enchantments. Walpole was not threatened by Kent's gardens, only by Kent's Gothick, so he could afford to be fair and wonderfully evocative.

On 18 May 1763, when Esher's grounds had matured and Kent was safely in the grave, no longer a rival, Miss Pelham, Henry Pelham's second daughter, gave a sophisticated Anglo-French entertainment there and Walpole, whose father had been Henry's closest political friend, was invited. His account deserves a full quotation because it catches the essence of the Rococo mood which had always been Kent's natural stylistic environment, despite the Palladian straitjacket into which Burlington tried half-successfully to clamp him. It was an entirely al fresco day:

> We had a magnificent dinner, cloaked in the modesty of earthenware: French horns and hautboys on the lawn. We walked to the belvedere on the summit of the hill, where a threatened storm only served to heighten the beauty of the landscape, a rainbow on a dark cloud falling precisely behind the tower of a neighbouring church, between another tower, and the building at Claremont. Monsieur de Nivernois, who had been absorbed all day and lagging behind, translating my verses, was delivered of his version, and of some more lines, which he wrote on Miss Pelham in the belvedere, while we drank tea and coffee. From thence we passed into the wood, and the ladies formed a circle on chairs before the mouth of the cave, which was overhung to a vast height with woodbines, lilacs and laburnums, and dignified by those tall shapely cypresses. On the descent of the hill were placed the French horns; the abigails, servants, and neighbours wandering below by the river – in short, it was Parnassus as Watteau would have painted it. Here we had a rural syllabub, and part of the company returned to town; but were replaced by Giardini and Onofrio, who with Nivernois on the violin and Lord Pembroke on the bass, accompanied Miss Pelham, lady Rockingham and the Duchess of Grafton who sang. This

> little concert lasted till past ten; then there were minuets; and as we had seven couple left, it concluded with a country dance – I blush again, for I danced, but was kept in countenance by Nivernois, who has one wrinkle more than I have. A quarter after twelve they sat down to supper, and I came home by a charming moonlight.[5]

There, perfectly encapsulated, is that fabled *douceur de la vie*, the aristocratic apogee which Talleyrand regretted so soulfully when the French Revolution had destroyed it. But, while appreciating the charm of this description of Esher written in a private letter, it has to be noted that Walpole slipped much vicious character assassination into his published writing: his *Memoirs of the Reign of George II*, that indispensable source book for all nineteenth-century and many twentieth-century historians of the period. Consider his slighting references to Henry Pelham, the Prime Minister, who had fought bravely in his youth at Prestonpans against the Jacobites in their first, 1715, rebellion; dealt wisely and justly with Scotland after their second rebellion in 1747; ended the 1739–48 war with France by an honourable peace, and, last of all, reduced the national debt by honest fiscal management. Pelham died in office, deservedly popular and widely regretted. Where Walpole was concerned Pelham had, however, denied him a pension and, worst of all, he had arranged for his daughter Catherine to marry Henry Fiennes Clinton, the handsome, strapping 9th Earl of Lincoln with whom Walpole had, for three years, been conducting an intense and happy homosexual relationship. Lincoln was the love of bachelor Walpole's life; but after that marriage all contacts were firmly ended by Lincoln's father-in-law, Pelham, whom Walpole never forgave. Consequently the *Memoirs* dribble spite, as in: 'All men thought Mr Pelham honest till he was in power', or 'nothing tended so much to unravel the mystery of devotion which the nation had conceived for Mr Pelham, as it appearing that it had not been the genius of the man, but the servility of the times which had established his authority'; worse still, 'He supplied the deficiency of genius by affected virtue; he had removed superiors by treachery, and those of whom he was jealous by pretexting or administering to the jealousies of his brother [the Duke of Newcastle, who succeeded him as Prime Minister]. He enjoyed the plenitude of his ministry but a short time [eleven years] and that short time was a scene of fretfulness [in fact, one of restored peace and prosperity].'[6]

A writer and historian who could so distort facts to gratify his frustrated affections had no difficulty in dismissing Kent's Gothick elevations to a rebuilt Esher, even though his quatrefoils, battlements and dripstones there would become the standard Gothick revival forms, a simple, easily copied medievalism fused with classical symmetries, which would satisfy most Gothick revivalists for the remainder of the century. For the jealous Walpole, however, 'The King's Bench at Westminster [Kent's 1739 Gothick screen for Westminster Hall] and Mr Pelham's house at Esher are proofs how little he conceived the principles or graces of that architecture.'[7] So which principles and what graces had Kent failed to conceive at Esher and what had inspired those revolutionary and thoroughly professional elevations?

It was Kent's appointment as Master Carpenter in 1726 that seems to have made him take architecture more seriously than painting and at least as seriously as interior decoration. His classical, but romantically ruined, Hermitage had been a great success in 1730. Exactly when he drew his rampageously Gothick gateways and castles to illustrate Spenser's archetypally Gothic poem, *The Faerie Queene*, is not certain.[8] The book would not be published, edited by Thomas Birch, until 1751, but the wicked hermit Archimago and his hermitage feature prominently in Book 1, as does Merlin in Book 3, so Kent probably made the drawings in the 1730s when he was designing the Queen's Gothick garden buildings at Richmond. They are far and away his liveliest book illustrations including several of his future garden buildings in the background. He also produced illustrations for Pope's *Odyssey*, Gay's *Poems* and *Fables*, Thomson's *Seasons*, Bunyan's *Pilgrim's Progress* and Tasso's *Gerusalemme Liberata*.[9]

Esher Place is dated 1733 on its surviving porch to Waynflete's Tower, and it was in 1732 that Kent was persuaded, by Sir Robert Walpole if his son's extremely unreliable and probably biased account is to be believed, to rebuild a gateway and the east range of the Clock Court at Hampton Court, not in a classical style, but in an associational Tudor-Gothic. In 1732 Pelham was Minister at War in the Walpole administration and the decision which he made at the same time over the style of his proposed new house at Esher suggests that it was Pelham rather than Sir Robert, the classical vulgarian, who pressed for an associational style rather than a classical solution at Hampton Court.

Kent originally prepared a conventional Palladian scheme for Pelham's Esher, one that Lord Burlington would have approved.[10] It would have been sited on the hilltop overlooking Waynflete's Tower down on the banks of the Mole. That suggests that it was entirely Pelham's brave decision to reject a perfectly adequate five-bay pedimented central block with quadrant arms and side pavilions, and commission Kent to refenestrate the Tower and rebuild the existing side wings in a committed, but disciplined Gothick. Among the Kent drawings for Esher, discovered by John Harris and Howard Colvin at Rockingham Castle, is one fascinating sketch showing how he hesitated over those side wings. Initially he was compromising, with an alternation of pedimented classical bays and narrow Gothick turrets, with some unconvincing three-light Gothick windows borrowed from his Hampton Court refurbishment.[11] He abandoned all that and settled for order. His entrance drive left Esher village between two neat Gothick boxes which are still standing and inhabited. Then it dived downhill, straight as an arrow to land a carriage in a courtyard overawed by the three towering bays and two ogee-capped turrets.

At this point it is necessary to be as fair to Horace Walpole's Strawberry Hill as Walpole was unfair to Kent's Esher Place. The Gothic and the classical represent two distinct human ways of handling architectural beauty. Gothic is romantically wild; it satisfies the fabled monsters of the Id. Classical is ordered, reassuring, harmonious, it imposes regularity and confines the spirit like a sedative. Kent shattered the classical mould by choosing Gothic forms but then, on the edge of revolution, consciously avoided asymmetry, deploying them in classical order and symmetry on both the main façades of Esher. He invented Gothick with a 'k', a compromise style for safe eighteenth-century builders. It was Walpole with his Committee of Taste, scholarly but free-thinking homosexual friends, who invented Gothic without a 'k' and eventually released the monsters of the Id upon nineteenth-century architecture. Kent's problem was that he had done no architectural homework and had no lively, camp friends, unless Alexander Pope qualifies, and Pope was soaked in classical proprieties, risking just one Gothic poem, 'Eloisa to Abelard', among thousands of predictable classical couplets – so he was no use.

Kent must have remembered vaguely those ogee arches on the west front of Bridlington Priory and he had mastered the easy, not essentially Gothic, geometry of quatrefoils. He settled for those and, with that limited vocabulary of forms, placed his memories in order at Esher. Beverley Minster, with all its glorious Gothic motifs, had been on his doorstep in the East Riding, but he seems not have explored, let alone sketched there. San Petronio in Bologna, where in 1540 Vignola and Giulio Romano laid out simple Gothic forms in classical symmetry, may have influenced him more than all the Gothic riches of England lying under his nose.

Walpole was more curious and, therefore, more fortunate. In his whimsical way he was a true scholar, getting into churches and houses all over England, noting details and developing an aesthetic of preferences. Kent had one single-minded friend, Burlington. Walpole gathered a whole gang of like-minded homosexuals about him for ideas and discourse on architecture as deviant as their sexual predilections. There was John Chute from The Vyne in Hampshire, the Georgian version of a screaming queen in twentieth-century parlance, and the owner of a very Gothic house. The poet Thomas Gray was a closet homosexual; and Richard Bentley, a talented artist and a married man, was sexually indeterminate, as ready to draw schoolboys' bottoms as they frolicked on the playing fields of Eton as an exquisite crocketed trefoil or a mouldering ogival arch. As a result Strawberry Hill was, behind a little regularity, a collection of interesting, jumbled Gothic bits and pieces, inside and out. It has charm; in its frail, tinpot way it is romantic and wild and disordered. The cleverness, the brilliance of Charles Barry and A.W.N. Pugin's Palace of Westminster is that it retains a reassuring, underlying classical symmetry beneath an exhilarating pandemonium of utterly asymmetrical towers. The Gothick and the Gothic can live together: the Houses of Parliament prove it in an ideal symbolism of national order and national aspiration. Exactly the same dual symbolism can be achieved in classical buildings. Sir John Vanbrugh proved that at Blenheim Palace where his military-style turrets rampage on the skyline above emphatic Baroque imperialism. That is why the nation's nervous rejection of Vanbrugh's style and its timid retreat to Palladian platitudes was such an artistic tragedy. In a century of so much wealth and aristocratic power England produced so little of note until the Prince Regent and John Nash came in at the last minute with some theatrical vitality at Brighton and Regent's Park.

This is where Kent was to blame. Esher was not a very attractive house. Its skyline of small ogee-capped turrets owed as much to the fifteenth-century work that remained as to Kent's additions. His patrons – Burlington, Sir Robert Walpole, Lord Lichfield, Pelham – were too important to take real risks, and his gang of drinking friends – Bryan and Ferdinando Fairfax and Sir Mark Pleydell – come across like an uninspiring bunch of Hooray Henrys. Only the dying General James Dormer gave Kent a chance to design imaginatively at Rousham. Yet he did try quite hard at Esher; he was artistically drawn towards the Gothic, but he simply knew very little about it. If he had just been pleasing a patron he would have fallen back on classical clichés in its interior décor; instead he threw himself uninhibitedly and clumsily into interiors best described as 'Gothical'.

His new vault for the Waynflete Tower has quarter sections of fan vaulting in the corners, supporting trefoiled beams reaching to the centre. The Rockingham papers have one complete design for an octagonal interior. Classical pediments hang over ogee-arched Gothick doors; there is a ceiling design with more of those trefoiled beams and trefoil interlacing; an ogee-arched chimneypiece has a monstrous overmantel of an octagon, a parallelogram and a broken pediment. Kent was feeling his way, with no friends to advise him and no sketchbook to supply details. Pope always claimed he was lazy, that actress mistress never made much mark on his life, and what might Kent's record have been if he and Batty Langley, another enthusiast for odd architecture, had got together and exchanged notes? Genius is often no more than a talent for friendship.

Whatever the failings of the house at Esher, Kent's handling of the grounds was masterly, or, more accurately expressed, it was painterly. We have Kip and Knyff's bird's-eye view of the estate in 1707, when Thomas Cotton was the owner,[12] and Rocque's map of 1737 to illustrate the Kentian transformation. In 1707 formal gardens lay between the house and the river, cutting off access and views; to the south beyond the kitchen gardens there was only a small wood with a Bowling Green on the hill above it and three avenues of trees. To the north, between the house and the rectangular Black Pond of Tudor date, there was a solid grove of trees and then more straight avenues: a disconnected, dull layout. By 1737 Kent had created two major vistas immediately around the house. Those formal gardens by the river with their twin pavilions had been swept away, leaving one great lawn down to the water. From the north end of the house Henry Pelham's favourite view had been opened up, the one he chose to have himself painted in, sitting with his secretary, the nervously deferential looking John Roberts.[13] They are working in the Fishing Temple, the most ambitious of the four garden buildings that Kent had designed by that time. The Belvedere Tower, which was the focus of the entertainment which Horace Walpole describes, was built later. From the wide arch of the Fishing Temple the vista sweeps across the Black Pond. That solid grove of trees has been completely felled and now the view extends over an extensive, smooth, tree-lined lawn to the north façade of the house which, surprisingly, is entirely classical and pedimented, though with the Gothic ogee turrets and battlements of the Waynflete Tower showing up behind it. Pelham sits with his documents in his hand, looking formidable, with signs of the overeating which would eventually carry him off. Did he insist that this one elevation of his house should be conventionally classical to match the Fishing Temple and did he cast a line for perch in between dictating letters? It is possible that the artist had been told to fake a classical front for convention's sake. Kent proposed and drew a plan for a water garden with elaborate flower beds in the area north of the Black Pond, but like his water garden at Chiswick nothing came of it.

This garden north of the house was Pelham's private place. All the gardens for entertainment lay south along the river on rising ground in a Wilderness not unlike Queen Caroline's at Richmond Lodge and distinctly arti-natural in character. Kent had pushed the gardens out some way further than they were on the 1707 view and, unpredictably, enclosed this new area with a Bastion Walk down to the river, the conclusion of a long winding vista path which climbed the hill up to the site of the later Belvedere. It is at this point that Kent made his most dramatic changes. In place of a diagonal avenue the whole hill slope has been turned into a vast lawn with a few natural seeming clumps of trees, very much the treatment which Capability Brown would soon make standard. There are no harsh Bridgemannick terraces, only two sections of steeper gradients. Evidently Pelham was not a bowls player, too much stooping probably; sedentary angling would have suited him better. All the trees from the square of the Bowling Green have gone: geometry was out.

Two broad avenues run through the Wilderness, one of them a goose foot, but its principal charm, one very apparent in Walpole's account, is the arti-natural maze of paths, leading, as Batty Langley had directed, to little clearings among the flowering bushes: lilac, laburnum and cherry with cypress spires rising between them. In Langley's book these clearings are to be occupied with haystacks, wood piles, barley fields and all the kitscherie of a *ferme ornée*, but this was scarcely suitable for a prime minister. In true Richmond Lodge fashion Kent and Pelham went for

Gothic escapism. A Tuscan Temple with wide projecting eaves, like those at Inigo Jones's St Paul's, Covent Garden, fronted the triple entrances to a Grotto; a little up the hillside a substantial classical arch fronted unconvincingly the Hermitage, which was apparently a pavilion where the French horns were played to take advantage of the acoustic, and it was here that a 'rural syllabub', an eighteenth-century milkshake, was served. The third garden building in the clearings, the Thatched Cottage, is the most interesting as it appears from Rocque's vignette to be the prototype for those strange triple domes of thatch which Kent would soon be raising, amid some controversy, over Merlin's Cave at Richmond Lodge. Perhaps this was where Walpole rested after minuets and a country dance.

Esher's garden was not large but there were points of interest in it everywhere and lawns with tree clumps were ousting those seventeenth-century straight avenues. Kent did propose to naturalise the banks of the geometric Black Pond but, if Pelham was a keen angler, that would have been sacred. He emerges from his chosen landscape as a sympathetic figure, one undeserving of Walpole's malice. In November 1739, shortly after Rocque's map was drawn, he lost his two small boys, both friends of Kent, to a throat infection, and two months later Lucy, one of his six daughters, died of the same illness. When one of his friends' children fell ill he wrote to his friend Sir Robert, 'These incidents renew too much in me what I ought and endeavour to forget but find I never shall.'[14] His own death in office devastated his brother, the Duke of Newcastle, who was another victim of Walpole's spiteful reporting. Between them these two brothers, both patrons of Kent, presided over the most expansive and prosperous years of Great Britain in the mid-eighteenth century, but neither has been given the assessment their organising drive and scrupulous honesty (both died poor) deserve.

From Esher it is an easy step back to Richmond Lodge; indeed, one Kent drawing in the Rockingham papers illustrates an elaborate domed Turkish Tent bearing the royal arms, which could have been put up temporarily at Esher for a royal visit, not from King George, who hated such occasions, but from Queen Caroline who liked to quiz her aristocrats' furnishings and gardens. If she did make a visit that Thatched Cottage would have caught her eye and, just as she indulged in four or five of Langley's wildernesses, so she indulged in not one but three thatched domes. The entrance to Merlin's Cave, built in 1735, two years after Esher was completed in all except the Belvedere, was an exact copy of the deeply inset ogee-arched entrance to Waynflete's Tower from the garden; so the links between the two layouts were strong.

If the Queen had interested the whole country with her classical Hermitage and its homage to the nation's intellectuals, rather than the usual admirals and generals, then when Kent had designed her Merlin structure with its obscure waxworks, all England was bewildered. With Merlin's Cave, which was not a cave at all but a big cottage with an interior space columned with tree trunks, the Gothick message became gnomic indeed, so obscure that Mrs Duck, ex-housekeeper to the Queen at Richmond, was permanently on hand to explain its significance.

Accounts vary, but what matters here is not so much the complexities of Queen Caroline's attempt at royal propaganda in those nervous years before the second Jacobite Rebellion of 1745, as Kent's involvement in it all. Judith Colton has written an exhaustively scholarly article on the 'Cave' and all its possible associations, but she may have underestimated Kent's role in the saga by dating his lively drawing of Merlin in his bat-haunted cave, to 1751, long after the Richmond Cave was built.[15] That drawing was one illustration among many, thirty-two in all, which Kent drew for the Thomas Birch edition of *The Faerie Queene*. While illustrating a book of adventures in an impossible faerie past, Kent was able to throw off the inhibitions that had tied him to the repetitious order of a few limited motifs on the façades of Esher. His Artegal fights a Saracen knight on an ogee-arched bridge by a version of the Castel Sant'Angelo which has sprouted balconies with ogee arches under dripstones.[16] Duessa's House of Pride in Book 1, canto 4, has ogee arches poised upon twin classical columns, and a peacock perches on its pastrywork parapet.[17] Kent was apparently so charmed by this invention that he reshaped it a little in 1739 to create a screen enclosing the Courts of Chancery and King's Bench inside Westminster Hall, and another version of it, in 1741, to make a choir screen for Gloucester Cathedral, this time featuring clustered Corinthian columns to support his ogees.[18]

That frivolous and wildly inappropriate invention seems, on stylistic evidence, to have inspired Richard Bateman, a friend of Horace Walpole, to commission an entire church design from Kent in the same style of ogee arches, acanthus friezes and Rococo-Gothick for his nephew, Lord Bateman, to build at Shobdon Court, the Bateman seat in Herefordshire.[19] Kent would be dead before the church was completed in 1756, but the fact that it was built under the direction of his co-architect in several joint ventures, Henry Flitcroft, strengthens the Kent attribution, as does the pulpit at Shobdon, a pretty, toy version of the almost authentically medieval pulpit that Kent designed for York Minster in 1740–41 and John Vardy drew for inclusion in *Some Designs of Mr Inigo Jones and Mr William Kent*. The attribution of Shobdon to Kent may be circumstantial, but anyone with an interest in his elusive character should make a pilgrimage there. In the interior a visitor will experience a harmless haunting by Kent's irreverent ghost, together with the authentic scent of Anglican religiosity in the Age of Reason. Crisply carved ogee arches nod down from the plaster ceiling without any visible means of support. There is nothing remotely numinous about it, no savour of sin or repentance, only a cheerful, cosy order of village society gathered together in elegant comfort to admire the squire and his relations. Kent usually laughs at his own architectural sketches with their dancing rabbits and rude dogs. Here in Shobdon he seems to have been taking the Divinity equally lightly, creating a setting for an 'At Home' with the Almighty. It is an interior that raises a question about Kent's range: was he ever serious enough to be a great designer, a great architect or a great artist? Mozart could combine great music with high spirits, but was Kent fundamentally a shallow artist? Did he always have to put two fingers up to the pomposities with which he was involved, and if so was that what the posturings deserved? Was Kent's function, therefore, positive?

The perfect instance of his undercutting stands in the chapel at Blenheim Palace on Rysbrack's mountain of black and veined white marble, the monument carved in 1733 to the great Duke of Marlborough.[20] Kent designed it and it is entirely unmoving. The angels of Fame and History support the Duke in Roman costume with selected members of his family. He is showing a fine muscular leg and his younger son bares a naked bottom. Duchess Sarah is looking up admiringly at her husband as if recalling those moments when he would return from the labours of campaigning to pleasure her with his boots on. But he is looking away somewhere else, nobly indifferent. Underneath the waiting coffin Kent has slipped in his scampering rabbit, this time a small, cross dragon representing Envy and sticking out a long rude tongue of protest at the gentry who are squashing him.[21] That baby wyvern and the Holy Drawing Room at Shobdon sum up Kentian spirituality.

The *Faerie Queene* edition would not come out until 1751, Colton's date, but Kent was probably drawing the illustrations at the same time as he was painting three canvases of the life of King Henry V for Queen Caroline. These attractively naive compositions were for many years kept in Kensington Palace, but they are now in Windsor and at Clarence House. They illustrate 'The battle of Agincourt', 'The meeting between Henry V and the Queen of France' and 'The Marriage of Henry V'.[22] They appear, from payments to Kent of £166.6.0 'for pictures' made in 1730 and 1731, to predate quite comfortably the projection of Merlin's Cave. If Kent was working on history pictures around 1729–30 he would have been in a medieval mood and the drawings for Birch's much-delayed book were probably done at the same time.

If this is correct, and the facts are admittedly speculative, then that illustration of Merlin's Cave could well have drawn the Queen's attention to the possibilities of Merlin's prophecies in *The Faerie Queene*. Kent's drawing, a gruesomely Gothic affair, has Merlin actually delivering those prophecies to Britomart and her maid Glaucè in Book 3 of Spenser's epic poem, and three of the waxwork figures in the Gothick niches of Merlin's Cave were Merlin, Britomart and Glaucè. The other three waxworks, all the creation of a Mrs Salmon, well known for such creations, represented Merlin's secretary, Queen Elizabeth of York, who was the wife of the first Tudor King, Henry VII, and Queen Elizabeth of Spanish Armada fame.

Queen Caroline had several objectives in view when she commissioned Kent to set up his triple Thatched Cottage. If she had restricted herself to one message, then the impact of the waxworks would have been clearer. Primarily she hoped to remind visitors that the Hanoverian line was in direct descent from the Tudors. Both Henry VII and his wife were of Welsh descent and had claimed to be able to trace their ancestry back to the marriage of Britomart and Artegal, and through them to King Arthur. According to Spenser, who was stealing his storyline from Ariosto's *Orlando Furioso*, Merlin had a magic mirror which could show virtuous maidens their future husbands. Merlin showed Britomart the image of Artegal and held forth at great length, prophesying the glories of their Tudor and, therefore, so Caroline hoped, their Hanoverian descendants. With Bonny Prince Charlie politically active in Rome and Paris, any reminder of the legitimacy of George II was welcome at court, though King George, hardly the typical Welshman, dismissed all his wife's well-intentioned propaganda as 'childish silly stuff'.[23] Kent probably thought the same but was reluctant to turn down a royal commission. The lines from Spenser which he elected to illustrate are those when the two girls,

> First entering, the deadful Mage there found
> Deepe busied bout worke of wondrous end,
> And writing strange characters in the ground,
> With which the stubborn feends he to his service bound.[24]

From the array of 'stubborn feends' crawling loathsomely up the wall of the Cave it seems Kent enjoyed his Gothic horrors: dragons, serpents, wolves, hounds as well as bats.

Caroline's second purpose may have been to engineer a reconciliation with her son, the Prince of Wales, persuade him to marry and so perpetuate this royal line of King Arthur. To that end a book was placed on Merlin's table of the prophecies of Duncan Campbell, a latter-day Merlin well known in contemporary London for seances in which he revealed the identity of ladies' future husbands. All of which is ridiculous but it does give the tone of the reign in all its Ruritanian oddity and William Kent did get the commission to build a palace for Prince Frederick and to lay out a highly influential garden for him, so Merlin's Cave was not without its repercussions.

While Caroline's Hermitage was generally greeted with respect, Merlin's Cave became something of a national joke, several public houses being named after it. Lord Bolingbroke never missed an opportunity to cause trouble and his journal, *The Craftsman*, printed an account, curiously prescient of Jerome K. Jerome's *Three Men in a Boat*, where a group of friends get rowed upriver to Richmond and are there persuaded to land at 'a certain Place with iron Palisades' to be shown 'fine gardens'.[25] Caleb continues the narrative: 'We were then led thro' a great Number of close Alleys, with clipt Hedges, without any Variety or Prospect': one of Caroline's Wildernesses. They come to the Hermitage, 'which I found to be an Heap of Stones, thrown into a very artful Disorder, and curiously embellish'd with Moss and Shrubs to represent *rude Nature*. But I was strangely surpriz'd to find the Entrance of it barr'd with a Range of *costly gilt Rails*.'[26] After viewing the 'Heads of several wise Men' and making silly jokes they were led on to Merlin's Cave,

> something like an *old Haystack, thatch'd over* . . . we then went thro' a gloomy Passage with 2 or 3 odd Windows which led to a Kind of circular Room supported with Wooden Pillars. In *This* too, as the *Hermitage*, are placed several hieroglyphical Figures, male and female, which I cannot interpret. I shall only say, God keep all our *fair maidens* out of the *Conjurers Circle*.[27]

As they are leaving, the waxwork of Merlin comes to life and delivers a long prophecy in rhyme which the article explains at tedious length with reference to current European history. While such an article might be expected in *The Craftsman*, it is surprising that it was reprinted in full in the *Gentleman's Magazine* in September 1735, an indication at least of national interest in Kent's creation, though hardly a flattering one. His commissions for Prince Frederick would do much more for his reputation but already he was established, if not as the nation's leading painter or architect, at least as the nation's prime garden designer.

18

Working for the opposition – Kent and Prince 'Fretz'

Frederick Louis, Prince of Wales, was the patron who could have rescued William Kent from his dependency upon Lord Burlington and the drag of Palladianism; but instead of achieving that escape Kent actually designed for the Prince his White House at Kew, one of the dullest buildings to which he ever set his hand.

It is one of the social clichés of English history that the Hanoverian monarchs never got on well with their eldest sons, but where relations between Prince Frederick – 'Fretz' as he was always known – and the rest of his family are concerned, there was an unexplained rift and an unreasonable fury far more intense than those future quarrels between George III and the Prince Regent or between Queen Victoria and her eldest boy, Albert Edward. As usual, Lord Hervey is our authority for the explosions of rage in this strange tension between the Prince and his parents, who were generally emotionally warm and loving in their relations with their other son and their four daughters. But Hervey is a suspect witness, as he turned from being the Prince's intimate friend, sharing a mistress, Anne Vane, with him, to a bitter enemy. The pages of Hervey's diary recording the course of that falling out were so scandalous that when Hervey's descendant, the 1st Marquess of Bristol, came to edit them, he tore the pages out and destroyed them. The surviving passages are sexually explicit enough, so the Prince Frederick pages must have been outrageous in the extreme.

Whatever the cause, Queen Caroline, a worldly wise woman, normally most tolerant in sexual matters, could not contain her hatred at the mere sight of her elder son. The most quoted outburst came as Hervey and the Queen were standing at a window in St James's Palace when the Prince, casually dressed, walked across the court:

> The Queen spied him, and said, reddening with rage: 'Look, there he goes – that wretch! – that villain! – I wish the ground would open this moment and sink the monster to the lowest hole in hell!'[1]

When Hervey expressed his surprise she continued: 'I can assure you if my wishes and prayers had any effect, and that the maledictions of a mother signified anything, his days would not be happy nor very many.'[2] Frederick's sister, Princess Caroline, joined her mother in this chorus of loathing:

> They neither of them made much ceremony of wishing a hundred times a day that the Prince might drop down dead of an apoplexy, the Queen cursing the hour of his birth, and the Princess Caroline declaring that she grudged him every hour he continued to breathe.[3]

Which made it all the more unfortunate when the Prince did die very suddenly and unexpectedly in 1751, if not of an apoplexy, of something very like it, with rumours spreading that his wife, Princess Augusta, might have poisoned him because she had fallen in love with Lord Bute, their son George's tutor and the future Prime Minister, the man who lost the American colonies.

Lord Hardwicke claimed that Sir Robert Walpole had told him of 'certain passages . . . of too high and secret a nature' between the Prince and his mother to be revealed, but which explained the quarrel.[4] Unfortunately, when Hardwicke's son quizzed his father again on the subject, many years later, the old gentleman claimed to have forgotten. Hervey asserted that, after his quarrel, the Prince had put about the story that Hervey had accused the King of having an improper relationship with his eldest and favourite daughter, the Princess Royal. It does seem that there must have been some sexual source for the violence of the feelings that Prince Frederick aroused.

In his everyday life the Prince was the most popular member of his family: extrovert, friendly and relaxed, looking in for a pint of ale at the local inn near his house at Cliveden, captaining a team to play cricket against other village teams and joining in the fun at fairs and festivals. Whether he deserved the reputation he acquired of being a Rococo Prince, devoted to French decorative styles, is not completely proven. Two of his closest friends and courtiers, Lord Lyttelton at Hagley, Worcestershire, and Sir Thomas Lee at Hartwell in Buckinghamshire, did, however, create beautiful and committed Rococo interiors for their houses in anticipation of the day when they would be entertaining a Rococo King.[5] So it does seem probable that the long, dull reign of the Palladian revival would have ended with a King Frederick, which makes it all the more puzzling that when Kent, usually so adept at handling rival patrons, was brought into the Frederick–Caroline conflict and asked to design a palace for the Prince, he designed the White House, so-called for its stucco cladding, not only in the most pedestrian Palladian, but overlooked from the garden of Queen Caroline's private retreat on Kew Green. Exactly why she wanted that plain five-bay house when she and her husband had Richmond Lodge half a mile away upriver is not clear; but it is described as 'The Queen's House' on the only known illustration of it, a vignette on Rocque's 1734 edition of his *Plan of Richmond Gardens*.[6]

What possessed Prince Frederick to lease an old timber-framed Tudor house on the other side of the ironically named Love Lane from his mother's private retreat is unclear. In March 1731, when he leased it officially, he had already been living in it for three months and had bought its contents, including a range of seventeenth-century portraits, so it was a considered action. His eldest sister, the Princess Royal, was living in the Dutch House next door. A family commune was building up, but not the commune of an affectionate, united family, so what exactly was Frederick's purpose? The most obvious answer is that he was trying to regain a place in his mother's affections. She had left him behind in Hanover as the family's token representative, to reassure their German subjects, when he was only seven years old. As a result he had grown up a virtual orphan in the company of household servants. At some point soon after his parents came to the throne in 1727 he was reunited with them in England and something went badly wrong in their relations. This must have been that mysterious passage of too high and secret a nature that Sir Robert revealed to Lord Hardwicke and that Hardwicke then forgot.

Kent moved into this fraught and stormy family colony in August 1732 when he was appointed as the Prince's architect, so he already had the experience of Esher with its garden buildings behind him and, as at Esher, he was building around the existing core of an earlier house. The link between this White House, as it came to be known, and Esher Place was rather with Esher's classical Fishing Temple than Waynflete's Gothic Tower. Kent's most distinctive and successful architectural form was that which he first produced in the Fishing Temple: a pediment sunken within another pediment, essentially a form where the roof dictates the fabric and the façades are secondary. He could have picked it up from Palladio's last church, the Redentore on the Giudecca at Venice, but Kent concentrated it brilliantly in a series of garden temples until it climaxed in his Worcester Lodge at Badminton. When, however, he attempted a composition of applied pediments strung out over a nineteen-bay elevation, as he did for Prince Frederick's White House, it failed completely.[7] The pediments needed to enclose each other in a compact, almost Baroque whole to succeed visually. There were no columns, no pilasters, no enrichments to the window surrounds, just the standard Palladian plat band and sill band. It was a most un-Kentian composition and, without a shred of evidence to prove the claim, it looks as if Lord Burlington had laid his heavy hand of discipline and purity on Kent's shoulders as he designed it. All existing views of the White House, which would be demolished in 1802, were drawn from the garden, so there is no record of the entrance front.

From comments by Sir William Chambers the interiors of the White House were livelier than its exterior. Kent had decorated its Gallery in blue and gold, its Drawing Room with Grotesque ornaments in reds, blues and gold, while the ceiling was centred with Kent's favourite classical rape: Leda and the Swan. John Vardy illustrated a bucolic Kent chimneypiece for the White House with hunting horns, fox masks, whips and stirrup chains around a portrait of the Prince on the hunting field – all very sportive.[8]

The garden to the White House was as disappointing as its elevations. Evidently, at this stage, the Prince did not favour an Arcadian informality. Twin statues dominated the two lawns of its forecourt and its garden was rigidly formal. A lawn with four statues was flanked by square boscage, after which a terrace stood above a much bigger lawn with two statues above four large quarter-beds of flowers. A vegetable garden was tucked away in the front of the house beside the stables and service buildings. In marked contrast, the grounds of the Queen's House across Love Lane were alive with curving paths in a little wilderness, a garden temple, a formal avenue and an orchard with a terrace overlooking the lane.[9]

Initially, while his new house was going up, the Prince and Kent found each other kindred spirits, sharing an enthusiasm for fancy dress and for riotous ornamentation of water transport. In 1731, Hervey, who disliked Kent, was debating, in letters to his beloved Stephen Fox, whether to accompany the Prince to a masquerade, dressed in the wildly camp Tudor huntsman's costume that Kent had devised for the party, or to attend the same function in normal costume and laugh at the masqueraders. The Prince himself was going as a shepherd, 'an Adonis, or an Apollo, I forget which',[10] and the eighteen huntsmen who were to accompany him were to be dressed in an outfit that obviously tempted the effete Hervey:

> In green waistcoats, leopard-skins and quivers at their backs, bows and arrows in their hands, tragedy buskins upon their legs, breeches trussed up like rope dancers, antique gloves with pikes up to their elbows, and caps and feathers upon their heads like a Harry the 8th by Holbein.[11]

Kent had a reputation for creating exotic outfits, his best known being a lady's petticoat adorned with columns of the five orders. The masquerade would obviously be much talked about. Hervey had, however, been dancing too much recently. He was a dedicated hypochondriac. 'I have tasted nothing but tea, bread, and hartshorn drops this four and twenty hours', he ended his letter to Fox, 'and nothing warm about me but that corner of my hart which you inhabit.'[12] So he decided he was not strong enough to enter a ballroom,

> with a mob of about four or five squeaking idiots in our train . . . I know it will be monstrous to go at all after refusing to go with him, but I cannot resist the curiosity I have to see this fraternity, I have deserted, run the gauntlet, and shall take a malicious pleasure in swelling the number of their persecutors.[13]

He did, in fact, attend and 'laughed, like Madame Sévigné, dessous ma coiffe' to see 'that fraternity I had deserted, lugged and twirled about as I imagined they would be'.[14] Not that Tudor huntsmen were impossibly exotic in such a masquerade ball; one of the liveliest at contemporary Versailles saw all the masqueraders dressed as clipped privet bushes.

In retrospect, these years in the early 1730s were when Kent could have slipped from the confines of Burlington and his Palladian obsessions and launched out as Prince Frederick's favourite designer in the new wave of French fashion, working for all those disaffected lords in expectation of a new, style-conscious monarchy. There would still have been twenty years to go before the Prince's sudden death in 1751. Kent himself died in 1748, but his last years could have been influential, swinging the country into the cultural orbit of France and Austria with an exuberant figurative decorative style perfectly suited to Kent's playful invention. Few artefacts convey as vividly what the country lost by Kent's failure to persuade his patrons towards another way as that State Barge which he designed in 1731–2 for Prince Frederick's water progresses. It rests now in the Maritime Museum in Greenwich, beached for ever.[15] The present Prince Charles understandably coveted it and hoped to row it out into the twentieth century, with all the contrast between its lean, functional elegance, powered by twenty-one muscular oarsmen, and the astonishing decorative flowering of the gilded woodwork that Kent devised for its stern, its acanthus-encrusted cabin and golden sea lions, snarling out like King Charles spaniels over the prow. Apparently it was too frail, or the Museum authorities were too nervous, to risk sending it out again on to the Thames. It is indeed an object of high art, Baroque in composition, Rococo in detail, and the authorities were right to be nervous. On each side of the stern, which rises to the Prince of Wales's feathers, enclosed in a scallop shell, a nubile mermaid reaches out an arm to grapple with a golden dolphin, the two sinuous fishes framing a Garter star. Wreaths, scallops, sea lions and a bold guilloche frieze line the sixty-three-foot hull, built sleek and streamlined for speed. In splendid contrast the royal cabin stands bolt upright and uncompromisingly square like a pedimented garden building alive with crowns, bell-drop chains, and yet more scallop shells. This was the inventive panache that George II's declining years desperately needed.

Yet even over this glittering vessel Lord Burlington had extended his influence. Kent included on the designs, in addition to a triton, a six-foot waterman in a livery lifted shamelessly from Inigo Jones's sketches for royal Stuart masques with feminine, feathery fringed sleeves, a tight jerkin to show off a well-muscled chest and a neat helmet above trim curls.[16] If Alexander Pope had ever seen the sketch he would have become morbidly suspicious of his amusing friend.

This perfect creation took to the water on 8 June 1732, with the Prince, his mother, his brother and all his five spiteful sisters on board, but not, sadly, King George. They sailed from Chelsea Hospital down to Somerset House with French horn players stationed among the gilded sea lions to warn lesser craft to keep their distance. It was the first of many such happy occasions, the last being a voyage to carry Queen Victoria's consort, Prince Albert, to open the Coal Exchange. Left-wing critics are always ready to praise any royalty, like the bicycling Dutch royal family, that behaves with an un-royal simplicity: Alfred burning the cakes, Louis XVI making locks, the present Prince William heaving logs around in Chile. But there are moments for magnificence and a poetry of display to remind witnesses that life is not necessarily brutish or short, and the Baroque was made for them: a new Pope coming out on the balcony above Bernini's colonnades or that unexpected opening to Queen Elizabeth II's fiftieth Jubilee, which had been predicted a fiasco, when the golden Coronation Coach, with more trumpet blowing tritons, rolled out quite briskly on to The Mall to the strains of Zadok the Priest and delighted hundreds of thousands with its cheerful pomp.

That State Barge was Kent's moment. Working for a prince it is one's business to create the legend and, with buskined huntsmen and golden mermaids, Kent was doing just that. Then in 1733, Lord Burlington, who had given him all his chances, opportunities sometimes beyond his deserving, sometimes well within his reach, took offence at not being given the white staff of the Royal Steward and resigned everything, including his strategic Lord-Lieutenancies and the Vice-Treasureship of Ireland.[17] The King had promised him the Stewardship, but then found that the Duke of Devonshire had a better claim. Kent had owed all his offices to Burlington's influence. From 1733 onwards he would have to rely on himself and it is clear from the records that there was some falling away in royal commissions. Not one of those impossibly heavy designs for a new Parliament Building came to anything; and not one stone was laid to realise Kent's pearwood model for a twenty-one-bay Doric palace on the Thames at Richmond.[18] George Vertue had always claimed that Kent owed more to influence than to merit, but one positive result of the loss of that influence was Kent's turning away from art and architecture towards garden design and his more lasting fame.

He would still retain one advocate in royal palaces. Burlington gave up all his royal offices in that fit of pique, but Lady Burlington remained a Lady of the Bedchamber, not, as Lord Hervey pointed out, from any sense of loyalty, 'but from a stronger passion of another kind. She liked the Duke of Grafton, and had she left the Queen she must have left her lover, or at least lost many favourable opportunities . . . which her own ingenuity more than her lover's assiduity always improved.'[19] How dull the social history of the century would be without the vigilant malice of those two sexual outsiders and society insiders, John, Lord Hervey, and Horace Walpole, two men alert to relish every scandal and suppose the worst on every possible occasion.

For one more year, 1733, the Burlington influence would linger, with Kent designing the Stanhope monument to set against the classical choir screen of Westminster Abbey and balance the Isaac Newton monument, which he had designed in 1731 on the other side of the choir entrance.[20] Those two pyramidally composed memorials signify Kent's status nationally. The soldier, Lord Stanhope, dreams in his marble tent with a helmeted Victory seated uncomfortably on its apex. Sir Isaac rests upon a pile of books with the great globe itself poised above him. He has two angel attendants to Stanhope's one, but Stanhope shows the better leg. Both men are in Roman costume. It would be in 1740, with his design for a Shakespeare memorial, that Kent would make the popular breakthrough and design the dead wearing the costume of their own time without a trace of Roman posturing.[21] His Shakespeare was carved by Scheemakers and with its romantic, swaggering stance did something positive for the playwright's image. The problem with sartorial authenticity would come when sculptors had to make something acceptable out of a pair of trousers, as in the lamentable statue to Earl Mountbatten of Burma in Horse Guards Parade.

It was Kent's work in two particular gardens, not necessarily his best, but his most observed and praised, that made his reputation in this divergent field: Carlton House in the middle of fashionable London and the Elysian Fields at Stowe in Buckinghamshire. Prince Frederick gave him his opportunity at Carlton House, but Kent, a natural trimmer, had begun work for a supporter of the Prince, the Whig politician Lord Cobham, at Stowe several years before planting out began at Carlton House in 1734. This was with a louche affair, a classical bordello no less, the Temple of Venus, a miniature Palladian composition, copied from Pirro Ligorio's reconstruction of ancient Rome, one of ten sheets of sixteenth-century engravings that John Talman had collected and sold to Lord Burlington.[22] Ligorio illustrated his three-part pavilion overlooking a small garden with four trees and one statue; Kent set his Temple of Venus more boldly on the edge of one of Bridgeman's geometric fortifications. It was in position before 1731, a contemporary, therefore, of Queen Caroline's Hermitage at Richmond, but rather less savoury in its associations. All the many visitors who wrote accounts of the multiple garden buildings of that amazing park noticed Venus, some with blushes, others with fascination.

Its exterior was set with busts of notorious sexual enthusiasts: Nero, Vespasian, Cleopatra and Faustina. On the frieze was carved a Latin inscription warning visitors what to expect within. Translated it read:

> Let him love now, who never lov'd before:
> Let him who always lov'd, now love the more.[23]

Anyone untutored in Latin would have a shock on entering, as the room was furnished with 'pleasuring couches'[24] and the walls were painted with scenes from Spenser's raunchiest episode in *The Faerie Queene*, an old favourite of Kent and one which he had obviously drawn to Lord Cobham's attention. Malbecco's wife Hellenore runs away from her old husband and takes up residence with a colony of lewd woodland satyrs. Chasing after her, poor Malbecco observes her taking part in an orgy, but when he urges her to return home she threatens to set the satyrs on him. Consequently he goes mad. It is not an improving tale, but offers an interesting side light on Kent.

An anonymous French visitor to Stowe in 1748, writing a description, *Les Charmes de STOW*, for a lady friend, was rapturous about the park. His account helps to explain the continental delight in these innovative new English gardens which would spread a garden form, that Kent had done much to popularise, across Western Europe. 'L'heureuse Nation que la Nation Angloise!', he exclaimed flatteringly: 'She has burst the iron chains that bind virtually the rest of humanity; she alone is a nation of true men.'[25] The Temple's inner room was 'toute ornée de Peintures *galantes* à la verité, mais néanmoins nullement *obscénes*'.[26] Though he did think that instead of 'tant de *Satyres* dont ce *Temple* est défiguré', it would have been better to have painted 'des Amans moins lascifs; & que

Cupidon y parût sous une forme plus digne de lui',[27] so modest praise with reservations. They were the work of Francesco Sleter, who had none of Kent's problems with Leda and the Swan.[28] These distressful scenes have since been painted over and the National Trust, which now controls the grounds of Stowe, has made no move to restore them. If English Heritage were in charge it might be a different story.

Putting such amusing oddities aside, it is important to give Stowe's pleasure grounds a central place in the William Kent canon. His association with that most celebrated of English landscapes of his time was hugely influential. Not only did he design several of its many garden buildings – the Temple of British Worthies (1735), the Temple of Ancient Virtue (1735–7), the Shell Bridge, the Grotto, Congreve's Monument (1736), the Oxford Gate and the Hermitage (very close in style to Queen Caroline's at Richmond Lodge) – but he applied in the Elysian Fields all the apparently easy but actually innovative graces of natural seeming lawns and lakelets with trees tastefully clumped and the Grotto adding a touch of mystery. Every visitor writing on Stowe praises Kent's work in the Elysian Fields. It spelt the final closure to formal gardens. Kent's work on the grounds of Esher was as good or even superior, but few noticed it and it has not survived. Stowe has remained a national delight from 1700 to the present day: the 'Albano glut' in perfected Nature.

If the Temple of Ancient Virtue, the central structure in the Elysian Fields, is correctly dated, then it is likely, with its attendant ruin, the Temple of Modern Virtue, to be a deliberate riposte to Queen Caroline's Hermitage of 1730 and Merlin's Cave of 1735.[29] It seems that Kent, who had already lost the support of Burlington at court in 1733, was putting himself even further away from possible royal patronage. Cobham was taking over some of the direction that Burlington had exerted. Kent's best gift to English architectural design, the pavilion that begins with a roof and works downwards in a satisfying theorem of dome, triangular pediments and cube, appears nowhere at Stowe. Cobham had his eye fixed upon a more correct classical Arcadia. The Temple of Ancient Virtue is beautiful but conventional. It imposes Arcady upon its glade of lawns, its Grotto and wandering river, but within that Arcadia stood emblems of contemporary political venom.[30] Pure white statues of Homer, Socrates, Epaminondas and Lycurgus reminded visitors of the comparative nobility of the poetry, philosophy, bravery and legal impartiality of the ancient world. A few yards away stood an ugly ruin, the Temple of

Modern Virtue, with a headless statue of Sir Robert Walpole to make his responsibility for the corruption of the British state abundantly clear. Quite how Sir Robert was identified without a head is not apparent; but a case could be made for restoring this lost twin to the surviving Temple of Ancient Virtue. The only authentic Kentism on the scene is that exedra of British Worthies, remembered from a drawing Kent had proposed for Chiswick but which Burlington had rejected. It provides a perfect talking point, and talking points are what these English Arcadian Gardens were all about. It offers some kind of definition to English history, very much as Caroline had attempted in her Hermitage. It was typical of Kent to undercut the serious sequence of sixteen Worthies with one of his scampering rabbit devices, in this case 'Signor Fido, an Italian' who,

> neither learnt nor flatter'd any Vice.
> He was no Bigot,
> Tho' he doubted of none of the 39 Articles.
> And, if to follow Nature,
> and to respect the Laws of Society,
> be Philosophy
> he was a perfect Philosopher;
> a faithful Friend,
> an agreeable Companion,
> a loving Husband,
> distnguish'd by a numerous Offspring.

And, of course, Fido turns out to be 'not a Man but a Grey-Hound'.[31] The affectionate sentimentality of the device is pure Kent. Fido's fellow Worthies are the hero figures of the Whig opposition to Sir Robert Walpole's administration:

> Those, who, by Arts invented, Life improv'd
> And, by their Merits, made their Mem'ries lov'd.[32]

They are: King Alfred, Edward, Prince of Wales, Queen Elizabeth, King William III, Sir Walter Raleigh, Sir Francis Drake, John Hampden, Sir John Barnard (who had put money into the party), Alexander Pope, 'Ignatius' Jones, John Milton, William Shakespeare, John Locke, Sir Isaac Newton and Sir Francis Bacon.

By daylight this Elysian glade has a satisfying green elegance, the tree planting apparently casual, though actually carefully contrived. To appreciate how the little valley would have worked at night for a 1770 reception given for Princess Amelia, in all the uncertainties of the English climate, Horace Walpole is the best authority, wickedly observant as ever, of human frailties, his own included. Seven years before, for that Anglo-French entertainment at Esher, it had all been so different:

> On Wednesday night a small Vauxhall was acted for us at the grotto in the Elysian fields, which was illuminated with lamps, as were the thickets and two little barks on the lake. With a little exaggeration I could make you believe that nothing ever was so delightful. The idea was really pretty, but as my feelings have lost something of their romantic sensibility, I did not quite enjoy such an entertainment al fresco so much as I should have done twenty years ago. The evening was more than cool, and the destined spot anything but dry. There were not half lamps enough, and no music but an ancient militia-man who played cruelly on a squeaking tabor and pipe . . . I could not help laughing, as I surveyed our troop, which instead of tripping lightly to such an Arcadian entertainment, were hobbling down by the balustrades, wrapped up in cloaks and great-coats for fear of catching cold . . . we were none of us young enough for a pastoral. We supped in the grotto, which is as proper to this climate, as a sea-coal fire would be in the dog-days at Tivoli.[33]

Such was Kent's contribution to the multiple attractions that made Stowe the archetypal 'Pleasure Garden', one offering ideal beauty as a background to easily absorbed instruction. Carlton House garden was less interesting, but because its twelve acres of *rus in urbe* were overlooked by the back gardens of some very distinguished people in Pall Mall, and because the ponderous Sir Thomas Robinson of Rokeby Park, Yorkshire, wrote a quotable analysis of its experimental nature, it had its impact.[34] Basically it was Pope's Twickenham garden, only very much more expensive. Kent's immediately celebrated new garden, 1250 feet long and 300 feet wide, lay at right angles to the house, which, therefore, commanded only a limited view of an existing Wilderness and one of Kent's most ingeniously spatial garden buildings. This was a domed 'Saloon' which contained statues of King Alfred and the Black Prince, to suggest the wisdom and nobility of King Frederick's future reign, set above an octagonal bath house, the Bagnio, on the ground floor.

From this equivocal haunt of pleasure, visitors would lose all sense of being in London, with a vista down a huge lawn, made private on either side by an undulant line of trees, 15,200 of them according to the accounts, concealing a system of winding pathways. After enjoying their Bagnio, the visitors could cross the Prince's cricket pitch and walk down a widening funnel of lawns to exedral flower gardens, left and right, with classical herms, half-moon pools and rich crescent beds of flowering shrubs. Lilac, laburnum, roses, jasmine, laurustinus and sweet briar gave a backing to hollyhocks, day lilies, pinks, tulips and carnations. Kent was in no way limited to Italian lawns, dark hedges and statuary; these were virtual cottage gardens, a foretaste of the nineteenth-century 'Gardenesque'. Beyond that flowery space the trees closed in about an informal pool. Hidden behind it, to give some focus to a garden walk, was an Aviary, deep in the trees concealing Marlborough House. After inspecting the birds, visitors could pick their route back through sinuous walks in a planting of yews, hornbeam, chestnut, firs, oaks and hollies, to Carlton House or tea in the Saloon.

Sir Thomas Robinson, whose own gardens at Rokeby had copied Castell's plans with Plinian exedras,[35] recognised that 'after Mr Kent's notion of gardening' everything would have to change.[36] The Carlton House garden had 'the appearance of beautiful nature'; now garden designers would have to 'work without either level or line', judging layouts with a painter's eye, so that 'one would imagine art had no part in the finishing'. Robinson claimed that, after Carlton House, 'the celebrated gardens of Claremont, Chiswick and Stowe [were] now full of labourers, to modernize the expensive works finished in them', which was flattering enough, though Burlington might have begun to feel more than a little passé.

19
Institutional failures – Ruritanian and gargantuan

The failures of William Kent will make for a short chapter in a life of multiple successes, but there were failures so they must be acknowledged. They were usually failures on a grand scale, associated with institutions around London, together with one house, Holkham Hall, which was conceived by an ill-assorted committee, more as an art institute than as a home. Given his unpretentious, cheerful nature Kent was happier thinking on a human rather than on an institutional scale. There was also the staccato quality to Palladian revival design which inclined to fussiness on any grand project, the awful prime instance of which was the 'goods-train', the 200-yard-long east front of Henry Flitcroft's Wentworth Woodhouse in Yorkshire.[1] It was usually necessary to borrow the embracing theatrical arms of the Baroque to counter this separation, but antique austerity and Berninesque hyperactivity were in opposition.

Kent did, however, fail on a human scale with that pearwood model that he prepared, around 1734, for a royal palace to replace homely, shoddy Richmond Lodge. With his eye on the Grand Trianon at Versailles he offered a twenty-seven-bay building that was essentially a vast single-storey sequence of state rooms for a king, George II, whom he should have known disliked lavish expense and preferred modest palaces like the Lodge or Kensington. His model had a basement and first floor, but the absence of a central dome suggests that one of Burlington's unsatisfactory skullcaps had been proposed, and the squat octagonal turrets, which Kent would propose again for Horse Guards, had a threatening, defensive air. It was a design better suited to a building for Parliament than the gargantuan barracks that Kent would design later for that national project.

It was typically Hanoverian that while both palaces and parliament designs got nowhere, a resoundingly palatial horse stable was built without financial hesitations on the site next to St Martin-in-the-Fields where the National Gallery now stands. The Royal Mews, or 'Muse' as Kent spelt it, went up between 1731 and 1733, a stabling for fifty-six horses to a design which Kent claimed as his own.[2] A spirited drawing for its south entrance, featuring stallions curvetting on the gate posts, has all the marks of Kent's style, but that was never built.[3] Isaac Ware was Clerk of Works for the Great Stable and its elevation, which copied the gate arch to Burlington House, looks to have been a joint compilation by Burlington and Ware.[4] It survived for less than a century though it seems from Fourdrinier's engraving to have had a loutish grandeur appropriate to Dunghill Mews.[5]

Kent's Treasury Building on the north side of Horse Guards Parade has been more fortunate and deserved its luck. Enthusiasts for Burlington's work often regret the demolition in 1935 of the heavily rusticated town house which he designed for General Wade in 1723 on Old Burlington Street.[6] But Kent's Treasury building, which went up ten years later, in 1733–7, preserves much the same richly correct textures of rustication, a pediment on engaged Ionic columns and windows inset within arcading on both floors. Metopes of alternate crowns and wreaths on the frieze below the *piano nobile* are a Kentian defiance of normal Ionic enrichments; but the best feature of the building is generally inaccessible to the public. This is the Treasury Board Room, where top decisions are supposed to be made. Kent infused an almost poetic majesty even into bureaucratic officialdom.[7] Coupled Composite columns support an exquisite frieze of fruit and flowers on the chimneypiece.[8] The table and all the chairs have his favourite lion masks and clawed legs. Term-shaped pedestals for busts are set against the walls together with a superb astronomical bracket clock by Charles Clay. Deep pediments on brackets emphasise the doors and, as a final touch, should the King wish to observe the proceedings, there is a throne with dolphin arms and crowning amorini either side of the royal monogram.[9] So the Moguls had their Peacock Throne, Japan its Chrysanthemum Throne and George II, as lord of the seas, had his Dolphin Throne. It was very much in Kent's nature to apply charm and figurative detail to such a desperately serious chamber.

This five-bay exoticism in Whitehall was originally intended to be the centrepiece of a seventeen-bay terrace of offices. It preceded the Horse Guards Parade range, which it now overlooks, by many more years than Kent, who contrived them both, could have anticipated. Some time before his death in 1748 he had designed a three-part range of buildings vaguely similar in its bay structure to what now confronts the open Parade for the Trooping the Colour with such a jaunty, unserious skyline. It is Ruritanian in its charm and wholly inappropriate to the War Office which it was built to contain. It is easy to imagine Rudolph Rassendyll and Colonel Sapt in there, discussing how to frustrate the rascally designs of Rupert of Hentzau and Black Michael, but not Wellington planning how to thwart Napoleon. Yet the first and second British Empires were projected successfully from these blocks of, again, typically Kentian humanity in scale. As the building now stands, centred by an impudently odd turret, it is such a tourist draw that it would be a pleasure to attribute it without reservation to Kent; but that is not possible.

His pre-1748 design[10] is not rusticated, has intrusive pediments and those squat octagonal turrets he briefly favoured. Then he died and a Board of Works – Flitcroft, Ripley, Henry Finch and William Oram – took over. It is to be hoped that they then worked from a later lost Kent design, heavily influenced by the Treasury Building next door, because what they built is much better. Kent was brilliant on fenestration, perceiving that in an austere staccato elevation a three-dimensional richness is essential to window surrounds to counter tedium. Both the rustication and the fenestration of the eventual Horse Guards range are taken from the Treasury Building which overlooks it, like a Chancellor of the Exchequer's private villa. The foundations of the Parade were laid in 1750 and, over 181 committee meetings, the Board of Works decided on the new, strongly centrist turret in 1752, built it in 1753 and completed the building in 1759 at a cost of £65,000, more than twice the estimate.[11]

Burlington may have lost his influence at court after that petulant resignation, but Lady Burlington was still at court and the Queen still favoured Kent. In 1734 he designed the 'velvet covered galleries and gilt lustres' to make the Chapel at St James's fit for that disturbing wedding of the Prince of Orange, though Isaac Ware was paid £2646 for 'deals, uphirs [upholsteries], baulks, standards &c', which indicates that, as usual, Kent left the hard work to someone else and just offered sketches.[12]

In 1737, in the nick of time before Caroline died, the Queen's Library, which Kent had designed for her, handsomely but conventionally arcaded, was completed.[13] Henry Fox, Surveyor of the King's Works, had told the dying Queen that her Library was finished when it was not; and Hervey wrote him a delightful rocket of a letter:

> To Henry Fox, Neglector of his Majesty's Works, St James, Thursday Night, 1737.
>
> Which of all the Devils in Hell prompted you to tell the Queen that everything in her Library was ready for putting up her Books? Thou abominable new broom that so far from sweeping clean, hast not removed one grain of Dirt and Rhubbish . . . go with me to scold all your odious dilatory subalterns.
>
> Bad Night.[14]

Which sounds as if Kent was included in the inefficiency; but he did complete for his Queen an exuberantly feminine seat supported by wreathed caryatids in Kensington Gardens, set on a mount from which the Rococo s-curves of her Serpentine, most Rococo of waters, could be enjoyed.[15] Her Rococo instincts in a Palladian country would be sadly missed.

These were, however, the reactionary years when Kent dumbed down Inigo Jones's garden front for Wilton House to create Devonshire House on Piccadilly, retaining those odd skirted window surrounds, but adding nothing vitalising or original: a demonstration of Burlington's continuing hold on his friend during the late 1730s.[16] It was proof of Kent's failure to animate an outworn tradition of design that need never have been revived in the first place. Eleven bays in the heart of fashionable London for the grandest of Whig ducal families should have given him an opportunity to educate and astonish.

Burlington had brought out his cherished *Fabbriche Antiche* in 1730, intending it to be the foundation of an English neo-classicism. Consequently, though his friend had lost much of his influence in 1733, Kent beavered away at ponderous elevations for the Houses of Parliament that got nowhere.[17] Three times, in 1733, 1735 and 1739, he drew up grandiose elevations for a mind-numbing Palace of Westminster with one façade to the Thames, the other for public entry; and three times they were consigned to the record cupboards. Internally the planning was logical and sound. The Commons would have argued in an arena much like that of the Senate in Washington today; the Lords would have met in a depressed rectangle with a grandly arcaded surround, much simpler than what Barry and Pugin would contrive in the next century.

It was on his exteriors that Kent's invention lost touch with reasonable models. Burlington seems to have insisted on a colonnade with at least twenty giant columns on a welcoming exedra. Saddled with that central feature on the landward elevation poor Kent flailed about wildly with strange double-decker columns set *in antis* and variations of his favourite pedimental features, open and closed. For the skyline of the 1739 version he invented a templar confection; for the 1733 version he had made do with those shallow skullcap domes. The foolish Earl of Shaftesbury had condemned Wren's St Paul's, so a normal Baroque dome with a drum was out of the question. It was a blessing that Lord Burlington had lost his powers of persuasion at court, saving the nation from a clumsy and unloveable central symbol of democratic government.

Throughout this decade of the 1730s, dismal as it might appear from his activities in the capital city, Kent was inventing from strength to artistic strength in his garden designs. He had set his seal upon Stowe and given Capability Brown, who became Head Gardener there in 1741, a method of landscaping which would become a park formula for the whole country over the next thirty years, though it would rarely be followed with Kent's subtle variations or quite his line in playful Arcadian fantasies. In 1733 Shotover would follow and, after 1738, Claremont and Rousham. In the meantime, vast, brooding and difficult to love, Holkham Hall, the 1st, and in that creation, the last Earl of Leicester's half-palace, half-institution, was taking shape in the most testing terrain that Kent would ever encounter for his Arcadian Garden formula: the sluggish undulations of East Anglia.

Holkham brought Kent back, in middle age, to an unsatisfactory relationship of his youth. As a young man in Italy he had never quite been able to charm Thomas Coke, a man more interested in things than in people. Coke had been the obsessive collector and self-styled 'virtuoso' who almost got Kent thrown out of the Papal States in 1716 over the illegal export of a headless Roman statue of Diana. He collected Leonardo drawings, rare manuscripts and antique statues. Consequently, on his return to England in 1718, loaded with glorious art treasures, he was desperate for a gallery, not a house, in which to display them. He was also, like Lord Burlington, caught up in Shaftesbury's version of a Roman architecture revived by a Whig oligarchy. To make him even harder to control he was an almost professional architect, having taken lessons in Rome from Kent's friend, Giacomo Mariari.

There was one major problem. In 1720 Coke lost huge sums of money in the South Sea Bubble fiasco. For the remainder of his life he would be pursuing a vision of a gallery-house, conceived when he was very wealthy, but with much reduced means. Holkham was the result of that tension. It is one of the strangest houses in England, impossible not to admire but difficult to like; it is, in addition, a battlefield of attributions. Coke and his local architect, the elder Matthew Brettingham, brooded for years over what they might build when the money was right. Lord Burlington became friendly with Coke, while always posing as a superior authority on matters architectural, and inevitably Kent became involved. Arguments have raged over the respective contributions of the four men, records of building are patchy, plans are often undated, recently a whole cache of letters from Coke to Brettingham was discovered.[18] However, the truth remains uncertain and it would be tedious to enter into an inconclusive debate.

As Coke, raised to the peerage in 1728 as Baron Lovell, spent his limited funds, first on the park before laying even a foundation for even part of Holkham's ultimate complex, it will be chronologically helpful to make a journey into the estate from the direction Kent intended, the south, making the most of an unrewarding topography. Holkham Park is not Kent's most successful garden achievement, but it tested him more than any other. If an Arcadia could be created in Norfolk it could be created anywhere except the Fens.

Kent drew the design for the first signifier of Holkham's importance, a triumphal arch lodge, with a donkey standing under the central of its three arches, an indication of frustration with Coke's obstinacy.[19] The building, more stage scenery than convincingly antique, lies between two groves of trees more than a mile from the house. Coke cut out the two side pyramids that Kent had drawn; they would reappear later at Badminton. From the arch the straight drive rolls away apparently to infinity. The trees lining it, largely sombre ilex, but mixed and splendidly mature, are set back respectfully to suggest an approach to an important lord. Eventually it reaches Kent's beckoning giant Obelisk in the middle of a wood, but at that point time has confused Kent's intentions. About a hundred yards to the left is a large domed Temple, handsome enough but plain, and it is completely invisible. The trees have screened it not only from the drive, where it should indicate Arcadia, but also from the house where it should be the focus to all southern views. This is a visual disaster. Landowners naturally love their trees, but Kent's Holkham works on a few, limited, grand simplicities and that Temple is one of them and a key item. Work had begun on the gardens in 1722, only two years after the South Sea crash, and between 1730 and 1733 John Parsons was building this Temple, the Obelisk and a 'Seat' on a mount.[20]

A return to the drive and the Obelisk and at last the house swings into view down what passes in Norfolk for a hill. On the left is a big natural seeming lake contrived out of a salt marsh and a tidal arm of the sea. Kent designed the bridge at its far end, but it is the extraordinary condominium of the house that holds the attention. In a design of 1726 Coke was still intending just a large central block, but by 1731 he had a change of mind from which Holkham has never recovered.[21] Either to achieve a Roman villa appearance or to allow for very high ceilings he cut out the usual attic storey entirely, losing a bedroom floor. In a cleverly functional, but expensive, solution to his self-created problem he determined to follow Palladio's precedent in his Villa Mocenigo and add a wing at each corner. But where Palladio added a pavilion, Coke added a house, four substantial, identical five-bay houses in the standard 1/3/1 Palladian bay rhythm. That gave his palace-gallery a staggering twenty-three bays facing south and north.

The disaster, visually apparent from the hillside, was that while Coke and Brettingham devised the central gallery block with, possibly, Burlington advising from his experience of Venetian windows in recessed arches at Chiswick and his gloomy turrets at Tottenham Park,[22] they let Kent design the five-bay houses at the corners economically in a different style that neither accords with nor dramatically clashes with the solemn centrepiece. There has to be a strong suspicion that Kent was behind the whole Mocenigo-style solution, because he drew, at some uncertain date, a very similar scheme for Horse Guards, which is why Holkham has been set here in this otherwise institutional chapter.[23] That first Kent drawing for Horse Guards had two five-bay wings cursorily attached to a central block with Venetian windows in recessed arches, and just the same Kentian scatter of open and closed pediments as a second-thoughts roofline. What clinches the attribution of these unsuitable wings to Kent is the fact, abundantly proven in these recently discovered letters, that Coke the masterful still left every detail of the internal fitting up of the first, south-west wing for Kent to draw.[24] This, of course, was the most important of the four wings, the one where Coke intended to live with his beloved library and where the Earl of Leicester lives today. It is entirely Kent-designed though the penurious Coke failed to decorate the Library ceiling with Kent's lively scroll work.

As the drive curls down the modest slope towards the house it passes closest to that family wing, then the north-west wing where Coke kept his guests in isolation, separated from the family by the long Statue Gallery and its two Tribunes. The north or entrance front of Holkham, lacking the south front's immense hexastyle portico, is even more gloomily institutional. Polite architectural critics use the word austere rather than gloomy, but even Christopher Hussey has to admit that 'bright sunlight, however, is required (whereas Blenheim or Seaton Delaval are best seen in grey weather)'[25] and Windsor Castle no doubt in a thunderstorm. But Holkham is glorious enough within to be able to withstand home truths about its dismal exterior.

Coke intended it to be golden with Bath stone. He seems not to have explored Walpole's solution of Whitby limestone. When Bath proved too expensive he remembered that in 1730 he had built that Temple of locally produced white bricks. For the house he managed to find a local clay that baked into dun-coloured bricks. These were declared authentically Roman and of these Holkham was built. Their texture is not attractive and Kent saw that the elevations would need a decorative lift. He produced a design for the south front that enriched the principal windows with blocked surrounds, gave all-over rustication for textural depth and added a frieze of swags and wreaths.[26] If his design had been followed those Venetian windows would have been inset within arched recesses, but when rustication is executed in brick thirty different moulds are needed to shape the bricks for a single rustication. Coke cut back on costs and his house was the permanent loser.

We must, however, forget all these lost opportunities and prepare to enter Kent's master stroke, the Marble Hall. Aesthetic assessments are always personal so, writing personally, this for me is one of the most exhilaratingly beautiful internal spaces, not just in England, but in Europe; and it is a measure of Kent's greatness that he did at least one even better, reserved for the next chapter. His Baroque affinities, acquired in Rome, crossed with Coke's reaching towards the Roman Antique, and resulted in a Baroque neo-classicism, full of movement, an apse within an apse, yet Roman in its dignified reserve and, most unexpected of all, translucent in colour with its Derbyshire alabaster columns and side panels and those insistent black and white key fret and guilloche friezes. How it can ever be described, as it often is, as 'cold' with all that coloured veining, defies reality. Its coffering swirls awesomely above an enriched frieze of naked boys and ox skulls; big daisy paterae star the ceiling compartments, classical statues, mostly nudes, stand in the niches and the ironwork balustrade curls like sea horses.

The genius behind the planning must have been Kent's. The second of these important letters, from Coke to Brettingham and written in 1734, records Burlington's approval and adds 'Kents outside is also vastly in favour & the going up steps from the hall also'.[27] It is that entry at ground level, which leaves the visitor sunken below the *piano nobile* level of the gallery on three sides, that makes all the difference spatially to the impact of the entrance. If we imagine the Hall with its floor at the level of the column bases, that soaring visual effect would be lost. Something even more dramatic, however, has been lost. As Kent designed the Marble Hall it was to have been dominated by a towering marble statue of Jupiter, bought in Rome in 1717 during Coke's Grand Tour, halfway up the stairs to the apse.[28] It would have been actively anti-Christian in impact, turning the Hall into a version of the ancient Capitolium vetus on the Quirinale, an actual Roman temple ready for sacrifice.[29] Jupiter's plinth would have divided concave steps, not the present convex flight, and Kent's projected columns were unfluted Corinthian, not the fluted Ionic that were eventually built. The alabaster deserves the flattery of fluting so Coke was right to make the change, but he did not risk raising Jupiter and the statue was eventually set up in the Smoking Room below the portico on the south front.[30] It is to be hoped that some future Earl of Leicester will have the courage to return him to Olympus.

If only the money flow had been easier and the work pace faster, a pure and amazing neo-Roman Antique interior could have surprised the country by 1740, two decades before Robert Adam achieved similar but less theatrical effects at Kedleston Hall in Derbyshire. Kent was our first and most successful neo-classicist; it just so happened that the house would not be completed until 1764, by which time Kent had died in 1748, Coke in 1759, and Adam had returned from Dalmatia to steal the fame with his 1764 *Ruins of the Palace of the Emperor Diocletian at Spalatro*, when Kent and Coke had already rebuilt part of that palace in Norfolk.

It would be foolish to describe the remaining fine rooms of Holkham as an anticlimax. They are a resounding staccato of varying styles: Burlington's Chiswick is surpassed in the cool serenity of the Statue Gallery, Houghton's velvet richness is at least equalled in Holkham's Saloon, and Holkham, unlike Houghton, has retained its original collection of paintings. There is no authentic Kentian connection with these rooms, but it is a testimony to Kent's influence that they could all have been fitted up by Kent, including Benjamin Goodison's golden furniture of Baroque birds, beasts and shells. Holkham's interiors are a demonstration of the complex, not easily defined, truth that Kent had created a style of interior decoration, opulent, profuse, allusive and indulgent, that would serve his country for the middle years of the century in default of a continental Rococo.

20

Success in the capital for the wrong patron

In their analysis of Kent's entrance hall at Holkham some writers discuss his superlative achievement there as if he had been a child learning to paint by numbers. They refer to coffered panels copied from Antoine Desgodetz's plates of the Pantheon in Rome,[1] to the frieze, borrowed from Fréart's 1650 *Parallèle de l'Architecture Antique et de la Moderne*, of the Temple of Fortuna Virilis, ceiling ribs taken from one of Lord Burlington's Inigo Jones drawings, and proportions filched from Burlington's Assembly Rooms in York.[2] What this intense scholarship fails to acknowledge is that Holkham's Entrance Hall is arguably superior to the master, Palladio's, sanctuary of San Giorgio Maggiore – more dramatic, more of a unity, warm and translucent. It should never have been described as a 'marble' hall, for the effect of fluted alabaster is quite different, livelier, more reflective of light and colour, so unprecedentedly un-English that many visitors take refuge in whimsical humour and claim it would work better as a swimming pool.[3]

The problem with Kent's reputation is that he does not exude the gravitas of a great architect; he simply produced, increasingly in the latter years of his maturity, great architecture, but without the legends and the aphorisms that posterity relishes. Kent should have lived to the biblical three score years and ten, not the grudging sixty-three that he was allowed. Assuming that he was forty-nine when he projected entry at ground level for this Alabaster Hall of Jupiter at Holkham; that he had laid out his most magical garden at Rousham by remote control when he was fifty-six in 1741; fifty-nine when he devised the matchless spatial subtleties of 44 Berkeley Square; sixty when he began the Great Room at 22 Arlington Street for the Prime Minister, and the same age when he designed for the Duke of Beaufort at Badminton the most perfect garden building in Britain. If these are all taken into account, 1748 was not the time to die with at least three projects – Horse Guards, Holkham and Wakefield Lodge – unfinished. But with all those to his credit who needs gravitas for greatness?

If ever proof were needed that Kent alone was responsible for the spatial drama of the Alabaster Hall, then the staircase hall of a small London town house, 44 Berkeley Square, is conclusive.[4] Without a hint of aid from Coke or Burlington and only a rich, sophisticated spinster to please, Kent thought up a Baroque space of bewildering subtlety, trimmed it with Rococo elegance and still managed to keep within the bounds of robust, correct Palladianism. Like the Alabaster Hall, his Stair Hall at Number 44 would go down as his greatest building if only he had not produced something even more challengingly perfect a year or two later. Kent was a great late developer who reached his professional prime in his sixties, then died too soon.

Lady Isabella Finch, the patron for whom he created this rare interior, was the daughter of the Earl of Winchilsea and Nottingham, Daniel Finch, who was the leader, along with Lord Carteret, of the opposition to Walpole's administration. It was curious, therefore, that the King's second daughter, Princess Amelia, had chosen her as First Lady of the Bedchamber; but Amelia was a law unto herself. She never married, rode furiously to hounds and swept into church services wearing riding clothes and carrying a dog under each arm; all of which sounds distinctly lesbian in tendency, except that she was also a notorious flirt and had a scandalous affair with the Duke of Grafton.[5] The couple used a hunt as a cover for a secret meeting. Queen Caroline was furious, but none of her last three children married. When Amelia died she was found to have worn concealed a miniature of King Frederick II of Prussia, to whom she had once been engaged.

With such connections the spinster Lady Bel, as she was known to her friends, will have entertained at the highest level and required Kent to provide her with a dazzling ambience for it. He must have found her a kindred spirit because he made a special mention of her in his will, bequeathing her 'my veined Alabaster Vase with brass ornaments gilt in ditto with vine leaves grapes etc', and, more surprisingly, an intellectual trophy:'my four models of Newton, Lock, Woollaston and Doctor Clark'.[6] These last mean that Lady Bel was a supporter of Kent's controversial Hermitage of British worthies in Richmond Park. Lord Cobham from the opposition and the Queen from the ruling administration could both have recommended Kent for the task. He began to engineer his paradise of forms behind a bland, three-bay, three-storey house in 1742, using the same team of craftsmen who had just been working for him on the first stage of his old friend and patron, Henry Pelham's town house at 22 (19 at that date) Arlington Street on the other, south, side of Piccadilly. That was to prove embarrassing, as the interiors which Kent produced for Lady Bel of the opposition were so infinitely superior to those he had contrived for Pelham that when, in 1743, Pelham became Prime Minister, he felt obliged to call Kent in again to add a third canted bay to his house overlooking Green Park with a Great Room as fine, if not finer, than the one Kent had produced for Lady Bel Finch. Pelham's new wing was not quite completed when Kent died in 1748, but the contretemps has resulted in two eccentrically brilliant Roman Antique-Renaissance-revival-style Kentian interiors, one on each side of Piccadilly. Only 44 Berkeley Square has a Baroque-Rococo-Palladian Stair Hall. Number 22 Arlington Street's stairs are fine but they mount in three conventional flights, rather like Henry Pelham himself. Does that tell something of Lady Bel's character?

Created for such a small house, the detailing of the Stair Hall at Number 44 might be expected to be delicate. The reverse is true. Joseph Pickford, mason and sculptor, and Robert Dawson, plasterer, worked on a scale of rich grandeur in gloriously confined spaces.[7] Only Benjamin Holmes, smith ('Rich Iron work to Railings Great Stairs £69.0.6'[8]), revived the Rococo-style sea-horse curves and husked enrichments of Kent's favourite design, which he had used for the balustrades of the Alabaster Hall at Holkham, to sound a feminine note.

The dark front corridor hall of Number 44 is the perfect preparation for the surprise of the Stair Hall at the end of it. This is made luminous by a large apsidal fanlight of delicate fan tracery set immediately overhead, above a breathtaking complexity of galleried and guilloched internal balconies. So much decorative detail embosses the walls in a high relief of gilded swags, wreaths, classical busts in deep round niches with swan-necked scrolls, that it takes a time to make sense of Kent's whirligig of stairs and landings. An imperial flight, only one person wide, leaps up between Holmes's s-scrolls and husks to an arched recess and paterae band. Here it divides steeply to reach Lady Finch's most ornate gallery and the entrance to her Great Room. Four fluted Ionic columns carry an apsidal cornice of the most exuberant enrichments. This crashes – there is no other word for the meeting – into its side walls to land on Ionic pilasters, just missing the bold projection of broken pediment to the doorcase of the Great Room. Behind the Ionic columns a flight of stairs slinks up diagonally through an apsidal space where the classical busts of naked athletes and heavily clothed philosophers are linked by drops and wreaths of fruit, lions' heads and bell flowers.[9] These gentlemen do, however, manage to assert a certain neo-classical authority upon their bedizened surroundings; Kent never quite forgets Lord Burlington or the Earl of Shaftesbury. Above them, outsailing on four golden acanthus brackets, are the razor-sharp apsidal curves of a second gallery and the panel-patterned, semi-dome of the ceiling, studded with paterae at every geometric junction.

The Great Room lives up superbly to the promise of its approach. Light reflects sumptuously from gilded mirrors and jewel-like glass drops are suspended on the walls like glittering necklaces. Every detail of its door surrounds, its acanthine modillioned cornice and its Roman Renaissance-style ceiling of interlaced lozenges, hexagons and squares,[10] has been enriched to the ultimate degree and gilded by William Almond. For the 'Ceiling, Cove & intablature in Great Room' the plasterer Dawson was paid £176.13.8'.[11] Princess Amelia might have felt humbled by it, for there was nothing in her father's palaces to equal it. As a bonus, she would, with her amorous disposition, have been aroused by the lewd loves of the Gods on their terracotta, blue and green backgrounds: the moon goddess pouncing upon a naked Endymion, Jupiter as a bull raping Europa and Ganymede having a bad time with an eagle. Do these account for that strange translation manuscript in the Bodleian Library of Ovid's *Metamorphoses* that Kent laboured over?[12] The accounts name Edward Wetherby as the painter, but when he was working to a miniature scale, as in these lubricious cameos, Kent himself could express character and attitude with dextrous economy. In one lozenge containing a man and a sheep he appears to have been making amends for that terrible Ulysses and the ram painting on the King's Gallery ceiling at Kensington twenty years before.

This ceiling must represent the most elegant sexual art in London. No wonder that 44 Berkeley Square is a popular Open Doors Day venue, and that Henry Pelham asked for a repeat performance, just as explicit, just as Roman Antique-Renaissance, and entirely outside the contemporary pattern of ceiling designs, for his Great Room at Arlington Street.[13] Kent rose to the challenge almost too sumptuously. The Arlington Great Room is even more rich and riotous in ornament than Lady Bel's Great Room. Whether it is as satisfying, as digested in its display, is questionable. It is larger and more complex in ground plan with deep recesses on either side of its chimneypiece. Even its doors are double. The coving, which has to navigate around those recesses on a system of garlanded brackets, is oppressively enriched with the hexagons and lozenges of the ceiling. Between the enriched frieze, the coving and the ceiling the eye has nowhere to rest and in its prime, before it was taken over sympathetically for offices, the walls were equally bedizened with Rococo mirrors, paintings in ornate frames and richly carved panelling. Under pressure from a prime minister and friend Kent had gone a little too far.[14] If it was Kent who worked on both ceilings, awkwardly suspended, it could well have shortened his life and explained why his patrons out in the country found it so difficult to get the Signior to attend regularly to his garden commissions. There would be no other work even remotely like the interiors of these two houses until Robert Adam's return from Italy ten years later, in 1758, and then a stricter Scottish propriety would be observed. They throw an interesting light upon Kent's tastes and the open-mindedness of both Hanoverian princesses and prime ministers, examples of how, in retrospect, we have Bowdlerised the whole period with our prim concept of 'the Georgian'.

21

Places, patrons and the wood of self-revelation

It is no criticism of Kent to remark that he had his Arcadias handed to him by a fortunate coming together of factors, but he was the first with the vision to take hold of those factors and shape them into what Christopher Hussey described, with a pardonable excess of zeal, as 'the earliest surviving ancestor of all the landscape gardens in the world'.[1] Hussey was writing about Kent's Rousham, which will be the central subject of this chapter, and while the Chinese and the Italians would have strong reservations to make on Hussey's claim, it still offers a useful starting point for a garden of bewildering and challenging subtlety. Rousham is, beyond any question, Kent's most important garden work, arguably his greatest and most influential.

A late seventeenth-century enthusiasm for tree planting in parks, as an investment when in a solid plantation, or as an ornament when in an avenue, had left the country around most large houses generously wooded but rather dull. Kent's contemporary, Charles Bridgeman, following to some degree the practice of the garden designers London and Wise, had developed a reputation by carving up these acreages of woodland into geometric patterns, long narrow allées, diagonals and circles. But the mood in gardening was changing and Kent picked up that mood quickly because, with his artistic training in Italy, he was more sensitive to the possibilities suggested in landscape paintings of the Poussins, Claude and Albani and any number of Italian and Dutch artists. In Horace Walpole's words, Kent was

> painter enough to taste the charms of landscape, bold and opinionative to dare and to dictate, and born with a genius to strike out a great system from the twilight of imperfect essays. He leaped the fence, and saw that all nature was a garden. He felt the delicious contrast of hill and valley changing imperceptibly into each other, tasted the beauty of the gentle swell, or concave scoop, and remarked how loose groves crowned an easy eminence with happy ornament . . . Thus the pencil of his imagination bestowed all the arts of landscape on the scenes he handled.[2]

A carefully sited classical garden building could, at a stroke, raise these picturesque compositions to the Arcadian, while a wider eclectic range of pavilions – Chinese, Turkish, Gothic – could give that Arcadia a national reputation. The existing topography would matter, as would the vision of the patron. England was wealthy, its philosophers – Shaftesbury and Locke – were genial and positive, even the climate could be welcoming, but only when characterful shelters were provided for the intervals between sunshine.

By the time he came in 1738 to Rousham, Kent had gained wide, recent experience at three other landscapes: Esher and Shotover, Oxfordshire, before 1733, and Claremont, Surrey, between 1728 and 1743. Rousham, begun in 1738, would be followed by Euston in Suffolk, where he worked episodically between 1738 and 1746. Then, in 1745 came Oatlands in Surrey[3] and Badminton in Gloucestershire.

At Shotover he found himself almost as closely tied to the tyranny of long, straight walks focused upon a single marker as he had been at Chiswick.[4] The Tyrrells' house there stood at the mid-point of an axial line between the Gothick Temple and an Obelisk that Kent was required to raise to complete the formalism. To the side of it was a Wilderness waiting for a poetic treatment which, as at Chiswick, Kent failed to provide. His additions were as geometric as the existing layout. On a mound he built a domed octagonal Temple, more conventional than his usual inventions.[5] From here five straight vista lines fan out: a Lime Walk to an iron gate, a vista to the house, another to his Obelisk, a fourth to the Octagonal Pond and the last to an access avenue. Colonel James Tyrrell was a friend of Colonel Robert Dormer of Rousham, but not of Robert's brother, the formidable General James Dormer, who would shortly lay his spell upon Kent and Rousham. Colonel Robert had employed Charles Bridgeman in 1725 to impose his geometry on the woods of Rousham, so Colonel Tyrrell was content with the same ordered military solutions for Shotover.

At Claremont, Kent was working for an energetic, controlling patron, the debt-ridden Duke of Newcastle, who found time, between his several spells as Prime Minister, to keep a close watch on garden developments and to catch fish in the lake that Kent had created for him.[6] Claremont was more rewarding than Shotover because Kent was working there in the shadow of Vanbrugh's own nightmarish carving up of woodland to concentrate the eye upon a dour, castellated Belvedere. Recognising its drama, Kent left Vanbrugh's garden alone, concentrating on Bridgeman's simplistic offerings. He widened Bridgeman's round pond into a large lake, picturesque with a wooded island and its Belisle Temple as a base for the Duke's dab fishing. Then, with a veil of trees, he softened the intrusive stepped amphitheatre that Bridgeman had cut into the hillside. To please the practical Duke, Kent designed a Bowling Green Temple, a Home Farm with model premises and a Bower similar to his Richmond Hermitage. Some trees he thinned to allow views through groves and an additional 2300 trees were planted in clumps to soften vistas, with more conifers than usual, Scotch fir, spruce, cypress and yew. These darker trees, a Cottage and an almost complete absence of statuary suggest that Newcastle was not a committed classicist, so Claremont is only intermittently Arcadian.[7]

Moving from duke to duke as his reputation rose, Kent designed his second grandest garden pavilion, the Temple, for the Duke of Grafton at Euston, to transform an unusually underwooded topography and a shallow valley. By 1743 Horace Walpole was reporting that Euston was

> one of the most admired seats in England – in my opinion, because Kent has a most absolute disposition of it. Kent is now so fashionable, that, like Addison's Liberty, he
>
> Can make bleak rocks and barren mountains smile.[8]

Euston was unusual in that Kent had little pre-existing woodland, only John Evelyn's mesh of avenues, to work upon.[9] He had, therefore, to make do with clumps, scorned by Walpole: 'Mr Kent's passion, clumps – that is, sticking a dozen trees here and there, till a lawn looks like a ten of spades. Clumps have their beauty; but in a great extent of country,

A chillingly pure staccato of Palladian incidents in Kent's Entrance Hall at Ditchley Park, Oxfordshire (1724-5) designed under the threat of an inspection by Henry Flitcroft.

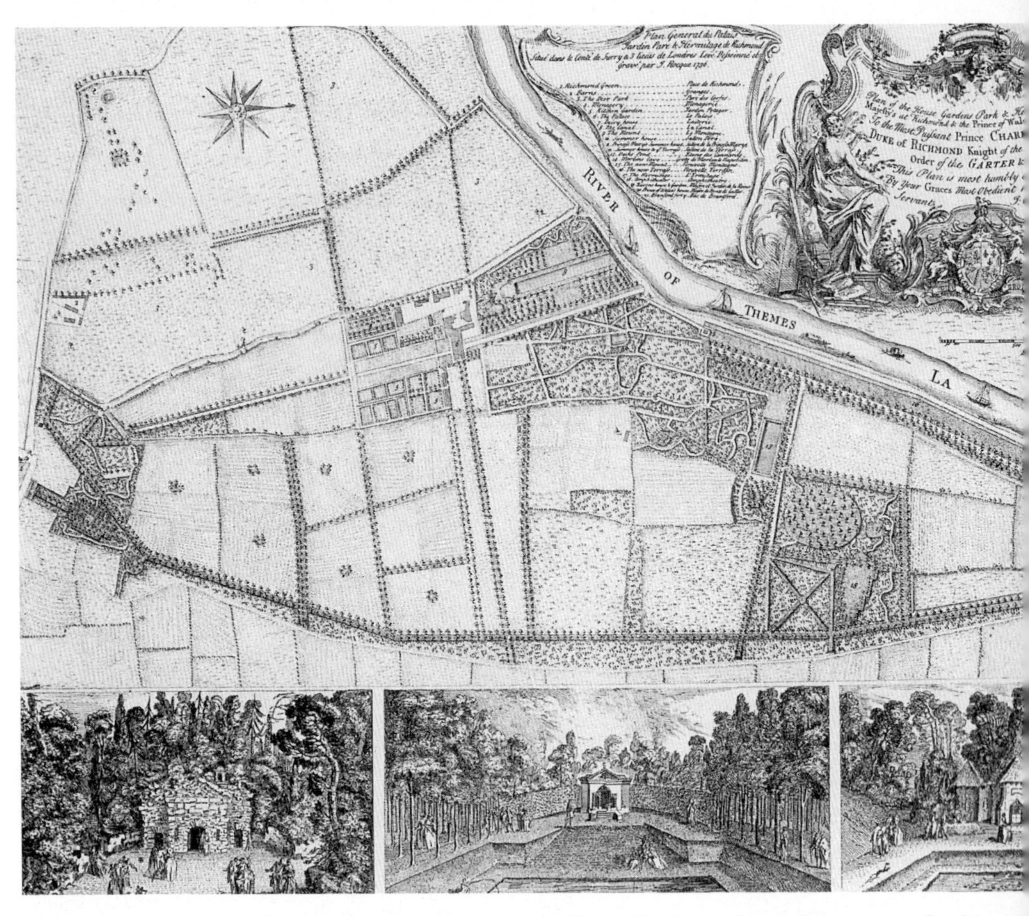

Rocque's 1736 plan of the royal park at Richmond (Kew Gardens) shows the scatter of wilderne
across fields retained for partridge shooting. Merlin's Cave stood next to the rectangular basin

Kent's flattering proposal sketch for a Hermitage at Richmond Gardens. A muscular satyr is kissing the hand of Queen Caroline as royal shepherdess.

Queen Caroline's Hermitage at Richmond, designed in 1732 by Kent in rocky Romantic classicism to contain marble tributes to British scientists and philosophers.

Kent's wildest and most notorious garden building was his Merlin's Cave, built in 1735 on the bank of the canal at Richmond.

These waxworks set within Gothick niches in Kent's Merlin's Cave were part of a group intended to demonstrate George II's descent from the Tudors and King Arthur.

Kent's drawing of himself with his arm around Alexander Pope in a largely fantasy version of the poet's back garden at Twickenham. An arch behind the Shell Temple gives a glimpse of the Thames seen through Pope's Grotto.

Henry Pelham, sitting with his secretary, John Roberts, in the pavilion of his garden at Esher Place, Surrey. The house, with its Kentian mixture of Gothick and classical forms, is visible across the lake.

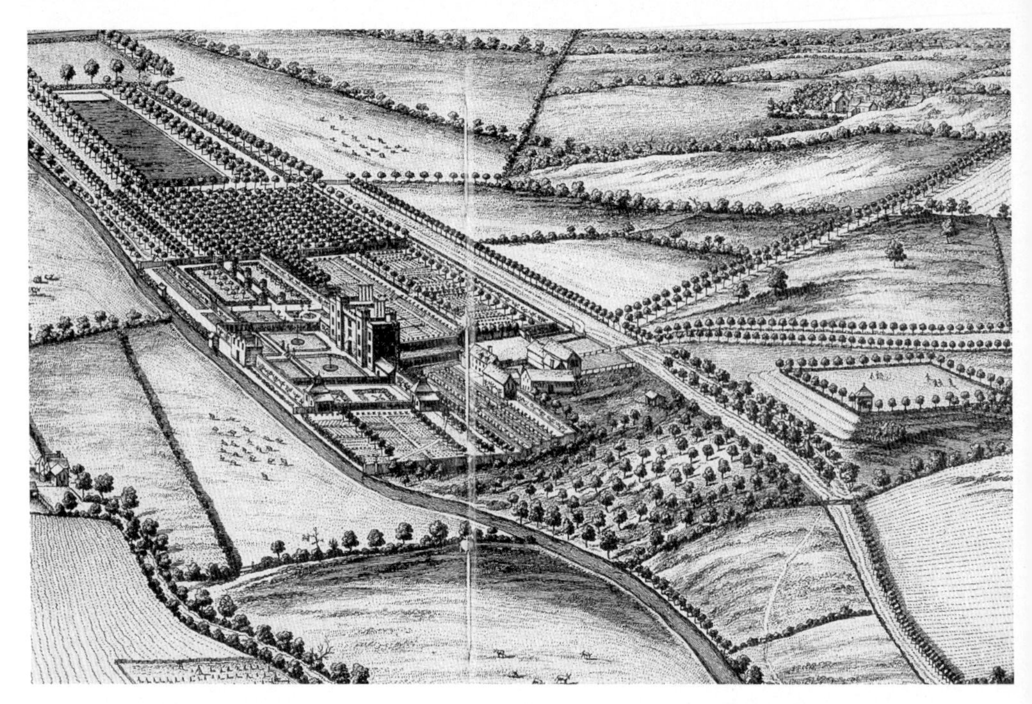

A 1708 view of Esher Place from *Britannia Illustrata* showing the laterally aligned formal gardens around Waynflete's Tower. Note the rectangular canal, the walled garden with its banqueting houses to the river and the elevated bowling green with its temple.

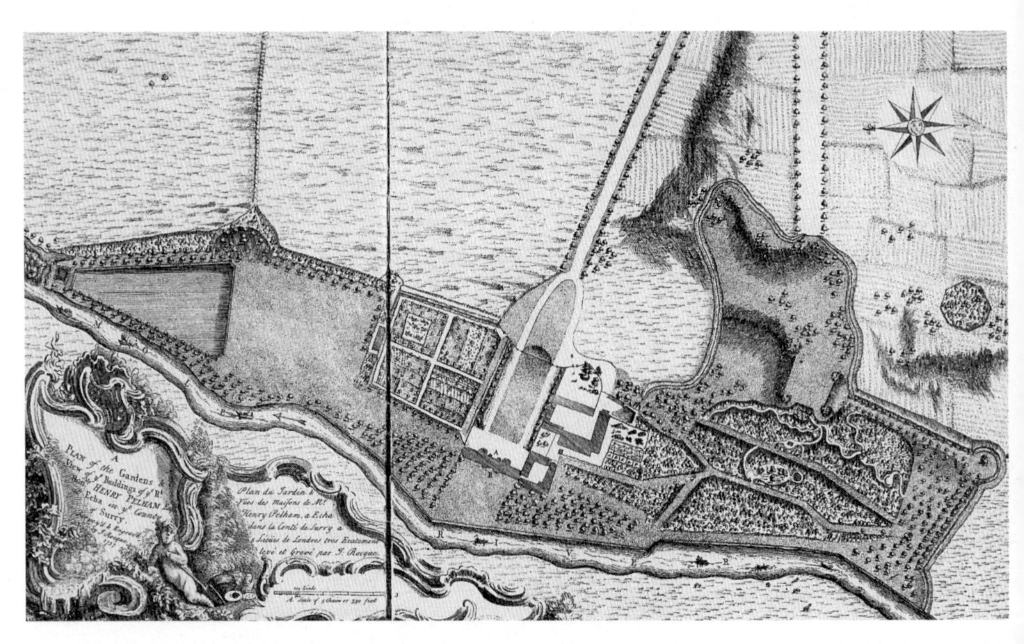

John Rocque's 1737 plan of Esher after Kent's softening of the geometries. The walled garden has been demolished, opening up a framed view from the house to the river, and the orchard has been threaded with serpentine paths which lead to new garden pavilions; the bowling green has disappeared and the canal is now a trapezoid lake with a temple at its head.

Kent's favoured Bridlingtonian ogee arches proliferated in his 1739 design for a Court of Justice within Westminster Hall.

Kent and Queen Caroline were both devoted to Edmund Spenser's *The Faerie Queene*. Here Kent has drawn Merlin in his bat-haunted cave prophesying royal descendants, George II among them, to Britomart.

The Bagnio, with a saloon above, which Kent designed in 1734 for Prince Frederick's garden behind Carlton House, was a brilliant Baroque distortion of a Palladian form.

The extraordinary staircase for Lady Bel Finch at 44 Berkeley Square shows Kent at his most eclectic best. Neo-Palladian detail is thrown around with a Baroque gusto, the balustrade and decorative swags are Rococo and the whole design conveys the richness of Imperial Rome. It is neo-classicism gone wild.

how trifling to scatter arbours, where you should spread forests!'[10] Kent's Temple at Euston, however, makes the point that a really memorable park building can raise the tone of undramatic topography.[11] For Euston's Bury St Edmund's Lodge, and even for Euston's Wash House, Kent kept to that Palladian simplicity which Lord Burlington would have approved, creating the noblest wash house in Britain.[12] But for his Temple, Kent remembered the Bagnio he had designed for Prince Frederick at Carlton House, pulled out the stops and produced an architectural jewel, infinitely grander than its parent house.[13]

A shallow dome sits on an octagon above a second pedimented octagon of elegant buff 'Woolpit White' brick with a bold vermiculated quoining of Suffolk flints. Side pediments in the Redentore manner shoulder the composition, and there is an extravagance of Chiswick-style flights of steps on two sides. Kent had planned the Temple to face the garden front of the main house,[14] but it was built instead on a ridge to the south-east of the house to utilise the foundations of an existing ice house, where it could serve as a grandstand overlooking an exedral hippodrome down in the valley. Simply to enter the banqueting room on the upper storey raises the spirits. It has noble proportions, two Kentian chimneypieces with guilloche friezes and overmantel mirrors, Corinthian enrichments to the archways and a transparency of great windows flooding in light from east and west.[15] With foreknowledge it is easy to feel Kent's eagerness to repeat this small triumph, but much heightened, at the next opportunity. The Temple is the Worcester Lodge at Badminton in embryo: Kent did not always pull out a new design.

For Lt General James Dormer, however, a very close friend and very special patron, a member of Burlington's convivial inner circle, Kent could be attentive, inventive and, it appears, sympathetic. General Dormer's reshaped house and garden at Rousham throw more light upon Kent's character and moral inclinations than anything else in his reserved and underchronicled life since those letters he wrote from Rome to Massingberd and Chester twenty years earlier.

Rousham House lies a few miles north of Oxford and its twenty-five acres of grounds cover the quite steeply rising west bank of the River Cherwell. It is a near miraculous survival of Kent's gardening, as if some benign, or more likely mischievous, garden god had determined that, though Esher might be lost and no documentary proof of Kent's activities at Stowe would survive, at Rousham at least we should know almost everything. Not only are most of the garden buildings of those intense five years, 1737–41, intact, but the General-haunted house is as Kent left it with most of the Cottrell–Dormer paintings and statuary still in place to record the General's curious tastes.

It would be too much to expect there to be anything in the way of Kent's own dyslexic writings to explain his aims and directions, but there is a revealing correspondence from the General's Steward and right-hand man, William White, relating the course of the improvements and asking, sometimes in vain, for Kent's presence or advice.[16] A plan of the grounds as Bridgeman left them in 1725 has survived, and a plan that illustrates exactly Kent's modifications to Bridgeman's garden.[17] Rarest of all there is an amusingly racy and enthusiastic description of how to enjoy a tour of the garden with all the delights, though not all the moral challenges, it had to offer.[18] It was written in 1750, two years after Kent's death, nine years after the General's, by John MacClary, the Head Gardener, in an effort to persuade the Cottrells, to whom the General had bequeathed the place, to come up from London more often. So it gives a valuable impression, if a Bowdlerised one, of what a mid-century landowner wanted from a landscape garden.

With all this information available, and well known since at least Christopher Hussey's full account of Rousham in *Country Life* in 1946,[19] there has been, not so much a conspiracy as an embarrassment, very English in its nature, though one shared by American writers, about the full moral implications of this beautiful and important garden. It is yet another instance of that 'No sex please, we're Georgians' syndrome mentioned earlier. At the risk of being considered lewd this author has no intention of either conspiring or of being embarrassed, because Rousham offers some rare insights into the nature of both William Kent and General James Dormer. The English have an abiding horror of homosexuality and bisexuality, perhaps because both are common. In the past, three English kings – William Rufus, Edward II and Richard II – have been murdered on the suspicion of the 'vice'. James I only escaped because he produced three remarkable children, William of Orange because he was Dutch and had rescued the country from Roman Catholicism, which was considered, marginally, worse. Oscar Wilde remains an obsession with writers and film-makers, the gay question splits the Church of England as a trendy new heresy, and even a suspicion of one-time gay activity is enough to destroy a political career. In earlier chapters it was noted that Kent could hardly have been gay, otherwise Alexander Pope would have outed him in a fit of moral righteousness. But then Pope, from his letters, was on excellent terms with the Dormer brothers, Colonel Robert and General James,[20] and Pope never married, so who knows what repressions might have been surging behind the whited sepulchre of his exterior. Readers will have to make their own judgements on the evidence or, if they are Georgians, skip on to the end of the chapter.

Kent's additions to Rousham House are quite the quirkiest and most surprising of his whole career, a sure sign of an idiosyncratic patron. Even the entrance drive plays a spectacular trick. A gap in the trees on the left reveals for a moment the Caroline front of the House, then hides it away. The Stable Block is entirely different: Kent in a mood of authoritative Roman simplicity with hangover Baroque details. A cheeky and inappropriate ogee-domed turret tries to undercut the masculine austerity, a very Kentian device, an architectural equivalent of those scampering rabbits in his garden sketches.

Walking around the west wing of the House the drama of the Bridgeman ha-ha strikes home. It runs within feet of Kent's pseudo-Caroline bow windows, and a herd of ferociously primeval long-horned cattle graze on the paddock, so close that their calves walk in the ha-ha ditch itself. Behind them, across the field, is the Castellated Barn, battlemented like the House, the Middle Ages at play next to the authority of a Classical Gateway built to give visitors their entrance to the park circuit. Much nearer at hand, closer even than the wild cattle, are the Gothick ogee-arched niches prepared by Kent in the walls of the west wing for the General's first blast of challenging nudity. A naked Venus half-covers her private parts with a revealing hand, and next to her a nude young male, Antinous or Apollo according to sexual preference, has the same air of posed exhibitionism and introduces Rousham's theme of paired qualities and the availability of moral choice.[21] On the east wing a Bacchanal and a Dancing Faun, stark naked and grinning, reinforce that choice. It is not quite a garden of Good and Evil, but more Rabelais's 'Do what you please' Abbey of Thelema, a place for self-discovery, haunted by unleashed desires.

After this disturbing introduction it is logical to enter the House to find out more about the man posing the choices. General James Dormer had enjoyed a gallant military career campaigning in Spain and been rewarded with the appointment of Minister to the Portuguese court in Lisbon. He was no ordinary soldier but a Merton College man, 'withall, a curious gentleman, and well skill'd in Books', Cicero and Chaucer being his favourites.[22] In Lisbon he showed another side to his nature.[23] Mr Burnett, a fellow Englishman living across the street from him, had put about stories that Dormer was to be recalled in disgrace, and further enraged him by holding lavish parties to which he was not invited. The General's response was to order his serving men to beat Burnett up. As a result Burnett went about with a brace of pistols and, when the General's bully boys tried to drag him out of his chaise, his own footmen pitched in with swords. In the deplorable fight that followed Burnett was wounded in the calf and on a hand. The King of Portugal was naturally horrified and ordered his courtiers to pay sympathetic visits to Burnett. The General was withdrawn from his post and retired to England with William White, one of his cronies. White had been involved in the fracas and would become the General's faithful and attentive Steward when his brother, Colonel Robert, died in 1737.

General James was not only interested in blood and hooliganism. Kent reported on 28 November 1738 that, though crippled by 'a regular fitt of the Gout he is still bronzo mad, & they have brought him the Quarter Shiavi of Gio: di Bolognia at Leghorn'.[24] The General's 'bronzo' madness is still evident in the first room shown of the House, the Parlour or Saloon, a low room panelled and painted in a pea green, with little bronze busts and full-length miniatures perched on Kentian brackets. A confident chimneypiece in Kent's best manner, with a glowering Medusa's head on its frieze, presides over a shameless collection of good copies of erotic originals: Francesco Parmigianino's *Cupid Shaping his Bow*, Titian's *Rape of Lucrece*, Antonio Correggio's *Education of Cupid*. One brazenly big, bare Cupid's backside positively dominates the room, a most bizarre thematic note.

On the ceiling is Kent's oil on canvas, a variation of that grotesque-work ceiling, quartered by broad red ribbons, which he painted for the Presence Chamber in Kensington Palace in 1724. The Raphaelesque wreaths and scrolls of harpies are exquisitely handled; Kent could be so good when he was working to a small scale. But instead of a centre-piece of Apollo's chariot pulled by a Saxon horse, this has an oval of Ceres and Bacchus sprawling uncomfortably in support of Venus and Cupid: *Corn and Wine sustain Beauty and Love*. It is an interpretation of a line from Terence: 'Sine Cerere et Baccho frigit Venus' – 'Without food and wine Love grows cold'.[25] This is the voice of the old General, chuckling as he gets his guests in the mood for a modest orgy. Among the ribbons, garlands and ribs of Kent's composition are two real rarities, medallions decorated with his landscapes. More significantly, there are also a nymph and a satyr, viewed first from the back and then from the front. So Kent had entered into the spirit of the General's curious household for those few years of self-exploration and expression. It would be fascinating to know how long he spent there and what he thought of the indoor and outdoor Thelema he was creating for his old, dying friend.

For the General *was* dying, of that all-purpose eighteenth-century illness, the gout, and there are indications that Kent was not an eager visitor. Steward White was forever writing to urge Kent to come down to Rousham to advise on the siting of a statue or the planting of a grove. In 1741 the General himself wrote pitifully to Lord Burlington: 'I hope Ld Burlington does not forget his word & if Kent can be persuaded to come I shall take it very kindly.'[26] It is unlikely that Kent came. He seems to have preferred to keep life at a distance, and with the old General's lifestyle that is understandable. He comes across over the years as a Magus figure out of the John Fowles novel, or perhaps an earlier version of Clough Williams-Ellis, the creator of poetic illusions at Portmeirion, someone sophisticated, autocratic but driven.

Kent's other extraordinary room, the Library in the west wing, is a structural, not a sexual, demonstration piece. It has a ceiling of airy ribs and vaults like no other he ever designed. It has been called 'Mauresque', but that is because no description really fits it. The General must have had some power of positive persuasion to lure him into the experiment. All the Rococo decorative frames around the walls are later, Cottrell-controlled, work, which suggests that the General may have coaxed Kent into some outrageous effects below that vaulting to create a setting for his patron's readings from Chaucer and the more esoteric classical myths like those of Ovid's lascivious *Metamorphoses*. Was he delving into Antique Roman erotica to amuse the old General?

If the interiors of Rousham exude a boozy sexuality then the gardens convey a nobler sensual atmosphere. A violent, self-indulgent old bachelor soldier is looking back upon what he has learned of life and its choices. The landscape works like a session of psychoanalysis with Kent taking down notes, not in writing, but in garden design.

Out on the garden front of the House, away from the wild cattle at the side, is the Bowling Green and a vista to the dreadful silhouette of an agonised horse, torn by a ravening lion. It was expressly ordered from Scheemakers by the General, a version of a work in the garden of the Villa d'Este at Tivoli: a bitter comment on life as he, the battle-hardened, had experienced the violence and the pain. Beyond them, so MacClary wrote to remind the absent Cottrells, 'your eye drops upon a very fine Concave Slope, at the Bottom of which runs the Beautiful River Charvell, and at the top stands two pretty Garden Seats'.[27] The Seats are still there, 'one on each side, backt with the two Hilloks of Scotch Firrs, here you sit down first in the one, and then in the other, from whence perhaps at this time you have the prettiest view in the whole World'.[28] Centring that view is the 'Temple of the Mill'. Kent could not remove the existing cottage so he added buttresses, quatrefoils and battlements to make it an acceptable feature.[29] A crude 'Giant Triumphant Arch in Aston Field'[30] should hold the eye at this point.[31] It is not one of Kent's most convincing efforts, but the wood has grown up to partially hide it. Two Herms stand nearby, one a goddess in militant and seductive mood, implying that this was a significant stopping place for pilgrims of the gardens, a place where wide views and moral choices are meant to infiltrate the mind. Kent naturalised the banks of the river where Bridgeman had canalised them. MacClary was not interested in moral choices, but wrote of 'Carriers Wagons, Gentlemen's Equipages, Women riding, Men walking, and sometime twenty Droves of Cattle goes by in a Day', on the 'Great Road' crossing Heyford Bridge, all to be seen from the Seats.[32] A gazebo was the eighteenth-century equivalent of a TV set, an important visual luxury.

Next, on a turn to the left, the General stated his only option, which was Death, in Scheemakers's Dying Gladiator: a movingly apt, Stoic reference, sited above the roof of the Praeneste Arcade. The balustrade behind him is flanked by two Herms: Hercules representing Duty, neighboured by Pan, the shepherd of self-indulgence. The Praeneste below was the General's literary pantheon and a reminder that life was not without uplifting lives and works. The path leads on with views on the left across the paddock and then, on the right, a surprise view down into Venus's Vale where Kent had turned Bridgeman's square pond into an octagon with rounded corners; a glimpse only – Love would come later. Then a winding woodland path leads down to the Serpentine Rill, much wider and bounded with stones in Kent's version, unlike the present concrete channel. It leads to the Cold Bath in deep shades with a Grotto changing room or seat for spectators of the General's Stoic plunges, some human nudity to accord with the next nude statue.

This is the 'Colossus', larger than life, the centrepiece of the General's new north garden with a Tuscan pavilion, the Townesend Building,[33] from which the giant nude youth could be enjoyed at leisure. The statue is the largest and most important iconically in the garden, yet MacClary, who faithfully lists every other scrap of carving in the circuit, ignores it completely.[34] Garden writers of a 'Georgian' complexion insist that it is a statue of Apollo, a respectable god. In fact it is Antinous, one of three representations that the General bought and obviously relished. Antinous was the Emperor Hadrian's beautiful boy lover who came to a mysterious death in the Nile and was subsequently deified, the ultimate gay icon. In this 'Colossus' form the boy is shown supported by a column of reeds from the river in which his life was ended, not by the sun symbols more appropriate to Apollo.

If the Townesend Building is approached from the river up the long, straight, Bridgeman-designed Elm Walk, the General would have enjoyed closer and ever closer views of Antinous's buttocks and torso. MacClary would have been well aware of the General's appetites and of the uneasy reputation Rousham had gained in his five-year tenure of it. That would explain why the Cottrells kept a nervous distance long after his death and why MacClary particularly addressed his appeal to Lady Cottrell, stressing the duck, turkey and guinea fowl she would enjoy, with pineapples and peaches, if only she and her family would settle in Rousham House and banish its demon past, for there were demons enough, or satyrs, in Venus's Vale.

Antinous stands alone, towering and unthreatened. Venus has company and Kent devised his finest water theatre for her display. The Vale is best reached back down the Elm Walk or along the riverbank. MacClary delights in its fountains, one fifty, one thirty feet high, and a 'Cascade, where the Water comes tumbling down from under three Arches, through Ruff Stones'.[35] An erotic statue of female modesty, Venus is flanked on the one side by Pan, and on the other by a predatory looking satyr by Van Nost with a face of demonic lechery. But there are Cupids 'riding upon swans Backs'[36] and, with its bowering trees, the Vale has a lilting Arcadian beauty. Without visiting Greece, Kent has caught our preferred image of that pagan country as Swinburne would evoke it with 'the breasts of the nymphs in the brake',[37] that world of flesh and grace for which the Emperor Julian apostasised. General James gave Venus better measure than he gave to Antinous, or was that Kent's subtle arranging? It should be remembered with dismay that in its naughty heyday virtually every statue at Rousham was painted in natural flesh colours. The effect would have been of a Madame Tussaud's gone nudist and startlingly different to the present garden where stone statues have weathered and lead ones have lost all but a trace of their first defiant realism.

From the foot of Venus's Vale the seven-arched Praeneste Arcade, Kent's most original garden feature at Rousham, can be seen at the head of one of Bridgeman's concave slopes. To understand its significance MacClary is the best source as vandals or the threat of burglary have stripped it of most of the General's treasured relics of antiquity and Kent furniture. In the woods beyond the Praeneste is another of his garden museums, the Pyramid. But where the Pyramid is dark, originally full of reminders of the noble dead – Julius Caesar and Calpurnia, Marcus Aurelius and Socrates, signs of the General's hopes for his reputation – the Praeneste is wholesome and full of light, polychromatic with ironstone, smooth freestone and rubble, and ochre-washed interior walls originally with dove blue and white seats prepared for young lovers.[38] MacClary list its busts, now mostly stolen: 'a young Cleopatra, Shakspeer, a Bacchanal, Alexander, the Roman Sistenor [Senator], and Niaba',[39] a mixed bag of heroes and heroines, a soldier's choice.

Beyond the Praeneste and Bridgeman's second concave the woods darken around the Pyramid of the noble, classical dead. MacClary was more interested in it as a viewpoint:

> here you goe in and set down, and have a very pretty view of the Meddow, the Road, and the Bridge, and two parrish Churches, together with the pretty naturial turnings and windings of the River, and the delightful naturial Cascade that falls down under the Wooden Bridge.[40]

Here the garden peters out intentionally in a gloomy corner where wall and sinister flowing river come together by the remains of a Gothic Seat. At no point is Kent's layout emotionally or visually inactive. Demands are always being made on any moving figure. It is a garden based upon motion yet with five or six places for sitting down, viewing the prospect and thinking. Each visitor is being controlled by two men, both long dead: General Dormer and William Kent. It is a moral time trip and a most memorable experience.

Appropriately, after so much solemn concentration upon death and the afterlife, come Kent's own challenging posthumous achievements: two grandstands for the civilised enjoyment of the hunt, both completed around 1750. These were Wakefield Lodge in the Duke of Grafton's Northamptonshire deer park, and the Worcester Lodge in the Duke of Beaufort's park at Badminton, Gloucestershire.

Wakefield is gauntly grand, a compact concentration of the essential elements of Inigo Jones's garden front to Wilton House, with viewing towers at each end and a vast galleried central Hall on its first floor, with the dimensions of Jones's Hall in the Queen's House at Greenwich.[41] Kent had clearly been told by the 2nd Duke to create a hotel for the reception of a large number of hard-drinking, hungry hunters, with rooms above for the Duke's family and humbler accommodation for the rabble in lofts over the grand Stable Block. Even today a herd of three hundred fallow deer make the rolling landscape of Whittlewood Forest magical with their presence, moving, if they are not disturbed, in a gentle, instinctive pilgrimage, east to west across the house as the sun sets. It is a place where that bucolic eighteenth-century interaction of gentry and half-wild beasts can still be appreciated. The Lodge stands on a long, axial drive-line that follows east to west the route the deer herd takes; and it overlooks a generous, Brownian-style lake.

Badminton is a landscape that Kent could never quite pull together because of its level topography, but where he was able to design, though not to see conceived in stone, his most supremely satisfying building: Euston's Temple grown twice as tall, in the Worcester Lodge to the Duke of Beaufort's design-resistant park.

The 3rd Duke had commissioned Bridgeman to deformalise the vast seventeenth-century garden around the house and he had already laid out a great lawn studded with obelisks before the north front when his patron died in 1745. Kent was brought in by the 4th Duke to try to make visual sense of this vast park and to connect the surviving tree avenues with classical temples. Canaletto's 1748 *Badminton Park from the House* shows this scheme with a lake in the left foreground spanned by a nine-arched bridge, an arched and pedimented cascade at the head of the lake and a circular colonnaded temple to the right of the central avenue leading to the Worcester Lodge.[42] It is unlikely, however, that anything came of it, and the 4th Duke was still trying to enliven the park, with the help of Thomas Wright, by adding Gothic garden structures – a Hermit's Cell, a Ragged Castle and the Castle Barn – after Kent's death.[43]

Anyone walking Badminton today will soon appreciate Kent's problem. It is a sun-soaked, wind-blasted plateau of thin soils upon hard limestone and is ducally vast. But the Worcester Lodge demands attention even from a mile away in the park. It raises the spirits by its challenging exploration of space however often it is passed on the A433 to Tetbury and whatever the weather. Kent has designed a building, quite small in ground plan, which can outface sunshine, driving rain or a thunderstorm, particularly a thunderstorm. 'Here', it proclaims, 'be Dukes, puissant and noble Princes'; and to build with such vision the 4th Duke of Beaufort must have been puissant indeed. It is the building where Kent managed to achieve everything he almost did at the Euston Temple and then some more.

The Lodge is topped with the standard Burlington skullcap dome on an octagon, shouldering out, Redentore-wise, but with roofs not pediments. A whole 1/3/1 bay house takes over from the octagon with a true pediment topping the huge transparency of a round-arched window, balconied as if to address cheering crowds rather than the green Cotswolds. A matching window to the rear floods light into the ducal banqueting room inside where there is a term-flanked chimneypiece and a spider's web of plasterwork on the ceiling with animals' heads, fruit and flowers, appropriate to a 'grand room where the duke dines in summer'.[44] As a house it is three-dimensionally lively in its own right of recesses and niches, but then Kent pulls a coup. He has jacked the whole structure up on another two rusticated storeys penetrated by a wide arch. It is as if he were showing Burlington's little arched Bagnio at Chiswick how it should have been built with style. To exaggerate the verticality of it all Kent indulged himself in the form he had hankered after in sketches. Two little rusticated pyramids act as dwarf wings on each side; while to compensate a great arc of low walling spreads out to small kiosks barely connected with the sensational height of the centrepiece. The Worcester Lodge is unquestionably the greatest park gate lodge in Britain, a triumphant exercise in a normally tame Palladian style.

If only Kent could have pulled off the same trick with the entrance front to Badminton House. He almost does it, but that fat central block which he inherited defeated him.[45] He gave a fat, wide house a fat, wide, bracketed pediment and topped the side wings with inappropriately jaunty cupolas recycled from one of his failed Horse Guards Parade designs. Like all architects, Kent had his strengths and his weaknesses: great on small works, floundering on grand ones. But if, as the estate records seem to reveal, the Worcester Lodge was a posthumous work,[46] what a trumpet call at a distant gate! And if William Kent died before he could see his most perfect, most aspiring design realised, how like him to slip away at the height of his powers, the master of two conflicting styles of architecture, and probably as a result of overindulgence in good food. The man who cooks for himself, as Kent seems to have done with his essential bachelordom and his special recipes, is always vulnerable to simple greed.

In his malicious, half-accurate account of Kent's successes, George Vertue moved in for the kill with a relish, yet was still unable to hide the fact that here was a man who died loved and cared for, not by family, not by a mistress, but by a friend of long standing, a partner in a quiet cultural revolution. Writing with a syntax almost as tortuous as Kent's own, Vertue related the end:

> By slow increase of his distemper suddenly over powerd & tended to a Mortification in his bowells & feet especially inflamd. attended he was with great care at Burlington hous. a fortnight or three weeks. when he died of a Mortification all over, on Tuesday April. Ye. 12. 1748. his age about 60.[47]

Vertue could not even get his age right. Kent was sixty-three and about four months. In a gesture of friendship and respect, which meant more then than it might today, Lord Burlington had his companion buried in the Burlington family vault at Chiswick. There at least was one love that did dare to speak its name, because it had nothing to hide and much to celebrate.

Notes

Preface

1. Kent Letters from the Devonshire Collection held at Chatsworth House, Derbyshire, 260.0-15, Letter O.

Introduction: Yet another royal wedding (pp. xv–xxii)

1. The wedding ceremony is described in detail by Hervey in Romney Sedgwick (ed.), *Some Materials Towards Memoirs of the Reign of King George II by John, Lord Hervey*, vol. 1, pp. 263–72.
2. The boarded gallery alone, which went across the garden to connect the Chapel with the Drawing Room, cost £3980: see H. M. Colvin (gen. ed.), *The History of the King's Works*, vol. 5 (1660–1782), p. 243.
3. Ibid., vol. 2, p. 581.
4. See chapter 5 of this study.
5. See Jenny Uglow, *Hogarth: A Life and a World*, pp. 233–5.
6. See Ronald Paulson, *Hogarth: His Life, Art, and Times*, pp. 42–3, for an illustration and analysis.
7. Uglow thinks it is a workman, Vertue records that it is Pope who had recently dedicated a book on Taste to Burlington: 'Vertue Note Books III', *The Walpole Society*, vol. 22 (1933–4), Oxford University Press, 1934, p. 56.
8. Ibid., pp. 63–5; plate 12.
9. For Jacobite iconography in Palladianism and this instance in particular,

see Jane Clark, 'Palladianism and the Divine Right of Kings', *Apollo*, April 1992, pp. 224–9.

10. The altarpiece was destroyed by fire in the Blitz, but had been brought out once a year to be set up in a local pub and toasted.
11. Sedgwick, *Memoirs*, vol. 1, pp. 271–2. The quotation is in French.

Chapter 1: Gothic Bridlington – the birthplace (pp. 1–9)

1. Bridlington acquired a mayor and the usual electoral processes in the late nineteenth century. For a full account of the Lords Feoffees see David Neave, *Port, Resort and Market Town: A History of Bridlington.*
2. He had been raised for his loyalty to the royal cause from the Irish peerage of 2nd Earl of Cork.
3. Quoted in *Yorkshire Historical Quarterly*, vol. 8, no. 1 (August 2002), p. 7.
4. Susan and David Neave, 'The Early Life of William Kent', *The Georgian Group Journal*, vol. 6 (1996), pp. 4–11; p. 4. I am most grateful to David Neave for his help and advice about Kent's origins in Bridlington.
5. The back wall has a datestone of 1693 with Esther and William senior's initials and emblems of their love.
6. 'Vertue's Note Book B. 4', *The Walpole Society*, vol. 22 (1933–4), Oxford University Press, 1934, pp. 87–142; p. 139.
7. Lincoln County Record Office, 2MM.B. 19A.
8. Ibid., Letter to Burrell Massingberd, 15 November 1719, from Paris but with no address.
9. Information from the Lords Feoffees' records: Manorial Court Rolls, 1680–1702, quoted by the Neaves in *The Georgian Group Journal*, p. 5.
10. Ibid., p. 5.
11. John Wardle, *Bridlington Priory Parish Church of St Mary*, Bridlington, no date, p. 5.
12. Ibid., p. 6.
13. Nikolaus Pevsner, *The Buildings of England, Yorkshire: York & The East Riding*, Penguin, 1972, p. 175.
14. Borthwick Institute of Historical Research, York, NOM, SM, 1704/2.
15. See the [Neaves'] article in *The Georgian Group Journal* for an admirably clear and detailed genealogical chart of the complex Hustler–Osbaldeston connections (p. 7).
16. *The Walpole Society*, vol. 22 (1933–4), p. 139.

Chapter 2: Politics and a pick-up in London (pp. 10–20)

1. Humberside County Record Office, Beverley, East Riding Registry of Deeds, A61/79, 80 and 81.
2. Bodleian Library, MS Eng. Misc. C.114: Kent to Samuel Gale, another London friend, 17 April 1712. Kent's only reason for writing was to ask Gale to pass a picture on to Sir William Wentworth.
3. Susan and David Neave, 'The Early Life of William Kent', *The Georgian Group Journal*, vol. 6 (1996), pp. 4–11; p. 6.
4. Sacheverell's 15 August 1704 sermon: 'Diabolical inspiration and non-sensical cant': one of several such contemporary instances quoted in *The Oxford English Dictionary*.
5. Bodleian Library, MS Eng. Letters a.34: 'Copies of Letters written by John Talman from Italy', f. 46; Graham Parry (ed.), 'The letter Book of John Talman', *The Walpole Society*, vol. 59 (1997), pp. 55–165.
6. John Harris and Martin Rix, *Gardens of Delight: The Rococo English Landscape of Thomas Robins the Elder*, Basilisk Press, 1978; see also Timothy Mowl, *Historic Gardens of Gloucestershire*, Sutton, 2002, pp. 83–8.
7. Bodleian Library, MS Eng. Letters e.34, ff. 46–7.
8. The drawings, seven in all with copious notes in Talman's hand, are in the Library of Worcester College, Oxford; see H. M. Colvin, *A Catalogue of Architectural Drawings of the 18th and 19th Centuries in the Library of Worcester College, Oxford*, Oxford University Press, 1964, figs 36–42. I am indebted to Joanna Parker for her help and advice over the Talman designs. Two of these are illustrated as colour plates 1 and 2 and fig. 36 in H. M. Colvin, *Unbuilt Oxford*, Yale University Press, 1983. Plate 1 proposes a palatial range of Fellows' rooms in typical Piedmontese Baroque with a shallow dome. Plate 2 shows the 'Romish' exterior to the Refectory.
9. Text on the drawing.
10. Ibid., ff. 46–7.
11. This identification was made by Richard Hewlings in the appendix to the Neaves' article on Kent in *The Georgian Group Journal*, vol. 6 (1996), pp. 10–11.
12. Ibid., p. 7.
13. According to Jonathan Swift, *The History of the Four Last Years of the Queen*, in Herbert Davis (ed.), *The Prose Works of Jonathan Swift*, 13 vols, Basil Blackwell, 1951, vol. 7, p. 9.
14. Quoted in H. M. Colvin, *A Biographical Dictionary of British Architects 1600–1840*, p. 950.

15. 'Vertue Note Books III', *The Walpole Society*, vol. 22 (1933–4), Oxford University Press, 1934, p. 139.
16. For a clear chart of the complex family relationships see the Neaves' *Georgian Group Journal* article, p. 7.
17. Bodleian Library, MS Eng. Letters, e.34, f. 174: from John Talman in Naples to Daniel Locke in Rome, 20 December 1710.
18. Ibid., f. 55: Talman to Oddy, 17 August 1709.
19. Ibid.
20. *The Walpole Society*, vol. 22 (1933–4), p. 139.
21. Ibid., p. 138.

Chapter 3: A foolish voyage (pp. 21–9)

1. Bodleian Library, MS Eng. Letters. e.34, f. 49. Talman was referring to the ship's longboat going ashore to Deal for fresh supplies and to carry any mail. A convoy system was necessary at this stage in the war.
2. Ibid. f. 36.
3. Ibid. f. 49.
4. Ibid. f. 53.
5. Ibid., f. 56.
6. Ibid., f. 60. At this point on the journey Talman was more interested in urging his father to buy Lord Ashburnham's house in Westminster, currently on the market, than in his Italian project. He had described the house in detail in an earlier letter.
7. Ibid., f. 76.
8. Ibid. f. 122.
9. Lincoln Record Office, 2MM. B. 19A: letter from Rome from Kent to Burrell Massingberd: 15 February 1717.
10. Brinsley Ford and John Ingamells, *A Dictionary of British and Irish Travellers in Italy, 1701–1800*, Yale University Press, 1997, p. 570.
11. Bodleian Library, MS Eng. Letters, e.34, f. 61.
12. Ibid., ff. 67–9.
13. See figures 23 and 30 in John Dixon Hunt, *William Kent, Landscape Designer*.
14. Bodleian Library, MS Eng. Letters, e.34, f. 91: part of a long letter brimming with impudent sexual curiosity.
15. Ibid. ff. 81–4.
16. Ibid., f. 45.

17. H. M. Colvin, *A Biographical Dictionary of British Architects 1600–1840*, p. 582. She lived in Covent Garden and is supposed to be one of the figures painted by Kent on the staircase of Kensington Palace. The claim to a mistress would have made Kent relatively respectable in his ambiguous condition as an ageing bachelor.
18. Michael I. Wilson, *William Kent: Architect, Designer, Painter, Gardener, 1685–1748*, pp. 5–6.
19. Bodleian Library, MS Eng. Letters. e.34, f. 20.
20. Ibid., f. 152.
21. Bodleian Library, MS Eng. Letters. e.34, f. 171.
22. Ibid., f. 173.
23. Ibid., f. 174.
24. The portrait is at Chatsworth and is illustrated as the frontispiece to Wilson's *William Kent*. For a list of portraits of Kent see Wilson, *William Kent*, appendix 1.

Chapter 4: Silk stockings from the Philosopher Earl (pp. 30–41)

1. The details of Kent's arrangements with Sir William Wentworth are revealed in the Kent–Massingberd correspondence in Lincoln Record Office, 2MM. B. 19A: Massingberd to Kent, 24 May 1713, by which time Wentworth's subsidy had sunk to £30 a year, but Kent was being sponsored by Burrell Massingberd and Sir John Chester of Chicheley at £20 apiece. That made £70 a year in all.
2. British Library, Wentworth Papers, Add. MS 22.229, ff. 89–91: Raby to Wentworth from Berlin, 25 February 1710: 'tho now I remember you having been at Rome before I need not trouble you with any to recommend lodgings or the like'.
3. Ibid., f. 95.
4. Quoted in Brinsley Ford and John Ingamells, *A Dictionary of British and Irish Travellers in Italy, 1701–1800*, Yale University Press, 1997, p. 951, from a letter of January 1708 written by Henry Trench to his patron, Sir John Perceval.
5. British Library, Wentworth Papers, Add. MS 22.229, f. 92: Wentworth to Raby from Padua, 20 March 1710.
6. Ibid., f. 84.
7. Ibid., f. 98.
8. Ibid., f. 95.

9. Bodleian Library, MS Eng. Misc. C.114. That was the letter where Kent assured Gale that for £50 one could live comfortably in Rome and still have money to buy books and prints.
10. Lincoln Record Office, 2MM. B. 19A, from Massingberd's draft of a letter to Kent of 9 December 1713, and only one of several such complaints.
11. Anthony Ashley Cooper, 3rd Earl of Shaftesbury, *Characteristicks of Men, Manners, Opinions, Times*, 3 vols, 1732, 3, p. 398. This is the fifth, corrected edition, which contains the 'Letter concerning Design'.
12. Though he does seem aware that the musical scene had improved recently. He does not mention Purcell by name.
13. Support for this claim that Vanbrughian styling was not simply for large houses will be found by an examination of the quite modest, but impressively subtle Vanbrugh-style town house in St Michael's Street, Oxford.
14. Shaftesbury, *Characteristicks*, vol. 3, p. 401.
15. Ibid., vol. 1, p. 23.
16. *The Spectator*, 20 vols, 1803, 5, no. 393, p. 373: 31 May 1712.
17. Shaftesbury, *Characteristicks*, vol. 2, p. 390.
18. Ibid., p. 391.
19. Ibid., vol. 3, p. 398.
20. Ibid., vol. 2, p. 345.
21. Ibid., p. 388.
22. Ibid., pp. 393–4.
23. Benjamin Read (ed.), *The Life, Unpublished Letters & Philosophical Regimen of Anthony, Earl of Shaftesbury*, 1992, p. 246.
24. Shaftesbury, *Characteristicks*, vol. 2, p. 282.
25. Ibid., vol. 1, p. 127.
26. For these, as for many other details of itineraries in Italy, I am indebted to the impeccable scholarship of the late Brinsley Ford and John Ingamells.
27. This is the frontispiece to the 1732 edition of Shaftesbury's *Works*.
28. Sheila O'Connell, 'Lord Shaftesbury in Naples', *The Journal of the Walpole Society*, vol. 54 (1988), pp. 149–219; p. 162.
29. Ibid., p. 150.
30. Ibid., p. 175.
31. Ibid., p. 177.
32. Ibid., p. 187, written on Friday 16 September 1712. Did Kent, one wonders, ever boast of the episode of the stockings in his conversations with Lord Burlington?

33. Ibid., p. 197.
34. Ibid., p. 197. Henry Trench, on the other hand, was paid 5 Pistoles 'for his Trouble in Agency about five Pieces of Painting bought by my Lord of Signor Porcinari.' So he was honest. At this period Trench's function seems to have been to shadow Kent and make him feel uneasy.
35. Shaftesbury, *Characteristicks*, 3, p. 399.
36. Ibid., 3, p. 400.

Chapter 5: Playing the patrons (pp. 42–58)

1. British Library, Print Room, 197* d.3: 'Drawings of Ecclesiastical Garments'. This is a collection of coloured drawings of ecclesiastical oddities like 'The Glove that St Appolinaris used when he celebrated Mass' and 'The Sandal which St Bernard Abbot of Valambrosa in Tuscany used when he celebrated Mass'. Being intensely pietistical, John Talman toured Italy to search out such relics believing that drawings of them would be received eagerly by the Catholic faithful in England. To have access to the Papal Sacristy was a crowning success.
2. From Talman's letter book in the Bodleian Library, MS Eng. Letters e.34, f. 199. Talman left out 'aboundance of particulars . . . because I intend to have it all drawn in colours'.
3. Ibid.
4. H. M. Colvin, *A Biographical Dictionary of British Architects, 1600–1840*, p. 755.
5. MS Eng. Letters e.34, ff. 199–201.
6. Ibid., f. 223.
7. Ibid., f. 204. Talman had described Naples in an earlier letter to Locke (f. 174) as 'more a siren y can yu imagin', implying sexual indulgence.
8. Ibid., f. 211.
9. Henry Hoare's Stourhead landscape garden had a Turkish tent and Hoare was, according to Bishop Pococke, proposing to build a mosque with a minaret on an island in the lake. There was also a Turkish tent at Charles Hamilton's Painshill and a Greek Temple of Bacchus. Stowe has a colossal Greek Temple of Concord and Victory at the head of the Grecian Valley.
10. Lincoln Record Office, 2MM. B. 19A: correspondence between Kent and Burrell Massingberd, thirty-five letters in all, plus four draughts from Massingberd to Kent; 25 June 1712.
11. Ibid., Kent to Massingberd, 13 August 1712.

12. Ibid., Kent to Massingberd, 5 November 1712. Kent added 'my Ld Herbert was very kind to me & has bespoke a very fine picture of Giuseppe Chiari', before leaving for Florence with Mr Newton.
13. Ibid., Kent to Massingberd, 20 July 1715.
14. Ibid., Kent to Massingberd, 5 November 1712.
15. Bodleian Library, MS Eng. Misc. C.114, f. 46: letter of 10 March 1718. Stukeley had not confessed to any entanglement, but Massingberd thought he detected the psychological symptoms of one.
16. Lincoln Record Office, 2MM. B. 19A: draft of a letter written by Massingberd to Kent, 5 July 1714.
17. Bodleian Library, MS Eng. Misc. C.114, f. 46: Massingberd to Stukeley, 10 March 1718.
18. Lincoln Record Office, 2MM. B. 19A: draft of a letter written by Massingberd to Kent, 5 July 1714.
19. Ibid. Kent to Massingberd, 8 June 1718. The painting survives in the entrance hall at Chicheley.
20. Ibid., Kent to Massingberd, 20 August 1720.
21. Bodleian Library, MS Eng. Misc. C.114, f. 4: Kent's very first surviving letter written from Italy to Samuel Gale.
22. Lincoln Record Office, 2MM. B. 19A: Kent to Massingberd, 15 February 1717. 'Mr Talman was here this morning & would have me do this ceiling after ye Grotesk manner but . . . am resolved to do a thought of my own.'
23. Ibid., Kent to Massingberd, 16 May 1714.
24. Ibid., Kent to Massingberd, 9 June 1716.
25. Ibid., Kent to Massingberd, 26 January 1714.
26. 'Vertue Note Books III', *The Walpole Society*, vol. 22 (1933–4), Oxford University Press, 1934, p. 138.
27. Lincoln Record Office, 2MM. B. 19A: Kent to Massingberd, 16 May 1714.
28. Brinsley Ford and John Ingamells, *A Dictionary of British and Irish Travellers in Italy, 1701–1800*, Yale University Press, 1997, p. 225.
29. Ibid.
30. Bodleian Library, MS Rawlinson, D.1162.
31. There is a microfilm of Jarret's accounts in the Bodleian Library, Holkham MS Film 304.
32. Bodleian Library, MS Rawlinson, D.1162, f. 2. They had arrived on 6 June. Kent also noted the ceiling painted in grotesques but Mr Winter, not Kent, drew the place and Kent's dates do not always agree with those of the meticulous Jarret.

33. Ibid., f. 3.
34. Ibid., f. 5.
35. Bodleian Library, Microfilm 304, 26/1/04, 'An Account by Ed. Jarret of money distributed upon account of his Master Thomas Coke Esq. . . . from 21 August 1712'.
36. Ibid.
37. Bodleian Library, MS Rawlinson D.1162, f.7.
38. Ibid., ff. 7–8.
39. Ibid., f. 8.
40. Ibid., f. 9.
41. Ibid., ff. 9–10.
42. Ibid.
43. Ibid., f. 12.
44. Ibid., f. 13.
45. Ibid., f. 14.
46. Ibid. The Farnese Theatre at Parma was the first in Europe to have a revolving stage. It was bombed in the Second World War, but has since been reconstructed.
47. Lincoln Record Office, 2MM. B. 19A: Kent to Massingberd, letter of 24 November 1714.
48. Ibid.
49. Ibid.
50. Ibid. Massingberd to Kent, draft letter of 5 July 1714.
51. Quoted in Ford and Ingamells, *Dictionary*, p. 160.
52. 'Vertue Note Books III', *The Walpole Society*, vol. 22 (1933–4), Oxford University Press, 1943, p. 138. Writing an obituary of Lewis Goupy, Vertue notes: 'he was tho. propper to be engaged by the young Earl of Burlington to go with him the tour of Italy & to Rome, as his singular favourit & painter – there he staid some time – but this noble Lord soon took into his favour other painters of this nation, Mr French & more <especially a Countryman of his> Mr Kent – a Yorkshire man there on his studyes'.
53. James Lees-Milne, *The Earls of Creation*, Hamish Hamilton, 1986, p. 91.
54. Lincoln Record Office, 2MM. B. 19A: Kent to Massingberd, 16 April 1715.
55. Ibid.
56. Ibid. Kent to Massingberd, 20 July 1715.
57. Ibid.
58. Ibid.
59. Ibid.

60. Ibid.
61. Ibid. Kent to Massingberd, 15 February 1717.
62. Ibid.
63. Ibid. Kent to Massingberd, 15 June 1717.
64. For illustrations of the church see Jan De Brabandere, Bart De Groof and Johan Ickx, *1000 jaar San Giuliano dei Fiamminghi*, Uitgeverij Stichting Kunstboek, 1996.
65. I am most grateful to the Rector of San Giuliano, Fr Hugo Vanermen, for my information on Kent's association with the church. The community preserves the legend that Kent actually had rooms over the church for a period, but paid no rent. This, considering his nature, is most likely. See also Edward Croft-Murray, 'William Kent in Rome', in Mario Praz (ed.), *English Miscellany*, vol. 1 (1950), p. 221.
66. A xerox of these pages was kindly supplied to me by Fr Vanermen from the originals in the Bodleian Library, MS Rawlinson D.1162. Kent had, no doubt, learnt the technique from Giuseppe Chiari.

Chapter 6: The wilful impatience of a would-be Palladian lord (pp. 59–70)

1. Lincoln Record Office, 2MM. B. 19A: Kent to Massingberd, 15 September 1717.
2. Ibid., Kent to Massingberd, 16 June 1718.
3. Ibid., Kent to Massingberd, 8 June 1718.
4. Ibid.
5. Ibid., Kent to Massingberd, 16 August 1718.
6. Ibid.
7. Ibid., Kent to Massingberd, 18 December 1718.
8. Ibid., Kent to Massingberd, 15 November 1719.
9. Ibid.
10. Ibid.
11. Ibid.
12. Ibid.
13. Dana Arnold (ed.), *Belov'd by Ev'ry Muse: Richard Boyle, 3rd Earl of Burlington and 4th Earl of Cork (1694–1753)* is a useful primer; see also John Wilton-Ely (ed.), *Apollo of the Arts: Lord Burlington and his Circle*, and Roger White (ed.), *Lord Burlington and his Circle*.
14. Jane Clark, 'The Mysterious Mr Buck', *Apollo*, May 1989, pp. 317–22.
15. Ibid.

16. For the Webb design see John Bold, *John Webb: Architectural Theory and Practice in the Seventeenth Century*, Oxford University Press, 1989, pp. 107–25.
17. Or to save the journey to Derbyshire, all that is needed to convey the difference between the Palladian and the Baroque is to go round Wentworth Woodhouse to its richly decorated but perfectly integrated west front of 1725: giant order late Baroque at its best, where every detail connects and fuses.
18. John Wilton-Ely, 'Lord Burlington in Italy', in Arnold (ed.), *Belov'd by Ev'ry Muse*, pp. 15–20; p.17.
19. Lincoln Record Office, 2MM. B. 19A, Kent to Massingberd, 14 January 1716.
20. Ibid., Kent to Massingberd, 20 March 1716.
21. Ibid., Kent to Massingberd, 9 June 1716.
22. Ibid.
23. The seal appears on several letters from Kent to Lady Burlington in the Chatsworth papers: 206.1–206.15.
24. Fountaine had given Burlington a letter of introduction to the Vicenzan nobility and it was only during this November visit that he was considering using it. His notes on his *Quattro Libri* speak of this as his second visit. His first had been in March 1715.
25. Burlington's copy of Palladio is in the Library at Chatsworth. Wilton-Ely, 'Lord Burlington in Italy', p. 17, gives the notes.
26. Clark, *Apollo*, p. 320.
27. Wilton-Ely, 'Lord Burlington in Italy', p. 17.
28. Wilton-Ely believes he did visit the Villa Maser: ibid., p. 17, but Eileen Harris, 'Alexander Pope, Lord Burlington and Palladio's *Fabbriche Antiche*', in Charles Hind (ed.), *New Light on English Palladianism*, pp. 10–13, states that the purchase was made in Venice. She cites Cinzia Maria Sicca, 'Il Palladianismo in Inghilterra', *Palladio La Sua Bredita Nel Mondo*, 1980, p. 39. Harris concludes that 'this contradicts the romantic legend related by Burlington in his preface to the *Fabbriche Antiche* of his exciting discovery of the drawings at the Villa Maser' (fn. 1, p. 13).

Chapter 7: In Paris 'to see the things' (pp. 71–8)

1. Lincoln Record Office, 2MM. B. 19A, Kent to Massingberd, 15 November 1719.

2. Ibid.
3. For a scholarly study of French design in this period see Katie Scott, *The Rococo Interior: Decoration and Social Spaces in Early Eighteenth-Century Paris*, Yale University Press, 1995.
4. Kent's well-known design for a lady's architectural dress is a version of Jean Bérain's and Nicholas Larmassins's similar designs of 1700 and 1699; see Scott, *Rococo Interior*, fig. 125 on p. 123; fig. 80 on p. 72.
5. Scott, *Rococo Interior*, fig. 127 on p. 125.
6. Ibid., fig. 131 on p. 129.
7. As in Claude Audran's cartoons for a tapestry series of the months in a Grotesque style drawn in the early 1700s before Kent's arrival. The tapestries are now in the Victoria & Albert Museum; for an illustration see Scott, *Rococo Interior*, fig. 198 on p. 182.
8. Lincoln Record Office, 2MM. B. 19A, Kent to Massingberd, 15 February 1717.
9. Ibid., Kent to Massingberd, 28 January 1718.
10. Grotesque garlands and masks on the present west front wall of William Talman's bowling-green pavilion at Chatsworth suggest that John Talman had influenced his father to experiment with auricular carving even on a chaste *neo-classical structure.*
11. See Scott, *Rococo Interior*, fig. 111 on p. 110 for an Oppenord design of about 1714 for the Salon d'Angle at the Palais Royal.
12. As in the suite of furniture he designed for the Double Cube Room at Wilton House.
13. For Antoine Coypel's *Death of Dido* see Scott, *Rococo Interior*, fig. 222 on p. 157.
14. Quoted in Brinsley Ford and John Ingamells, *A Dictionary of British and Irish Travellers in Italy, 1701–1800*, Yale University Press, 1997, p. 160.

Chapter 8: What good thing ever came from a Campbell? (pp. 79–90)

1. Burlington House was off Piccadilly, which at that time was known as Portugal Street and half-suburban.
2. Horace Walpole, *Anecdotes of Painting*, vol. iv (1771).
3. For biographical information on Campbell see H. M. Colvin, *A Biographical Dictionary of British Architects, 1600–1840*, pp. 209–11; and also Howard Stutchbury, *The Architecture of Colen Campbell*, Manchester University Press, 1967.

4. See H. M. Colvin, 'A Scottish Origin for English Palladianism', *Architectural History*, vol. 17 (1974), pp. 5–13.
5. Much of Campbell's façade survives today under nineteenth-century additions by Sydney Smirke and the firm of Banks and Barry.
6. It was originally painted for Consul Smith as an overdoor to his villa at Treviso. George III added it to the Royal Collection.
7. See *The Walpole Society*, vol. 7 (1918–19), p. 137, for Charles Stoakes's claim that his uncle Nicholas Stone both 'desined and built' it.
8. This is still in situ in the Council Room of the Fine Rooms, though cut down.
9. See John Cornforth, 'A Pantheon in Piccadilly', *Country Life*, 1 April 2004. However, the coloured illustration of a reconstruction of this stair hall should not be taken on trust as Ricci's paintings are shown without frames, filling entire wall spaces, which they are not large enough to do.
10. Lincoln Record Office, 2MM. B. 19A: Kent to Massingberd, 10 December 1719.
11. Ibid.
12. Ibid., Kent to Massingberd, 19 January 1720.
13. Ibid.
14. In a petition of about 1715–16 to George I, Campbell claimed that he had 'studied Architecture here and abroad for several years', which could mean anything. Quoted in Colvin, *Biographical Dictionary*, p. 209.
15. See *The Survey of London: Parish of St James Westminster*, Part II, *North of Piccadilly*, Athlone Press, 1963, vol. 32, pp. 390–438.
16. Lincoln Record Office, 2MM. B. 19A: Kent to Massingberd, 19 January 1720.
17. Ibid., Kent to Massingberd, 30 January 1720.
18. Ibid.
19. Ibid.
20. Ricci was in England from 1711 to December 1716. *The Survey of London* suggests that structural alterations to the staircase early in 1715 were done to facilitate Ricci's painting.
21. See Margaret Jourdain, *The Work of William Kent: Artist, Painter, Designer and Landscape Gardener*, p. 89, for the text of his will. It implies, but never actually states, that Elizabeth Butler had been his mistress and that he was the father of her children.
22. With the exception of his painting of *The Marriage Banquet of Cupid* on the ceiling of the Saloon which is undergoing prolonged restor-ation.
23. In some of Palladio's villas this is where the frescoes would have been

painted, not on the ceilings. But the Countess Juliana had set an unhappy precedent by framing the Ricci and Pelegrini canvases on the walls.

24. See the 1714 edition of Shaftesbury's *Characteristicks*, vol. 3, chapter 5, p. 400, for his attack on Wren.
25. For an analysis of the publishing history of the project see Eileen Harris and Nicholas Savage, *British Architectural Books and Writers, 1550–1785*, pp. 139–48; see also Rudolf Wittkower, *Palladio and English Palladianism*, pp. 103–5.
26. 'Ongoing' (2004–5), unpublished Ph.D. research at the University of Bristol, to which I am most indebted.
27. *Vitruvius Britannicus*, vol. iii (1725), plate 26: 'the first essay of his Lordship's happy invention', dated 1717. See also John Harris, *The Palladian Revival*, p. 57.
28. The painting is in the National Portrait Gallery, London, and illustrates the front cover of Dana Arnold (ed.), *Belov'd by Ev'ry Muse: Richard Boyle, 3rd Earl of Burlington and 4th Earl of Cork (1694–1753)*.
29. For Benson, Herrenhausen and Wilbury see Timothy Mowl, *Historic Gardens of Wiltshire*, Tempus Publishing, 2004, pp. 81–2. I am much indebted to Carole Fry's Ph.D. researches on Benson and early Palladianism.

Chapter 9: Kensington – Kent's innovative but unfortunate palace (pp. 91–108)

1. The sequence is as follows: Cupola Room ceiling (1722); Privy Chamber and the King's Bedchamber, now lost (1723); Presence Chamber and the Council Chambers, now lost (1724); Cupola Room walls (1725); King's Gallery, Great and Little Closets, now lost, and the King's Staircase (1725–7). See H. M. Colvin (gen. ed.), *The History of the King's Works*, vol. 5, p. 201.
2. I am indebted for much of my information on King George to Ragnhild Hatton's scholarly and revisionist study, *George I Elector and King*; also to Carole Fry's draft Bristol University Ph.D. thesis chapters on early Palladianism.
3. As his mother was one of fifteen children of Elizabeth, the Winter Queen of Bohemia, there were some other great-grandchildren, though not many.
4. Freiherr Friedrich Wilhelm von der Schulenburg, who was the King's *Kammerjunker*, notes that Thursday was the King's fixed day for cabinet

councils in 1717–18. See Görtz Archive, 121/6; cited in Hatton, *George I*, pp. 129–32.

5. For discussion of this topic see Hatton, *George I*, pp. 129–31.
6. The Galerie had been intended as a simple orangery. It was Georg's mother, the Electress Sophia, who insisted on turning it into a Festival Hall.
7. See Jürgen Prüser, *Die Göhrde*, 1969, chapter 5, for an account of the complex.
8. For an illustration of their 1970s replacements see Dietmar Horst (ed.), *The Royal Gardens of Herrenhausen, Hannover*, p. 30.
9. Horace Walpole ascribes the White Lodge to Pembroke in his *Anecdotes of Painting*, 1862 edition (ed. Wornum), vol. 3, p. 772; see Colvin, *King's Works*, vol. 5, p. 230; *Vitruvius Britannicus*, vol. iv (1767), gives it to Morris.
10. See Richard Hewlings, *Chiswick House and Gardens*, English Heritage, 1989.
11. For the Wilton bridge see Timothy Mowl, *Palladian Bridges: Prior Park and the Whig Connection*, Millstream Books, 1993; for Kent's Worcester Lodge see Timothy Mowl, *Historic Gardens of Gloucestershire*, Tempus Publishing, 2002, pp. 77–9.
12. For Kent's work at Canons see C. H. Collins Baker and M. Baker, *The Life and Circumstances of James Brydges 1st Duke of Chandos*, Oxford University Press, 1949, p. 81.
13. For illustrations of the building see *The Wren Society*, vol. xi (1934), plates 8–28.
14. See *The Walpole Society*, vol. 18 (1930), p. 101.
15. Ibid., p. 100.
16. The library on Piccadilly was described by Macky as 'the finest in Europe, both for the disposition of the Apartments as of the Books', quoted in Colvin, *King's Works*, vol. 5, p. 72, fn. 3.
17. *The Walpole Society*, vol. 6 (1955), p. 23.
18. J. Holland, *History of Worksop*, Sheffield, 1826, pp. 176–7.
19. Ilaria Toesca, 'Alessandro Galilei in Inghiliterra', in Mario Praz (ed.), *English Miscellany*, vol. iii, 1952, pp. 217–18.
20. A letter from Molesworth to Stanhope, dated 5 October 1717, asks him to persuade Sunderland as First Lord of the Treasury to allow 'Mr Hewett, my eldest son, Signor Galilei & I & (if you can engage him) Sir George Markham who are the new Junta for Architecture to show the King Galilei's designs': Chevening House, Stanhope Archives, Cupboard C34.1, cited in Colvin, *King's Works*, vol. 5, p. 72.

21. John Beattie, *The English Court in the Reign of George I*, Cambridge University Press, 1967, pp. 257–61.
22. Colvin, *King's Works*, vol. 5, p. 72, fn. 4.
23. See H. M. Colvin, *A Biographical Dictionary of British Architects, 1600–1840*, p. 608.
24. For Leoni's edition of Palladio see Rudolf Wittkower, *Palladio and English Palladianism*, pp. 79–85.
25. Colvin, *Biographical Dictionary*, p. 492.
26. See Timothy Mowl, *Stylistic Cold Wars: Betjeman Versus Pevsner*, John Murray, pp. 76–92.
27. Michael I. Wilson, *William Kent: Architect, Designer, Painter, Gardener, 1685–1747*, believes that the idea of the coffering was stolen from Thornhill and cites (p. 44) a drawing in the Victoria & Albert Museum Print Room (no reference given) for 'the ceiling of the Great Room at Kensington'. It seems likely that Thornhill painted this once he learned that a neo-classical design had been favoured. His own preferences were for Baroque figures.
28. Baker and Baker, *James Brydges*, p. 172, locate the painting to the ceiling of Closet number 36.
29. Ibid., p. 81.
30. These are, in fact, replacements of the 1970s. Two of the original statues survive in Hanover's Historisches Museum. They were made by P. van Empthusen, gilded by Gips Blei. I am indebted to Annabet Roellig, metalwork restorer, for this information.
31. *The Walpole Society*, vol. 22 (1933–4), p. 19.
32. Lincoln Record Office, 2MM. B. 19A: Kent to Massingberd, 15 February 1717: 'Mr Talman was here this morning & would have me done this ceiling after ye Grotesk manner.' Kent refused.
33. The decoration of the ceiling was also a backward glance to the de Critz Grotesque work in Inigo Jones's Queen's House at Greenwich.
34. *Kensington Palace: The Official Guide Book*, 2001, based on an original text by John Haynes, revised and edited by Clare Murphy.
35. Colvin, *King's Works*, vol. 5, p. 199.
36. His name was only found on the reverse of a canvas during restor-ation.
37. See Hatton, *George 1*, pp. 100, 338.
38. Horace Walpole, a shrewd judge, noticed the difference. He described those Staircase figures as 'the least defective work of his pencil'; quoted by Wilson, *William Kent*, p. 53. But whose pencil?

Chapter 10: The remarkable achievements of an apparent failure (pp. 109–22)

1. H. M. Colvin (gen. ed.), *The History of the King's Works*, vol. 5, p. 72, fn. 4.
2. *The Walpole Society*, vol. 22 (1933–4), pp. 55–6, 138–41.
3. Ibid., p. 140.
4. Ibid., p. 139.
5. Ibid., p. 140.
6. Ibid.
7. Ibid., p. 55.
8. Ibid., p. 141.
9. Ibid.
10. Ibid., p. 141.
11. Ibid.
12. See Margaret Jourdain, *The Work of William Kent: Artist, Painter, Designer and Landscape Gardener*, pp. 89–91; p. 89: 'unto my sister Esther Pearson one Annuity or yearly sum of Fifty Pounds to be paid her half yearly for and during her natural life out of the Rent of my House in Saville Street'. For Kent's indeterminate role in the development of the street see *Survey of London*, vol. 32, pp. 449–52, where it is stated that he 'seems normally to have let' the house 'at £100 per annum' (p. 451). Peter Willis, 'William Kent's letters in the Huntingdon Library, California', *Architectural History*, vol. 29 (1986), pp. 158–67, suggests that the house was rented out for the whole period of Kent's leasehold. It is likely, therefore, that Kent spent his time between his private apartments in Burlington House and his mistress's house in the parish of St Paul's, Covent Garden.
13. *The Walpole Society*, vol. 22 (1933–4), p. 140.
14. Ibid.
15. For a catalogue of Kent's landscape drawings, most of which are at Chatsworth, see John Dixon Hunt, *William Kent, Landscape Designer.*
16. Ibid., catalogue no. 23.
17. Ibid., catalogue no. 27.
18. Ibid., catalogue no. 30.
19. Ibid., catalogue no. 43. The Negro may be James Cambridge, Lady Burlington's black servant.
20. Ibid., catalogue no. 55.
21. Ibid., catalogue no. 66.
22. Ibid., catalogue no. 65.

23. Ibid., catalogue no. 22.
24. See Timothy Mowl, *Historic Gardens of Wiltshire*, Tempus Publishing, 2004, p. 95.
25. *Historic Manuscripts Commission*, Hastings MSS, vol. III, 1934, p. 26. The editors felt constrained to correct his spelling.
26. Ibid.
27. Jourdain, *William Kent*, p. 89.
28. Ibid.
29. *The Walpole Society*, vol. 22 (1933–4), p. 140.
30. Ibid., p. 138.
31. G. Sherburn (ed.), *The Correspondence of Alexander Pope*, vol. 4, p. 67.
32. James M. Osborn (ed.), *Joseph Spence, Observations, Anecdotes, and Characters of Books and Men*, 2 vols, Oxford University Press, 1966, vol. 1, p. 80, Anecdote 188, quoting Pope in April 1739: 'Addison and Steele [were] a couple of H-S. I am sorry to say so.'
33. From Alexander Pope's 'Epistle to Dr Arbuthnot'.
34. Sherburn, *Correspondence*, vol. 4, pp. 149–50.
35. Ibid., vol. 3, p. 517.
36. Jourdain, *William Kent*, p. 89.
37. Kent Letters, Chatsworth, 260.0
38. Quoted by Wilmarth S. Lewis (ed.), *The Yale Edition of Horace Walpole's Correspondence*, vol. 30, p. 24, fn. 23, citing George Edward Cokayne, *The Complete Peerage*, 13 vols (1910–59), vol. 2, p. 433.
39. Sherburn, *Correspondence*, vol. 4, p. 163.
40. Ibid., p. 43.
41. Ibid., p. 154.
42. Ibid., pp. 139–40.
43. Ibid., pp. 323–4.

Chapter 11: Across the Thames a princess creates a Rococo moment (pp. 123–30)

1. For a very lively account of the reign see Charles Chenevix Trench, *George II*, Allen Lane, 1973.
2. Ragnhild Hatton, *George I Elector and King*, p. 207, adds that the more injurious words used against Newcastle were that he had acted 'en cette affaire en malhonnête homme'.

3. Lady Mary Wortley Montagu had brought the serum back from Turkey.
4. From a letter by Swift to Lady Betty Germaine, January 1733, quoted in Irwin Ehrenpreis (ed.), *Dean Swift*, 3 vols, Methuen, 1983, vol. 3, p. 478.
5. He had been exiled for his support of the Old Pretender in the 1715 Jacobite Rebellion.
6. G. Sherburn (ed.), *The Correspondence of Alexander Pope*, vol. 2, p. 14.
7. Illustrated in *Vitruvius Britannicus*, vol. iv, 1739, plate 8/9.
8. Caroline's reconciliation audience with her father-in-law is recorded in *The Diary of Mary Countess Cowper, Lady of the Bedchamber to The Princess of Wales 1714–1720*, 1864, p. 149.
9. Ibid., p. 150.
10. *Historical Manuscripts Collection*, Egmont Diaries, HMSO, 2 vols, 1923, vol. 2, p. 138: entry for Tuesday 31 December 1734.

Chapter 12: Burlington's neo-classical counterattack at Chiswick (pp. 131–8)

1. Jacques Carré, *Lord Burlington*, Adosa, Clermont-Ferrand, 1993.
2. We know for certain from John Macky's *A Journey through England in 1724*, that by then 'Every Walk terminates in some little Building', one where 'my Lord often dines instead of his House', most likely the Bagnio; quoted in John Harris, *Palladian Revival*, pp. 78–9.
3. John Harris's scholarly detective work on the Earl's coronet on the design held in the Royal Institute of British Architects (hereafter RIBAD) collection (CA (24) 8) revealed the sequence of events; see *Palladian Revival*, p. 133.
4. As in the 'Therme di Agrippa' of Burlington's own *Fabbriche Antiche desegnate da Andrea Palladio Vicentio*, 1730.
5. A pen and wash plan and elevation is in the RIBAD collection: XVII/1r.
6. For illustrations of these villas see Vincenzo Scamozzi, *L'idea della architettura universale*, 1615.
7. The drawing is in the RIBAD collection: XVII/15r.
8. The drawing is at Chatsworth: 26A, 35.
9. Kent's design is in volume 2, plate 72 and illustrated in Harris, *Palladian Revival*, p. 148.
10. The manuscript, 'Breve Compendio delle Metamorfosi di Ovidio Istoricamente spiegate e descritte da GUGLIELMO KENT', is in the Bodleian Library, MS Rawlinson, D.540.

11. At Syon House, Kenwood and Newby Hall in Yorkshire. See Eileen Harris, *The Genius of Robert Adam: His Interiors*, Yale University Press, 2001.
12. Much comment rages over the source of this very odd ceiling. Cinzia Maria Sicca urges that Kent saw one like it in the ducal palace at Mantua; see 'On William Kent's Roman Sources', *Architectural History*, vol. 29 (1986), pp. 134–57; figs 2 and 3. However, a pen and watercolour sketch in the John Talman collection at Chatsworth (25.A2) seems to offer a Burlington source. Either way it is a spatial disaster.
13. Hervey, 'Verses on the E – of B – & His House at C – K by the Author of the Nobleman's Epistle to Dr Sherwyn', British Library, Add. MS 8127, f. 21; quoted in Harris, *Palladian Revival*, p. 107.
14. Earl of Ilchester (ed.), *Lord Hervey and his Friends 1726–38*, p. 186.
15. Romney Sedgwick (ed.), *Some Materials Towards Memoirs of the Reign of King George II by John, Lord Hervey*, vol. 2, p. 574.

Chapter 13: Chiswick – the garden as a learning experience (pp. 139–49)

1. For an account of Castell see Eileen Harris and Nicholas Savage, *British Architectural Books and Writers, 1550–1785*, pp. 149–54, from which this quote is taken (p. 151).
2. Robert Castell, *The Villas of the Ancients Illustrated*, 1728 on title page, though actually published in July 1729, Preface.
3. Harris and Savage, *British Architectural Books*, p. 150.
4. John Fleming, *Robert Adam and his Circle in Edinburgh and Rome*, John Murray, 1962, p. 28.
5. Harris and Savage, *British Architectural Books*, p. 150.
6. Ibid., p. 151.
7. For Temple see Timothy Mowl, *Gentlemen and Players: Gardeners of the English Landscape*, Sutton, 2000, pp. 64–5. See also Ciaran Murray, *Sharawadgi: The Romantic Return to Nature*, International Scholars Publications, 1999.
8. Castell, *Villas*, pp. 116–17.
9. Ibid., p. 117.
10. Ibid., p. 59.
11. Horace Walpole, *The History of the Modern Taste in Gardening*, p. 43.
12. Castell, *Villas*, p. 83.
13. Ibid., pp. 86–7.

14. Ibid., pp. 80–81.
15. Ibid., pp. 89–90.
16. See John Harris, *The Palladian Revival: Lord Burlington, His Villa and Garden at Chiswick*, catalogue no. 98, p. 236 where the hedge of the Exedra is shown rising no higher than the waistlines of the statues.
17. Ibid., catalogue nos 106–10, pp. 244–8.
18. Quoted in Cinzia Maria Sicca, 'Lord Burlington at Chiswick: Architecture and Landscape', *Garden History*, vol. 10, no. 1 (Spring, 1982), pp. 36–69; p.66.
19. Harris, *Palladian Revival*, catalogue nos 92 and 93, pp. 230–31.
20. John Dixon Hunt, *William Kent, Landscape Designer*, does, however, give a catalogue of these, but not reproduced in their original pen and brown wash.
21. Ibid., catalogue no. 108, p. 246.
22. Ibid., catalogue no. 99, p. 237.
23. Ibid., catalogue no. 96, p. 234.
24. Ibid., catalogue no. 97, p. 235.

Chapter 14: From antique brilliance to sumptuous decadence (pp. 150–67)

1. M. Verney and P. Abercrombie, 'Letters of an Eighteenth-Century Architect pt. III', *Architectural Review*, vol. LX (1926), p. 51.
2. Michael Wilson is especially good on Kent's furniture: see his *William Kent: Architect, Designer, Painter, Gardener, 1685–1747*, chapter 5, pp. 88–126.
3. Margaret Jourdain, *The Work of William Kent: Artist, Painter, Designer and Landscape Gardener*, p. 82.
4. See particularly the six settees of gilt wood in the Double Cube Room at Wilton which Wilson, *William Kent*, p. 120, attributes convincingly to Kent.
5. Ibid., p. 82, quoting William Chambers, *Decorative Part of Civil Architecture*.
6. W. H. Pyne, *Royal Residences*, 3 vols, 1819; vol. 2, p. 84.
7. Jourdain, *William Kent*, p. 84.
8. *HMC*, Portland MSS, vol. vi, 1900, p. 160.
9. For a full account of the building history see Christopher Hussey, *English Country Houses: Early Georgian 1715–1760*, pp. 66–71; also John Cornforth, 'Ditchley Park, Oxfordshire', *Country Life*, 24 October 1985.
10. Quoted by Cornforth, *Country Life*, 24 October 1985.
11. Ibid.

12. H. M. Colvin, *A Biographical Dictionary of British Architects, 1600–1840*, p. 366, quotes Dr Pamela Kingsbury as his authority for this romantic episode.
13. Hussey, *Early Georgian*, p. 69.
14. Mereworth Castle had been bequeathed to that branch of the Tree family by the Hon. Peter Beatty.
15. Romney Sedwick (ed.), *Some Materials Towards Memoirs of the Reign of King George II by John, Lord Hervey*, vol. 1, p. 80.
16. Ibid., pp. 86–7.
17. Ibid.
18. Ibid.
19. Ibid.
20. Ibid., vol. 1, p. 85.
21. *HMC*, Portland MSS, vol. vi, p. 160.
22. Hervey was writing to Frederick, Prince of Wales, in a letter of 21 July 1731, during one of those brief spells when he and the Prince were on good terms. Quoted in Earl of Ilchester (ed.), *Lord Hervey and his Friends 1726–38*, p. 74.
23. John Harris, 'James Gibbs, Eminence Grise at Houghton', *The Georgian Group Symposium*, 1988, pp. 5–9.
24. Hussey, *Early Georgian*, p. 72.
25. *HMC*, Portland MSS, vol. vi, 1900, p. 160.
26. Ibid., pp. 160–61.
27. Ilchester, *Lord Hervey*, p. 72: letter of 14 July 1731 to Frederick, Prince of Wales.
28. Ibid.
29. Sedgwick, *Memoirs*, vol. 1, p. 18, footnote.
30. Ibid., vol. 2, p. 421.
31. Quoted, significantly, by a woman historian, Betty Kemp, *Sir Robert Walpole*, Weidenfeld & Nicolson, 1976, p. 133.
32. Ibid., p. 38.
33. Ibid., p. 39.
34. Ibid., p. 38.
35. A term popularised by Osbert Lancaster, *Homes Sweet Homes*, John Murray, 1939, p. 64.
36. Ilchester, *Lord Hervey*, p. 74.
37. For Wilton Garden see Timothy Mowl, *Historic Gardens of Wiltshire*, Tempus Publishing, 2004, pp. 30–41.
38. Hussey, *Early Georgian*, p. 80.
39. Ibid., p. 81.

Chapter 15: Queen Caroline and a landscape on the cusp at Richmond Lodge (pp. 168–75)

1. For Vanbrugh see Christopher Ridgway and Robert Williams (eds), *Sir John Vanbrugh and Landscape Architecture in Baroque England 1690–1730*, Sutton, 2000.
2. H. M. Colvin (gen. ed.), *The History of the King's Works*, vol. 5, pp. 97–8; plate 67.
3. For Bridgeman see Peter Willis, *Charles Bridgeman and the English Landscape Garden*, Elysium Press Publishers, 2002.
4. For Addison see Timothy Mowl, *Gentlemen and Players: Gardeners of the English Landscape*, Sutton, 2000, chapter 7, pp. 79–92.
5. For Switzer see Mowl, *Gentlemen and Players*, chapter 7, pp. 79–92.
6. Earl of Ilchester (ed.), *Lord Hervey and his Friends 1726–38*, p. 76.
7. Ibid.
8. John Macky, visiting Ormonde Lodge in 1714, recorded: 'There is a fine avenue that runs from the front of the house to the Town of Richmond at a half a mile distance one way [known as the Wild Chestnut Walk], and from the other front to the Riverside; see Ray Desmond, *The History of the Royal Botanic Gardens Kew*, Harvill Press, 1998, p. 2. Desmond illustrates John Lawrence's engraving, the frontispiece from his 1726 *A New System of Agriculture*, of the George London layout (p. 4).
9. For Southcote and ornamental farms see David Jacques, *Georgian Gardens: The Reign of Nature*, pp. 18–25.
10. The first indication that Bridgeman was working at Richmond comes in a letter from Pope to the Earl of Oxford of 22 March 1725: '[I have] just turfed a little Bridgmannick Theatre myself. It was done by a detachment of His workmen from the Prince's [the Prince of Wales at Richmond]'.: G. Sherburn (ed.), *The Correspondence of Alexander Pope*, vol. 2, p. 14.
11. Colvin, *King's Works*, vol. 5, p. 218.
12. For an illustration of this building see Ray Desmond, *The History of the Royal Botanic Gardens Kew*, p. 10.
13. For a full account of the Hermitage see Judith Colton, 'Kent's Hermitage for Queen Caroline at Richmond', *Architectura*, 2 (1974), pp. 181–91.
14. Sedgwick, *Memoirs*, vol. 2, p. 501.
15. Sherburn, *Correspondence*, vol. 3, p. 329.
16. John Dixon Hunt, *William Kent, Landscape Designer*, catalogue no. 70.

17. For Herrenhausen see Dietmar Horst, *The Royal Gardens of Herrenhausen, Hannover.*

Chapter 16: Twickenham – a real garden designer and a poet who claimed to be one (pp. 176–87)

1. Mavis Batey, *Alexander Pope: The Poet and the Landscape*, Barn Elms Publishing, 1999.
2. Alexander Pope, 'To Richard Boyle, Earl of Burlington: On the Use of Riches', lines 55–60.
3. Alexander Pope, 'Eloisa to Abelard', lines 150–51.
4. See John Dixon Hunt, introduction to *William Kent, Landscape Designer*, pp. 15–29.
5. Ibid., p. 26.
6. Wilmarth S. Lewis (ed.), *The Yale Edition of Horace Walpole's Correspondence*, vol. 9, p. 122: Walpole to Montagu, 22 July 1751. Walpole was referring to Francesco Albani, sometimes known as Albano (1578–1660), a Bolognese painter whose idealised landscapes with mythical figures and classical buildings pre-date those of Claude Lorraine (1600–82), Gaspard Dughet (1615–75) and his brother-in-law, Nicolas Poussin (1594–1665). In a further letter to John Chute of 4 August 1753 (Lewis, *Correspondence*, vol. 35, p. 75) Walpole writes: 'I have been here [Stowe] these two days, extremely amused and charmed indeed. Wherever you stand you see an Albano landscape. Half as many buildings I believe would be too many, but such a profusion gives inexpressible richness.'
7. Ibid., vol. 10, p. 315: Walpole to Montagu, 7 July 1770.
8. Hunt, introduction to *William Kent, Landscape Designer*, p. 42, quotation from Horace Walpole, *A History of the Modern Taste in Gardening*.
9. See John Harris, 'The Artinatural Style', in Charles Hind (ed.), *The Rococo in England: A Symposium*, Victoria & Albert Museum, 1986, pp. 8–20.
10. This has been partly remedied by Eileen Harris and Nicholas Savage in their section on Langley in *British Architectural Books*, pp. 262–80.
11. Batty Langley, *The New Principles of Gardening*, 1728, Introduction, p. ii.
12. Ibid., p. xi.
13. Ibid.
14. Ibid.
15. Ibid., p. iii.

16. Ibid., p. x.
17. Ibid., p. vi.
18. Ibid., p. vii.
19. Ibid., p. vii.
20. Ibid.
21. See particularly Morris Brownell, *Alexander Pope and the Arts of Georgian England*, Oxford University Press, 1978.
22. George Gilfillan, *The Poetical Works of Alexander Pope*, 2 vols, James Nichol, Edinburgh, 1856, vol. 1, Introduction, p. xxiv.
23. Alexander Pope, 'An Essay on Criticism', lines 68–73.
24. See *Alexander Pope's Villa. Views of Pope's villa, grotto and garden: a microcosm of English landscape*, Greater London Council, 1980; also Anthony Beckles Willson, 'Alexander Pope's Grotto in Twickenham', *Garden History*, 26, no. 1 (Summer, 1998), pp. 31–59.
25. For illustrations of both maps see Batey, *Pope*, pp. 59, 68–9.
26. Langley, *New Principles*, p. x.
27. Ibid., p. vii.
28. Ibid., p. iii.
29. Horace Walpole, *A History of Modern Taste in Gardening*, p. 44.
30. Lewis, *Correspondence*, vol. 10, p. 42: Walpole to Montagu, 24 September 1762.

Chapter 17: First for a prime minister and then for a queen – a forgotten Gothick revival (pp. 188–203)

1. See Marcus Binney, *Sir Robert Taylor: From Rococo to Neo-Classicism*, Allen & Unwin, 1984.
2. H. Avray Tipping, 'Esher Place', *Country Life*, 6 January 1900.
3. See J. M. Crook, 'Strawberry Hill Revisited', *Country Life*, 7, 14 and 21 June 1973; also Timothy Mowl, *Horace Walpole: The Great Outsider*.
4. Horace Walpole, *A History of the Modern Taste in Gardening*, pp. 43–4.
5. Wilmarth S. Lewis (ed.), *The Yale Edition of Horace Walpole's Correspondence*, vol. 10, pp. 72–3: Walpole to Montagu, 19 May 1763.
6. Horace Walpole, *Memoirs of the Reign of George II*, 3 vols, edited by John Brooke, Yale University Press, 1985, vol. 1, p. 247.
7. Ibid., vol. 2, p. 6.
8. For illustrations of these see Michael I. Wilson, *William Kent: Architect, Designer, Painter, Gardener, 1685–1748*, plates 58–61.

9. Ibid., plates 10–19; see also John Dixon Hunt, *William Kent, Landscape Designer*, plates 16–19 (Thomson's *Seasons*).
10. For the Palladian scheme and Kent's other designs see Michael Symes, 'The Landscaping of Esher Place', *Journal of Garden History*, 1988, vol. 8, no. 4, pp. 63–96; fig.11. See also John Harris, 'Esher Place', *Country Life*, 14 May 1959.
11. Illustrated in *Country Life*, 6 January 1900.
12. From *Britannia Illustrata*, 1707 (1984, Paradigm Press, Bungay, eds, John Harris and Gervase Jackson-Stops), pp. 152–3.
13. The portrait, by an unknown artist, is illustrated in Symes, 'Esher Place', fig. 6, p. 71.
14. *DNB*.
15. Judith Colton, 'Merlin's Cave and Queen Caroline: Garden Art as Political Propaganda', *Eighteenth-Century Studies*, vol. 10 (1976), pp. 1–19; pp. 12–13.
16. For an illustration see Wilson, *William Kent*, plate 59.
17. Ibid., plate 61.
18. The Westminster screen is illustrated in Wilson, *William Kent*, plate 62; the Gloucester screen is illustrated in Michael McCarthy, *The Origins of the Gothic Revival*, Yale University Press, 1987, plate 191.
19. For Shobdon see McCarthy, *Gothic Revival*, pp. 149–54, who gives the design jointly to Kent and Richard Bateman; see also Julia Ionides, 'Shobdon Church – Who Done it?', *The Picturesque*, no. 4 (Autumn, 1993), pp. 1–4.
20. Kent remembered Rysbrack in his will with a mourning ring so their relationship was friendly.
21. Copied from a more formidable beast on the tomb of Pope Gregory XIII in St Peter's, Rome.
22. For illustrations see Roy Strong, *'And when did you last see your father?' The Victorian Painter and British History*, Thames & Hudson, 1978, plates 15, 16 and colour plate 1.
23. Sedgwick, *Memoirs*, vol. 2, p.501.
24. Edmund Spenser, *The Faerie Queene*, Book 3, canto 3.
25. Quoted in *Gentleman's Magazine* for September 1735, pp. 532–3, but reprinted from *The Craftsman*.
26. Ibid.
27. Ibid.

Chapter 18: Working for the opposition – Kent and Prince 'Fretz' (pp. 204–16)

1. Romney Sedgwick (ed.), *Some Material Towards Memoirs of the Reign of King George II by John, Lord Hervey*, vol. 3, p. 681.
2. Ibid.
3. Ibid., p. 671.
4. Ibid., vol. 1, Introduction, p. xxxi.
5. See Michael Snodin (ed.), *Rococo: Art and Design in Hogarth's England*, Victoria & Albert Museum, 1984; see also Timothy Mowl and Brian Earnshaw, *An Insular Rococo: Architecture, Politics and Society in Ireland and England, 1710–1770*, Reaktion Books, 1999.
6. Illustrated in Ray Desmond, *The History of the Royal Botanic Gardens Kew*, p. 7 (top left-hand vignette).
7. The White House is illustrated in Desmond, *Kew*, p. 22.
8. In John Vardy, *Some Designs of Mr Inigo Jones and Mr William Kent*, 1744, Gregg Press, Farnborough, 1967, plate 34.
9. All the details from Rocque's plan of 1748 have been helpfully enlarged in Desmond's *Kew*, p. 25.
10. Earl of Ilchester (ed.), *Lord Hervey and his Friends 1726–38*, p. 116.
11. Ibid.
12. Ibid., p. 114.
13. Ibid., p. 116.
14. Ibid.
15. Illustrated in Michael I. Wilson, *William Kent: Architect, Designer, Painter, Gardener, 1685–1748*, plates 50–51. See Geoffrey Beard, 'William Kent and the Royal Barge', *Burlington Magazine* (August, 1970), pp. 488–93.
16. Illustrated in Wilson, *William Kent*, plate 49.
17. For Burlington's complex relations with Kent and his other protégés at this time see Rudolf Wittkower, *Palladio and English Palladianism*, chapter 8, pp. 114–34. See also the adverse criticism of the York Assembly Rooms which may have contributed to Burlington's decision to give up his posts and, therefore, his controlling influence in the official Palladian revival: Wittkower, *Palladio*, chapter 9, pp. 134–46; also John Harris, *The Palladian Revival*, pp. 169–72.
18. The model is preserved at the Dutch House in Kew and is illustrated in Wilson, *William Kent*, plate 70.
19. Sedgwick, *Memoirs*, vol. 1, p. 189.

20. For an illustration of the monuments in their original setting see Wilson, *William Kent*, plate 54.
21. Kent's Shakespeare is discussed in detail by Wilson, *William Kent*, pp. 141–2. Scheemakers made a replica of it for the 9th Earl of Pembroke, which still stands in the entrance hall at Wilton.
22. The Ligorio engraving is illustrated in John Dixon Hunt, *William Kent, Landscape Designer*, fig. 4. A wooden version of the Temple was set up after Kent's death at Oatlands Park, see Michael Symes, 'New Light on Oatlands Park in the Eighteenth Century', *Garden History*, vol. 9, no. 2 (Winter, 1981), pp. 136–56.
23. From Benton Seeley's 1744 *A Description of the Gardens of Lord Viscount Cobham at Stow in Buckinghamshire*, in George B. Clarke (ed.), *Descriptions of Lord Cobham's Gardens at Stowe: 1700–1750*, p. 126.
24. Information from Kate Felus.
25. Clarke, *Stowe*, p. 160.
26. Ibid.
27. Ibid.
28. Sleter was a Venetian artist who painted the Long Gallery at Mereworth Castle and also worked at Moor Park in Hertfordshire.
29. For the political iconography behind the Elysian Fields see Patrick Eyres (ed.), *New Arcadian Journal*, vol. 43/44: 'The Political Temples of Stowe', New Arcadian Press, Leeds, 1997.
30. See George Clarke, 'Grecian Taste and Gothic Virtue: Lord Cobham's Gardening Programme and its Iconography', *Apollo*, June 1973.
31. From Seeley's *Description*, quoted in Clarke, *Stowe*, p. 140.
32. Ibid. Originally in Latin, translated by Clarke, p. 138.
33. Wilmarth S. Lewis (ed.), *The Yale Edition of Horace Walpole's Correspondence*, vol. 10, pp. 314–15: Walpole to Montagu, 7 July 1770.
34. See David Coombs, 'The Garden at Carlton House of Frederick Prince of Wales and Augusta Princess and Dowager of Wales', *Garden History*, vol. 25, no. 2 (Winter, 1997), pp. 153–77. See also Mark Laird, *The Flowering of the Landscape Garden: English Pleasure Grounds 1720–1800*, pp. 41–2, 198–200.
35. See Giles Worsley, 'Rokeby Park, Yorkshire', *Country Life*, 19 March 1987.
36. Robinson's appreciation of Kent is quoted in full in Harris, *Palladian Revival*, pp. 196–7; see also Timothy Mowl, *Gentlemen and Players*, Sutton, 2000, p. 117.

Chapter 19: Institutional failures – Ruritanian and gargantuan (pp. 217–26)

1. See Christopher Hussey, *English Country Houses: Early Georgian 1715–1760*, pp. 147–54.
2. A Kent note, Bodleian Library, MS Rawlinson, D.540, claims that he took the King and Queen 'to look upon that Building of my Designe'.
3. H. M. Colvin (gen. ed.), *The History of the King's Works*, vol. 5, plate 21B.
4. Ibid., plate 21C.
5. See Michael I. Wilson, *William Kent: Architect, Designer, Painter, Gardener, 1685–1748*, plates 65 and 66.
6. See *Vitruvius Britannicus*, vol. iii (1725), plate 10.
7. For a full, illustrated account of this remarkable room see *The Survey of London: The Parish of St Margaret, Westminster* – Part III, Batsford, 1931, vol. 14, pp. 31–6, plates 11–35.
8. Ibid., plate 21.
9. Ibid., plate 23.
10. Illustrated in Colvin, *King's Works*, vol. 5, plate 65.
11. Ibid., pp. 433–40.
12. Ibid., p. 243, fn. 2.
13. See Wilson, *William Kent*, plate 48.
14. British Museum, Add. MS 51396, f. 185; quoted in Colvin, *King's Works*, vol. 5, p. 242.
15. Illustrated in John Vardy, *Some Designs of Mr Inigo Jones and Mr William Kent*, plate 38.
16. See John Cornforth, 'Devonshire House, London – II', *Country Life*, 20 November 1980.
17. See Colvin, *King's Works*, vol. 5, plates 59–65.
18. See Christine Hiskey, 'The Building of Holkham Hall: Newly Discovered Letters', *Architectural History*, vol. 40 (1997), pp. 144–58.
19. See Hussey, *Early Georgian*, plate 210.
20. Hiskey, *Architectural History*, pp. 148, 156. Kent's drawing of the view to the southwest across the lake with the Seat on the Mount is illustrated in Leo Schmidt, 'Holkham Hall, Norfolk – II', *Country Life*, 31 January 1980, fig. 3.
21. For illustrations of the 1726 proposal and Kent's south front see Leo Schmidt, 'Holkham Hall, Norfolk – I', *Country Life*, 24 January 1980, figs 3 and 11; see also Hussey, *Early Georgian*, pp. 131–46.
22. For Tottenham Park see John Harris, 'Serendipity and the Architect Earl', *Country Life*, 28 May 1987.

23. See Colvin, *King's Works*, vol. 5, plate 65A.
24. See Hiskey, *Architectural History*, Letters 7, 9, 10 and 12.
25. Hussey, *Early Georgian*, p. 137.
26. Ibid., plate 213.
27. Hiskey, *Architectural History*, p. 147.
28. For Kent's drawing see Hussey, *Early Georgian*, plate 219.
29. Schmidt, *Country Life*, 31 January 1980, figs 6 and 7, cites the Temple of Venus and Roma as illustrated by Palladio as one Antique source for the Marble Hall.
30. I am indebted to the Holkham archivist, Christine Hiskey, for information on the statue. The Jupiter was almost two metres tall and was left lying in various builders' yards in London before being brought to Holkham. Joseph Wilton did some restoration work on the arms and hands after 1755, and by 1765 it was in the 'Portico Room' (Smoking Room). By 1861 it had been moved to the newly built conservatory and remained there until the 5th Earl (1949–76) removed it. The restored head of the Jupiter is still in the Smoking Room and its torso lies in Samuel Wyatt's old Game Larder.

Chapter 20: Success in the capital for the wrong patron (pp. 227–31)

1. From his *Les Édifices Antiques de Rome* of 1682, an intensely thorough demonstration of French scholarship which contemporary England could only marvel at. Cinzia Maria Sicca detects the influence of Giulio Romano's Palazzo del Tè in Mantua on the Marble Hall: 'On William Kent's Roman Sources', *Architectural History*, vol. 29, 1986, pp. 138–9.
2. See Leo Schmidt, 'Holkham Hall, Norfolk – II', 31 January 1980.
3. Indeed, it featured recently (2005) in a television advertisement fronted by the sports commentator Desmond Lynam, where he parted the waters in the Hall, as if in the Red Sea, and descended the stairs.
4. Most aficionados of architecture know of 44 Berkeley Square, but as it is a very superior private club, The Clermont, with a 1963 Gothick pavilion by Fowler and Jebb in its back garden, not many have experienced it. The house is, however, accessible on some Open Doors days. I am most grateful to the staff at the Clermont for allowing me access.
5. John Van Der Kiste, *King George II and Queen Caroline*, Sutton, 1997, p. 129.

6. Margaret Jourdain, *The Work of William Kent*, pp. 90–91.
7. See John Harris, 'William Kent's 44 Berkeley Square', *Apollo*, August 1987, pp. 100–104. See also Mark Girouard, '44 Berkeley Square, London', *Country Life*, 27 December 1962.
8. Ibid., quoting from the Account Book in Sir John Soane's Museum.
9. Girouard, *Country Life*, 27 December 1962, suggests that the originals may have been the four models that Kent left to Lady Bel in his will.
10. Girouard, ibid., cites the High Renaissance work in the Villa Madama, Rome, and the Doge's Palace at Venice as typical sources for Kent's two ceilings at Berkeley Square and Arlington Street.
11. Ibid., p. 104.
12. Cinzia Maria Sicca, *Architectural History*, vol. 29, 1986, p. 139, relates the design of the honeycomb coffering to Giulio Romano's Sala di Psiche at the Palazzo del Tè in Mantua.
13. See Clifford Musgrave, '22 Arlington Street, London', *The Connoisseur*, June 1964, pp. 74–80.
14. Early photographs in the National Monuments Record show this rich profusion.

Chapter 21: Places, patrons and the wood of self-revelation (pp. 232–45)

1. Christopher Hussey, 'Rousham, Oxfordshire – II', *Country Life*, 24 May 1946.
2. Horace Walpole, *A History of the Modern Taste in Gardening*, pp. 43–4.
3. For Kent's vestigial work at Oatlands see Michael Symes, 'New Light on Oatlands Park in the Eighteenth Century', *Garden History*, vol. 9, no. 2 (Winter, 1981), pp. 136–56.
4. See Mavis Batey, 'An Early Naturalistic Garden, Shotover, Oxfordshire – 1', *Country Life*, 22 December 1977.
5. Kent's design is illustrated in John Dixon Hunt, *William Kent, Landscape Designer*, plate 100.
6. For Claremont see Roy Strong, *The Artist and the Garden*, pp. 232–9; also *Claremont*, National Trust, 2000, and Phyllis M. Cooper, *The Story of Claremont*, published privately, 2000.
7. Kent's achievement is best viewed in a series of paintings by the 'Master of the Tumbled Chairs' illustrated in John Harris, *The Artist and the Country House: A History of Country House and Garden View Painting in Britain 1540–1870*, Sotheby Parke Bernet, 1979, plates 192a–e.

8. Wilmarth S. Lewis (ed.), *The Yale Edition of Horace Walpole's Correspondence*, vol. 18, pp. 254–5.
9. Evelyn wrote: 'The tufts of firr and much of the other wood were planted by my direction'; quoted in Arthur Oswald, 'Euston Hall, Suffolk – III', *Country Life*, 24 January 1957.
10. Lewis, *Correspondence*, vol. 18, p. 255.
11. I am much indebted to Philip Gunn and his wife, Tibouche, for their kind hospitality at Euston.
12. Kent's drawing for the Lodge is illustrated in Hunt, *William Kent, Landscape Designer*, catalogue no. 48, where it is captioned as a 'triumphal arch'.
13. See 'A Georgian Gem', *Architectural Digest*, March 2005, pp. 50–58.
14. See his drawing of a new house with the Temple to the rear in *William Kent, Landscape Designer*, catalogue no. 49.
15. There are also two plaques with the Grafton cipher and two recording the date of completion: 1746.
16. See Kenneth Woodbridge, 'William Kent's Gardening: The Rousham Letters', *Apollo*, October 1974, pp. 282–91; also Ulrich Müller, 'Rousham: A Transcription of the Steward's Letters, 1738–42', *Garden History*, vol. 25, no. 2 (Winter, 1997), pp. 178–88.
17. These are both illustrated in Woodbridge, *Apollo*, 1974, plates 2 and 3. The Bridgeman plan is in the Bodleian Library and the later plan is preserved at the house.
18. See Mavis Batey, 'The Way to View Rousham by Kent's Gardener', *Garden History*, vol. 11, no. 2 (Autumn, 1983), pp. 125–31.
19. Two articles on the house (17 and 24 May), and two specifically on the gardens: 'A Georgian Arcady: William Kent's Gardens at Rousham, Oxfordshire' (14 and 21 June). See also Kenneth Woodbridge, 'William Kent as Landscape-Gardener: A Re-Appraisal', *Apollo*, August 1974, pp. 126–37.
20. Primarily with Colonel Robert for whom he wrote a fine epitaph.
21. I am much indebted for her interpretation of the iconographic programme at Rousham to Dr Susan Gordon's unpublished doctoral thesis, 'The Iconography and Mythology of the Eighteenth-Century English Landscape Garden', University of Bristol, 1999.
22. Quoted in David Coffin, 'The Elysian Fields of Rousham', *Proceedings of the American Philosophical Society*, vol. 130, no. 4 (1986), pp. 406–23; p. 422.
23. This biographical episode is given in Gordon, Ph.D. thesis, p. 44, citing British Library, Eg. MA. 927.

24. G. Sherburn (ed.), *The Correspondence of Alexander Pope*, vol. 2, p. 188: Kent to Pope.
25. Gordon, Ph.D. thesis, p. 43, citing Terence, 'Eunuch', 4, 735.
26. Quoted by Woodbridge, *Apollo*, October 1974, p.284.
27. Batey, *Garden History*, p. 127.
28. Ibid.
29. Kent's drawing for the conversion is given in Woodbridge, *Apollo*, October 1974, fig. 6.
30. Ibid., p. 128.
31. Kent's drawing for this view is preserved at the house and illustrated in Hunt, *William Kent, Landscape Designer*, plate 106.
32. Ibid.
33. Named after the master mason, but designed by Kent whose first version elevation and plan is illustrated in Hunt, *William Kent, Landscape Designer*, plate 107. The final version is illustrated in John Vardy, *Some Designs of Mr Inigo Jones and Mr William Kent*, 1744, Gregg Press, Farnborough, 1967, plate 39.
34. See Coffin, *Proceedings of the American Philosophical Society*, pp. 416–18.
35. Batey, *Garden History*, p. 130.
36. Ibid.
37. Algernon Charles Swinburne, 'Hymn to Proserpine', line 24.
38. These last have been removed to the House for security.
39. Batey, *Garden History*, p. 130.
40. Ibid.
41. See Marcus Binney, 'Wakefield Lodge, Northamptonshire', *Country Life*, 2 August 1975; also Richard Hewlings, 'Wakefield Lodge and other houses of the Second Duke of Grafton', *The Georgian Group Journal*, 1993, pp. 43–61.
42. See Michael Liversidge and Jane Farrington (eds), *Canaletto and England*, Merrell Holberton Ltd, 1993, fig. 5.
43. See Eileen Harris, 'The Architecture of Thomas Wright', *Country Life*, 19 August, 2 and 9 September 1971; see also Michael McCarthy, *The Origins of the Gothic Revival*, Yale University Press, 1987, pp. 42–8.
44. Remarked by Bishop Pococke, who visited Badminton in 1754; quoted in Hussey, *Early Georgian*, p. 166. The chimneypiece is a fugitive from Stoke Park, the Beauforts' dower house near Bristol; the original is now in the Dining Room at Badminton. The convex mirror, presumably designed by Kent, has also been removed to Badminton House.
45. Kent's involvement in the complex building history of Badminton is

ably conveyed by Andor Gomme, 'Badminton Revisited', *Architectural History*, vol. 27 (1984), pp. 163–82.

46. See Nicholas Kingsley, *The Country Houses of Gloucestershire*, vol. 2: *1660–1830*, Phillimore & Co., 1992, p. 60, which records that the Lodge was built after Kent's death under the direction of Stephen Wright and completed in 1750 at a cost of £721. The main contract drawings in the hand of Stephen Wright are in the Beaufort drawings at Gloucester Record Office, D. 2700.
47. *The Walpole Society*, vol. 22 (1933–4), p. 140.

Select Bibliography

Primary Sources: Kent-Related Manuscripts

Bodleian Library, MS. Rawlinson, D.1162: Kent's diary of his Italian tour with Thomas Coke

Bodleian Library, Holkham MS Film 304: Edward Jarret's accounts for Thomas Coke's Grand Tour

Bodleian Library, MS Eng. Letters e.34: John Talman's Letter Book

Bodleian Library, MS Eng. Misc. C.114: Stukeley Correspondence

Bodleian Library, MS Rawlinson, D.540: Kent's translation of Ovid's *Metamorphoses*

Lincoln Record Office, 2MM. B. 19A: Kent–Burrell Massingberd *Correspondence*

British Library, Print Room, 197* d.3: John Talman's Book of Prints, 'Drawings of Ecclesiastical Garments'

British Library, 197 c.2: Talman's Book of Prints

British Library, Add. MS22.229: Wentworth Papers

Borthwick Institute, York, NOM SM 1704/2: Hustler Papers

Chatsworth, Materials from the Devonshire Collection: Kent Burlington Letters, 260.0–15

Huntingdon Library, California: Kent–Countess of Huntingdon Correspondence

Primary Sources: Theses

Jacques Carré, 'Lord Burlington', University of Dijon Ph.D., 1980

Susan Gordon, 'The Iconography and Mythology of the Eighteenth-Century English Landscape Garden', University of Bristol Ph.D., 1999

Gordon Higgott, 'Lord Burlington and William Kent: A study in Proportion', London, Courtauld MA, 1978

G. Lester, 'The Interior Designs of William Kent', London, Courtauld MA, 1973

Verity Smith, 'Thomas Coke – Was He the Architect of England's First Neo-classical House, Holkham Hall?', University of Bristol BA, 2003

Primary Sources: Books (Publication place London unless otherwise specified)

Richard Boyle, 3rd Earl of Burlington, *Fabbriche Antiche disegnate da Andrea Palladio*, 1730

Matthew Brettingham, *The Plans, Elevations and Sections of Holkham in Norfolk, the Seat of the late Earl of Leicester*, 1761

Robert Castell, *The Villas of the Ancients Illustrated*, 1728/July 1729; Garland Publishing, New York and London, 1982

George B. Clarke (ed.), *Descriptions of Lord Cobham's Gardens at Stowe: 1700–1750*, Buckinghamshire Record Society, Dorchester, 1990

Anthony Ashley Cooper, Earl of Shaftesbury, *Characteristicks of Men, Manners, Opinions, Times*, 3 vols, 2nd corrected ed, 1714

The Diary of Mary Countess Cowper, Lady of the Bedchamber to The Princess of Wales, John Murray, 1864

Earl of Ilchester (ed.), *Lord Hervey and his Friends 1726–38, based on letters from Holland House, Melbury, and Ickworth*, John Murray, 1950

William Kent, *The Designs of Inigo Jones, Consisting of Plans and Elevations for Public and Private Buildings*, 1727

Batty Langley, *New Principles of Gardening or The Laying Out and Planting Parterres, Groves, Wildernesses, Labyrinths, Avenues . . . After a More Grand and Rural Manner than has Been Done Before*, 1728

——, *Ancient Architecture Restored and Improved*, 1741–2; re-issued as *Gothic Architecture*, 1747

Wilmarth S. Lewis (ed.), *The Yale Edition of Horace Walpole's Correspondence*, 48 vols, Yale University Press, New Haven and London, 1937–83

Andrea Palladio, *The Four Books of Architecture*, Dover Publications, New York, 1965

Vincenzo Scamozzi, *L'idea della architettura universale*, 1615

Romney Sedgwick (ed.), *Some Materials Towards Memoirs of the Reign of King George II by John, Lord Hervey*, 3 vols, King's Printers, 1931

G. Sherburn (ed.), *The Correspondence of Alexander Pope*, 5 vols, Oxford University Press, 1956

Stephen Switzer, *The Nobleman, Gentleman, and Gardener's Recreation*, 1715; revised and enlarged as *Ichnographia Rustica, or, The Nobleman, Gentleman, and Gardener's Recreation*, 1718

John Vardy, *Some Designs of Mr Inigo Jones and Mr William Kent*, 1744, Gregg Press, Farnborough, 1967

Vitruvius Britannicus or The British Architect, Benjamin Blom, New York, 1967

Horace Walpole, *A History of the Modern Taste in Gardening*, 1782; Ursus Press, New York, 1995

Secondary Sources: Books (Publication place London unless otherwise specified)

James S. Ackerman, *Palladio*, Penguin, Harmondsworth, 1966

A Gothick Symposium, The Georgian Group, 1983

Dana Arnold (ed.), *Belov'd by Ev'ry Muse: Richard Boyle, 3rd Earl of Burlington and 4th Earl of Cork (1694–1753)*, The Georgian Group, 1994

Philip J. Ayres, *Classical Culture and the Idea of Rome in Eighteenth-Century England*, Cambridge University Press, 1997

Mavis Batey, *Alexander Pope: the Poet and the Landscape*, Barn Elms, 1999

Mavis Batey and David Lambert, *The English Garden Tour: A View into the Past*, John Murray, 1990

Geoffrey Beard, *Decorative Plasterwork in Great Britain*, Phaidon, 1975

——, *Craftsmen and Interior Decoration in England 1660–1820*, John Batholomew, Edinburgh, 1981

David Bindman, *Hogarth*, Thames & Hudson, 1981

Anthony Blunt, *Guide to Baroque Rome*, Granada Publishing, St Albans and London, 1982

John Bold, *Wilton House and English Palladianism: Some Wiltshire Houses*, HMSO, 1988

Morris Brownell, *Alexander Pope and the Arts of Georgian England*, Oxford, 1978

Jacques Carré, *Lord Burlington*, Adosa, Clermont-Ferrand, 1993

Edward Chaney *The Evolution of the Grand Tour: Anglo-Italian Cultural Relations Since the Renaissance*, Cassell, 1998

David Coffin, *The English Garden: Meditation and Memorial*, Princeton University Press, 1994

H. M. Colvin (gen. ed.), *The History of the King's Works* (6 vols), vol. 5 (1660–1782), HMSO, 1976

——, *A Biographical Dictionary of British Architects, 1600–1840*, Yale University Press, New Haven and London, 1995

John Cornforth, *Houghton Hall, Norfolk*, Jarrold Publishing, Norwich, 1996

Ray Desmond, *The History of the Royal Botanic Gardens Kew*, Harvill Press, 1998

Patrick Eyres (ed.), *New Arcadian Journal: The Political Temples of Stowe*, vol. 43/44, New Arcadian Press, Leeds, 1997

John Fowler and John Cornforth, *English Decoration in the 18th Century*, Barrie & Jenkins, 1978

Robert Halsband, *Lady Mary Wortley Montagu*, Oxford University Press, 1956

——, *Lord Hervey: Eighteenth-Century Courtier*, Oxford University Press, 1973

Eileen Harris and Nicholas Savage, *British Architectural Books and Writers, 1550–1785*, Yale University Press, London and New Haven, 1990

John Harris, *The Artist and the Country House: A History of Country House and Garden View Painting in Britain 1540–1870* Sotheby Parke Bernet, 1979

——, *The Palladian Revival: Lord Burlington, His Villa and Garden at Chiswick*, Royal Academy of Arts, London, and Yale University Press, New Haven and London, 1994

John Harris and Gordon Higgott, *Inigo Jones Complete Architectural Drawings*, The Drawing Center, New York, 1989

John Harris and A. A. Tait, *Catalogue of the Drawings by Inigo Jones, John Webb and Isaac de Caus at Worcester College Oxford*, Oxford University Press, 1979

Ragnhild Hatton, *George I Elector and King*, Thames & Hudson, 1978

John Haynes, *Kensington Palace: The Official Guidebook*, Historic Royal Palaces, 2001

Christopher Hibbert, *The Grand Tour*, 1987

Charles Hind (ed.), *New Light on English Palladianism*, The Georgian Group, 1990

Dietmar Horst (ed.), *The Royal Gardens of Herrenhausen, Hannover*, Hanover Tourist Board, 2000

John Dixon Hunt, *Greater Perfections: The Practice of Garden Theory*, Thames & Hudson, 2000

——, *The Picturesque Garden in Europe*, Thames & Hudson, 2002

John Dixon Hunt and Peter Willis (eds), *The Genius of the Place: The English Landscape Garden 1620–1820*, MIT, 1988

——, *William Kent, Landscape Designer: An Assessment and Catalogue of his Designs*, Zwemmer, 1987

Christopher Hussey, *English Country Houses: Early Georgian 1715–1760*, Antique Collectors Club, Woodbridge, 1955

Edward Impey, *Kensington Palace: The Official Illustrated History*, Merrell, 2003

John Ingamells and Brinsley Ford, *A Dictionary of British and Irish Travellers in Italy 1701–1800*, Yale University Press, New Haven and London, 1997

David Jacques, *Georgian Gardens: The Reign of Nature*, Batsford, 1983

Margaret Jourdain, *The Work of William Kent: Artist, Painter, Designer and Landscape Gardener*, Country Life, 1948

Mark Laird, *The Flowering of the Landscape Garden: English Pleasure Grounds 1720–1800*, University of Pennsylvania Press, Philadelphia, 1999

James Lees-Milne, *The Earls of Creation: Five Great Patrons of Eighteenth-Century Art*, Hamish Hamilton, 1986

Earl of Leicester, *Holkham*, Clifford Press, Coventry, 2004

Edward Malins, *English Landscaping and Literature 1600–1840*, Oxford University Press, 1966

Naomi Miller, *Heavenly Caves: Reflections on the Garden Grotto*, George Allen & Unwin, 1982

Timothy Mowl, *Horace Walpole: The Great Outsider*, John Murray, 1996

David Neave, *Port, Resort and Market Town: A History of Bridlington*, Hull Academic Press, Hull, 2000

Ronald Paulson, *Hogarth: His Life, Art, and Times*, Yale University Press, New Haven and London, 1974

——, *Hogarth*, 3 vols, Lutterworth Press, Cambridge, 1991

Catherine R. Puglisi, *Francesco Albani*, Yale University Press, New Haven and London, 1999

Kimerly Rorschach, *The Early Georgian Landscape Garden*, Yale Center for British Art, New Haven, 1983

Roy Strong, *'And when did you last see your father?' The Victorian Painter and British History*, Thames & Hudson, 1978

——, *The Artist and the Garden*, Yale University Press, New Haven and London, 2000

John Summerson, *Architecture in Britain 1530–1830*, Penguin, Harmondsworth, 1977

Robert Tavernor, *Palladio and Palladianism*, Thames & Hudson, 1991

Charles Chenevix Trench, *George II*, Allen Lane, 1973

Jenny Uglow, *Hogarth: A Life and a World*, Faber & Faber, 1997

John Van Der Kiste, *King George II and Queen Caroline*, Sutton Publishing, Stroud, 1997

Roger White (ed.), *Lord Burlington and his Circle*, The Georgian Group, 1982

Michael I. Wilson, *William Kent: Architect, Designer, Painter, Gardener, 1685–1748*, Routledge & Kegan Paul, 1984

Andrew Wilton and Ilaria Bignamini (eds), *Grand Tour: The Lure of Italy in the Eighteenth-Century*, Tate Gallery Publishing, 1996

John Wilton-Ely (ed.), *Apollo of the Arts: Lord Burlington and his Circle*, University Gallery, Nottingham, 1973

——*A Tercentenary Tribute to William Kent*, Ferens Art Gallery, Hull, 1985

Rudolf Wittkower, *Palladio and English Palladianism*, Thames & Hudson, 1974

Kenneth Woodbridge, *Landscape and Antiquity: Aspects of English Culture at Stourhead 1718 to 1838*, Clarendon Press, Oxford, 1970

Giles Worsley, *Classical Architecture in Britain: The Heroic Age*, Yale University Press, New Haven and London, 1995

Secondary Sources: Articles

Mavis Batey, 'The Way to View Rousham by Kent's Gardener', *Garden History*, vol. 11, no. 2 (Autumn, 1983), pp. 125–32

Geoffrey Beard, 'William Kent and the Royal Barge', *Burlington Magazine*, August, 1970, pp. 488–93

Marcus Binney, 'Wakefield Lodge, Northamptonshire', *Country Life*, 2 August 1975

Jane Clark, 'The Mysterious Mr Buck', *Apollo*, May 1989

——, 'Palladianism and the Divine Right of Kings', *Apollo*, April 1992

George Clarke, 'Grecian Taste and Gothic Virtue: Lord Cobham's Gardening Programme and its Iconography', *Apollo*, June 1973

——, 'William Kent: Heresy in Stowe's Elysium', Peter Willis (ed.), *Essays on the History of the English Landscape Garden in Memory of H.F. Clark*, 1974

David Coffin, 'The Elysian Fields of Rousham', *Proceedings of the American Philosophical Society*, vol. 130, no. 4, 1986, pp. 406–23

Judith Colton, 'Kent's Hermitage for Queen Caroline at Richmond', *Architectura*, 2 (1974), pp. 181–91

——, 'Merlin's Cave and Queen Caroline: Garden Art as Political Propaganda', *Eighteenth-Century Studies*, vol. 10 (1976), pp. 1–19

Howard Colvin, 'Georgian Architects at Badminton', *Country Life*, 4 April 1968

David Coombs, 'The Garden at Carlton House of Frederick Prince of Wales and Augusta Princess and Dowager of Wales', *Garden History*, vol. 25, no. 2 (Winter, 1997), pp. 153–77

John Cornforth, 'Houghton Hall, Norfolk', *Country Life*, 30 April and 7 May 1987

John Cornforth and Leo Schmidt, 'Holkham Hall, Norfolk IV', *Country Life*, 14 February 1980

Andor Gomme, 'Badminton Revisited', *Architectural History*, vol. 27 (1984), pp. 163–82

Eileen Harris, 'Alexander Pope and *Fabbriche Antiche*', *The Georgian Group Symposium*, 1988, pp. 10–13

John Harris, 'A William Kent Discovery: Designs for Esher Place, Surrey', *Country Life*, 14 May 1959

——, 'The Artinatural Style', in Charles Hind (ed.), *The Rococo in England: A Symposium*, Victoria & Albert Museum, 1986, pp. 8–20

——, 'Esher Place, Surrey', *Country Life*, 2 April 1987.

——, 'Serendipity and the Architect Earl', *Country Life*, 28 May 1987

——, 'James Gibbs, Eminence Grise at Houghton', *The Georgian Group Symposium*, 1988, pp. 5–9

——, 'Some Disputatious Thoughts upon Chiswick', *The Georgian Group Journal*, 1993, pp. 86–90

Richard Hewlings, 'Wakefield Lodge and other houses of the Second Duke of Grafton', *The Georgian Group Journal*, 1993, pp. 43–61

Christine Hiskey, 'The Building of Holkham Hall: Newly Discovered Letters', *Architectural History*, vol. 40 (1997), pp. 144–58

Francis Johnson, 'William Kent and Bridlington', *Country Life*, 9 July 1948

Bernhard Kerber, 'Giuseppi Bartolomeo Chiari', *The Art Bulletin* vol. 1 (1968), pp. 74–86

Hal Moggridge, 'Notes on Kent's garden at Rousham', *Journal of Garden History*, vol. vi (1986), pp. 187–226

Ulrich Müller, 'Rousham: A Transcription of the Steward's Letters, 1738–42', *Garden History*, vol. 25, no. 2 (Winter, 1997), pp. 178–88

David Neave, 'Lord Burlington's Park and Gardens at Londesborough, Yorkshire', *Garden History*, vol. 8, no. 1 (Spring, 1980), pp. 69–90

Susan and David Neave, 'The Early Life of William Kent', *The Georgian Group Journal*, vol. 6 (1996), pp. 4–11

Cinzia Maria Sicca, 'Lord Burlington at Chiswick: Architecture and Landscape', *Garden History*, vol. 10, no. 1 (Spring, 1982), pp. 36–69

——, 'On William Kent's Roman Sources', *Architectural History*, vol. 29 (1986), pp. 134–57

Michael Symes, 'The Landscaping of Esher Place', *Journal of Garden History*, vol. 8, no. 4 (October–December, 1988), pp. 63–96

H. Avray Tipping, 'Four Unpublished Letters of William Kent in the Possession of Lord Spencer', *Architectural Review*, vol. LXIII (January–June, 1928), pp. 180–82, 209–11

Laurence Whistler, 'The Authorship of the Stowe Temples', *Country Life*, 29 September 1950

Roger White, 'Saved by the Landmark Trust: Laughton Place, East Sussex', *Country Life*, 5 May 1983

Peter Willis, 'William Kent's Letters in the Huntingdon Library, California', *Architectural History*, vol. 29 (1986), pp. 158–67

Kenneth Woodbridge, 'William Kent as a Landscape-Designer: A Re-Appraisal', *Apollo*, August 1974, pp. 126–37

——, 'William Kent's Gardening: The Rousham Letters', *Apollo*, October 1974, pp. 282–91

Giles Worsley, 'Riding on Status: The Stables at Houghton', *Country Life*, 27 September 1990

——, 'Houghton Hall, Norfolk', *Country Life*, 4 March 1993.

Index

Index